D1449982

Global Information Technology and Competitive Financial Alliances

Yutaka Kurihara
Aichi University, Japan

Sadayoshi Takaya
Kansai University, Japan

Nobuyoshi Yamori
Nagoya University, Japan

IDEA GROUP PUBLISHING

Hershey • London • Melbourne • Singapore

Acquisitions Editor:	Michelle Potter
Development Editor:	Kristin Roth
Senior Managing Editor:	Amanda Appicello
Managing Editor:	Jennifer Neidig
Copy Editor:	Dawne Brooks
Typesetter:	Sharon Berger
Cover Design:	Lisa Tosheff
Printed at:	Integrated Book Technology

Published in the United States of America by
Idea Group Publishing (an imprint of Idea Group Inc.)
701 E. Chocolate Avenue
Hershey PA 17033
Tel: 717-533-8845
Fax: 717-533-8661
E-mail: cust@idea-group.com
Web site: http://www.idea-group.com

and in the United Kingdom by
Idea Group Publishing (an imprint of Idea Group Inc.)
3 Henrietta Street
Covent Garden
London WC2E 8LU
Tel: 44 20 7240 0856
Fax: 44 20 7379 0609
Web site: http://www.eurospanonline.com

Library of Congress Cataloging-in-Publication Data

Global information technology and competitive financial alliances / Yutaka Kurihara, Sadayoshi Takaya and Nobuyoshi Yamori, Editors.
     p. cm.
  Summary: "This book discusses information technology and its underdeveloped use in financial institutions despite some efforts to improve and upgrade their systems with new systems"--Provided by publisher.
  Includes bibliographical references and index.
  ISBN 1-59140-881-4 (hardcover) -- ISBN 1-59140-882-2 (softcover) -- ISBN 1-59140-883-0 (ebook)
  1. Financial institutions--Data processing. 2. Financial institutions--Technological innovations. 3. Information technology. I. Kurihara, Yutaka, 1962- II. Takaya, Sadayoshi. III. Yamori, Nobuyoshi, 1963-
  HG104.G56 2006
  332.1068'4--dc22
                              2005035296

British Cataloguing in Publication Data
A Cataloguing in Publication record for this book is available from the British Library.

All work contributed to this book is new, previously-unpublished material. The views expressed in this book are those of the authors, but not necessarily of the publisher.

Global Information Technology and Competitive Financial Alliances

Table of Contents

Section II: Financial Markets in the IT Age

Section III: Financial Innovations and IT

Preface

The world economy has grown rapidly since World War II. The most remarkable example is Japan, which grew annually at more than 10% during the 1950s and 1960s. One of the reasons that Japan could grow so fast is that Japan could learn necessary technologies from advanced countries, mainly the United States, during the catch-up process. This is consistent with the growth theory literature that predicts global convergence among nations in terms of per capita gross domestic product (GDP). That is, the richer the country is, the more slowly it grows. However, the experience in the 1990s tells a different story. Figure 1 shows the United State's real GDP growth rate since the 1960s.

The United States has been the richest country since World War II and it had been expected to grow more slowly than before. However, the U.S. economy has a strong foundation because the IT sector is strong. Actually, for the period from 1970 to the mid-1980s, the United State's annual growth rates, approximately only 3%, were not so high. However, the United State's growth rates increased around 2000. Furthermore, Table 1 shows that other developed countries also recorded high economic growth rates around 2000. It is often said that the development of information technology (IT) contributed to these high growth rates. Some argue that after the IT revolution, the "new economy" came into being.

Now, IT is used in diverse business areas. For example, because firms can manage their inventory in real time by using a point-of-sale system, they do not accumulate dead stock. Financial companies can offer a new product that requires tremendous calculations of risks. So, IT has a significant effect on most advanced countries.

Although many developed countries lack natural resources, they have accumulated tremendous human capital. In the IT world, knowledge and wisdom are key resources for steady economic growth and a bright future. Therefore, because IT relies little on natural resources but heavily upon the "brain assets" of wisdom and intelligence, the advanced economies have a comparative advantage in the development of new IT.

However, Japan in the 1990s is a striking exception, as shown in Table 1. Of course, as we discuss in this book, Japanese companies and banks have developed and adopted various information technologies. In spite of their efforts, Japan recorded very low, sometimes negative, growth rates in the late 1990s. The main reason was its fragile financial system. In particular, huge, non-performing loans prohibited Japanese banks from investing sufficient funds in IT. Therefore, Japanese banks were said to be a few years behind U.S. and European banks. A main reason for big bank mergers since 2000 in Japan was that Japanese banks had to ensure enough funds for developing information technologies. Therefore, IT has a large impact on the Japanese economy.

Figure 1. U.S. real GDP growth rate (5-year moving average) (Source: 2005 Economic Report of the President)

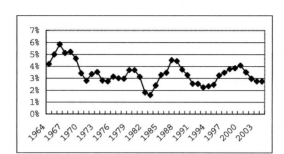

All figures are forecasts as published by International Monetary Fund. For United States, advance estimates by Department of Commerce show real GDP grew 4.4% in 2004. Source: 2005 Economic Report of the President

What are the reasons behind this lack of development? Where do we stand? Where should we go? This book addresses these issues and future options for growth and development relative to conditions in the world's countries.

Unfortunately, IT in the area of finance is underdeveloped even though financial institutions have worked to improve and upgrade their systems. Of course, almost all of the financial institutions have adopted IT for many aspects of their businesses. Another point is that IT has made it possible to process high-volume trading. Finally, only IT can accommodate processing the large volumes of files needed to store information and data.

But the revolution is not limited to customer service. Efficient management systems and high quality analysis using IT have been adopted and developed further in recent years. Financial derivatives, for example, are not possible without the support of IT. Modern financial theory and financial engineering have rapidly developed. This, combined with IT in the 1980s, greatly changed the character of finance business. The necessity of developing risk management can and should be pointed out. Instead of taking a statistical approach to credit risks, financial institutions used to evaluate risks based on experience. This caused an outbreak of bad debt problems for banks in some countries.

IT has introduced very interesting aspects. Financial alliances have appeared all over the world. The IT revolution has made it possible for financial enterprises to ally with each other, and moreover, to increase efficiency and profit as well as to develop more fruitful business concepts and practices. Along with the IT revolution, alliances have become indispensable and necessary.

Some readers are unfamiliar with the situation of the world financial system and of the spreading use of IT. In fact, there seem to appear to be numerous areas of misunderstanding. To clear up the misconceptions, this book addresses customer service, the interface between IT and other fields, and efficiency and quality improvements that can

Table 1. Growth rates in real GDP, 1986-2004 (Percent Change of Annual Rate)

Area and country	1986-1995	1996	1997	1998	1999	2000	2001	2002	2003	2004
World	3.3	4.1	4.2	2.8	3.7	4.7	2.4	3	3.9	5
Advanced Economies	3.0	3.0	3.4	2.7	3.5	3.9	1.2	1.6	2.1	3.6
United States	2.9	3.7	4.5	4.2	4.5	3.7	0.8	1.9	3	4.3
Japan	3.1	3.5	1.8	-1.2	0.2	2.8	0.4	-0.3	2.5	4.4
United Kingdom	2.5	2.8	3.3	3.1	2.9	3.9	2.3	1.8	2.2	3.4
Canada	2.3	1.6	4.2	4.1	5.5	5.2	1.8	3.4	2	2.9
Germany	2.7	0.8	1.4	2	2	2.9	0.8	0.1	-0.1	2
France	2.1	1	1.9	3.6	3.2	4.2	2.1	1.1	0.5	2.6
Italy	2.1	1.1	2	1.8	1.7	3	1.8	0.4	0.3	1.4
Regional Groups:										
Africa	1.9	5.7	3.2	3.1	2.7	2.9	4	3.5	4.3	4.5
Central and Eastern Europe	0.8	4.8	4.2	2.8	0.4	4.9	0.2	4.4	4.5	5.5
Commonwealth of Independent States		-3.9	1.1	-3.5	5.1	9.1	6.4	5.4	7.8	8
Russia		-3.6	1.4	-5.3	6.3	10	5.1	4.7	7.3	7.3
Developing Asia	7.7	8.2	6.5	4.1	6.2	6.7	5.5	6.6	7.7	7.6
China	9.9	9.6	8.8	7.8	7.1	8.0	7.5	8.3	9.1	9
India	5.7	7.5	5	5.8	6.7	5.4	3.9	5	7.2	6.4
Middle East	2.7	4.6	5.3	3.8	2.4	5.5	3.6	4.3	6	5.1
Western Hemisphere	2.8	3.7	5.2	2.3	0.4	3.9	0.5	-0.1	1.8	4.6
Brazil	2.5	2.7	3.3	0.1	0.8	4.4	1.3	1.9	-0.2	4
Mexico	1.6	5.2	6.8	5	3.6	6.6	-0.2	0.8	1.3	4

All figures are forecasts as published by International Monetary Fund. For United States, advance estimates by Department of Commerce show real GDP grew 4.4% in 2004. Source: 2005 Economic Report of the President

be garnered by introducing IT functions. Each chapter includes a general view. The book also addresses implications for future growth that are engendered by alliances between IT and financial fields, and examines the related situations in the world.

The content of this book is ultramodern and ambitious. However, the content is also original and very basic. We can easily imagine that that the progress of IT brings about changes in financial institutions. Financial alliances are a natural outgrowth of IT progress. In most developed nations, mergers and acquisitions and partnerships of financial institutions are emerging, and the progress of IT is considered one of the causes. However, neither the academic literature nor the popular press has addressed the relationship between IT and financial enterprise alliances to any depth. Therefore, readers will find this strange situation while examining some kinds of databases. The importance of and interest in the topic, as well as this scarcity of literature on the topic, is the main incentive behind the publication of this book.

All of the authors in this book deserve our attention and our praise. Some of them have published many books. Others have published manuscripts in highly reputable, international journals. The authors are well known and deserve their fine reputations in each field. We are deeply grateful for their contributions to this project.

Scholars in diverse fields (economics, IT, business/marketing), policy makers and business persons are the target audience for the book.

This book is organized into 17 chapters. The following briefly describes each of the chapters.

Section I: Financial Institutions, Alliances, IT, and Economic Growth

Over time, a large variety of tools have appeared that have added value to traditional financial functions, such as financial intermediation (deposit and lending) and settlement. Banks will find that these added values are destined to dwindle. The volumes of financial intermediation and settlements are not increasing. Banks are therefore trying to produce new value by forming alliances with other banks, financial institutions and industries. During this process, IT plays an important role and becomes an effective weapon.

Chapter I: Investment in IT and the Business Performance of Financial Companies. The purpose of this chapter is to empirically investigate the relationship between investment in IT and the business performance of financial companies. IT and competitive financial alliances are helping to remake business circumstances. IT and well-functioning financial markets play a crucial role in increasing economic growth and prosperity. The author uses a vector autoregressive (VAR) model to test two hypotheses: (Hypothesis 1) Spending on IT improves financial performance, and (Hypothesis 2) High financial performance increases spending on IT — with the assumption that stock price returns can provide an adequate measure of financial performance. The analysis includes control variables for general business cycle conditions. The results show that the greatest benefits from increases in technology accrue to insurance and other financial companies. Managers of these companies may increase their business performance by using strategic investment and IT.

Chapter II: Recent Development of Information Technology in Japanese Banks. Leading international banks have spent a great deal of money on information technology since the 1990s. For example, the largest commercial banks in the United States are estimated to spend as much as 25% of their total expenses on IT. Although Japanese banks have suffered from huge, non-performing loans since the burst of the bubble, they have also invested a huge amount of money on their information facilities. Japanese banks are expected to spend $11.9 billion on technology in the 2004 fiscal year. This chapter discusses in detail recent developments in IT in Japanese banks. First, it provides a brief explanation of the current Japanese banking environment. Then, the chapter discusses how Japanese financial institutions have dealt with new IT. This chapter is unique in providing a detailed discussion on new Internet banks and the Internet banking services of existing banks. Because information investment has an external effect, government assistance is necessary, and this chapter also discusses what the government has done to encourage IT usage in financial services.

Chapter III: Payment Systems of Financial Institutions: Current State and Future Prospects. Economic activity is always accompanied by payment. Payment systems, which are the subject of much recent discussion, are an indispensable part of the infrastructure that supports the entire economy. Of recent interest are issues of increasing payment risk and the severe situations of financial institutions in some developed countries. The costs associated with setup and operation of payment systems is high, and market participants expect efficiency. Many problems are associated with bond payments. The spread of delivery-versus-payment (DVP) systems and IT-based transactions are also impacting payment systems. Links between payment systems are also important and have prompted concerns about systemic risk if time-designated net settlements coexist with real-time gross settlements (RTGSs), which can alter outcomes, thereby increasing systemic risk. If RTGSs and the net payment system are not operated by a single rule, this problem worsens. Unification of settlement systems, rules and dealings custom is critical. Financial alliances are urgent problems. The complex legal frameworks that govern payment activity would benefit from structural revisions.

Chapter IV: Financial Innovation and Economic Growth: Some Further Evidence from the UK, 1900-2003. This chapter assesses the contribution of financial development to savings and economic growth in the UK in the 20th century. Financial development has grown by leaps and bounds along with a number of infamous crashes. Using annual time-series data for the whole century, this chapter finds that financial growth has helped savings and economic growth in the UK throughout the 20th century. The unprecedented increase in money holdings in the 1960s and various forms of financial innovation and liberalization initiated in the 1980s raised both the level and the rate of economic growth. There are long-run and unique cointegrated relations of GDP with productivity of capital and financial depth in the 20th century. The financial crash known as Black Monday in 1987 upset equilibrium relations and led to a negative money-stock elasticity of economic growth.

Section II: Financial Markets in the IT Age

Changes in business processes and systems will eventually contradict existing management styles. Eventually, old styles will transform themselves into new management systems. IT is one typical example that has affected financial markets greatly. New needs will be generated, which will lead to adopting the next IT solution. In return, these solutions will generate changes to financial systems. The linkages among financial markets have tied very closely. Of course, although these linkages have good aspects, there are also bad aspects. Large capital movements occur in a short time. Exchange rates and other stock prices fluctuate greatly. Recently, we could not prevent the Asian currency crisis and its spread. Alliances of various kinds are needed to solve such problems more effectively.

Chapter V: Malliavin Calculus for the Estimation of the U.S. Dollar/Euro Exchange Rate When the Volatility is Stochastic. The tendency of exchange rates to fluctuate sharply and regularly is often referred to as currency market volatility. The extent of currency market volatility is a major element of market risk. For financial transactions, volatility is a source of both profits and costs. Increased currency market volatility implies higher currency option premiums and, therefore, higher hedging costs for investors and importers/exporters. However, interestingly for banks and other investment houses dealing in options, an increase in option prices may contribute to higher profits. It has been well documented that the volatility of exchange rates varies over time. In recent years, the literature has proposed various stochastic volatility models that try to capture the dynamics of exchange-rate volatility. In turn, several methods have been developed to estimate the parameters of such stochastic volatility models, with varying results. This chapter proposes another method for parameter estimation of an exchange rate function when the volatility follows a stochastic process, using a geometric Brownian motion to represent stochastic volatility. Using Malliavin calculus, this chapter presents an explicit expression for the likelihood function of the observations. Numerical integration methods (Monte-Carlo simulations) and numerical optimization methods (generic algorithms) enable us to find an estimate for the unknown parameters and the volatility. Using weekly U.S. dollar/Euro exchange rates, the calculation obtains estimates of the parameters of the U.S. dollar/Euro exchange rate function (i.e., the constant of the drift) and the assumed stochastic volatility model (i.e., the constants of the diffusion process). Application of the estimated model to out-of-sample data for the U.S. dollar/Euro exchange rate shows a significantly high accuracy of the proposed method.

Chapter VI: Evolution of the Euro and Currency Competition in the Global ICT Age. This chapter investigates competition of the key currencies as foreign exchange vehicles, which has a character of the network externality. After January 2002, the Euro has been used in our daily lives, with significant competition between the Euro and the U.S. dollar as the dominant international currency. The author presents the currency competition model with a decreasing transaction cost that reflects the character of the ICT network externality, to investigate the competition between the Euro and the dollar. The findings suggest that the impact of the Euro's introduction may cause competition for the Euro to emerge as the key currency in international settlements. Further, the author indicates the importance of policy coordination between the U.S. and the Euro area in terms of ensuring stable international capital flows, exchange rates and a key currency regime.

Chapter VII: Co-Integration of the International Capital Markets with the Use of Information Technology: The Case of Europe. The purpose of this study is to analyze the "revolution" that was caused by the rapid spread of IT in terms of the development and integration of financial markets, especially capital markets. The main issue is that IT progress and facilities enabled efficient transactions in capital markets, and this phenomenon resulted in the ability to offer investors a variety of investment options. This chapter focuses from a theoretical and practical framework on the European capital markets and the impact of IT on important activities implemented by the capital markets: the structure of the trading platforms, the cross-border cooperation of the markets and the financial intermediaries.

Chapter VIII: International Capital Movements, Currency Crisis and ICT Innovation. This chapter investigates the effects generated by the currency crisis. The countries that have experienced currency turmoil have confronted financial crisis, economic deterioration and increased unemployment. This chapter empirically examines the effect of currency depreciation on the real GDP and the unemployment rates in those countries by using the Structural Vector Autoregressive Model, which attempts to clarify whether identified supply or demand shocks can be caused by exchange rate depreciation. This study suggests currency crisis might generate demand shock, resulting in harmful impacts to the real economy in those countries that may be deemed negative effects of information and communication technology (ICT) innovation.

Chapter IX: Volatility Spillover Structure of Stock and Foreign Exchange Market between Korea, Japan and Hong Kong. IT can be a source of volatility spillover between markets located in other countries. In this chapter, the author investigates the interrelationship between stock returns in North East Asian countries and the effect of foreign exchange rate volatility on the relationship between stock returns. This chapter elucidates simultaneous interrelationship between stock return and foreign exchange volatility. Focusing on the covariance of each asset return, if foreign exchange rate volatility is not taken into account, the portfolio risk might be undervalued. The analysis shows that foreign exchange market turbulence might be accompanied by an increase in covariance between stock returns. Just after the Asian Currency Crisis, the relationship between stock returns and foreign exchange turbulence may have changed. For managing international portfolio risk during the age of IT, foreign exchange risk and structural change in covariance between stock returns should be considered.

Section III: Financial Innovations and IT

The lack of progressive dynamism in financial systems in some fields has been serious. On the contrary, recently innovation has been rapid. Since the 1980s, innovative movements in finance have grown rapidly and continuously. The source of added value depends on innovation. Some innovative changes have arisen from IT, which has introduced much innovation into our daily lives and into the business world. IT has gradually changed financial institutions, job descriptions and alliances among institutions. Technology is cumulative in some fields such that it is difficult to catch up with more aggressive competitors. These changes also suggest the formation of new kinds of alliances in the near future.

Chapter X: Trade Liberalization and International Performance of Australian Manufacturing Industries and ITs. Trade liberalisation has played a pivotal role in improving the export orientation of the various Australian manufacturing industries. IT is not an exception. However, those industries subjected to industry-specific assistance measures (e.g., textiles, clothing, footwear and the machinery and equipment industries) have exhibited a superior export-oriented performance. The important lesson emanating from this result for the IT sector is that although it is subjected to these measures, their expansion can help alleviate the weak and stagnant export performance in IT-related goods, thereby helping to combat the projected large balance-of-trade deficit. Moreover, stronger output and employment growth will occur because of the significant contributions of these goods to the economy.

Chapter XI: Recent Developments of Digital Cash Projects in Japan. In this chapter, the authors examine the factors involved in the recent spread of digital cash and the problems with digital cash projects in Japan that still remain to be solved. In the 1990s, many Japanese banks and other non-bank enterprises have conducted forward-looking projects despite their financial difficulties. One of these projects has been to develop digital cash technology and promote its usage. Efforts to establish digital cash projects made discernible progress in the early 2000s, and digital cash is more commonly used now in Japan than in other IT-advanced countries. This chapter provides an overview of the recent development of digital cash projects in Japan and discusses the issues involved in the further growth of digital cash usage.

In this chapter, the authors first took into account the history of digital cash projects in Japan during the past decade, ranging from the initial experiments to the recent commercialization efforts. Then they discuss what factors led to remarkable progress in digital cash usage in the early 2000s. They find that cooperation between the government and private companies has been the most important factor leading to the recent diffusion of digital cash. At the same time, the authors point out that the manufacturing costs of smart cards were significantly reduced through expansion of IC-card markets and technological improvements. Furthermore, the other important factors for diffusing the digital cash are (1) increasing convenience of digital cash usage, (2) expansion of available districts of digital cash, (3) innovations in ID technologies, and (4) close cooperation between the public and private sectors. Finally, the chapter describes the remaining issues that must be addressed to enable further growth of digital cash usage.

Chapter XII: Money is What Money Does: Prospects for an Electronic Money Payment System in Japan. Contrary to expectations, digital money has not been spreading. Despite the amazing progress in IT that has occurred in recent years, electronic money failed to live up to expectations and has made little headway into payments systems. The gap between expectations and reality is especially pronounced in Japan. The author compares the cases of Japan and Germany. The reason behind the failure of electronic money in Japan is two-fold. First, typical use of electronic money is in general rather limited as long as conventional money is required as a unit of account and a store of value for the official operation. Second, Japanese financial institutions chose a very limited standard for their electronic money systems and these could not compete with the near-monopolistic positions that credit card companies enjoy in cashless payment markets. On the contrary, Germany adopted a broad standard that fully utilizes the advantages of electronic money as a medium of payment.

Chapter XIII: Investment in IT Stocks by Japanese Life Insurers. Insurance companies have introduced IT from the early stages. This chapter analyzes the relationship between Japanese life insurers' investment in IT stocks and conventional financial statistics, such as return on return on equity (ROE) and dividend yield. The analysis shows that Japanese life insurers do not necessarily formulate their portfolios based on recent data. In particular, insurers who invested in low-ROE stocks tended to be financially unstable. These findings confirm that even after the Japanese financial crisis of the late 1990s, the primary objective of stock investment by Japanese life insurers continued to be the maintenance of business relationships with client firms, and not the maximization of investment performance.

Chapter XIV: The Roles of IT in the Conduct of Modern Monetary Policy. This chapter reviews the roles of IT from two perspectives. First, from the macroeconomic perspective, the IT revolution induced output growth and new financial innovations such as asset-backed securities and electronic money. However, these phenomena complicate the conduct of monetary policy, but they do not totally diminish its effectiveness. Second, from the operational level, IT applications are currently used to enhance operational efficiency, bolster the decision-making process, and increase the innovative practices of monetary authorities in central banks throughout the world. The degree of implementation of IT applications in the conduct of monetary policy, in turn, may become another determinant of monetary policy frameworks in the future.

Chapter XV: The Role and Future of Local Currency and IT. The use of local currency, introduced by non-governmental organizations (NGOs) or other organizations in particular regions of some countries, has spread gradually since the 1990s in many countries. In countries around the world, nonprofit organizations (NPOs) and other similar groups have introduced local currencies. Recently, one local currency related to preventing environmental problems has appeared, and local currencies have also been implemented in the protective and nursing industries. In some countries, expectations for economic recovery have been supported by the introduction of a local currency. Various problems are involved with the spreading use of local currencies. It is important, however, to promote the spread. Given a good relationship among users, the advantages of local currencies are considerable. Use of local currency does not create major obstacles to interfere with other economic activity as long as the sizes of transactions do not increase greatly, so governments and financial authorities have little reason to prohibit its use unless the currency issue authority in the country is seriously threatened. The use of IT is an important point. The merits from introducing IT into a local currency are quite large. Linkages and alliances are important.

Section IV: Security, Law, and IT

It is a fact that the Internet originated as a network for the military. After that, it evolved into an academic field and then transformed into a business network. Financial institutions are also heavy users. However, a lot of serious problems are occurring. We cannot ignore this fact. Not only policy makers but also financial institutions should make concerted efforts to prevent these issues. Alliances are much needed to solve these problems.

Chapter XVI: Integrity and Security in the E-Century. E-commerce offers an enormous range of solutions to payment and settlement problems. However, e-commerce also poses a myriad of regulatory issues. Understanding the issues regarding technology, taxation and economic institutions posed by e-commerce that impact the ability to provide such services aids in comprehending the vast integrity and security issues surrounding this innovation. This chapter examines the effect of this technological innovation in the light of theories of regulation that postulate a struggle between attempts to control innovation and further innovation and regulation. To illustrate how regulation of e-commerce may be counterproductive, the chapter introduces a case study of the evolution of regulation of derivatives to test a hypothesis concerning social and avoidance costs. The author then examines a comparative case study of regulation of e-commerce to suggest a policy approach using a private-sector solution within a public policy matrix that is similar to the system used for private deposit insurance.

Chapter XVII: Legal Concerns Against Auctions and Securities Conventions: A Japanese Perspective. This chapter introduces the two newly emerging issues in the C2C and B2B areas in Japanese IT law: antifraud measures in Internet auctions and treatment of the Hague Securities Convention. The author discusses the law in some countries and areas. The liability of auction providers for a tenant's fraud beyond the freedom of contracts is not clear. If consumers bear the risks, adequate disclosure should be promoted. In addition, because this issue is complex, several measures, including advertisement regulations against small business consumers and development of escrow payment techniques, should be promoted. Regarding the Hague Securities Convention, the United States has pushed other countries to ratify it, but the EU has hesitated to conform. This chapter proposes that the ratification of the Hague Convention regarding unification of conflicting laws and the UNIDROIT Convention for unification of the substantive laws should be done simultaneously to avoid some side effects.

Acknowledgments

The editors would like to acknowledge the help of all involved in the collation and review process of the book. Without their support, this project would not have been satisfactorily completed.

Most of the authors of the chapters also served as referees for articles written by other authors. We thank all those who provided constructive and comprehensive reviews. They helped us greatly. We also thank Akihiro Amano, Seiichi Fujita, Hisashi Harui, Kunihiko Ito, Koichiro Morikawa, Tsutomu Muramoto, Eiji Nezu, Hiromasa Okada, Hitoshi Okada, Hiroshi Osada, Jun-ichi Senda, Katsuya Ue, and Ichihiro Uchida for their constructive suggestions and advice.

Special thanks go to the publishing team at Idea Group Inc., in particular to Kristin Roth, who continuously provided guidance via e-mail to keep the project on schedule, and to Mehdi Khosrow-Pour, whose enthusiasm motivated us initially to accept his invitation to work on this project. Their work was great and should be highly admired.

Finally, we wish to thank all of the authors for their insightful and excellent contributions to this book. Yamori and Kurihara appreciate the Institute for Advanced Research, Nagoya University. The first director of the institute was Professor Ryoji Noyori, who won the Nobel Prize for chemistry in 2001. Yamori has belonged to the Institute since 2003. This project initially started when Kurihara was a visiting scholar at the Institute.

The editors,

Yutaka Kurihara
Sadayoshi Takaya
Nobuyoshi Yamori

Section I

Financial Institutions, Alliances, IT, and Economic Growth

Chapter I

Investment in IT and the Business Performance of Financial Companies

Irene Henriques, York University, Canada

Perry Sadorsky, York University, Canada

Abstract

Global information technology and competitive financial alliances are helping to reshape the business landscape. Information technology (IT) and well functioning financial markets play a crucial role in increasing economic growth and prosperity. The purpose of this study is to empirically investigate the relationship between investment in IT and the business performance of financial companies. A vector autoregressive (VAR) model is used to test hypotheses one (increased spending on IT increases financial performance) and two (increased financial performance increases spending on IT) where financial performance is assumed to be adequately measured by stock price returns. Control variables for general business cycle conditions are included in the analysis. Our results show that the greatest benefits from increases in technology accrue to insurance and other financial companies. Managers of these companies could increase their business performance through strategic investment and use of IT.

Introduction

Technological progress can lead to process innovation (lower cost ways of producing existing products) or product innovation (the development of new products). According to neoclassical economic growth theory, technological improvements are the only way to increase the living standards in countries that have reached the golden rule. An increase in technology raises the production function and increases the steady state amounts of capital stock and output. In terms of economic performance, maximizing productivity growth is the single most important objective for a country to have since increases in productivity growth lead to higher living standards. More productive workers receive higher wages and salaries and this translates into higher disposable income which can be used to purchase additional goods and services or increase savings. The exact split between consumption and savings depends upon the marginal propensity to consume. Both of these conditions (higher wages and salaries and higher disposable income) are desirable because strong consumer demand from increased consumption of goods and services fuels increased business performance which in turn increases profits. Higher profits can be used to pay higher wages, salaries and dividends and hire more workers (which creates more jobs in the economy). Increased savings raises the amount of funds available for business investment (either expanding existing businesses or creating new ones).

Information technology (IT) plays a crucial role in increasing economic growth and prosperity. Currently, media, telecommunications and computing are converging towards the Internet. This can be visualized by imagining three spokes (represented by media, telecommunications and computing) connecting to a hub (the Internet). The Internet has thus become a multipurpose medium of information and knowledge exchange. This convergence is occurring against a backdrop of efficient financial capital markets. Countries or regions with highly efficient capital markets will see this convergence occur faster than countries or regions with less efficient or less developed financial capital markets. Institutional arrangements (an example of social capital), like regulation, are very important to financing the new economy (Mayer, 2002).

Companies engaged in banking, insurance and other financial services are the drivers of efficient financial markets. IT can impact banking, insurance and financial services companies in a number of different ways. For example, increases in IT investment lead to the installation of automatic teller machines (ATMs) and Internet banking, both of which provide more convenience to consumers and can be offered at lower costs than traditional bricks and mortar financial companies. ATMs are particularly interesting because they share positive network effects. Positive network effects are very important in the development and adoption of IT because this means that the value of a product to one user depends on how many other users there are (Shapiro & Varian, 1999). As more and more users employ ATM services, the more indispensable the service becomes. This is particularly relevant in the discussion of the benefits and costs of using digital cash (Kurihara, 2005).

In an interesting recent study, Kim and Davidson (2004) use a balanced scorecard (BSC) approach to empirically investigate the effects of IT expenditures on Korean bank's business performance. The balanced scorecard approach identifies four BSC indicators measuring the strategic role of information technology in banking services. The four BSC indicators are: (1) perspective learning and growth (improved efficiency and effectiveness), (2) internal perspective (increased labour productivity), (3) customer perspective (increased customer satisfaction and market share), and (4) financial perspective (improved financial performance and competitive advantage). They find a relationship between IT expenditures and banks' financial performance. In particular, they find that for banks with high IT expenditures, IT expenditures (1) increased labour productivity, (2) decreased payroll expenses, and increased operating and total administrative expenses, (3) increased market share, and (4) increased revenue and profit. Kim and Davidson (2004) suggest that it would be useful for bank managers to use the balanced scorecard approach to measure the business performance of both management and IT strategies. Their results clearly indicate that effective use of IT increases market share and profits and reduces payroll expenses.

Increases in IT also lead to competitive advantages for the top tier banks that need more sophisticated trading platforms for their derivatives trading business (The Banker (2004a)). Innovation in trading technology is growing rapidly but many in the industry expect credit derivatives trading to follow in the sluggish footsteps of the fixed income markets where electronic trading has been used for the past five years and yet there is only a 10%-15% penetration rate.

Meanwhile, increased access to electronic communications networks (ECNs) is also making business more difficult for many companies involved in wealth management. While the wealth management sector is growing globally, so too is the competition as the expansion of ECNs means that, while more information is being collected on consumer tastes and preferences, it is also more difficult to use this information effectively since so many companies have access to the same or similar databases. Technology trends point towards faster and more automated decision making. Rewards will go to the firms that can successfully use the leading edge technology. Failure will result to those firms that fall behind (*The Banker,* 2004b). As is the case in all industries, competitive advantage is gained by exploiting new markets or technologies. Competitive advantage is maintained through innovation (Porter, 1985).

Shiller (2003) proposes combining information technology with financial engineering to better manage risks faced by people in the normal course of their lives. Economic risks affect people's health, education choice, career choices, and the growth and well being of countries. Imagine spending many years in school training for a job that may become obsolete ten years after starting the profession. This is an example of a real economic risk that today cannot be managed in any coherent manner. One possible solution for this economic risk is to provide a contract that insures against adverse employment opportunities in the future. According to Shiller (2003), one of the greatest opportunities for financial economics is in designing information databases, markets and contracts (insurance policies, futures contracts) to help individuals and countries better manage their risks. This provides an enormous opportunity for financial services companies to expand into new areas of business.

Globally, the financial services industry is currently spending and expected to continue to spend large amounts of money on IT solutions. TowerGroup expects that external IT spending to account for 57% of total global IT spending in the financial services industry and sees total global IT spending to increase from $198bn in 2004 to $224bn in 2006 (*The*

Banker, 2004c). TowerGroup estimates that total global IT investments on risk and compliance solutions will total $51bn in 2004 as new governance rules come into effect.

Despite the increases in IT and the Internet, however, most financial services are still delivered locally and that, in retail banking, the performance of commercial banks is strongly determined by the growth of their home markets (Grosse, 2003).

The purpose of this study is to empirically investigate the relationship between investment in IT and the business performance of financial companies. Increased investment in IT leads to process innovation which translates into reduced costs of doing business and increased financial performance. Increased investment in IT can also lead to new products being developed, which in itself, will not lead to reduced business costs, but will expand the choice of products available to consumers. This is particularly evident in the wealth management segment of the financial services industry. As long as new products or services are valued by consumers then increased profit opportunities exist.

But what are the profit opportunities in a saturated market like financial services? The standard economic model for a company to grow its profits has been traditionally based on the following cycle. Innovate a product, market the product, sell the product in the home market until saturation, sell the product globally, engage in mergers and acquisitions to cut costs, raise prices if possible, and repeat the cycle (Slywotzky & Wise, 2003). This has been the basic business model for the past hundred years. The problem today is that the global market has become saturated with brand names and all of the wealthy international markets have been exploited. Banking has become a "product" and like other established products faces stiff competition. Slywotzky and Wise (2003) suggest that companies can still grow even when the overall market is not growing by focusing on what they term "demand innovation". Demand innovation centres on inventing new and better ways to serve customers and create value. Demand innovation is a business design similar to a process innovation that focuses on serving the customer after the basic product has been sold. In the future, process innovation not product innovation is the key to sustaining profit growth. In the financial services sector, information technology is the most important type of technology and process innovation and demand innovation stems from investment in information technology. Hence:

Hypothesis 1 (H1): Increased spending on IT increases financial performance.

Increased financial performance means that a firm has more money to budget towards expenditures on IT. In the United States, TowerGroup expects IT spending by U.S. consumer banks to grow by more than 5% in 2004 at a time when banking revenue grew 9% in 2002-2003 (*The Banker,* 2004d). The recent profit performance of U.S. corporations has been very impressive (*The Economist,* 2005). U.S. corporate profits are now more than 9% of GDP. This is close to the record high achieved in 1929 and slightly larger than the near record high in the 1960s. Since 1982, the profits of U.S. financial firms have grown from 4% of overall corporate profits to more than 40% today. Currently, the U.S. financial industry accounts for 40% of U.S. stock market capitalization. This "finance based economy" is currently being sustained by the Federal Reserve via very low interest rates (*The Economist,* 2005). Furthermore, loose U.S. monetary policy is being exported around the globe as other countries like Japan and China print their own money in order to buy U.S. treasuries to hold down their currency exchange rates against the U.S. dollar. In addition, the U.S. banking sector is currently going through a wave of mergers and acquisitions which itself is providing a stimulus to cut costs through more automatic banking and widespread adoption of technology. Hence:

Hypothesis 2 (H2): Increased financial performance increases spending on IT.

Hypotheses 1 and 2 indicate a possible feedback relationship between spending on IT and a firm's financial performance.

The main objective of this study is to determine the relationship between IT expenditures and financial performance in the financial services industry. A vector autoregressive (VAR) model is used to test hypotheses one and two where financial performance is assumed to be adequately measured by stock price returns. Control variables for general business cycle conditions are included in the analysis. In the following sections, the methodology, data, and empirical results are presented and discussed. Concluding remarks and managerial implications are also provided.

Methodology

A vector autoregression (VAR) is used to empirically investigate the relationship between financial performance and technology. One of the advantages of using a VAR is that the researcher does not need to provide prior assumptions about endogeneity and exogeneity because in a VAR all variables are treated as endogenous. This means that in a VAR, each variable depends upon the lagged values of all the variables in the system. This allows for a much richer data structure that can capture complex dynamic properties in the data (Brooks, 2002). VAR models are justifiable on theoretical grounds because as Zellner and Franz (1974) show, any multivariate theoretical model is a reduced form representation of some econometric model. Multivariate Granger causality tests on VAR models are also more powerful than in the single equation approach (Nelson & Schwert, 1982).

A vector autregression can be written as:

$$y_t = \sum_{j=1}^{p} B_j y_{t-j} + u_t, \qquad \Sigma(u_t u_t^{'}) = \Sigma$$

where y is a n vector of endogenous variables and B_j is a n×n matrix of regression coefficients. In the above equation for a VAR, there are $n^2 p$ free parameters. Consequently, the selection of the appropriate lag length, p, is important. If the lag length is set too large relative to the sample size (T), degrees of freedom will be used up and this will lead to large standard errors on the estimated coefficients. If the lag length is set too low, then there may not be enough lags in the VAR to adequately capture the dynamic properties of the data. One approach to determining the lag length, p, is to use a likelihood ratio test statistic ($LR = T(\log|\Sigma_R| - \log|\Sigma_U|)$, where Σ_R (Σ_U) is the covariance matrix from the restricted (unrestricted) model to test models with different lag lengths. Ideally the chosen model should also have no serial correlation in the residuals.

Because of the large number of estimated coefficients in a VAR, the coefficients in themselves are not that interesting to look at. VAR models are mostly used to test Granger causality (do lags of one variable help explain the current value of some other variable?) and describe the dynamics of the data. Granger causality tests can be constructed from likelihood ratio tests that compare restricted models with unrestricted models. Model dynamics can be studied using either impulse response functions or variance decompositions.

Impulse response functions are the dynamic response of each endogenous variable to a shock in the system. An impulse response separates the determinates of the endogenous variables into shocks (or innovations) which are identified with specific variables and then traces the effect on current and future values of the endogenous variable. Impulse responses are very useful for describing persistence. In general, innovations are correlated and this makes it difficult to interpret the impulse response functions. The usual way to solve this problem is to apply a transformation Q to the innovations to make them uncorrelated.

$$v_t = Qu_t \sim (0, D)$$

where D is a diagonal covariance matrix. In our impulse responses we compute generalized impulses which do not depend upon the ordering of the variables in the VAR model.

Variance decompositions provide a similar but alternative method for examining dynamics in a VAR model. Variance decompositions separate the proportion of the movement in the dependent variable into its own effect and the effects from the other variables. Because of the adding up constraint that own and other effects sum to one (or 100%) an orthogonal decomposition (like Cholesky which depends upon the ordering of the variables) is required.

Data

U.S. stock market data were collected over the period February 1984 to December 2003, on an information technology index, banking index, insurance index, and other financial services index. We used the Pacific Stock Exchange (PSE) Technology Index to measure the stock market performance of information technology firms because the PSE represents a pure play on technology. Unlike NASDAQ, all of the companies in the PSE index are technology related and the index includes companies listed on leading stock exchanges as well as over the counter shares. The PSE Technology Index is a price-weighted, broad-based index which is comprised of 100 listed and over-the-counter stocks from 15 different industries including computer hardware, software, semiconductors, telecommunications, data storage and processing, electronics and biotechnology (www.pacificex.com). Ideally we would like to have some way to measure the value of information technology. The problem is that IT is comprised of both tangible and non-tangible factors making it impossible to have one widely accepted measure of IT. In this chapter, we create a value for IT by using an equity based measure of IT. Our approach to measuring IT is to start with an IT stock market index like the PSE and then remove general stock market effects from this index by regressing the PSE index on a general stock market index and saving the residuals. These residuals reflect only the variation in IT and are the measure of IT we use in our vector autoregressions.

The financial performance of banking, insurance and other financial services can be measured using the NASDAQ sub stock market indices for these three industries (www.nasdaq.com accessed on February 10, 200). The NASDAQ Bank Index contains 525 NASDAQ listed companies classified according to the FTSE™ Global Classification System as Banks. It includes banks providing a broad range of financial services, with significant retail banking and money transmission. The NASDAQ Insurance Index contains 63 NASDAQ listed companies classified according to the FTSE™ Global Classification System as insurance or life assurance. They include insurance brokers, non-life insurance, re-insurance, other insurance, and life assurance. The NASDAQ Other Finance Index contains 106 NASDAQ listed companies classified according to the FTSE™ Global Classification System as investment companies, real estate, specialty and other finance, or investment entities. They include real estate holding and development, property agencies, asset managers, consumer finance, investment banks, mortgage finance, other finance including financial holding companies, security and commodity exchanges, and other financial companies. By comparison, the NASDAQ composite index contains 3,227 companies.

Macroeconomic and financial variables like interest rates, interest rate spreads, inflation rates, and unemployment rates are used as measures of general economic conditions and reflect movement along the business cycle (Keim & Stambaugh, 1986; Fama & French, 1988, 1989, 1993; Chen, 1991). In this way, an empirical model is built to test hypotheses.

Figure 1 shows the time series plot of the PSE Technology index and the NASDAQ Bank Index (NBK), NASDAQ Other Financial Index (NFN), and NASDAQ Insurance Index (NIS). The stock price data are available from Reuters. For easy comparison, each of these indexes is normalized equal to 100 in February 1984. The PSE index peaked in February 2000 and again a few months later in August of 2000 before falling to less than half of its value in September 2002. The Financial index peaked in April 1999 and bottomed in September 2002. The Bank and Insurance indexes have, for the most part, continued to trend upwards and avoided the volatility that characterized technology stock prices in the late 1990s. These four stock market indexes show some very strong (greater than 0.79) correlations (Table 1). The PSE is most highly correlated with the NFN and NBK is most highly correlated with NIS.

BANK is the continuously compounded return on the NBK index. FINE is the continuously compounded return on the NFN index. INSUR is the continuously compounded return on the NIS index. The technology data series (TECH) is constructed from the

Figure 1. Time series plot of stock prices in the technology and financial services sectors

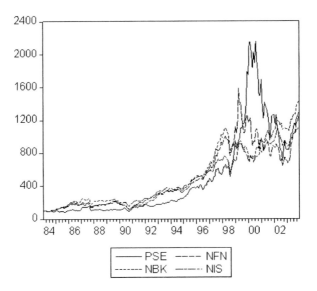

residuals of an ordinary least squares (OLS) regression of the continuously compounded PSE Technology returns on the value weighted CRSP continuously compounded market return. This regression yielded a statistically significant (at the 1% level) beta value of 1.52, indicating that the PSE Technology stock price index is 52% riskier than the U.S. market. This regression equation fits well (adjusted R squared of 0.75 and Durbin Watson statistic of 2.00).

In order to capture general business cycle conditions and changes in equity risk premiums, a number of macroeconomic control variables are included in the analysis. DIVYLD is the continuously compounded rate of return on the S&P 500 dividend yield series. Dividend yields are related to long term business cycle conditions and are therefore likely to be useful for predicting stock returns (Fama & French, 1988). SIR is the continuously compounded rate of return of the U.S. three month T bill. Short term interest rates reflect monetary policy and are included to capture the short term

Table 1. Correlations between the stock prices of technology and financial firms

	PSE	NBK	NFN	NIS
PSE	1			
NBK	0.797715	1		
NFN	0.882329	0.914987	1	
NIS	0.836357	0.980818	0.926922	1

Notes: Sample period is Feb 1984 to Dec 2003. The four stock indexes are; PSE Technology Index (PSE), NASDAQ Bank Index (NBK), NASDAQ Other Financial Index (NFN), and NASDAQ Insurance Index (NIS).

Table 2. Summary statistics

	BANK	FINE	INSUR	TECH	DIVYLD	SIR	ISPREAD	UNEMP	UNINFL
Mean	1.12	1.06	1.02	0.00	-0.43	-0.98	0.00	-0.13	-0.01
Median	1.43	1.78	1.40	0.07	-0.41	-0.40	0.00	0.00	-0.02
Maximum	15.27	33.49	12.68	16.29	15.62	12.19	0.82	7.41	0.60
Minimum	-24.08	-23.95	-22.68	-10.57	-16.34	-25.31	-1.01	-8.89	-0.57
Std. Dev.	4.72	6.28	4.69	3.99	3.83	5.08	0.26	2.57	0.18
Skewness	-1.26	-0.35	-0.80	0.30	0.34	-1.38	0.25	0.13	0.04
Kurtosis	8.30	7.72	6.08	3.97	6.21	7.38	3.84	3.64	3.92
Jarque-Bera	340.95	226.28	119.07	12.82	106.62	265.50	9.52	4.75	8.57
Probability	0.00	0.00	0.00	0.00	0.00	0.00	0.01	0.09	0.01
Observations	238	238	238	238	238	238	238	238	238
Unit Root Tests									
ADF	-11.7	-13.18	-12.93	-15.32	-13.21	-9.56	-7.68	-6.92	-15.54
PP	-11.67	-13.08	-12.74	-15.52	-13.06	-9.54	-10.28	-17.3	-15.56
KPSS	0.09	0.06	0.04	0.73	0.14	0.26	0.1	0.21	0.11

Notes: Data definitions discussed in the text. For the Augmented Dickey and Fuller (1979) (ADF) and Phillips and Perron (1988) (PP) unit root tests, the null hypothesis is unit root while for the Kwiatkowski, Phillips, Schmidt and Shin (1992) KPSS test, the null hypothesis is no unit root (stationarity). For the ADF and PP tests, the 1%, 5% and 10% critical values are -3.458, -2.873, and -2.573 respectively. For the KPSS test the 1%, 5% and 10% critical values are 0.739, 0.463, and 0.347 respectively. The number of lags in the ADF is chosen using the Schwarz information criteria. The PP and KPSS tests use a Bartlett kernel and the bankwidth at zero frequency is selected using the Newey and West (1994) approach.

investment opportunities. ISPREAD is the one month change in the spread between the ten year U.S. Government note and the three month U.S. T bill rate. The spread between long term Government bond yields and short term Government bond yields reflects movements along the yield curve and has been shown to contain considerable predictive power for forecasting GDP growth rates (Estrella & Mishkin, 1996; Harvey, 1997). UNEMP is the logarithmic difference of the unemployment rate. Unemployment rates are included in VAR models to reflect general economic conditions. UNINFL is the unantici-pated one month inflation rate. This variable is constructed from the one month percentage change in the U.S. CPI and a one month forecast (Brooks, 2002). The one period forecast was constructed from an ARIMA(2,1,1) model fitted over the entire data set. This model was chosen based on parsimony and lack of serial correlation in the residuals. The macroeconomic data are available from the Federal Reserve Board of St. Louis (http://research.stlouisfed.org/fred2/). The data on S&P 500 dividend yields are available from DRI McGraw Hill and various issues of the Federal Reserve Bulletin.

Summary statistics for the data indicates that each series has a large standard deviation in relation to its mean value (Table 2). Each of the series exhibits some degree of skewness and/or kurtosis. Unit root tests from regressions with a constant but no trend component are used to establish stationary. For the Augmented Dickey and Fuller (1979) (ADF) and Phillips and Perron (1988) (PP) unit root tests, the null hypothesis is unit root while for the Kwiatkowski, Phillips, Schmidt and Shin (1992) KPSS test, the null hypothesis is no unit root (stationary). Unit root tests confirm that each series is stationary (lower panel of Table 2).

The average annual returns, over the period February 1984 to December 2003, on the PSE, NBK, NFN, and NIS were 12.87%, 13.39%, 12.68%, and 12.18% respectively. In comparison, the average annual return on three month T bills was 5.32%. Risk adjusted returns are measured using the Sharpe ratio. Higher values of the Sharpe ratio are preferred to lower values. Sharpe ratios for the PSE, NBK, NFN, and NIS were 0.27, 0.49, 0.34, and 0.42 respectively. The Sharpe ratios for the financial stock market indexes were each larger than the Sharpe ratio for the PSE technology index suggesting that, for the period under consideration, investments in financial companies were preferable to investments in technology firms.

Results

In our analysis, three VAR models were estimated (one each for the variables BANK, FINE and INSUR). Likelihood ratio tests were used to determine the appropriate lag length for each VAR model. These tests selected 6, 24 and 21 lag lengths for models 1 (BANK), 2 (FINE) and 3 (INSUR) respectively. Hypothesis 1 which predicts a statistically significant effect of an increase in technology on financial performance (measured here by bank stock price returns) is rejected (first panel of Table 3). Furthermore, Granger causality tests indicate that it is very difficult to explain the variation in bank stock price returns using the other variables in the model. This indicates that variables on interest rates, inflation, unemployment rates and dividend yields do not contain enough information about business cycle conditions and/or risk premiums to help explain bank stock returns. Hypothesis 2 which predicts a significant relationship between financial performance and technology is partially supported at the 10% level of significance. In comparison, lagged values of the technology variable do have a statistically significant impact on the stock price returns of other financial services companies, and thus, partially supporting hypothesis one (second panel of Table 3). Lagged values of unanticipated inflation and unemployment rate are also useful drivers of stock price returns of financial services companies. Lagged values of FINE do not, however, impact TECH indicating that hypothesis two is not supported. Lagged values of the technology variable do have a statistically significant impact on the stock price returns of insurance companies and thus partially support hypothesis one (third panel of Table 3). In addition, lagged values of dividend yields, unanticipated inflation and unemployment rates each have predictive power for the stock price returns of insurance companies. Lagged values of INSUR do not, however, impact TECH. While Granger causality tests are useful for testing the existence of a relationship between two variables it does not necessarily indicate the direction of the relationship. For this impulse response functions are more useful.

Table 3. Granger causality tests

From				To			
	BANK	TECH	SIR	ISPREAD	DIVYLD	UNINFL	UNEMP
BANK		0.0657	0.0060	0.1135	0.0000	0.1310	0.5652
TECH	0.4941		0.7243	0.0753	0.4403	0.0660	0.1901
SIR	0.2477	0.2372		0.3871	0.8312	0.0225	0.0869
ISPREAD	0.4720	0.3655	0.0076		0.4550	0.2589	0.6549
DIVYLD	0.7549	0.4435	0.1379	0.2321		0.4419	0.8788
UNINFL	0.6325	0.4898	0.0211	0.3337	0.5665		0.2745
UNEMP	0.1453	0.4194	0.0042	0.5462	0.1844	0.8031	

From				To			
	FINE	TECH	SIR	ISPREAD	DIVYLD	UNINFL	UNEMP
FINE		0.1304	0.5650	0.0422	0.0017	0.1209	0.1435
TECH	0.0444		0.9153	0.8244	0.0002	0.0678	0.0005
SIR	0.1694	0.5683		0.4153	0.0140	0.2551	0.0092
ISPREAD	0.3451	0.4411	0.2230		0.0001	0.0366	0.0786
DIVYLD	0.1383	0.1988	0.3033	0.0329		0.2347	0.1300
UNINFL	0.0360	0.3079	0.8090	0.8329	0.2906		0.0845
UNEMP	0.0558	0.1807	0.8306	0.2458	0.0040	0.0643	

From				To			
	INSUR	TECH	SIR	ISPREAD	DIVYLD	UNINFL	UNEMP
INSUR		0.1908	0.4249	0.4684	0.0019	0.2229	0.2526
TECH	0.0003		0.2592	0.8517	0.0864	0.5654	0.0378
SIR	0.6502	0.9590		0.3956	0.5974	0.2562	0.1290
ISPREAD	0.5001	0.5786	0.0358		0.1441	0.0599	0.0048
DIVYLD	0.0328	0.5339	0.1845	0.2964		0.6499	0.5969
UNINFL	0.0035	0.7642	0.1977	0.5571	0.6360		0.1649
UNEMP	0.0807	0.2165	0.7901	0.1383	0.1929	0.2644	

Notes: Probability values of Wald test statistics are shown.

Table 4 reports the results from model fit and testing the VAR model residuals for serial correlation. The fit of model 1 (BANK) is relatively poor compared to the fits of models 2 (FINE) and 3 (INSUR). The adjusted R-squared values for FINE (0.31) and INSUR (0.22) are easily three times larger than the adjusted R-squared values for BANK (0.06). The tests for serial correlation are multivariate lagrange multiplier (LM) tests (null hypothesis is no serial correlation). Overall, the test results shown in Table 4 indicate little evidence of serial correlation which provides evidence that the VAR models are adequately specified.

Figure 2 shows the response of the BANK variable to generalized one standard deviation innovations in the variables in the VAR model 1. Confidence bands, calculated using 1000 Monte Carlo simulations, are provided to gauge statistical significance. Not surprising, a one standard deviation shock to the BANK variable has a large and statistically

Table 4. Model fit and VAR residual serial correlation LM tests

Model 1	BANK	TECH	SIR	ISPREAD	DIVYLD	UNINFL	UNEMP
R-squared	0.23	0.22	0.49	0.40	0.28	0.24	0.27
Adj. R-squared	0.06	0.04	0.38	0.26	0.12	0.07	0.11
S.E. equation	4.61	3.94	4.02	0.21	3.61	0.18	2.43
Model 2	**FINE**	**TECH**	**SIR**	**ISPREAD**	**DIVYLD**	**UNINFL**	**UNEMP**
R-squared	0.85	0.81	0.86	0.88	0.88	0.83	0.89
Adj. R-squared	0.31	0.11	0.32	0.42	0.44	0.21	0.48
S.E. equation	5.39	3.76	4.24	0.19	2.93	0.16	1.86
Model 3	**INSUR**	**TECH**	**SIR**	**ISPREAD**	**DIVYLD**	**UNINFL**	**UNEMP**
R-squared	0.75	0.69	0.81	0.78	0.78	0.73	0.77
Adj. R-squared	0.22	0.04	0.39	0.30	0.30	0.15	0.28
S.E. equation	4.14	3.89	3.99	0.21	3.28	0.17	2.22

	Model 1		Model 2		Model 3	
Lags	LM-Stat	Prob	LM-Stat	Prob	LM-Stat	Prob
1	63.6013	0.0785	39.3353	0.8366	42.7908	0.7216
2	64.1279	0.0721	38.4956	0.8598	42.4482	0.7342
3	68.0695	0.0370	60.9290	0.1180	58.9485	0.1562
4	41.2636	0.7759	44.0554	0.6734	39.5638	0.8299
5	61.1726	0.1138	59.6821	0.1411	54.3974	0.2765
6	40.8691	0.7891	71.1203	0.0211	34.0891	0.9478
7	63.6801	0.0775	35.8385	0.9196	46.2201	0.5865
8	53.5025	0.3056	45.9579	0.5972	45.9328	0.5982
9	58.7978	0.1594	42.4398	0.7345	35.3286	0.9287
10	35.1781	0.9313	50.4858	0.4146	45.5573	0.6135
11	48.2353	0.5041	49.2383	0.4636	55.9436	0.2304
12	42.7581	0.7229	50.9271	0.3977	60.9129	0.1182
13	48.1456	0.5077	52.9634	0.3238	49.9723	0.4345
14	39.0323	0.8452	36.7135	0.9022	38.6401	0.8559
15	54.3766	0.2772	47.1830	0.5471	51.1867	0.3879
16	45.1794	0.6288	56.5097	0.2149	60.1788	0.1315
17	76.2998	0.0075	63.1945	0.0837	62.3311	0.0956
18	48.7066	0.4849	54.9214	0.2603	36.3505	0.9097
19	40.5538	0.7994	57.6494	0.1858	40.1156	0.8132
20	44.4173	0.6592	58.4267	0.1676	42.0909	0.7471
21	38.4928	0.8599	52.9819	0.3232	55.2691	0.2499
22	58.1002	0.1751	54.1074	0.2857	37.5531	0.8834

Notes: Probability values calculated from a chi-square distribution with 49 degrees of freedom (df). Model 1 (BANK), Model 2 (FINE) and Model 3 (INSUR).

Figure 2. BANK response to generalized one S.D. innovations ±2 S.E

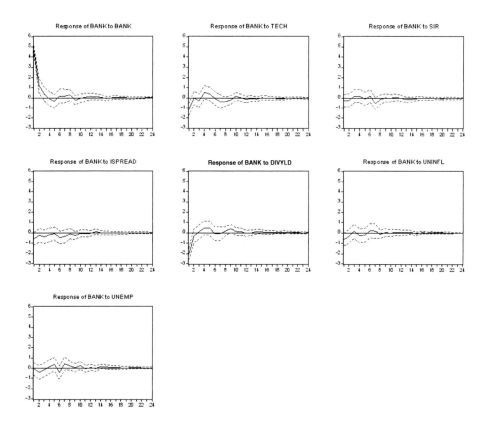

significant (confidence bounds do not contain zero) impact for three months after which time the impact of the shock dissolves. A one standard deviation shock to TECH has a negative and statistically significant impact on BANK for a period of two months. This result is not supportive of hypothesis one which predicts a positive impact between increases in technology and financial performance. One possible explanation for this is that the costs of purchasing and adopting new technology weigh heavier on the firm's financial performance than the gains from increased revenues resulting from the benefits of new technology. Shocks to short term interest rates or unemployment rates have virtually no impact on bank stock returns. A one standard deviation shock to the yield curve (ISPREAD) or the unexpected inflation rate has an initial negative and significant impact on BANK but these effects disappear very rapidly. A one standard deviation shock to dividend yields has a negative and statistically significant impact on BANK for two months before the response dissipates.

FINE responds positively and significantly to a shock to itself (Figure 3). FINE responds negatively and significantly to a shock to TECH, SIR, or DIVYLD although the effects of these shocks wane after a few months. Shocks to ISPREAD, UNINFL, or UNEMP have very little impact on FINE.

Figure 3. FINE response to generalized one S.D. innovations ±2 S.E.

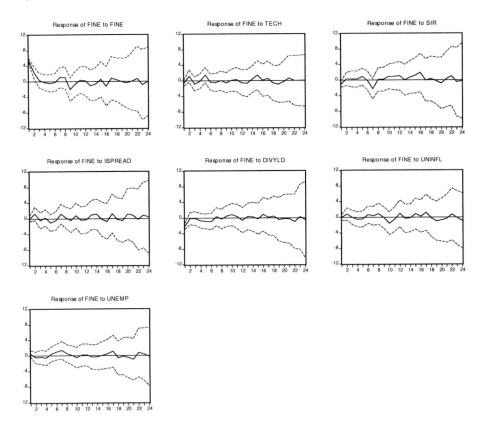

As expected, INSUR responds positively and significantly to a shock to itself (Figure 4). Shocks to technology, dividend yields, the unemployment rate, or interest rate spreads each have negative and statistically significant impacts on INSUR but these effects only last for a few months. Shocks to short term interest rates and unexpected inflation have no significant impact on INSUR.

Summarizing the results in Figures 2-4, shocks to technology or dividend yields each have negative and significant impacts on stock prices in all three models. The impact of these shocks, however, dissipates after a few months. Shocks to other variables like inflation and unemployment have little impact on stock prices while shock to the interest rate variables have somewhat different effect on stock prices and depend upon which stock price index is being studied.

Impulse responses for TECH in each of the three VAR models are not shown but summarized. A shock to BANK leads to a negative and non-significant initial impact on TECH. A shock to FINE leads to a positive initial and statistically significant impact on TECH which supports hypothesis two. A shock to INSUR leads to a negative initial and statistically significant impact on TECH which partially supports hypothesis two.

Figure 4. INSUR response to generalized one S.D. innovations ±2 S.E.

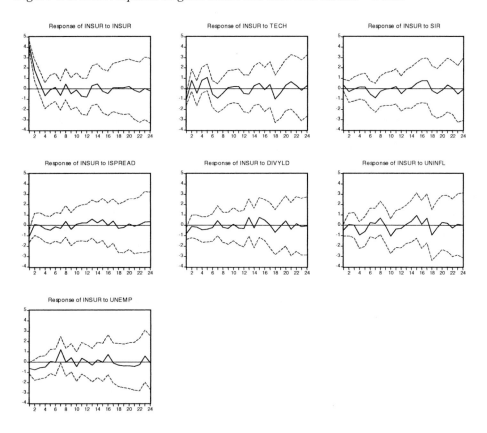

Variance decompositions provide another way of characterizing the dynamic behavior of a system of variables. Standard errors constructed from 1,000 Monte Carlo simulations are reported immediately below the values for the variance decompositions. The variance decompositions for the BANK variable (first panel of Table 5) show that its own effect dominates the decomposition up to 48 months (4 years). This result is consistent with the findings from the Granger causality tests. Unfortunately, different results are obtained with a different ordering of variables (second panel of Table 5). When the ordering of the variables used in the Cholesky decomposition is reversed, own effects explain approximately 62% of BANK and dividend yields explain approximately 18% of the variance in BANK. TECH explains about 7% of the variance and this is statistically significant. Unfortunately, in this case changing the ordering of the variables used in the Cholesky decomposition can and does affect the results. The results from Granger causality tests can be different from those of variance decompositions because variance decompositions are similar to exogeneity tests, they include both contemporaneous and lagged values whereas Granger causality tests only include lagged values of a variable. Variance decompositions are thus stronger restrictions in that current and lagged shocks to the explanatory variables may influence the variable of interest.

Table 5. Variance decompositions functions for BANK

Period	S.E.	BANK	TECH	SIR	ISPREAD	DIVYLD	UNINFL	UNEMP
1	4.6068	100.0000	0.0000	0.0000	0.0000	0.0000	0.0000	0.0000
		0.0000	0.0000	0.0000	0.0000	0.0000	0.0000	0.0000
3	4.8572	96.4062	0.5100	0.3144	0.4564	0.9209	0.3188	1.0734
		3.0950	1.2218	1.0704	1.3266	1.6787	1.1531	1.6633
6	5.0563	89.5878	2.0216	0.5889	1.4299	3.1273	1.0131	2.2315
		4.4874	2.2577	1.5741	2.1233	2.7801	1.6794	1.9752
9	5.2044	85.2016	2.9864	1.5958	2.6034	3.8008	1.2782	2.5338
		4.8756	2.4088	1.9573	2.5564	2.9075	1.8601	1.9115
12	5.2254	84.6047	3.1034	1.5977	2.6085	3.9976	1.3050	2.7832
		5.1203	2.4454	2.0132	2.5659	3.0127	1.8828	2.0278
18	5.2466	83.9801	3.1567	1.8175	2.6385	4.1265	1.3731	2.9078
		5.4505	2.4925	2.1923	2.6001	3.1502	1.9158	2.0937
24	5.2513	83.8363	3.1902	1.8544	2.6358	4.1739	1.3800	2.9293
		5.6842	2.5538	2.2771	2.6238	3.2507	1.9342	2.1354
36	5.2528	83.7903	3.1998	1.8675	2.6348	4.1867	1.3828	2.9382
		6.0293	2.6487	2.4162	2.6548	3.3986	1.9609	2.1848
48	5.2529	83.7870	3.2003	1.8685	2.6347	4.1876	1.3830	2.9388
		6.3294	2.7306	2.5633	2.6756	3.5274	1.9791	2.2201

Cholesky Ordering: BANK TECH SIR ISPREAD DIVYLD UNINFL UNEMP
Standard Errors: Monte Carlo (1000 repetitions)

Period	S.E.	BANK	TECH	SIR	ISPREAD	DIVYLD	UNINFL	UNEMP
24	5.2513	62.3946	7.5592	3.1606	2.9060	17.7373	2.8238	3.4185
		5.4847	3.0586	2.6585	3.0329	3.9330	2.2964	2.7071
36	5.2528	62.3605	7.5630	3.1698	2.9048	17.7427	2.8255	3.4338
		5.6373	3.1400	2.7648	3.0908	3.9678	2.3111	2.8433
48	5.2529	62.3580	7.5631	3.1705	2.9047	17.7432	2.8256	3.4349
		5.7450	3.2131	2.8330	3.1251	3.9893	2.3182	2.9169

Cholesky Ordering: UNEMP UNINFL DIVYLD ISPREAD SIR TECH BANK
Standard Errors: Monte Carlo (1000 repetitions)

Notes: Standard errors reported below variance decomposition values.

Variance decompositions for the FINE variable show that after two years own effects explain about 40% of the variance while technology explains about 9% of the variance in FINE (first panel of Table 6). The two interest rate variables taken together explain about 24% of the variance in FINE after two years. After four years the own effect is further weakened and the contributions of the most of the other variables slightly increased. Notice that the variance decompositions are not that sensitive to the ordering of the variables as the results in panel two of Table 6 are very similar to the results in panel one of Table 6.

Table 6. Variance decompositions functions for FINE

Period	S.E.	FINE	TECH	SIR	ISPREAD	DIVYLD	UNINFL	UNEMP
1	5.3905	100.0000	0.0000	0.0000	0.0000	0.0000	0.0000	0.0000
		0.0000	0.0000	0.0000	0.0000	0.0000	0.0000	0.0000
3	6.3408	86.3896	6.4896	1.2495	3.2634	0.6789	0.2887	1.6404
		7.7326	4.6289	3.9820	4.3929	2.9534	2.5615	3.5068
6	7.1893	67.7342	9.3263	1.8872	6.0299	6.2847	3.7488	4.9888
		7.9324	4.8471	4.5854	5.4551	5.6205	3.9225	4.4172
9	8.1589	62.0047	8.2968	8.0438	6.2167	6.1849	4.3348	4.9183
		7.8013	4.7229	5.7208	5.1567	5.0578	4.0488	4.0607
12	8.8261	53.7100	7.5790	10.6737	6.6947	6.4002	10.3297	4.6126
		7.2920	4.9608	5.9321	5.3465	4.8594	5.1292	3.8832
18	9.9864	46.0118	9.4082	12.9824	9.7077	5.7820	10.1892	5.9186
		7.0620	5.2808	6.3840	6.0033	5.2352	4.5238	4.2195
24	10.7937	40.5145	9.2212	13.3390	10.6864	6.3615	12.8751	7.0023
		7.2045	5.8999	7.0473	6.2423	5.8552	5.1713	4.6092
36	12.0041	35.3783	9.9586	13.9916	9.8160	8.1254	15.0170	7.7131
		8.3947	7.0475	9.0819	7.7051	7.0315	5.6472	5.6537
48	13.2055	32.7511	10.0633	15.9546	10.0999	9.7073	13.6998	7.7239
		9.7110	8.6308	11.077	9.1863	7.9303	6.4093	6.5130

Cholesky Ordering: FINE TECH SIR ISPREAD DIVYLD UNINFL UNEMP
Standard Errors: Monte Carlo (1000 repetitions)

Period	S.E.	FINE	TECH	SIR	ISPREAD	DIVYLD	UNINFL	UNEMP
24	10.7937	37.6666	7.8955	13.9843	14.8622	9.1719	8.7353	7.6842
		7.3307	5.3680	7.1874	6.5052	5.6670	5.5018	4.7839
36	12.0041	33.8439	8.3438	14.3190	13.0513	9.7063	12.2717	8.4641
		8.7048	6.3166	9.2412	7.5614	6.6257	6.7366	5.8100
48	13.2055	31.8293	8.7040	16.5582	12.1244	10.2412	12.0922	8.4507
		9.9466	7.3318	10.5508	8.8250	7.9284	7.6490	6.5690

Cholesky Ordering: UNEMP UNINFL DIVYLD ISPREAD SIR TECH FINE
Standard Errors: Monte Carlo (1000 repetitions)

Notes: See Table 5.

Variance decompositions for the INSUR variable show that after two years INSUR and TECH explain approximately 47% and 16% of the variation in INSUR (Table 7, first panel). After four years the own effect is down to 40% and the contributions of the other variables slightly increased. The combined effect of the two interest rate variables (18%) is slightly larger than the effect from technology. The variance decompositions are not that sensitive to the ordering of the variables used in the Cholesky decomposition because the results in panel two of Table 7 are very similar to the results in panel one of Table 7.

Table 7. Variance decompositions functions for INSUR

Period	S.E.	INSUR	TECH	SIR	ISPREAD	DIVYLD	UNINFL	UNEMP
1	4.1409	100.0000	0.0000	0.0000	0.0000	0.0000	0.0000	0.0000
		0.0000	0.0000	0.0000	0.0000	0.0000	0.0000	0.0000
3	4.8605	87.9661	7.3282	1.5112	0.3406	0.3492	0.0288	2.4760
		6.7334	4.3741	3.0038	2.3921	1.9891	2.1003	3.5499
6	5.3658	73.7653	12.5729	2.1267	3.5564	0.8333	4.3234	2.8221
		7.4939	5.1167	3.6019	4.5719	3.2103	3.7954	3.6546
9	5.8423	64.6966	14.4511	3.3150	5.1031	1.8441	5.3847	5.2054
		7.0314	5.7193	4.2411	4.7191	3.5378	4.2650	3.9868
12	6.2065	60.3201	14.0732	3.3806	4.6049	3.0873	9.1170	5.4168
		6.7798	5.5295	4.1267	4.6529	4.0144	4.8896	3.7277
18	6.8956	50.0983	15.2909	5.8640	6.6373	5.4206	10.6131	6.0756
		6.1280	5.5336	4.6258	4.9774	4.3924	4.8547	3.8269
24	7.1475	47.1106	15.9183	6.5550	6.6417	5.9908	10.3390	7.4445
		6.1124	5.7723	4.9591	5.1240	4.7749	5.1376	3.9688
36	7.7702	41.5591	16.7298	7.1802	9.5211	7.0974	10.5939	7.3185
		6.8483	6.5258	6.0051	5.9908	5.7553	5.5856	4.4676
48	8.1106	39.8346	16.2659	8.5502	9.7303	7.3123	10.6810	7.6257
		7.9028	7.5366	7.2288	7.1048	6.9070	6.7947	5.1400

Cholesky Ordering: INSUR TECH SIR ISPREAD DIVYLD UNINFL UNEMP
Standard Errors: Monte Carlo (1000 repetitions)

Period	S.E.	INSUR	TECH	SIR	ISPREAD	DIVYLD	UNINFL	UNEMP
24	7.1475	45.1212	15.3166	7.8147	4.4755	6.1086	11.4076	9.7559
		5.5674	5.0641	5.4079	4.1413	4.1287	5.4119	4.3455
36	7.7702	40.1641	15.9257	8.1663	8.2781	6.7021	11.4743	9.2895
		6.3164	6.1648	6.2829	4.9114	4.9803	6.3509	4.8797
48	8.1106	38.3862	15.6465	9.4792	8.3742	7.0899	11.5372	9.4867
		7.6754	7.0531	7.3375	5.6030	5.9504	7.2811	6.0351

Cholesky Ordering: UNEMP UNINFL DIVYLD ISPREAD SIR TECH INSUR
Standard Errors: Monte Carlo (1000 repetitions)

Notes: See Table 5.

Variance decompositions for the technology variable (TECH) show some interesting results. The tables are not shown to save space (but available from the authors upon request). For VAR model 1 (BANK), TECH explains 76.32% of its own variation after a period of 48 months (four years). The next most important variable is BANK which explains 10.98% of the variation in TECH. Each of these variance decompositions is statistically significant at the 5% level (one tail test). For model 2 (FINE), TECH explains 33.71% of its own variation after four years. FINE, the next most important variable, explains 15.38% of the variation in TECH after four years. Each of these variance

Table 8. Summary of results

Hypothesis one. Increased spending on IT increases financial performance.

From:	To:		
	Granger Causality tests (p values shown)		
	BANK	FINE	INSUR
Lagged TECH	0.49	0.04**	0.00**
	Generalized Impulse Responses		
	BANK	FINE	INSUR
One standard deviation shock to TECH	(-) **	(-)**	(-)**
	Variance Decompositions after 4 years		
	BANK	FINE	INSUR
TECH contribution to Variance Decomposition	3.20	10.66**	16.27**

Hypothesis two. Increased financial performance increases spending on IT.

From:	To:		
	Granger Causality tests (p values shown)		
Lagged	TECH (Model 1)	TECH (Model 2)	TECH (Model 3)
BANK (Model 1)	0.07		
FINE (Model 2)		0.13	
INSUR (Model 3)			0.19
	Generalized Impulse Responses		
One standard deviation shock to	TECH (Model 1)	TECH (Model 2)	TECH (Model 3)
BANK (Model 1)	(-)		
FINE (Model 2)		(+)**	
INSUR (Model 3)			(-)**
	Variance Decompositions after 4 years		
contribution to Variance Decomposition	TECH (Model 1)	TECH (Model 2)	TECH (Model 3)
BANK (Model 1),	10.98**		
FINE (Model 2)		15.38**	
INSUR (Model 3)			11.20**

*Notes: ** denotes statistically significant at the 5% level*

decompositions is statistically significant at the 5% level. For model 3 (INSUR), TECH explains 40.65% of its own variation after 48 months. INSUR is the next most important variable explaining 11.20% of the variation in TECH. Each of these variance decompositions is statistically significant at the 5% level.

The results from Tables 5-7, summarized in Table 8, show that after a reasonable length of time (two to four years) the variations in the variables FINE and INSUR can be partially explained by the technology variable but that the technology variable plays no role in explaining the variation in the variable BANK. One possible explanation for this is that compared to banks, companies in the insurance and other financial services categories tend to have a more limited scope of products and services making it easier to visualize a relationship between IT adoption inputs and company outputs. Banks on the other hand, tend to offer a wider array of products and services across a much larger portfolio of different types of customers. This makes it more difficult for banks to engineer strategic IT solutions. These results, which are for the most part consistent with the Granger causality tests and the information contained in the impulse responses, provide some evidence in support of hypothesis one. The problem is that according to the impulse responses in Figures 2-4, a shock to the technology innovation actually lowers financial performance in the first few months which is the opposite of what hypothesis one predicts. One explanation for this is that while a technology shock does have a negative impact on stock returns over one to two months, perhaps the accumulated effect of the shock is positive over a longer period of time. While we don't investigate this idea any further in this paper, it does seem very plausible especially in the context that expenditures on IT impact firm performance with variable lengths of time.

We also find some support for hypothesis two in the case of model 1 (BANK) and model 2 (FINE). For model 1, it is the case that the results from the Granger causality tests are in general agreement with the variance decompositions. For model 2, impulse responses and variance decompositions support Hypothesis two (Table 8).

Our study does have some limitations that need to be pointed out. First, we have no direct measure of technology and have consequently measured technology as the unexplained component from a capital asset pricing model. Second, we have measured financial performance using stock price data. There are other ways of measuring financial performance (like Tobin's Q for example) but stock prices remain the most widely used and easily accessible measure of financial performance. Stock prices are also the most visible and interesting measure of firm performance for investors (both individual and institutional). As behavioral finance researchers have shown, however, stock markets can become miss-priced and deviate from fundamentals because of investor emotion (which leads to bubbles and fads).

Conclusions

Global information technology and competitive financial alliances are helping to reshape the business landscape. Information technology (IT) plays a crucial role in increasing economic growth and prosperity. Currently, media, telecommunications and computing are converging to the Internet. The Internet has thus, become a multipurpose medium of information and knowledge exchange. This convergence is occurring against a backdrop of efficient financial capital markets. Countries or regions with highly efficient capital markets will see this convergence occur faster relative to countries or regions with less efficient or developed financial capital markets. Companies engaged in banking, insurance and other financial services are the drivers of efficient financial markets.

The growth in the financial services sector is particularly evident in the United States. Since 1982, the profits of U.S. financial firms have grown from 4% of overall corporate profits to more than 40% today. Currently, the U.S. financial industry accounts for 40% of U.S. stock market capitalization. One concern is that this "finance based economy" is currently being sustained by the Federal Reserve through very low interest rates. Increased profits means that firms have money to increase wages and salaries, dividends, invest in their own business strategies (like IT), hire more workers, and pursue financial alliances. Increases in IT can lead to increased labour productivity, greater market share and higher profits.

The main objective of this study was to determine the relationship between IT expenditures and financial performance in the financial services industry. For this chapter, a vector autoregressive (VAR) model was used to test hypotheses one (increased spending on IT increases financial performance) and two (increased financial performance increases spending on IT) where financial performance is assumed to be adequately measured by stock price returns. Control variables for general business cycle conditions were included in the analysis. Results from Granger causality tests revealed that lagged values of the technology variable helped explain current values of FINE and INSUR. Lagged values of BANK helped explain the technology variable. Granger causality tests are useful for determining whether the lagged values of one variable can help explain the movements of another variables but Granger causality tests do not indicate the sign (positive or negative) of the direction. For this, generalized impulse responses are more useful.

A one standard deviation shock to the technology variable led to a negative and statistically significant impact on the stock price variable in each of the three models. Clearly technology shocks did impact the business performance of financial companies but not in the way suggested by hypothesis one. A shock to BANK led to a negative and non-significant initial impact on TECH. A shock to FINE led to a positive initial and statistically significant impact on TECH which supported hypothesis two. A shock to INSUR led to a negative initial and statistically significant impact on TECH which partially supported hypothesis two.

Variance decompositions showed that after 48 months the technology variable had a statistically significant impact in explaining the variance decomposition of the insurance company stock price variable and the other financial services stock price variable. In comparison, each of the stock price variables had a statistically significant contribution to the variance decomposition of the technology variable in each of the three models.

Taken collectively, our results indicate that the relationship between technology and financial performance is murky and not as straightforward as some would believe. Changes in technology do have some impact on the business performance of insurance companies and other financial services companies but little impact on the financial performance of banks. In comparison, changes in financial performance (as measured by stock prices) do have some impact on technology in the models for banks and other financial companies. Our results show that the greatest benefits from increases in technology accrue to insurance and other financial companies. Managers of these companies could increase their business performance through strategic investment and use of IT.

References

The Banker (2004a). Credit goes to the innovators. Retrieved May 11, 2004, from www.thebanker.com

The Banker (2004b). Market trends create key challenges and solutions. Retrieved May 11, 2004, from www.thebanker.com

The Banker (2004c). FSIs to up external IT spending. Retrieved May 11, 2004, from www.thebanker.com

The Banker (2004d). Retail banking spurs IT drive. Retrieved May 11, 2004, from www.thebanker.com

The Banker (2004e). IT saving of $71bn up for grabs. Retrieved May 11, 2004, from www.thebanker.com

Brooks, C. (2002). *Introductory econometrics for finance*. UK: Cambridge University Press.

Chen, N. (1991). Financial investment opportunities and the macroeconomy. *Journal of Finance, 46*, 529-554.

Dickey, D., & Fuller, W. (1979). Distribution of the estimators for autoregressive time series with a unit root. *Journal of the American Statistical Association, 74*, 427-31.

The Economist. (2005, February 12-18). A world awash with profits. *373*(8413), 62-63.

Estrella, A., & Mishkin, F. S. (1996). The yield curve as a predictor of U.S. recessions, Federal Reserve Board of New York. *Current Issues in Economics and Finance, 2*, 7.

Fama, E., & French, K. (1988). Dividend yields and expected stock returns. *Journal of Financial Economics, 22*, 3-25.

Fama, E., & French, K. (1989). Business conditions and expected returns on stocks and bonds. *Journal of Financial Economics, 25*, 23-49.

Fama, E., & French, K. (1993). Common risk factors in the returns on stocks and bonds. *Journal of Financial Economics, 33*, 3-56.

Grosse, R. (2003). *The future of global financial services*. UK: Blackwell.

Harvey, C. R. (1997). The relation between the term structure of interest rates and Canadian economic growth. *Canadian Journal of Economics, 1*, 169-193.

Keim, D., & Stambaugh, R. (1986). Predicting returns in the stock and bond markets. *Journal of Financial Economics, 17*, 357-390.

Kim, C., & Davidson, L. F. (2004). The effects of IT expenditures on banks' business performance: Using a balanced scorecard approach. *Managerial Finance, 30*(6), 28-45.

Kurihara, Y. (2005). The spreading use of digital cash and its problems. In H. Kehal & V. P. Singh (Eds.), *Digital economy: Impacts, influences and challenges* (pp. 84-97). Hershey, PA: Idea Group Publishing.

Kwiatkowski, D., Phillips, P. C. B., Schmidt P., & Shin, Y. (1992). Testing the null hypothesis of stationary against the alternative of a unit root. *Journal of Econometrics*, *54*, 159-178.

Mayer, C. (2002). Financing the new economy: Financial institutions and corporate governance. *Information Economics and Policy*, *14*, 311-326.

Nelson, C. R., & Schwert, W. G. (1982). Tests for predictive relationships between time series variables: A Monte Carlo investigation. *Journal of the American Statistical Association*, *77*, 11-18.

Newey, W., & West, K. (1994). Automatic lag selection in covariance matrix estimation. *Review of Economic Studies*, *61*, 631-53.

Phillips, P. C. B., & Perron, P. (1988). Testing for a unit root in time series regression. *Biometrika*, *75*, 335-46.

Porter, M. (1985). *Competitive advantage: Creating and sustaining superior performance*. New York: The Free Press.

Shapiro, C., & Varian, H. (1999). *Information rules: A strategic guide to the network economy*. Boston: Harvard Business School Press.

Shiller, R. J. (2003). *The new financial order: Risk in the 21st century*. Princeton, NJ: Princeton University Press.

Slywotzky, A., & Wise, R. (2003). *How to grow when markets don't*. New York: Warner Business Books.

Zellner, A., & Franz, P. (1974). Time series analysis and simultaneous equation econometric models. *Journal of Econometrics*, *2*, 17-54.

Chapter II

Recent Development of Information Technology in Japanese Banks

Nobuyoshi Yamori, Nagoya University, Japan

Kozo Harimaya, Sapporo Gakuin University, Japan

Yoshihiro Asai, Nagoya University, Japan

Abstract

Although Japanese banks have suffered from huge, non-performing loans since the burst of the bubble, they have invested as much as possible in information technology. However, due to the shortage of available funds, each bank has felt that its investment was not high enough to compete with leading U.S. and European banks. This is one important reason why major Japanese banks have been merging with each other in recent years. Information technology has now become a key issue in the Japanese banking business. This chapter discusses the recent development of information technology in Japanese banks in detail. The section titled Changing in the Business Model *provides a brief explanation of the current Japanese banking environment. In* The Steady Progress of New Information Technology in Financial Institutions, *we discuss how Japanese financial institutions, mainly banks, have dealt with new information technology. The section on* Internet Banking *provides a detailed discussion of new Internet banks and the Internet banking services of existing banks. As information investment has an external effect, the market will fail without government assistance. Therefore, in* Government Efforts: E-Japan Strategy, *we explain what the Japanese government has done in terms of IT usage in financial services. Finally, the* Conclusions *section concludes this chapter.*

Introduction

It is commonly agreed that financial transactions are inevitably accompanied with so-called asymmetric information problems. For example, lenders are not sure whether applicants are honest and will do their best to pay back their loans. Because information issues may make transactions in the financial markets impossible, financial institutions play a crucial role in solving these issues.

As pointed out in the literature, there are two kinds of information — hard information and soft information (see Boot, 2000; Berger & Udell, 2002; Onega & Smith, 2000; Petersen & Rajan, 1995; Scott, 2004; Stein, 2002). Soft information, such as considering an owner's motivation, is important in small business loans. Usually, loan officers who maintain daily contact with borrowers are able to produce soft information. Soft information is difficult to quantify and verify to a third party. In contrast to soft information, hard information includes verifiable figures, such as financial ratios calculated from firm's financial statements and stock market prices. These figures are easy to quantify and verify by using a computer, and due to the rapid development of information technology, the usage of hard information has become highly advanced. For example, money market mutual funds require daily interest payments. Huge calculation tasks have become possible by using high-performance computers, and financial institutions recognize that information technology is a key technology for their business, because strategic technology investment reduces costs, increases efficiency and enables institutions to offer value-added and competitive products and services.

Leading international banks have spent a great deal of money on information technology. For example, CELENT (2002), a consulting and research firm, pointed out that the largest commercial banks in the United States spent as much as 25% of their total expenses on information technology, and certain specialist banks spent even higher percentages[1]. In addition, CELENT (2002) reported that U.S. banks spent more than U.S. $34 billion on technology in 2002. Citigroup's IT budget for 2002 was U.S. $5.1 billion. JP Morgan Chase followed Citigroup, with an IT budget of U.S. $4.7 billion. Bank of America, with an IT budget of U.S. $3.3 billion, was third, fourth was Wells Fargo with an IT budget of U.S. $2.0 billion, and fifth was Bank One with an IT budget of U.S. $1.9 billion. Furthermore, CELENT (2005) indicated that IT spending in the North American banking industry will continue to rise at a moderate rate from U.S. $42.6 billion in 2004 to U.S. $47.9 billion in 2007.

Regarding European banks, CELENT (2004) estimates that they spent EU 44.6 billion in 2004. The largest IT investor among European banks was HSBC Holdings, which spent EU 3.05 billion as an IT investment, followed by Deutsche Bank (EU 2.64 billion), UBS (EU 2.63 billion), ABN Amro (EU 2.26 billion), the Royal Bank of Scotland (EU 1.68 billion), Credit Suisse (EU 1.44 billion), ING (EU 1.41 billion) and BNP Paribas (EU 1.37 billion).

Figure 1. Non-performing loans and write-off costs of Japanese banks

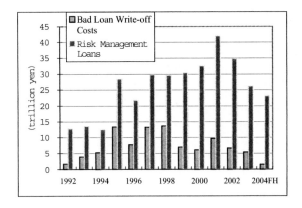

Notes: Figures from FY 1992 to FY 1994 cover only major banks (i.e., city banks, long-term credit banks and trust banks). Figures since FY 1995 cover all banks (i.e., the first- and second-tier regional banks, as well as major banks). The figures for FY 2004 are those as of the end of the first half of FY 2004. The data source is Financial Services Agency.

Although Japanese banks have suffered from huge, non-performing loans since the burst of the bubble (see Figure 1), they have also invested a huge amount of money on their information facilities. However, due to a shortage of available funds, every bank has felt that its investment was not high enough to compete with leading U.S. and European banks[2]. This is reported to be one of the main reasons why large Japanese banks chose to merge with other banks[3]. CELENT (2003) estimated that Japanese banks would spend U.S. $11.9 billion on technology in the fiscal year 2004. Mizuho Holdings spent U.S. $1.94 billion, followed by Sumitomo Mitsui Banking Corporation (SMBC) (U.S. $1.065 billion), Mitsubishi-Tokyo Financial Group (U.S. $930 million), UFJ Holdings (U.S. $895 million) and Resona Holdings (U.S. $735 million). The recent mega-mergers in Japan have enabled Japanese banks to spend as much on IT as major U.S. and European banks.

Changing in the Business Model

The traditional business model of financial institutions, such as banks and Shinkin banks (credit associations), is that they collect funds as a form of deposits, which are usually protected by government-supported deposit insurance, and extend loans to those who need funds. During the rapid economic growth period of the 1980s, Japanese households were net savers, and non-financial corporations were borrowers. Therefore, Japanese banks intermediated funds between households and non-financial corporations during that period. Since there were a lot of profitable investment opportunities in the fast-growing economy, a number of firms wanted to borrow as many funds as possible, and it was easy for Japanese banks to find promising borrowers. As the amount of loans that banks could extend were restricted by their ability to attract customers to open savings accounts and therefore amass savings during the rapid economic growth period, the most important consideration for financial institutions was how much money they could amass in savings. Therefore, the ability to amass savings was the most critical source of competitive advantage in financial industries. In that circumstance, the larger a bank was, the more profitable and stronger it was. Naturally, the hierarchy of Japanese banks was dependent on the amount of deposits.

However, the economic environment has changed since the 1980s. The Japanese economy has grown at lower rates than during the rapid growth period. Furthermore, as large Japanese firms have grown and accumulated their own funds, they have not needed to borrow funds from banks as often as before. In addition, the development of financial markets has accelerated the disintermediation of large firms, which means that large firms are increasingly less dependent on bank loans for financing and actively use financial markets. Thus, financial institutions do not always find prospective customers even if they have the ability to absorb funds. Therefore, the ability to absorb deposits does not necessarily mean the ability, anymore, of making profits. In summary, the source of the competitive power of financial institutions has changed from the ability to absorb deposits to the ability to create lending (i.e., find good borrowers).

Unfortunately, because of the tendency to absorb as many deposits as possible was an established practice by Japanese banks, some financial institutions could not adapt themselves to the new economic environment. They did not change their business model, and were recklessly active in absorbing deposits during the bubble period (i.e., in the late 1980s). As these institutions faced difficulties in finding traditional industrial borrowers, they were forced to increase loans to real estate companies and construction companies, which seemed prosperous during the asset price appreciation period. Yamori (2004) finds that financial institutions that went bankrupt after the burst of the bubble economy had increased their deposits during the bubble period more rapidly than sound financial institutions. Furthermore, the stagnant deflation and the Bank of Japan's substantial credit relaxation in the 1990s made the ability to create loans even more important. In sum, the ability to absorb deposits that is not accompanied by a decent ability to create loans is not a source of competitive power, and may in fact be a cause of bank failure.

While funds in the money market were superabundant in the late 1990s and financial institutions claimed that it was increasingly difficult for them to find good borrowers, many small- and medium-sized enterprises (SME) ironically had serious trouble with banks' reluctance to lend (i.e., credit crunch). In the extreme, several small firms suffered because banks peeled off their loans. In other words, Japanese financial institutions have not been able to perform an essential role (intermediary role), and Japanese financial institutions might lose their roles in financial business in the future.

In March 2003, the Council on Financial Services, which is the advisory council of the Financial Services Agency (FSA), released its report, "In preparation for reinforcing the function of relationship banking." This report recommended that regional financial institutions, such as regional banks, Shinkin banks and credit unions, develop the ability to give loans to regional customers. That is, the report suggested that regional financial institutions have no other choice but to do relationship banking — a banking business model in which banking with customers is conducted using soft information accumulated through long-term and close relationships. Previous studies found that a closer relationship between banks and borrowers leads to lower interest rates on loans (e.g., Berger & Udell, 1995; Harhoff & KoÈrting, 1998), more favorable collateral requirements (e.g., Berger & Udell, 1995; Harhoff & KoÈrting, 1998), smaller dependency on expensive trade credits (e.g., Petersen & Rajan, 1994, 1995), less volatile interest rates on loans (e.g., Berlin & Mester, 1998) and larger credit availability (e.g., Cole, 1998; Elsas & Krahnen, 1998).

Berger and Udell (2002) pointed out that small institutions are more suited to provide relationship banking services than large banks, because small institutions can handle soft information more efficiently than large institutions. Therefore, whether small regional financial institutions can adequately assess credit risks regarding local businesses through bank-firm relationships is a key condition for their survival. Of course, the importance of relationships in regional banking services was well recognized before the Council's report was published, but the Council on Financial Services stressed that the ability of many regional institutions to establish such relationships was not satisfactory, and that financial institutions should develop this ability immediately.

One of the reasons that Japanese banks are poor at screening loan applications and judging the credit risks of borrowers is that these functions have often been routinely performed based on each staff member's personal experience, and that the "know-how" to screen applicants and to judge each applicant's risk has not been adequately shared in the organization. Of course, soft information is not easily shared, but if hard information that can be shared easily is used to make loan decisions, a poor outcome is more likely to result. Therefore, banks should construct an information system to enable all officers of the institution to use common "know-how." Whether regional financial institutions can use information technology better or not in terms of loan creation is critical.

The Steady Progress of New Information Technology in Financial Institutions

After the burst of the bubble economy, Japanese financial institutions became preoccupied with the disposal of bad loans. As Figure 2 shows, banks' capital investments were considerably curtailed and the amounts of investments in 2002 were below the 60% level of fiscal year 1995. However, this decrease of capital investments of Japanese banks does not necessarily mean that there were no forward-looking investments. In this regard, it is notable that many banks sold off real estate, such as branch offices and employees' apartments. As these restructuring sales were regarded as negative capital investments, the total capital investments in the late 1990s tended to be small or even negative.

We would like to emphasize the fact that banks' mechanization investments, which are almost the same thing as IT investments nowadays, remained unchanged until the fiscal year 1999 and significantly increased after the fiscal year 1999. For example, the Financial Information System Center (2003) studied the implementation circumstances in terms of Internet banking services. According to the Financial Information System Center (2003), only 11.1% of surveyed financial institutions as of March 2002 reported that they had already provided Internet banking services to business customers, while as of March 2003, 36.8% of them reported either that they had already provided Internet banking services to business customers or that they were planning to start the services in 2003, and 40.0% of them reported that the matter was "under study." That is, the introduction of Internet banking for business customers has been proceeding smoothly. However, the following issues must be considered.

First, the IT implementation rates for corporate businesses vary substantially across bank categories. For example, while the IT implementation rate for city banks, which are the largest banks and play an important role in the Japanese Keiretsu, is 100%, that of the first regional banks is 18.3%, that of the second-tier regional banks is 6.5%, and that of the Shinkin banks is 9.6%. It is generally said that many regional financial institutions start Internet-banking services for corporate businesses not because regional banks want to curtail expenditures by using Internet banking, but because they are afraid that major commercial banks and pure-Internet-play banks could deprive regional banks of settlement services (N. K. Shimbun, personal communication, December 12, 2003). Financial institutions that cannot introduce these minimum IT services will find themselves in increasingly tight spots.

Second, IT implementation in financial industries for corporate customers is far behind that in other industries. The Ministry of Economy, Trade and Industry (METI) conducted a research survey on the market size of electronic commerce. According to the METI's report, the size of the e-commerce market, which is defined by how many business enterprises purchase raw materials and partly-finished goods through the Internet, namely the so-called electronic B2B market, increased to 43.6 trillion yen for the fiscal year 2002. In contrast, the size of electronic B2B financial transactions (including insurance) was only 4 billion yen. The electronic transaction rate in B2B financial transactions has stayed at just 0.01%, while the electronic transaction rate of the entire Japanese economy is 6.99%. It is apparent that IT implementation in financial industries lags far behind that in other industries.

Third, while banks have invested substantial funds into information technology in order to reduce expenditures, future IT investments should be used to enhance the loan creation ability, which is the *raison d'etre* of regional financial institutions. For example, the report of the Council on Financial Services mentioned above demands that every financial institution set interest rates on loans at the level reflecting the borrower's true credit risk. Financial institutions have to prepare a reliable statistical database and then set the interest rates on loans at the level that is derived from the data analysis. If financial institutions set interest rates on loans without a satisfactory explanation and a statistical base, customers will not be convinced that the interest rate is fair.

Finally, small- and medium-sized enterprises (SME) want a rapid decision to be made on their loan applications. According to "The special questionnaire on functions and roles of financial institutions that industrial firms expect," conducted and released by the Nagoya branch of the Bank of Japan in December 2003, SME regarded "the expeditious

Figure 2. Trend of capital investment and IT investment of banks

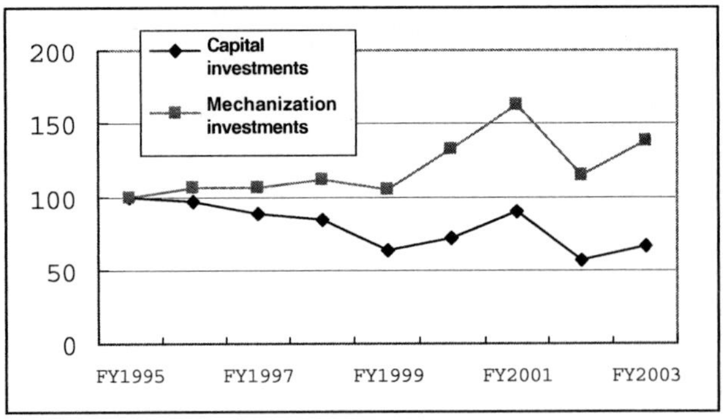

*Notes: The figure is based on the Bank of Japan's "short-term economic observation. (*Tankan *in Japanese)." In* Tankan, *the amounts of investments of financial institutions are reported. We drew up this figure by setting the fiscal year 1995 as the base year, and using annual rates of change to calculate each year's relative level. All values except for fiscal year 2003 were actual ones, but we had to use a planned value for fiscal year 2003 because the questionnaire was changed after 2004.*

offer of money" as the third most important service and function of financial institutions, while a "lower borrowing rate of interest" and a "stable supply of money" were the first and second. If financial institutions can speed up loan screening by developing an IT system, they can accurately accommodate these SME's needs. Moreover, if a loan contract is computerized, borrowers do not have to pay the documentary stamp tax. Actually, UFJ Bank is already making use of this fact, and is using it as an advertising tool to attract new customers (N. K. Shimbun, personal communication, October 28, 2003).

Regarding banking services for individuals, convenient access is particularly important. The Postal Services Research Institute, a division of Japan Post, has been conducting "a survey on the way households use financial institutions" every two years since 1989. The June 2004 result shows that 21.0% of surveyed persons (multiple answers allowed) answered, "Internet banking is convenient because we can use it for 24 hours," and 20.4% of them answered, "We can enjoy the services without visiting branch offices." Information technology surely enhances the convenience for individuals in terms of using financial services.

However, we should recognize that 52.8% of persons answered that they do not need Internet banking services, 25.6% answered that they were worried about settlement only through the Internet, and 22.0% answered that they were worried about Internet security. Therefore, to encourage the spread of Internet banking services for individuals, banks should make efforts not only to make their services safer, but also to convince individual customers that they are well protected when they use Internet banking services.

Internet Banking

Pure-Internet-Play Banks

Although almost no banks except foreign subsidiary banks were established in Japan after the World War II, several new banks recently began operation due to deregulation. Even though these new banks do not necessarily specialize in providing settlement services on the Internet, they share common management attributes. For example, they do not have physical branch offices, but offer the same kinds of services as existing banks through the Internet[4]. In the following paragraphs, we will compare existing banks with these new banks.

Table 1 summarizes the basic management figures of new entry banks at the end of March 2004. The Financial Services Agency (FSA) required these banks to obtain net profits within three years from their establishment. March 2004 was the time limit for this requirement for these four new banks. However, as shown in Table 1, the only bank out of the four to achieve net profits was the IY Bank. Despite the fact that the other three banks failed to fulfill the requirement, the FSA did not take any actions against them because they significantly reduced deficits for this fiscal year, which indicates that they will obtain profits in the near future.

The IY Bank's main service is its settlement operation through the ATM network that is installed in affiliated convenience stores (i.e., Seven-Eleven Japan). Seven-Eleven is the largest convenience store chain and an owner of IY Bank. The number of IY Bank ATMs has increased by 49% compared to the previous year, and these ATMs have substantially contributed to IY's black-ink balance. The others are pure-Internet-play banks, and the number of accounts at these banks has been increasing steadily. This shows that pure-Internet banks have become popular, and Internet banking services are widespread among individual customers.

Here, we further scrutinize the details of each pure-Internet-play bank, because each bank has business attributes that are significantly different from the others, even though they are all pure-Internet-play banks. As Table 1 shows, Japan Net Bank and Sony Bank actively engage in extending loans and eBank specializes in settlement operations over the Internet. In particular, Sony Bank positions the offer of asset management services to individuals as its main business, and Sony Bank holds home mortgages of 60.4 billion yen in its portfolio, which corresponds to 95% of its loan portfolios. However, Sony Bank's deposit-loan ratio is just 16.6%, far lower than the average of all banks in the same year (i.e., 73.4%). With regards to asset management, Japan Net Bank and Sony Bank commonly invest substantial funds into marketable securities. The deposit-security ratios for Japan Net Bank and Sony Bank are 99.2% and 88.2%, respectively. However, the deposit-loan ratios for IY Bank and eBank are 17.9% and 6.3%, respectively. These two banks have been operating with a focus on settlement services. Therefore, they hold most assets in cash and deposits, because they need their assets to be safe and liquid[5]. In summary, a big difference between Japan Net Bank and Sony Bank and IY Bank and eBank can be seen.

Table 1. Basic figures of new banks (for fiscal year 2003)

	Japan Net Bank	IY Bank	Sony Bank	eBank
Inaugural date	October, 2000	May, 2001	June, 2001	July, 2001
Current income (billion yen)	6.8 (4.0)	29.1 (11.5)	7.4 (4.0)	2.8 (0.6)
Profits and losses for this term (billion yen)	-1.7 (-2.7)	5.0 (-8.1)	-2.2 (-4.4)	-2.9 (-4.2)
The number of accounts (thousand accounts)	840 (650)	160 (100)	260 (190)	710 (480)
The number of workers	63 (65)	145 (140)	78 (72)	70 (72)
Operating cost (billion yen)	4.5 (4.7)	23.0 (18.4)	5.8 (5.3)	4.1 (4.6)
Deposit (billion yen)	153.4 (119.3)	122.4 (75.9)	378.8 (248.7)	158.0 (11.6)
Loaned money (billion yen)	16.2 (17.4)	0.0 (0.0)	63.0 (22.4)	0.0 (0.0)
Marketable securities (billion yen)	152.3 (94.8)	22.0 (22.6)	333.4 (211.5)	10.0 (0.0)
Total assets (billion yen)	203.7 (169.7)	259.6 (159.9)	489.4 (320.4)	169.4 (15.5)

Notes: Figures in the parentheses indicate figures for the previous year.

Compared with traditional banks, we find that the labor productivity of new entry banks is extremely high. Even though deposits per bank clerk at the IY Bank, which employs more than 100 persons, is 840 million yen, those of the other three banks are more than 2 billion yen, which are comparable to those of seven city banks in the same year. With respect to the first regional banks and the second-tier regional banks, only the Bank of Yokohama records deposits per bank clerk of more than 20 billion yen (i.e., 26.6 billion yen) and all other regional banks are lower than the three new banks in terms of deposits per bank clerk.

New banks can absorb huge deposits by paying higher interest rates and charging lower commission fees to their customers[6]. They can pay higher interest rates on deposits because they do not have expensive branches. With respect to the settlement operations, a larger number of accounts and large balances in those accounts naturally lead to larger commission incomes, resulting in higher profit performance. Thus, it is natural for these new banks to actively attract new customers by paying higher interest rates on deposits and charging lower commission fees to customers.

Internet Banking Services Provided by Existing Banks

Of course, not only pure-Internet-play banks but almost all banks are offering banking services through the Internet. Actually, the emergence of new banks into the market has spurred existing financial institutions to increase capital investments in IT. An article published by the Kinzai Institute for Financial Affairs on December 13, 2004, says that the basic services offered via Internet banking in Japan are various reference services, such as confirming deposit balances, withdrawal history and money transfer. In addition, customers of some advanced banks can buy fixed-period deposits, foreign currency deposits and mutual funds over the Internet. While city banks offer wide kinds of services through the Internet, most regional banks offer only basic services such as remittance and money transfer.

It is notable that there are many differences in commission services, interest rates and business hours among different banks. We have to take these differences into account when comparing the quality and prices of services that different banks offer. For example, as of December 2004, the Bank of Tokyo-Mitsubishi, UFJ Bank and Resona Bank set their commission fees on money transfers through the Internet at lower levels than those applied to ATM card transfers, while Mizuho Bank and Sumitomo Mitsui Banking Corporation set Internet transfer and ATM transfer commission fees at the same level. Almost all city banks offer Internet banking services without any accounting management charges, while more than half of regional banks offer Internet banking services with some charges. Moreover, even regional banks that offer only basic banking services such as remittance and money transfer charge management fees for Internet banking. Regional banks are inactive in offering Internet banking services, partially because most regional banks, except those in metropolitan areas, do not have a large potential demand for Internet banking services, while the costs involved in offering various services through the Internet are not negligible for these banks.

The Future of Internet Banks and Internet Banking in Japan

As mentioned above, Internet banking services have become increasingly common, and pure-Internet-play banks have grown. In this sub-section, we would like to point out several remaining issues that have to be overcome in order to make Internet banking services more convenient and reliable.

First, in terms of settlement operations, it is expected that if new entry banks obtain an additional number of accounts, the competition between traditional banks and new entry banks will accelerate. Some observers point out that the number of accounts at pure-Internet-play banks will exponentially increase because many firms offering electronic commerce to consumers (B2C) select these pure-Internet-play banks as settlement service providers. However, we expect that new entry banks that have no, or at best a very weak, relationship with commercial firms will face difficulties once mega banks that have strong relationship with commercial firms through loans and stock holdings actively offer Internet settlement services to these firms. If this occurs, the high-growth trend for new entry banks might be slowed. In this regard, the strategy of mega banks for consumer loans markets is suggestive. That is, mega banks do not provide consumer loans by themselves, but purchase consumer finance companies. Likewise, mega banks may not expand their own Internet banking services, but instead purchase new entry banks or establish a subsidiary bank to strengthen the Internet services in their financial group[7].

Second, we do not know how fast and how much the cashless society will progress. Above all, new entry banks will not offer all settlement services that are necessary for daily life. For example, the installation of IY Bank's ATMs depends on local circumstances and therefore varies significantly across regions[8]. It is conceivable that regional financial institutions will keep their dominant role in a regional society, especially in areas in which Internet banking will not be important in the future. It might be said that pure-Internet-play banks play an important role only in urban areas, even though Internet transaction is referred to as a borderless service. Thus, this difference between metropolitan areas and rural areas will remain.

Government Efforts: E-Japan Strategy

As we mentioned above, it is essential for financial institutions to put IT into practice to survive. Financial institutions may introduce and improve IT because of their own self-interests. However, as IT accompanies significant externality, it often happens that the effort of only one financial institution will not contribute to the improvement of its operating effectiveness as a whole. That is, the private market may fail. In this case, governmental efforts are desirable and necessary.

In fact, the Japanese government set up a "Strategic Headquarters Forming Advanced Information and Communications Network Society," and has been developing an "e-Japan strategy" to make Japan the world's most advanced IT nation. The "e-Japan Priority Policy Program" published in August 2003 clearly declared that the use of IT should be widespread, especially in such fields as healthcare, food, daily life, small business financing, knowledge, employment/labor and administrative services.

In this section, we will focus on small business financing as e-Japan policy objectives. The above government document maintains that diversifying credit sources and streamlining procedures improve financing environments for small- and medium-sized enterprises (SMEs), and also reduces the risks of collecting trade credits. The government expects that a society in which SMEs actively operate their businesses will emerge as a result. That is, the government believes that information technology is a promising tool to improve SMEs' financing environment.

The following aims are specified in the e-Japan program.

a. **Computerized Credit Accommodation**. Loan and guarantee contracts and other credit-related services (e.g., computerized bill services) can be processed electrically through the Internet. By developing this computerized credit accommodation, the clerical burden on SMEs for providing financial contracts will be substantially reduced.

b. **Establishing procedures regarding credit guarantees online**. In Japan, many small- and medium-sized enterprises obtain credit guarantees from public credit guarantee corporations. According to the National Federation of Credit Guarantee Corporations, approximately two million SMEs, or about half of all existing SMEs in Japan, used public credit guarantees in 2003. Small firms can ask the Credit

Guarantee Corporation to guarantee their borrowings by paying insurance premiums[9]. Currently, the basic premium rate is 1.35% for no-collateral loans and 1.25% for collateral loans. Although this public guarantee scheme alleviates the economic difficulties experienced by SMEs, many SMEs complain that the procedures involved are burdensome. The government has found it necessary to reduce the procedures required for financing. The government plans to make it possible for the application for public credit guarantee to be processed online by 2005.

c.   **Standardized and Computerized Credit Information regarding SMEs**. The government plans to develop an infrastructure for standardizing and computerizing credit information, contract information, and monitoring information for SMEs. Standardized and computerized credit information will enable financial institutions to make the right decisions about whether they should lend or not based on appropriate and accurate information.

d.   **Establishment of electronic receivable market**. The government will establish a new market where receivables can be sold and purchased online. Small- and medium-sized enterprises and financial institutions will obtain necessary funds through the electronic receivable market.

After the e-Japan Priority Policy Program was released, several related advisory bodies of the Ministry of Economy, Trade and Industry advanced various efforts to materialize this program. The financial industry is also engaging in several activities to support this program. For example, Shinkin Central Bank actually began offering online payment services in January 2004. In summary, the infrastructure for e-Japan has been steadily developing under the government's initiatives.

Conclusions

Now, financial institutions have to change the out-of-date business model in which banks collect money as deposits and lend it to large industrial firms, even though this business model worked very well during the rapid growth period. Only a bank that efficiently collects and processes soft and hard information can gain prosperity. In other words, nowadays the financial industry can be considered one branch of the information industry. However, financial institutions do not necessarily have a comparative advantage as an information industry. Other industries can deprive financial institutions of the roles they have played, if the financial institutions do not make immediate changes. In fact, general trading companies (*Sogo-Shyosha* in Japanese) and leasing companies have actively entered this field.

Of course, the authors of this chapter believe that it is highly probable that financial institutions that have accumulated customer information and experiences regarding financial technology can survive. As we have reiterated in this chapter, the immediate key condition is whether banks can successfully take measures to achieve progress in making use of information technology. Finally, we should note that if the use of information technology becomes widespread, then a competitive advantage can only be obtained through those services that cannot be computerized, namely, relationship banking functions. Therefore, although financial institutions should advance the use of IT, fostering personnel who can produce valuable soft information is vital for making regional financial institutions strong.

Acknowledgments

The authors appreciate professor Yutaka Kurihara's valuable comments. Nobuyoshi Yamori also appreciates the Japan Society of the Promotion of Science for its financial supports (grant-in-aid for scientific research).

References

Berger, A., & Udell, G. F. (1995). Relationship lending and lines of credit in small firm finance. *Journal of Business, 68*(3), 351-82.

Berger, A. N., & Udell, G. F. (2002). Small business credit availability and relationship lending: The importance of bank organizational structure. *Economic Journal, 112*(477), 32-53.

Berlin, M., & Mester, L. (1998). On the profitability and cost of relationship lending. *Journal of Banking and Finance, 22*(6-8), 873-97.

Boot, A. W. A. (2000). Relationship banking: What do we know? *Journal of Financial Intermediation, 9*(1), 7-25.

CELENT. (2002). *IT budgets at U.S. banks continue to grow, despite recession.* Retrieved, January 11, 2002, from http://www.celent.com

CELENT. (2003). *IT spending trends in Japanese banking.* Retrieved April 3, 2003, from http://www.celent.com

CELENT. (2004). *Celent expects IT spending at European banks to exceed EU 44.6 billion in 2004.* Retrieved April 26, 2004, from http://www.celent.com

CELENT. (2005). *A North American perspective: IT spending at U.S. and Canadian banks.* Retrieved February 3, 2005, from http://www.celent.com

Cole, R. (1998). The importance of relationships to the availability of credit. *Journal of Banking and Finance, 22*(6-8), 959-77.

Elsas, R., & Krahnen, J. (1998). Is relationship lending special? Evidence from credit-file data in Germany. *Journal of Banking and Finance, 22*(6-8), 1283-316.

Financial Information System Center. (2003). *Steps and action assignments of Japanese Financial institutions on IT investment.* White book 2003 fiscal year on financial information system (in Japanese).

Harhoff, D., & KoÈrting, T. (1998). Lending relationships in Germany: Empirical results from survey data. *Journal of Banking and Finance, 22*(6-8), 1317-54.

Ongena, S., & Smith, D. C. (2000). Bank relationships: A review. In S. A. Zenios & P. Harker (Eds.), *Performance of financial institutions* (pp. 221-258). Cambridge, UK: Cambridge University Press.

Petersen, M., & Rajan, R. (1994). The benefits of firm-creditor relationships: Evidence from small business data. *Journal of Finance, 49*(1), 3-37.

Petersen, M., & Rajan, R. (1995). The effect of credit market competition on lending relationships. *Quarterly Journal of Economics, 110*(2), 407-43.

Scott, J. A. (2004). Small business and the value of community financial institutions. *Journal of Financial Services Research, 25*(2-3), 207-230.

Stein, J. (2002). Information production and capital allocation: Decentralized vs. hierarchical firms. *Journal of Finance, 57*(5), 1891-1921.

Ukai, Y. (Ed.). (2005). *Economic analysis of information system investment in banking industry.* Tokyo: Springer-Verlag.

Yamori, N. (2004). *Crisis of regional financial system and small business finance: The role of credit guarantee program and the governance of Shinkin bank.* Tokyo: Chukura-Shobo (in Japanese).

Endnotes

[1]   See CELENT's homepage at http://www.celent.com.

[2]   Actually, many Japanese banks have recorded net losses since the late 1990s. Concretely speaking, the net current profits or losses of Japanese banks as a whole were +908 billion yen for fiscal year 1999, -176 billion yen for FY2000, -4,199 billion yen for FY2001, -4,851 billion yen for FY2002 and -780 billion yen for FY2003.

[3]   In 1990, there were 13 city banks. In 2005, there were five city bank groups — four mega bank groups and Resona Holding. The four Japanese mega bank groups are Mitsubishi-Tokyo Financial Group, Sumitomo Mitsui Financial Group, UFJ Holdings and Mizuho Financial Group. All five city bank groups were established in the 2000s.

[4]   An exception regarding existing banks is Orix Trust and Banking, which has been operating through Internet transactions without a branch office network. Orix Trust and Banking was established by purchasing stocks of the now-defunct Yamaichi Trust and Banking.

[5]   For instance, IY Bank's cash and deposits paid are 203.7 billion yen in total, which is 53.7% of IY Bank deposits received.

[6]   For example, the interest rates on large denominated time deposits for one year for eBank, Sony Bank and the Japan Net Bank were 0.35%, 0.22% and 0.10%, respectively, while all city banks offered the same deposits with interest rates of 0.03%.

7   The largest shareholder of Japan Net Bank has been Sumitomo Mitsui Banking Corporation from its establishment. In addition, Sumitomo Mitsui Banking Corporation also has substantial shares of Sony Bank.

8   IY Bank, which is installing ATMs in convenience stores, does not necessarily install ATMs in all affiliated convenience stores.

9   The maximum guaranteed amount of standard program is 280 million yen.

Chapter III

Payment Systems of Financial Institutions:
Current State and Future Prospects

Yutaka Kurihara, Aichi University, Japan

Shigeaki Ohtsuka, Kwansei Gakuin University, Japan

Abstract

Economic activity is always accompanied by payment. Payment systems, which are the subject of much recent discussion, are an indispensable part of the infrastructure that supports the entire economy. Progress in the field of information technology (IT) has spurred new developments in hardware and software that affect payment systems. Of recent interest are issues of increasing payment risk and the severe situation of financial institutions in some developed countries. The costs associated with setup and operation of payment systems is high, and market participants expect efficiency. Many problems are associated with bond payments. The spread of delivery vs. payment (DVP) systems and IT-based transactions are also impacting payment systems. Links between payment systems are also important and have made concerns about systemic risk if time-designated net settlements coexist with real-time gross settlements (RTGSs), which can alter outcomes or cause cancellations, thereby increasing systemic risk. If RTGSs and the net payment system are not operated by a single rule, this problem worsens. Unification of settlement systems, rules and dealings custom is critical. The complex legal frameworks that govern payment activity would benefit from structural revisions.

Introduction

The topic of payment[1] has recently been the subject of considerable attention. Economic activities of enterprises and households are always accompanied by payment. The payment system is an indispensable infrastructure that supports the entire economy.

Payment systems have been changing recently. For example, for many years paper checks were the most frequently used non-cash payment instrument in the United States.

Although the check remains the predominant type of non-cash payment instrument, the number of check payments, as well as the percentage of the total payments made by this method, has declined.

Payment systems have attracted considerable recent attention. One reason for this increased interest has been new developments in hardware and software that support payment systems that have arisen as a result of progress in the IT field. Another reason for this upsurge is the issue of growing payment risk.

Recently, large numbers of financial transactions have been completed. Financial derivatives, for example, create much more risk. More, the volume of financial transactions has been far much larger than the GDP. A third concern is the difficult situation of many financial institutions.

The international financial system is also changing rapidly. The euro has come into use and a new payment system has been introduced. A real-time gross settlement system (RTGS)[2] has been introduced in almost all developed countries. This chapter introduces the structure of the European payment system, Trans-European Automated Real-time Gross settlement Express Transfer (TARGET), which began operating on January 1, 1999. Changes to the payment system have not been limited to TARGET. This chapter also introduces the mechanism of payment systems of other than European countries, including the continuous linked settled (CLS) bank, that has come into use, and analyzes the relationship between payment systems and monetary/prudential policy. Finally, this chapter explains the structure of the new European settlement system, TARGET, and the mechanism of other payment systems.

TARGET System

This section describes the TARGET system, which now operates in Europe. This system is epoch-making in a lot of ways, and a suggestive one to for other countries. Financial alliances are well established.

Payment systems usually serve a single country. The TARGET system, the RTGS system for the euro, however, is an example of a system that links several countries by providing connection between the payment systems of various subscriber countries.

Since TARGET began operations in 1999, it has been one of the world's largest high-value payment systems for money market, foreign exchange and securities transactions.

According to the European Central Bank (ECB), with almost 1,100 direct participants and more than 48,000 banks — including branches and subsidiaries — accessible through the system. Using branches of the RGTS system, financial institutions can interact with the RTGS system of their own country and other countries.

Consider a case in which country A's "a" bank remits to country B's "b" bank. "a" bank in country A could remit to "b" bank using country B's RTGS through a branch or through a corresponding bank in country B. The TARGET system facilitates remittance to country B's central bank or to "b" through country A's central bank.

In the TARGET system, payment instructions are conveyed to the home country's central bank through that country's RTGS system. If there is enough capital, the order is settled by pulling down the ordered amount from the financial institution's account with the central bank. Afterward, the country A's central bank remits payment to country B's central bank, which in turn transfers the funds to an account of "b" bank with the central bank (BIS, 1997). Country B's central bank sends the payment order to "b" bank through the home country's RTGS to complete the payment. Settlements can be performed immediately, and payment orders can usually be completed within two to three seconds. Note that TARGET is a settlement system and not a clearing system.

Table 1 shows the number of European banks linked with TARGET as of 2002.

Table 1. TARGET in EU countries using settlement by RTGS (end of 2002)

Country	Number of Banks Participating
Belgium	93
Germany	1382[*]
Spain	239
France	705
Ireland	22
Italy	844
Luxembourg	31
Netherlands	158
Austria	71
Portugal	37
Finland	17
Denmark	96
Greece	41
Sweden	13
England	44

Notes: From "Payment and security system of European Union, April 2004" by ECB, April, 2004.
* Includes only direct participants of Deutsche Bundesbank.

Operating Time

The TARGET system uses ECB standard time, which is Frankfurt, Germany, summer and winter time. Basically, operating time is 11 hours a day, 7 a.m.- 6 p.m., which is longer than the operating hours for settlement systems for other countries such as the United States and Japan. The reason is to provide greater time overlap with the operations of other financial markets. This strategy reduces the settlement risk between different kinds of countries. In addition, unifying the closing time helps avoid the interest differential in the region (since the introduction of the euro, European countries adhere to a single, unified financial policy).

Days of Operation

TARGET operates daily, Monday through Friday, and is closed only on Saturday, Sunday, New Year's Day and Christmas. TARGET operates whenever the RTGS system in more than two countries in the EU region is operating. However, each country's central bank determines the days of operation of the RTGS in its own country (EMI, 1996).

Charges

Fees for use of the system vary between 0.80 to 1.75 euros per transaction depending on the total number of transactions, as shown in Table 2. The fees are paid by the financial institutions and are collected by the central banks on the remittance side. There are no joining fees or other basic charges.

Purpose and Development of TARGET

The primary purpose of the TARGET system is reduction of systemic risk and equalization of the settlement system. The designated-time net settlement system (DNS) was formerly the main payment system in each country. Concerns regarding systemic risk as a result of increased payment amounts and increases in international payments, especially using networks, elevated RTGS into the mainstream in every country throughout the world.

Table 2. TARGET fees per transaction

# of Transactions per Month	Charge per Transaction (in euros)
1–100	1.75
101–1000	1.00
1001+	0.80

Movement toward introducing RTGS began around 1992. The EU agreed to its introduction in 1993.

For the EU, a unified financial policy was influential to the introduction of TARGET. The globalization of international monetary transaction grew rapidly in the 1990s, giving rise to the need for global standards for transactions. In hindsight, the introduction of some kind of RTGS system was inevitable under the circumstances and its development helped to prompt the introduction of the TARGET.

In addition, the ECB payment mechanism (EPM) was established as the ECB's payment system in January 1999. Euro-based net payments have been performed since then.

Structure of the International Settlement System

This section describes the structure of the international settlement mechanism mentioned in the previous section. Many diverse factors influenced the development of the payment system. Many financial intermediaries provide payment, clearing and settlement. Table 3 provides details of the payment systems for many developed countries.

Table 3. Payment systems of developed countries

	Name of System	System Start Date	Owner	Operated by	RTGS or Net Settlement
Belgium	ELLIPS	1996	Central Bank	SWIFT	RTGS
Canada	LVTS	1997	CPA	CPA	Net
England	CHAPS	1984	CHAPS	CHAPS	RTGS
EU	Euro 1	1986	Euro Bank Society	SWIFT	Net
France	TBF	1997	Central Bank	SWIFT	RTGS
	PNS	1997	CRI	CRI	Net
Germany	RTGSplus*	2001	Central Bank	Central Bank	RTGS
	ELS*	1996	Central Bank	Central Bank	Net
	RPS	2003	Central Bank	Central Bank	Net
Italy	BIREL	1997	Central Bank	SIA	RTGS
Japan	BOJ-NET	1988	Central Bank	Central Bank	RTGS
	Zen-gin system	1973	Tokyo Bank Society	Tokyo Bank Society	Net
Netherlands	TOP	1997	Central Bank	Central Bank	RTGS
Sweden	ERIX	1986	Central Bank	Central Bank	RTGS
Switzerland	SIC	1987	Central Bank	Telekurs Co.	RTGS
USA	Fedwire	1918	Central Bank	Central Bank	RTGS
	CHIPS	1970	NYCHA	NYCHA	Net

*Notes: * RTGSplus, the new RTGS system, opened November, 2001. At this time, EAF (net settlement) was closed.*

In the United States, financial institutions and their customers use two major large-value payment systems to make transfers: Fedwire and CHIPS. Fedwire is operated by the Federal Reserve and is a real-time gross settlement system that enables participants to send and receive final payments through the central bank. The Fedwire Funds Service provides a real-time gross settlement system in which more than 9,500 participants make funds transfers that are immediate and final. Participants that maintain a reserve or clearing account with a Federal Reserve Bank can directly use Fedwire to send payments to, or receive payments from, other account holders. Participants initiate Fedwire to handle large-value, time-critical payments, such as payments for the settlement of interbank purchases and sales of federal funds; the purchase, sale and financing of securities transactions.

Since 1998, CHIPS has been owned and operated by CHIPCo. Bilateral and multilateral netting are being used for maximum liquidity. In addition, financial institutions may use separate communication systems to send payment instructions for transfers. Payment instructions submitted to the CHIPS payment queue that remain unsettled at the end of the day are tallied and funded on the multilateral net basis prior to releasing the payments. CHIPS processes more than 273,000 payments a day with a gross value of over $1.39 trillion now. CHIPS is the only large value, premier payments platform system in the world that has the capability of sending extensive remittance information for payments of U.S. dollars serving the largest banks from around the world, representing 21 countries.

The Society for Worldwide Interbank Financial Telecommunication (SWIFT) is the financial industry-owned, limited liability co-operative society set up under Belgium law. This society is controlled by its member banks (including central banks) and other financial institutions with offices around the world. Its worldwide community includes banks, brokers, dealers, and investment managers, as well as their market infrastructures in payments, securities, treasury, and trade. SWIFT supplies secure, standardized messaging services and interface software to 7,638 financial institutions in more than 202 countries to improve automation of financial transaction processes and to provide a forum for financial institutions (March 1, 2005). The headquarters are located near Brussels.

Japan uses four major payment systems for clearing and settling interbank payments. The BOJ-NET is the central bank's funds transfer system and is used to settle interbank obligations including net obligations of participants in the private sector. The Zen-gin system clears retail credit transfers, the Foreign Exchange Yen Clearing System (FXYCS) clears mainly yen legs of foreign exchange transactions, and the Bill and Check Clearing System (BCCS) clears bills and checks. The Bank of Japan serves as the central securities depository for Japanese government bonds and a number of registrars make up the settlement and depository systems. As for the management of the settlement system by the central bank, the degree of participation is considerably different among countries, with the United States having the greatest. On the other hand, private institutions manage the systems in Canada and Britain.

Private Settlement Systems

Private settlement systems, which often involve the participation of the central bank, also are important. In Japan, private systems include the Zen-gin system and the foreign exchange clearance system. Other private systems include CHIPS in the United States, Euro1 in Europe, ELS in Germany and PNS in France.

Among these, the Zen-gin system uses the standard nomenclature of a nationwide bank data communications system to provide the inland exchange (transfer, etc.) between the financial institutions in Japan. The management is subject to The Tokyo Bankers' Association.

Zen-gin system chiefly handles fund settlements between financial institution customers, whereas the Bank of Japan financial network system and foreign exchange yen settlement system accommodate large settlements. Small business transactions are handled by centers.

Net Settlement Systems

The pros and cons of RTGS were presented above along with the description of the new payment system, TARGET. However, net settlement is still an important system. The system is usually a designated time or deferred payment system.

In this system, balancing accounts for lending and borrowing between financial institutions involving payment of two or more transactions are calculated in the settlement, which uses the designated-time net system. Differences (net balance) between the total receipt and total payment by each financial institution are often settled through the central bank checking account. Settlements are performed collectively at a fixed time. This system uses multilateral netting to calculate net amounts.

This approach decreases the liquidity risk, and, to great advantage, the settlement amounts, and the settlement frequency. Thus, net payment is particularly useful in the case of frequent payments of small sums. Note, however, that when there are lags in the settlement, the credit risk increases greatly.

Managing Risk

Some authorities believe that rapid improvement of the expansion of derivatives transaction in recent years and the IT revolution, including telecommunications systems, increase credit risk (U.S. Department of Commerce, 2000).

Moreover, the problem of systemic risk occurs. When participants cannot perform settlements, it spreads to other system participants one after another and the operation of the entire system stops (Rochet & Tirole, 1996). Concerns about systemic risks may have accelerated movement to the RTGS as previously described.

With payments using RTGS, the full amount of money is settled at once for each transaction. At this time, settlement through the central bank avoids the concentration of the credit risk between transaction participants. Moreover, the settlement in the case of default, thus limits the liability and greatly reduces systemic risk (BIS, 1998).

However, the liquidity risk is concentrated, which raises the problem of the costs associated with securing liquidity. RTGS is inferior to the designated-time net payment in terms of efficiency of funds operations.[3]

The following discussion considers methods of reducing payment risk.[4] Methods of risk reduction include shortening the length of time from contract to settlement and simultaneous settlement. RTGS has merit for both approaches. Other approaches to risk reduction include setting of granting of credit and setting credit limits or caps. The system can automatically exclude transactions that exceed a specified limit so that other measures can be applied to determine whether the participant is in a position to complete the transaction.

In the case of bonds, if two or more transactions with the same date of delivery are completed in a time-designated net settlement, the system calculates the lending and borrowing balance of the accounts. The accounts are settled by transferring each participant's bond account to a specific bond-keeping organization.

In the United States, most securities are immobilized at the Depository Trust Company, which is a member of the Federal Reserve System and a registered clearing agency of the Securities and Exchange Commission (SEC). SEC can seek a variety of sanctions through the administrative proceeding process.

Administrative proceedings differ from civil court actions in that they are heard by an administrative law judge (ALJ), who is independent of the commission. The ALJ presides over a hearing and considers the evidence presented by the parties to the proceeding.

Following the hearing and the submission of briefs, the ALJ issues an *initial decision* that contains findings of fact, legal conclusions, and an order that often contains a sanction. Possible sanctions include, but are not limited to, imposition of a cease-and-desist order, suspension or revocation of a broker-dealer or investment adviser registration, an order of censure, a bar from association with a broker or dealer or investment adviser, payment of civil monetary penalties, and disgorgement of ill gotten gains. The parties may appeal all or any portion of the initial decision to the commission.

Many countries are investigating RTGS as an option for bond transactions. Price fluctuations in bonds and real estate, so-called the economic macro risk, may also contribute to systemic risk. The Euroclear System is operated by Euroclear Bank SA, a Belgian credit institution. Euroclear is the world's premier settlement system for domestic and international securities transactions, covering bonds, equities and investment funds.

Market owned and market governed, Euroclear provides securities services to major financial institutions located in more than 80 countries. In addition to its role as the leading International Central Securities Depositary (ICSD), Euroclear also acts as the Central Securities Depository (CSD) for Dutch, French, Irish and UK securities.

CIK, the CSD of Belgium, is expected to join the group later in 2005. The system uses the delivery vs. payment (DVP) technique in gross simultaneous settlements of securities and funds transfers. The system is based on the concept of book-entry settlements. The securities deposited by the participants in the Euroclear System are sub-deposited with a network of more than 70 custodians.

Eurex is the world's leading futures and options market for euro denominated derivative instruments. Its electronic trading platform provides access to a broad range of international benchmark products. With market participants connected from 700 locations worldwide, trading volume at Eurex exceeded 1.07 billion contracts in 2004.

Eurex Clearing AG further offers central counterparty services for instruments traded on the Eurex exchanges, Eurex Bonds and Eurex Repo as well as the Frankfurt Stock Exchange (Xetra and Floor).

Settlement risks include credit risk, liquidity risk, systemic risk, and so on, as mentioned above, and a legal risk is excluded. Legal risks are both critical and uncertain because insufficient legislation causes the credit risk and the liquidity risk.

Recent progress in computers and IT may increase certain aspects of risk. Operational risks can arise from clerical errors and computer system breakdowns as well as from decreases in reputation and evaluation. Clearly legal and operational risks increase with expanding globalization and the future spread of telecommunication system (Brynjolfsson & Hitt, 1998, 2000; Deloitte Research-Research Manufacturing Institute, 2000).

Payment Systems and Prudential Policy

The guarantee of liquidity is important in open market operations, which are often central to prudential policy. The market mechanism determines the relative merits of measures by which to ensure liquidity. If capital is efficiently distributed, daytime liquidity will not be charged.

To complete daily transactions, liquidity should be adequate to accommodate payment, and price determinations and dealings must proceed smoothly. However, such a market hardly exists in every country in the world now.

Capital should be freely moved on the same day. Arbitrage with the market mechanism is indispensable for financial stability. Keeping RTGS efficiently, such system should be developed. For some payment systems, penalty rate should be considered to prevent participant's purposely delaying payment.

As we mentioned above, there are differences between the RTGS system and the net settlement system. For instance, some countries' payment systems are not the same as others.

On the other hand, since payment against international trade has increased owing to globalization, the linkage between the settlement systems has been strengthened due to standardization.

There are, however, some problems. There could be a high possibility of systemic errors and/or systemic trouble taking into account the high volume of trade. Though both banks in a given transaction use net settlement systems, time differences affect settlement time, so there are risks — for example, market risks, settlement risks and so forth. As for international settlements, the unification and standardization of payment systems are important issues. Therefore, IT solution would help to solve these problems. In addition, some problems will be solved by CLS banks. We will discuss this further in the next section.

CLS Bank

The Bank of Credit and Commerce International (BCCI) event and the Bearings Company event spurred the development of the CLS Bank. BIS recognized the necessity of reducing the foreign exchange settlement risk by this measure. Seventeen countries and 65 financial institutions collaborated in the founding of the CLS Bank. Its goal is to reduce foreign exchange risk for banks that specialize in settlement. CLS was formed to provide multicurrency payment services that reduce substantially the risk to financial institutions of setting foreign exchange contracts.

CLS provides simultaneous settlement of foreign exchange transactions to eliminate the principal risk of only one leg of a foreign exchange transaction being settled. Because this bank was established in London in 1997, the connection with each country of Europe is also large and deep. Table 4 provides a list of key dates and milestones in the operation of the CLS Bank.

The CLS Bank links to each country with the central banks and has accounts with each central bank. When a settlement participant pays into the CLS Bank, it then pays into the CLS account of the central bank using the RTGS system in each country.

The settlement process starts at 7 a.m. The CLS Bank receives money through each country's RTGS system then transfers money to the member's account using the described transfer queue system. Next, the CLS Bank confirms whether the payment is possible and disburses payment to each member's account in the central bank via each country's RTGS.

The CLS Bank became Bank of Japan's choice for checking account dealings in May 2002. The CLS bank participates directly with Fedwire, which is the RTGS for the United States.

Table 4. CLS Bank operational timeline

Date	Activity
July 1997	CLS established in London
April 1998	System development; operations design
May 1999	Beginning of integration testing
April 2001	Implementation test on small sum dealings
October 2001	Commencement of operations
March 2002	All participants began to use the CLS Bank

The CLS Bank has the settlement account for a federal bank in New York. Among the CLS Bank's many advantages, substantial is reduction of the Herstatt risk from settlement time lags because final participant positions are settled by checking account transfers from each country's central bank between the participant and CLS, thus reducing credit and operational risks.

Finally, because the amount of money settled in the CLS bank is a net part of the foreign exchange dealings, efficient settlements become possible. There is some possibility that dealings through CLS will be activated. Problems remain with matters of liquidity management, exchange rate changes, correspondent arrangements, the system and so on. Much attention has been focused on the resolution of these problems.

Specialty Banks

Recently, settlement and net specialty banks have appeared to provide a new means for dealing with settlement issues. The settlement specialty bank does mainly settlement business and does not engage in lending.

Settlement specialty banks place ATMs in convenience stores and other retail locations. This strategy has the advantage of reducing the bank's personnel needs, but the nature of their business requires these banks must subscribe to the settlement system. Many problems, such system stability and cost, arise with this type of bank.

Net specialty banks also have the advantages of decreased costs associated with retail locations and decreased labor cost. Financial alliances can be easily established. Moreover, user benefits and convenience are considerable with the use of the Internet and cellular phones.

Problems with this type of system include decreased settlement commissions by the intensification of competition, the load increase of the cost, problems with the management environment, making of the settlement system, and poor competitive standing relative to traditional banks.

Conclusions

The payment system plays an important role in supporting economic activity. The payment can be accompanied to the economic activity. The success of the system depends upon smooth and efficient operation.

With the creation of a new market, it is necessary to invest in the development of new systems. Setup costs are very high, and market participants expect efficiency. The reason that the day time liquidity market is small is because there is not adequate private economic subject.

Problems with bond payments can be combated with increased use of DVP and IT-based transactions. International Standard ISO 15022 was prepared by Technical Committee ISO/TC68, Banking, Securities and Related Financial Services, Sub-Committee SC4, Securities and Related Financial Instruments. It replaces the previous standards for electronic messages exchanged between securities industry players, ISO 7775 - Scheme for message types and ISO 11521 - Scheme for interdepository message types. ISO 15022 sets the principles necessary to provide the different communities of users with the tools to design message types to support their specific information flows. These tools consist of a set of syntax and message design rules, a dictionary of data fields and a catalogue for present and future messages built by the industry with the above mentioned fields and rules.

The link among payment systems is also important. The first concern is the systemic risk generated when time-designated net settlement coexists with RTGS and results in different outcomes and transaction cancellations.

This problem worsens when RTGS and the net payment system are operated by different rules or lack a common infrastructure. It is necessary to unify the settlement system, rules and protocols as much as possible in each country. Increased disclosure would also be beneficial. The legal framework governing payment activity as well as the regulatory structure for financial institutions that provide payment services is complex and should be structured more logically and clearly.

Finally, innovation and competition have led to the use of new instruments and systems that rely increasingly on electronic payment mechanisms. IT development in the field is promising.

Acknowledgment

Financial support from Aichi University is greatly appreciated.

References

BIS. (1997, March). *Real-time gross settlement systems*. Report presented by the CPSS, 1-66.

BIS. (1998, March). *Risk management for electronic banking and electronic money activities*. Report presented by Basel Committee on Banking Supervision, 1-35.

BOE. (1996). *Practical issues arising from the introduction of Euro*. 3.

Borio, C. E. V., & Van den Berg, P. (1993). The nature and management of payment system risks: An international perspective. *BIS Economic Papers*, 36.

Brynjolfsson, E., & Hitt, L. M. (1998). *Beyond the productivity paradox*. Retrieved March 1, 2005, from http://ecommerce.mit.edu/erik/

Brynjolfsson, E., & Hitt, L. M. (2000). Computing productivity: Firm-level evidence. *Social Science Research Network*. MIT Sloan Working Paper, 4210-01. Retrieved February 15, 2005, from http://papers.ssrn.com/sol3/papers.cfm/abstract_id=290325

Deloitte Research Manufacturing Institute. (2000). *Digital royalty networks*. London: Delloitte Consulting and Delloitte and Touche.

ECB. (2000, February). *Payment systems in the European Union*. Press release, 1-211.

EMI. (1996). *First progress report on the TARGET project*. Press release, 1-719.

Hancock, D., & Wilcox, J. A. (1996). Intraday management of bank reserves: The effect of caps and fees on daylight overdrafts. *Journal of Money, Credit and Banking, 28*(4), 870-908.

Rochet, J., & Tirole, J. (1996). Controlling risk in payment systems. *Journal of Money, Credit and Banking, 28*(4), 733-762.

U.S. Department of Commerce. (2000). *Digital economy 2000*. Washington, DC: U.S. Department of Commerce.

Endnotes

[1] Payment is the process of sending an order for payment and its receipt. Clearing is a calculation for settlement. Netting and confirming a position are included in this process. Settlement is a transfer of money that should be final.

[2] The RTGS systems in each EU country began to be constructed in these 2-3 years. The Bank of Japan made checking account and government bond settlements RTGS among the Bank of Japan settlements on January 4, 2001, and has extended the operating time for online checking account transfers.

[3] Temporary liquidity deficits may result for variety reasons, such as bankruptcy and computer downtime, at the time of the settlement, which affects the creditor's receipt.

[4] This risk causes irrecoverable damage, along with the settlement breach, due to the deterioration of a financial situation of business contacts. Principal risk (principal or capital risk) and price fluctuation risk (market risk) are included in this (BIS, 1997). The Herstatt risk often indicates foreign exchange settlement risk with a time difference. The 1991 BCCI event is a representative example.

Chapter IV

Financial Innovation and Economic Growth:
Some Further Evidence from the UK, 1900-2003

Anita Ghatak, University of Greenwich, UK

Abstract

In this chapter, we assess the contribution of financial development to saving and economic growth in the UK in the 20th century. Financial development in this century has been by leaps and bounds along with a number of infamous crashes like the ones in the 1920s and in 1987. Using annual time-series data for the whole century, we find that financial growth has helped saving and economic growth in the UK throughout the 20th century. The unprecedented increase in money holding in 1965 and various forms of financial innovation and liberalisation initiated in the 1980s raised both the level and the rate of economic growth. Money-stock elasticity of GDP has been positive and statistically significant. There are long-run and unique co-integrated relations of GDP with productivity of capital and financial depth in the 20th century. The financial crash of Black Monday in 1987 upset equilibrium relations and led to a negative money-stock elasticity of economic growth.

Introduction

Keynes held the view that history of money was the history of civilisation. Schumpeter thought development of financial institutions was an essential ingredient of economic development. Entrepreneurship would be encouraged by existence of monopoly profits, but a well-developed banking system would be needed to support entrepreneurs and investment (Schumpeter, 1933). The view that financial factors influence speed, direction and stability of economic growth is shared among a large group of development economists, although degree of reliance on the all pervasive role of the banking system, varies in this group (Garshenkron, 1962; Cameron, et.al., 1967; Ghatak, 2003). The greater the degree of economic backwardness, the stronger would be the role of financial institutions in initiating, promoting and sustaining economic growth and development; the banking system of a developing country is likely to be much stronger than non-economic institutions but many of these institutions including government, religious institutions, the education system, ethics and aesthetics all influence the operation of the banking system. These issues remain only in the background for our purpose as we are considering a developed country like the UK in the 20th century.

Financial development and the phenomenon called financial innovation are closely related. In the recent decades, however, financial innovation has been more closely related to the role of information technology. The term innovation usually means introduction of a new product into the market or a new way of producing an existing product and financial market does not have to be an exception to this. There has been a massive growth of literature on financial innovation and how it affects economic growth and various other aspects of economic life. Two of the best-known papers full of *originality* are by Silber (1983) and Tobin (1984). In the later decades of the 20th century, the role played by technology, which makes exchange of information around the financial world much easier and much faster, has been assigned a major role in financial liberalisation. The international payments system was already revolutionised by a high degree of automation made possible by a much-improved telecommunications and computer system. SWIFT, Fedwire, CHIPS, CHAPS[1] and the like have contributed significantly to the growth of international banking and finance. Financial markets have been more widely publicised in the 1980s and have assumed a larger role in popular culture than in any previous period, with the possible exception of the late 1920s. In this chapter, we make special reference to the years that have affected finance and money in the UK; for example, the quantity of money holding increased substantially during the period from 1965-1999. Nominal money holdings increased from £17 billion in 1965 to £873 billion in 1999; the price level also increased substantially in the same period; the real money holding, as a result, increased four fold. Real GDP also more than doubled (Begg, Fischer, & Dornbusch, 2000). In the following section, we discuss the theoretical background and our methodology.

Theory and Methodology

Theory

Financial development can contribute to economic growth in at least three ways:

1. Financial development can reduce the loss of resources in the allocation of capital. Greater use of banks and financial intermediaries replacing direct intermediation reduces costs of financial intermediation.

2. Financial development can increase the savings ratio by providing various savings products, savings outlets of easier access.

3. Financial development can raise productivity of capital providing portfolio diversification and liquidity.

Relevant issues can be discussed in the context of growth models. Macroeconomic growth models to explain the nexus between financial and economic development was popularised by Shaw (1973). In honour of Edward Shaw, McKinnon provides an excellent collection of the Shavian models almost thirty years ago (McKinnon, 1976). In this edited volume, Spellman explains the relation between growth and financial intermediation, assuming such financial intermediation is performed by a depository financial institution. If this sector is sufficiently competitive such that no monopoly profits are earned, then the wealth owners' rate of return is given by:

$$r = Yf_k - \delta \tag{1}$$

where r is a deposit rate, Y is output, f is the production function and f_k is the partial derivative of the production function indicating marginal product of capital of the financed economy, and, δ is the real unit cost of finance per period. In equation (1), the unit financial costs constitute the difference between marginal productivity of capital and the deposit rate. From this simple equation, it follows that the more efficient the financial system is, the lower would be the unit costs of finance, the higher would be the r curve and the greater will be the equilibrium capital intensity, or, the capital-output ratio, K/Y (Spellman, 1976, pp. 17-18).

The later contributions on models of growth are available in Pagano (1993), Gylfason (1999), Santomero and Seater (2000), Theil (2001) and so on. Assuming only one good, Y, and one factor input, capital, K, Theil (2001) uses the growth model as:

$$Y_t = AK_t \tag{2}$$

where t stands for time period and A for capital productivity.

Using the definition of investment as net capital formation, we can write:

$$I_t = K_t - K_{t-1} + d K_{t-1} \tag{2a}$$

where $0<d<1$ is the rate of depreciation.

The relation (2a) can be rewritten for capital as:

$$K_t = I_t + (1-d) K_{t-1} \tag{2b}$$

We assume a constant saving ratio, s, as typical in growth models:

$$S_t = s Y_t, \ 0<s<1 \tag{2c}$$

We view capital as non-consumed resources, and assume that channelling of savings to investment implies the loss of a share of savings, $(1-\delta) >0$, due to intermediation costs; then the funds available for investment can be rewritten as:

$$I_t = \delta s Y_t \tag{2d}$$

Growth rate, g, is usually defined as the proportion:

$$g = [(Y_t - Y_{t-1}) / Y_{t-1}] \tag{2e}$$

In the steady state, output and capital grow at the same rate, implying:

$$g \ = \ [(K_t - K_{t-1}) / K_{t-1}] \tag{2f}$$

Steady state growth rate can, therefore, be rewritten as:

$$g = [(A*\delta* s) - d] / (1 - A*\delta* s) \tag{2g}$$

For small values of $(A*\delta*s)$, steady state growth can be approximated by:

$$g \approx [(A*\delta* s) - d] \tag{3}$$

Equation (3) indicates three possible channels of transmission from finance to growth. The rate, δ, stands for various costs of financial intermediation, such as, transactions costs, search costs, verification costs, monitoring costs, and the like (Heffernan, 2001). Such costs explain the differential between the interest paid on deposits and interest charged to the borrowers. So, one of the determinants of δ, is such interest differentials. Similarly, the degree of risk involved in lending will also influence the value of δ. The degree of competition in the financial market, efficiency of the financial market will reduce the value of δ. Tax imposed on profits of the financial sector will raise the value of δ. Efficiency of the financial sector in general reduces the loss of resources in transferring savings into investment and, thereby, can increase rate of growth.

The net effect of financial development on saving ratio itself is inconclusive (Ghatak, 2003; Theil, 2001). It depends on the relative strength of the *income* and the *substitution* effects. If financial development either lowers risks and/or improves prospects of higher returns on savings, there can be two kinds of effects:

1. Same returns can be secured from a lower volume of savings in which case savings would fall (and consumption would rise).

2. Higher returns from savings also mean that the price of present consumption increases and, therefore, present consumption should decrease and future consumption or savings should increase.

The net effect of higher returns resulting from a secure and well-developed financial market will depend on the relative strength of the two effects.

Financial development can lead to reduced risks offering a wider choice of financial assets and a diversified portfolio; as a result savings can increase with reduced volatility of returns.

Such arguments however, are given in a macro sense and not in a micro sense. In a microeconomic analysis of risks and returns, generally, risks and returns are inversely correlated. This is why a portfolio has to be diversified in the first place. A reduced risk pattern is likely to induce a direction of savings into higher risks /higher return assets with no resulting increase in total savings for a risk aversive investor. Also reduction of risks can reduce the level of precautionary savings.

Finally we are on the effects of financial development on the productivity of capital, A, on savings and on investment. An efficient financial sector can increase productivity of capital, A, in at least three ways: by selecting the most profitable investment projects, providing liquidity and by reducing risks. Search, verification, monitoring and similar functions performed by financial intermediaries can raise productivity of capital by selection of the most profitable investment project. It can also go some way in reducing principal agent problem. The financial intermediaries will be better at evaluating the credit worthiness of the debtor than private individual borrowers and lenders dealing directly.

Provision of liquidity by the financial sector can make the best combination of savings assets viable by matching the period of maturity of various assets with demand for withdrawals. Preferred habitat of lenders is short-term lending and that of borrowers is long-term borrowing and an efficient financial sector is a prerequisite for solving this "fundamental mismatch" between assets and liabilities (Hicks, 1939).

Long-term projects are often more profitable than short-term ones; there are different ways in which projects can be ranked, say by net present values (NPV), by profitability indices or by benefit-cost ratios and capital rationing or available investment opportunities influence these outcomes. Generally provision of liquidity raises the duration of investment projects and, thereby, raise productivity of capital.

Similarly, possibility of portfolio diversification encourages investment in riskier assets with higher returns and such diversification and consequent selection of specialised projects can be more profitable. This is especially true of investment in the foreign assets. International risk-sharing effects economic welfare directly and thereby stimulates growth (Obstefield, 1994). Global portfolio diversification shows a link between financial openness and economic growth clearly. Obstefield (1994) provides a number of calibration exercises using consumption and stock market data and these exercises imply that most countries reap large steady-state welfare gains from global financial integration. Total investment may not increase but productivity of capital increases due to financial development (Theil, 2001).

The Econometric Models

Following the above theoretical discussion, we have decided to estimate a number of equations to assess the effect of financial development on economic growth and to also assess the effect of financial development on saving. The latter can be handled by means of auxiliary regressions as indicated in equation (4). We have used annual time-series data for the UK economy, from the beginning of the 20th century. The sources of data are discussed in a later section.

Our first model is to measure the impact of financial growth on the saving ratio. The positive impact on rate of growth, as explained above, is transmitted through saving and productivity of capital. The regression equation we consider in this context is:

$$s = a + b_1 r + b_2 (M/Y) + b_3 P + u \qquad (4)$$

where the variables, the ratio of money stock to GDP, M/Y, can measure the degree of financial depth (Ghatak, 2000), and the industrial share price index, P, will be a measure of portfolio choice and diversification. We also take different interest rates by turn to assess whether sensitivity of saving is significantly different to different interest rates. However, the data on some interest rates are not available for the whole 20th century but they are available from the nineteen fifties or later, for example, the lending and deposit rates. The data on treasury bill rates, short-term and long-term government bond yields, and, the bank rate are available for the entire period under our study, 1900-2000. We have indicated in the relevant tables which interest rate has been used as an explanatory variable in the equation (4). Whether response of saving ratio is significantly different is assessed by ordinary t-tests for the null hypothesis:

$H_0: b_{1i} = b_{1j}$ for $i \neq j$, against the alternative hypothesis
$H_1: b_{1i} \neq b_{1j}$ for $i \neq j$, $i, j = 1, 2, \ldots 7$

where i and j stand for any two different interest rates. We use all interest rates on which data are available in the UK, such as treasury bill rate, r; Euro dollar rate, • \$; deposit rate, Dr; lending rate, Lr; government bond yields, short-term str; and long term, ltr; and bank rate. Br, which was renamed minimum lending rate in the UK. The bank rate or the minimum lending rate (MLR) is the interest rate that the Bank of England charges or used to charge when the commercial banks want to borrow money. It was an important weapon of monetary control in the UK in the 1950s and in the 1960s. The policies named in the document CCC, introduced in 1971 also retained the MLR although various other controls were relaxed.

Statistical significance of such t-ratios can be regarded as indication of different response of saving ratio to different interest rates. The latter, in turn, can be regarded as implying significance of various transactions costs and/or financial intermediation costs. In addition to this we use the difference between Lr and Dr as a measure of costs of intermediation, δ, and assess its influence on saving ratio. The data on Dr and Lr are available only from 1960 onwards.

In the next stage, we choose a simple model where growth of GDP is assumed to depend on saving ratio, financial depth, and a measure of capital productivity, PK:

$$g = a + b_1 s + b_2 (M/Y) + b_3 PK + u \tag{5}$$

We measure productivity of capital by the ratio of GDP to investment. Assuming net investment, I, as new capital formation, capital stock and investment are related as:

$$K_t = K_{t-1} + I_t$$

Productivity of capital, PK, therefore, can be taken as:

$$K_t/GDP = (K_{t-1}/GDP) + I_t/GDP.$$

Usually the capital stock and investment at the earliest time period for which data are available, are assumed to be equal and, future estimates are derived using the definition, (5). For example:

$K_{1900} = I_{1900}$ meaning $K_{1901} = I_{1900} + I_{1901}$; $K_{1902} = I_{1901} + I_{1902}$; and, so on.

However, we avoid this method for two reasons:

1. It would introduce random walk element and/or first order autocorrelation in the capital productivity variable, even if random walk element were not present originally.
2. We also observe that the GDP-to-investment ratio would be close to the reciprocal of the product of transactions costs and the saving ratio, as indicated in (2d). So, we will avoid the multicollinearity problem, to some extent, between s and PK, which are included in the regression (5).

We also exclude saving ratio from growth regression and check whether this leads to misspecification:

$$g = a + b_2 (M/Y) + b_3 PK + u \tag{6}$$

As the growth rate, g, is a stationary variable, we re-estimate regressions in the natural logarithms of GDP and money. Regressions in natural logarithms of variables complies with the standard procedure in the time-series analysis for exploring growth patterns (Box & Tiao, 1975). Denoting logarithms of variables by a prefix, L, our estimating equation for growth can be written as:

$$LY = a + b_2 LM + b_3 PK + u \tag{7}$$

In equation (7), therefore, the coefficient b_2 measures the elasticity of GDP with respect to that of money stock.

Finally, to make special reference to the various changes in the money and financial sector in the UK, we include dummy variables to our growth equations. Excessive growth of money holding after 1965, change of banking sector regulations by means of CCC in 1971, financial innovation and financial liberalisation supposed to have been set in motion in 1980, and, the financial crisis occurring in 1987, are accommodated by defining dummy variables in 1965, in 1971, in 1980 and in 1987. These dummy variables are introduced for both the intercept and the slope changes. The first subscript is 0 for intercept and 1 for the slope change:

$$LY = a + b_1 PK + b_2 LM + b_3 D_{0i} + b_4 D_{1i} + u \tag{8}$$

i=1,2,3,4, where the dummy variables are defined as:

$D_{01} = 0$, for 1900-1964 and $D_{01} = 1$ for 1965-2004
$D_{11} = 0$, for 1900-1964 and $D_{11} = M/Y$ or LM, for 1965-2004

$D_{02}=0$, for 1900-1971 and $D_{02}=1$ for 1972-2004

$D_{12}=0$, for 1900-1971 and $D_{12}=M/Y$ or LM, for 1972-2004

$D_{03}=0$, for 1900-1980 and $D_{03}=1$ for 1981-2004

$D_{13}=0$, for 1900-1980 and $D_{13}=M/Y$ or LM, for 1981-2004

$D_{04}=0$, for 1900-1987 and $D_{04}=1$ for 1988-2004

$D_{14}=0$, for 1900-1987 and $D_{14}=M/Y$ or LM, for 1988-2004

Statistical significance of the dummy variables will imply significance of the financial innovation process.

We estimate all the equations of our models by MICROFIT4. Following time-series methodology, we test all variables for stationarity. The tests used to detect stationarity are the popular augmented Dickey-Fuller t-tests (ADF) (Dickey & Fuller, 1979). In the next stage we check if the regressions listed above in equations (4) to (8) are equilibrium relations. The tests to be applied in this context are well known as the tests for cointegration. For multiple regressions, cointegration must be checked by Johansen's method (1988). In case the variables in the same equation pass the tests for a unique cointegration vector, we can take the relevant regression results as reliable, and not spurious.

The Sources of Data

We have used three main sources for getting the annual time-series data for the UK covering the period from 1900-2003.

1.   Liesner (1983). This source publishes data for the period 1900-1983 for a large number of variables, including the ones we have used in this study.
2.   International Financial Statistics Yearbooks, 1970, 1980, 2000 and 2003 published by the IMF.
3.   Economic Trends, 2000, published by the CSO.

Interpretation of Estimates

The results of stationarity tests given in Table 1 demonstrate that rate of growth of GDP, saving to GDP ratio, money stock to GDP ratio and the transactions costs are stationary. Most other variables are non-stationary and, therefore we apply stationarity tests to their first difference. The augmented Dickey-Fuller-t values in column (4) of Table 1 indicate

Table 1. Results of stationarity tests in annual time-series data for the UK, 1900-2003

Variable	ADF-t	First difference	ADF-t
Saving-GDP ratio	-4.1845*	Not required(NR)	NR
Money-GDP ratio	-4.7399*	NR	NR
Treasury bill rate	-2.3406	Δr	-8.1309*
Industrial share price index in natural logarithm	-1.7830	ΔLP	-7.5179*
GDP	-2.9722	ΔGDP	-9.2425*
g	-7.6197*	NR	NR
PK	-2.9722	ΔPK	-9.0624*
€$ r	-2.0298	Δ€$ r	-5.4141*
Deposit rate,Dr	-2.0653	ΔDr	-6.1377*
Lending rate,Lr	-2.2581	ΔLr	-5.0634*
Government bond yield, short-term str	-1.6159	Δstr	-7.8682*
Government bond yield, long-term ltr	-1.4655	Δltr	-7.3206*
Bank rate, Br	-1.9865	ΔBr	-7.2762*
Log(GDP)	-2.3316	ΔLog(GDP)	-9.5813*
Log(M)	-2.7976	ΔLog(M)	-6.0615*
δ	-4.4669*	NR	

that all the seven measures of the interest rate, GDP, money stock and, industrial share price in natural logarithm, GDP, and productivity of capital are stationary in their first difference.

The results of multi-cointegration tests by Johansen's method are given in Table 2.

We apply the trace test as this is more difficult to meet and, therefore it reduces the probability of Type II error or the error of accepting a false hypothesis. MICROFIT4 software provides the critical values of the cointegration and stationarity test statistics. We have indicated the relevant critical values in respective contexts. Critical values are different only when have a different sample size and/or a different number of explanatory variables. We indicate the new critical value only, as and when it is relevant. The results in column 4 of Table 2 suggest that the saving ratio equation holds an equilibrium relation only when we use the lending rate as the interest rate variable. The growth rate equation does not hold a unique co-integrated relation at all unless we regress natural logarithm of the GDP. Natural log of GDP holds a unique co-integrated relation with saving ratio, capital productivity, and logarithm of money stock. Equilibrium and unique cointegration properties are retained when transactions costs replace saving ratio in the log (GDP) regression.

When dummy variables are introduced after 1965 and 1980, unique cointegration vectors exist even if saving and transactions costs variables are excluded from the regression of log (GDP) on capital productivity and log (M). In each case of a unique cointegration

Table 2. Results of multi-co-integration tests by Johansen's method

Regression and Conclusion	Null Hypothesis H_0:	Alternative Hypothesis H_1:	Trace-Test statistic	Critical value at the 5% level and conclusion
S r m P No unique cointegration	H_0: n=0	H_1 : n>=1	150.2713*	58.93
	H_0 : n<=1	H_1 : n>=2	85.5945*	39.33
	H_0 : n<=2	H_1 : n>=3	38.3936*	23.83
	H_0 : n<=3	H_1 : n>=4	9.4616	11.54
S €$ r m P No unique cointegration	H_0: n=0	H_1: n>=1	88.8596*	No unique
	H_0 : n<=1	H_1 : n>=2	45.0271*	cointegration
	H_0 : n<=2	H_1 : n>=3	14.4109	vector exists
S Dr m P	H_0: n=0	H_1 : n>=1	82.9553*	No unique
	H_0: n<=1	H_1 : n>=2	39.4471*	cointegration
	H_0: n<=2	H_1 : n>=3	13.0789	vector exists
S Lr m P	H_0: n=0	H_1 : n>=1	62.3457*	A unique
	H_0: n<=1	H_1: n>=2	29.7164	cointegration vector
S str m P	H_0: n=0	H_1 : n>=1	141.7684*	No unique
	H_0: n<=1	H_1: n>=2	81.6139*	cointegration
	H_0: n<=2	H_1: n>=3	35.0697*	vector exists
	H_0: n<=3	H_1: n>=4	6.0405	
S ltr m P	H_0: n =0	H_1: n >=1	138.594*	No unique
	H_0: n<=1	H_1: n>=2	79.8793*	cointegration
	H_0: n<=2	H_1: n>=3	33.6085*	vector exists
	H_0 : n<=3	H_1: n>=4	4.7805	
S Br m P	H_0: n =0	H_1: n >=1	105.7245*	No unique
	H_0: n<=1	H_1 : n>=2	59.9114*	cointegration
	H_0: n<=2	H_1 : n>=3	23.1428*	vector exists
	H_0: n<=3	H_1: n>=4	13.0034	
Ly s PK m	H_0: n =0	H_1: n >=1	113.9772*	No unique
	H_0: n<=1	H_1 : n>=2	59.5959*	cointegration
	H_0: n<=2	H_1 : n>=3	10.9100	vector
g s PK m	H_0: n =0	H_1: n >=1	223.1214*	No unique
	H_0 : n<=1	H_1 : n>=2	78.5973*	cointegration
	H_0 : n<=2	H : n>=3	38.3503*	vector
Ly s PK Lm	H_0: n =0	H_1: n >=1	75.4919*	A unique
	H_0: n<=1	H_1 : n>=2	21.0939	cointegration vector
LY PK LM	H_0: n =0	H_1: n >=1	30.2458	Not Cointegrated
LY PK LM D_{01} D_{11} in 1965	H_0: n =0	H_1: n >=1	86.9373*	82.23
	H_0: n<=1	H_1: n>=2	48.0729	A unique cointegration vector exists
LY PK LM D_{02} D_{12} in1971	H_0: n =0	H_1 : n >=1	57.92	No cointegration
LY PK LM D_{03} D_{13} in 1980	H_0: n =0	H_1 : n >=1	102.1780*	A unique
	H : n<=1	H : n>=2	52.4884	cointegration vector exists
LY PK LM D_{04} D_{14} in 1987	H_0: n =0	H_1: n >=1	122.2324*	No unique
	H_0: n <= 1	H_1: n>=2	71.6729*	cointegartion
	H : n<=2	H : n>=3	43.0429*	vector
	H n<=3	H : n>=4	20.2367	
LY PK LM δ D_{01} D_{11} in 1965	H_0: n =0	H_1 : n >=1	118.0935*	109.18
	H : n<=1	H : n>=2	77.6213	A unique cointegration vector exists
LY PK LM δ	H_0: n=0	H_1: n>=1	61.7640*	A unique
	H_1: n<=1	H_1: n>=2	26.7281	cointegration vector exists

Table 3. Main results of estimated regressions: the UK, 1900-2004

Coefficients with t-values underneath

Regression	Intercept	Coefficient of variable number 1	Coefficient of variable number 2	Coefficient of variable number 3	Adjusted R^2 and Durbin-Watson statistic respectively
S r m P	a =-0.0832* -2.0688	b_1= 0.0161* 2.3336	b_2 = 0.1516 1.2912	b_3 = 0.00079* 6.2645	0.4824 2.0406
S • $ m P	a = -0.30893* -2.6408	b_1 =0.035646* 2.9157	b_2 =0.30429 1.7346	b_3 =0.00086* 4.8280	0.45204 2.3037
S Dr m P	a = -0.29495* -2.3143	b_1 =0.037554* 2.6759	b_2 =0.27965 1.5012	b_3 =0.00094* 4.8603	0.42135 2.3722
S Lr m P	a=-0.5032* 2.2971	b_1 = 0.05037* 2.5494	b_2 =0.27093 1.3354	b_3 = 0.00097* 4.2605	0.37643 2.3908
S ltr m P	a = -0.0657 -1.2578	b_1 =0.0076 0.957	b_2 = 0.1949 1.579	b_3=0.00088* 7.0236	0.4515 1.9448
S str m P	a=-0.0912 -1.8707	b_1=0.0136 1.7732	b_2=0.1769 1.4965	b_3=0.00083* 6.6185	0.46716 1.9816
S Br m P	a = -0.2248* -2.1699	b_1 =0.02198* 2.1767	b_2 =0.2811 1.6672	b_3 =0.0009* 5.5462	0.42645 2.1199
Ly s PK M	a=10.7514* 63.7961	b_1=0.6315 1.4437	b_2= 0.0660* 3.5603	b_3= 0.000013* 3.7574	0.34544 0.6861
g s PK m	a =0.6415 1.8196	b_1= -0.3385 -0.59535	b_2= -0.0288 -0.8461	b_3= -1.0651 -1.1198	-0.01253 2.0103
Ly s PK Lm	a = 5.4219* 6.8766	b_1=0.15897 0.44315	b_2= 0.0970* 5.8979	b_3=0.60831* 7.0561	0.52534 0.57
Ly PK Lm	a=5.234* 7.9121	....	b_2=0.0974* 5.9621	b_3=0.63218* 9.2100	0.53005 0.51304
LY δ PK LM	8.2220* 10.649	0.0673 1.3984	0.4767* 12.8402	0.1871* 2.2098	0.9116 0.9699

vector, the trace test statistic rejects the null hypothesis of no cointegration vector against the alternative hypothesis of at least one cointegration vector but it cannot reject the null hypothesis of less than or one cointegration vector. The implication of this combination of results is, therefore, that there exists a unique cointegration vector in this regression.

In Table 3, the estimates of the coefficients of equations (4)-(8) are given.

We only discuss the results of the estimates of the co-integrated equations. In the saving ratio equation (4) for r = Lr, all the explanatory variables are statistically significant at the 5% level and have the expected positive sign. Saving ratio increases with interest rate,

Table 4. Values of t-statistics for testing differences in coefficients of various interest rates in the regression of saving ratio

**Values of t-statistics for testing differences in coefficients
of various interest rates in the regression of saving ratio**

	r	$	Dr	Lr	Ltr	Str	Br
r	....	3.6672*	3.0048*	2.6628*	1.07	3.1987*	1.8375
$	3.6672*	....	0.1359	1.95	6.5528*	4.8441*	6.4559*
Dr	3.0048*	0.1359	......	2.2378*	4.9185*	3.7656*	3.9530*
Lr	2.6628*	1.95	2.2378*	....	23.54*	5.5980*	2.4019*
Ltr	1.07	6.5528*	4.9185*	23.54*	....	22.24*	6.6883*
Str	3.1987*	4.8441*	3.7656*	5.5980*	22.24*	....	3.4687*
Br	1.8375	6.4559	3.953*	2.4019*	6.6883*	3.4686*	....

financial depth and share price index. In all these saving ratio regressions there is a negative intercept, which is to be expected as there is negative saving at a low-income level. The positive sign of the coefficient of the money stock to GDP ratio supports our hypothesis that financial development increases the saving ratio by providing various ways of successful transmission of surplus funds into the sector with deficit. The positive sign of interest rate supports the idea that interest is a reward for saving. The positive and statistically significant coefficient of the industrial share price index supports the idea that saving can follow a portfolio management exercise and an upturn of share price index, therefore, acts as an incentive to saving. These regressions all have a similar value of the adjusted R-square. Coming to the cointegration issue, we find that only when lending rate is included as the interest rate that the saving ratio regression

Table 5. Dummy variables added for assessing significance of financial innovation

Coefficients with t-values underneath

Regression Ly PK LM $D_{01} D_{11}$	Intercept	Variable PK	Variable LM	Variable D_{0i}	Variable D_{1i}	Adjusted R-square and DW
Year of break,1965	13.0019* 10.6876	0.0811* 5.9113	-0.3460*- 2.3453	-8.7170* -4.9061	1.0946* 5.5938	0.7077 0.9085
Year of break, 1971	10.1835* 10.7557	0.0870* 6.5567	-0.003 -0.0262	0.0607 1.7667	1.4232* 4.2683	0.6845 0.78
Year of break, 1980	9.1671* 11.5684	0.07044* 5.7582	0.15677 1.8485	4.2222* 2.1085	-0.2218 1.1416	0.7449 1.0272
Year of break, 1987	6.9006* 10.7646	0.0856* 6.7217	0.4246* 6.0807	6.2576* 2.7552	-0.4595* -2.1178	0.7008 0.78

Table 6. Regressions with dummy variables and transactions costs

Coefficients with t-values underneath

Regression LY δ LM PK D$_{01}$ D$_{11}$	Intercept	Variable δ	Variable LM	Variable PK	Variable D$_{0i}$	Variable D$_{1i}$	Adjusted R-square and DW
Break year 1965	2.7659 0.0964	0.05591 1.0230	0.7816 0.2413	0.4702* 12.0643	-0.5886 -0.1816	5.5593 0.1937	0.8888 0.6602

Notes: a) In all the tables, one asterisk denotes statistical significance at the 5% level. b) Critical values of t at 5% level of significance are, respectively, 2.06, 2.042, 2.021, 2.0 and 1.98 for 25, 30, 40, 60 and 120 degrees of freedom.

has a unique cointegration vector. None of the other saving ratio regressions can sustain the idea of long-run equilibrium relations between these variables. In the growth equations, when economic growth is measured by log (GDP), the coefficients of saving ratio, capital productivity and financial depth are all positive and all but one are statistically significant at the 5% level. The coefficient of the saving ratio has the expected positive sign but an insignificant ordinary t-value. However, the lack of statistical significance of s can be explained by its effect being swamped, to some extent, by the GDP-investment ratio, as already discussed. That the saving ratio is important for explaining equilibrium growth is indicated in the lack of cointegration among the variables, LY, PK and LM , when saving ratio is excluded. The null hypothesis of no cointegration vector cannot be rejected at the 5% level in the regression of LY on PK and LM. GDP shows positive and statistically significant elasticities with respect to money stock in all the relevant regression with capital productivity and with or without saving ratio and transactions costs.

Before going on to check how the various changes in the financial sector affected economic growth and money-stock elasticity of GDP, we look at the response of saving ratio to different types of interest rates. The results of estimates of the coefficient of r in the equation (4) are given in Table 3. From the relevant coefficients and respective standard errors of estimates, we calculated the ordinary t-values and these t-values are given in Table 4. These t-values for testing:

H_0: $b_{1i} = b_{1j}$ for $i \neq j$, against the alternative hypothesis

H_1: $b_{1i} \neq b_{1j}$ for $i \neq j$, $i, j = 1,2,...7$

are significant in 17 out of 21 cases. This constitutes some indirect proof of the importance of various costs of financial intermediation in the saving behaviour.

The results given in Table 5 reveal that the huge increase in money holding in 1965 exerted a significant influence on growth of GDP; similarly, the changes initiated in the process of financial liberalisation in 1980 also have a significant effect on money elasticity of GDP.

In both cases, the dummy variables for the intercept and the coefficient of money stock are significant at the 5% level; more importantly, both equations show existence of a unique cointegration vector. We do not need to include the saving ratio or the transactions costs as an additional explanatory variable to achieve unique cointegration. As already discussed, there is an inverse relation between productivity of capital as measured by GDP-investment ratio and the product of saving ratio and transactions costs; as a result, the coefficients of saving ratio, transactions costs, and productivity of capital are not clearly separable. We, therefore, are inclined to take the regression equation (8):

$$LY = a + b_1 PK + b_2 LM + b_3 D_{0i} + b_4 D_{1i} + u$$

as the more correctly specified equation, where the dummy variables are defined from the year, 1965, and 1980. The dummy variables introduced after the introduction of CCC or after the financial crash in 1987 do not yield equilibrium relations, although there are significant short-term fluctuations: After the crash in 1987, the influence of financial growth becomes negative (0.4246-0.4595 = -0.0349) and all the variables including the dummy variables are statistically significant at the 5% level. However, the equation (8) when breaks are included in 1987, is not an equilibrium regression as there is no unique co-integrated vector. Regression (8) shows unique cointegration vector only when dummy variables are defined from 1965 and from 1980. All the coefficients in the equation (8) are statistically significant at the 5% level when the break year is taken to be 1965. The level of the growth equation was reduced from 13 to 4.2849 (=13.0019-8.7170) after 1965 but the impact of money growth on growth of GDP increased to 0.7486 (=-0.3460+1.0946) after 1965. Productivity of capital shows a significant and positive influence on growth of GDP as well. After 1980, the year earmarked for financial liberalisation, the level of the GDP growth is increased significantly, both intercepts, before and after 1980 are positive and significant, which implies that the various aspects of financial liberalisation offering more choice of financial products and assets raise the level of economic growth. This can be taken as the feel good factor generally rendering a positive impact on economic growth. The growth of money stock, however, is not statistically significant at the 5% level either before or after 1980. Productivity of capital has a positive influence on growth and it is statistically significant. The value of the adjusted R-square is reasonably high in all the growth regressions with dummy variables. Measuring transactions costs, δ as the difference between the lending and the borrowing rate, we re-estimate the growth regressions. The transactions costs variable is stationary and these are available from 1961 onwards. We report the main results of only a couple of regressions, one without the dummy variables in Table 3 and one with the dummy variables introduced in 1965 in Table 6. The transactions costs variable has a positive sign but it is statistically insignificant. The same arguments can be given against including δ as an explanatory variable along with GDP-to-investment ratio as for not including the saving ratio. While the addition of δ as measured by the difference between the lending and deposit rates, achieves unique cointegration, it renders all but one coefficient statistically insignificant. Only the productivity of capital as measured by the GDP-to-investment ratio has a positive and statistically significant coefficient.

Conclusions

Economic growth has long-run equilibrium relation with productivity of capital, and financial growth when the massive increase in money holding in the year 1965 and changes due to financial innovation and financial liberalisation in the UK economy are taken into account. The cointegration analysis suggests that there is a unique cointegration vector between growth of GDP, productivity of capital and financial growth if we allow for breaks in the level and slope after 1965 and after 1980. Money-stock elasticity of GDP is positive, statistically significant and it increases after 1965 and after 1980.

Unique cointegration is also achieved when saving ratio, or transactions costs are added as explanatory variables. Productivity of capital as measured by the GDP-to-investment ratio, in the economic growth literature, can be derived as reciprocal of the product of saving ratio and transactions costs of financial intermediation; so, one has to be alerted to possible specification error in growth equation with all three as explanatory variables.

In the auxiliary regressions of saving ratio on the various interest rates, financial depth, and, industrial share price index, we find that the response of saving ratio varies between different interest rates as expected and, such variations are statistically significant in seventeen out of twenty one cases. This implies the influence of transactions costs. The process of financial liberalisation is expected to increase competition, ensure a free flow of information, and, such like, and, thereby, expected to reduce such transactions costs. Saving ratio shows a long-run equilibrium relation when the lending rate is used as the interest rate. Transactions costs as measured by the difference between lending rate and the deposit rate are not statistically significant in any regression; however, the addition of these costs retain the cointegration properties of all regressions.

References

Begg, D., Fischer, S., & Dornbusch, R. (2000). *Economics*. London: McGraw Hill.

Box, G. E. P., & Tiao, G. C. (1975). Intervention analysis with applications to economic and environmental problems. *Journal of the American Statistical Association, 70*, 70-79.

Cameron, R., et.al. (1967). *Banking in the early stages of industrialisation*. Oxford: Oxford University Press.

Dickey, D. A., & Fuller, W. A. (1979). Distribution of the estimators for autoregressive time series with a unit root. *Journal of the American Statistical Association, 74*, 427-31.

Engle, R. F., & Granger, C. W. J. (1987). Co-integration and error correction: Representation, estimation and testing. *Econometrica, 55*, 251-276.

Engle, R. F., & Yoo, B. S. (1991). Forecasting and testing in co-integrated systems. In R. F. Engle & C. W. J. Granger (Eds.), *Long-run economic relationships: Readings in cointegration*. Oxford: Oxford University Press.

Garshenkron, A. (1962). *Economic backwardness in historical perspective: A book of essays.* Cambridge, MA: Harvard University Press.

Ghatak, A. (2003). Financial dynamics and economic growth: Lessons for India from the twentieth century. In P. S. Banerjee & F. J. Richter (Eds.), *Economic institutions in India: Sustainability under liberalization and globalization.* Houndmills, Basingstoke: Palgrave.

Gowland, D. H. (1991). Financial innovation in theory and practice. In C. J. Green & D. T. Llewellyn (Eds.), *Surveys in monetary economics, volume 2: Financial markets and institutions.* Oxford: Basil Blackwell.

Gujarati, D. N. (2003). *Basic econometrics.* Boston: McGraw Hill.

Gylfason, T. (1999). *Principles of economic growth.* Oxford: Oxford University Press.

Heffernan, S. (2001). *Modern banking in theory and practice.* London: Wiley.

Hicks, J. R. (1939). *Value and capital.* Oxford: Oxford University Press.

Johansen, S. (1988). Statistical analysis of cointegration vectors. *Journal of Economic Dynamics and Control, 12*, 231-254.

Levine, R. (1997). Financial development and economic growth: Views and agenda. *Journal of Economic Literature, XXXV*, 2.

Liesner, T. (1984). *The economist: Economic statistics, 1900-1983.*

McKinnon, R. I. (Ed.). (1976). *Money and finance in economic growth and development: Essays in honour of Edward S. Shaw.* Stanford: Marcel Dekker.

Obstefield, M. (1994). Risk-taking, global diversification, and growth. *The American Economic Review, 84*, 1310-1329.

Pagano, M. (1993). Financial markets and growth: An overview. *European Economic Review, 37*, 613-622.

Santomero, A. M., & Seater, J. J. (2000). Is there an optimal size for the financial sector? *Journal of Banking and Finance, 24*, 945-965.

Schumpeter, J. A. (1936). *Theory of economic development.* Harvard: Harvard University Press.

Shaw, E. S. (1973). *Financial deepening in economic development.* Oxford: Oxford University Press.

Silber, W. (1983). The process of financial innovation. *American Economic Review, Papers and Proceedings*, 89-95.

Spellman, L. J. (1976). Economic growth and financial intermediation. In R. I. McKinnon (Ed.), *Money and finance in economic growth and development: Essays in honour of Edward S. Shaw.* Stanford: Marcel Dekker.

Theil, M. (2001). Finance and economic growth: A review of theory and the available evidence. *Economic Paper,* 158.

Tobin, J. (1984). On the efficiency of the financial system. *Lloyds Bank Review, 153*, 1-15.

Endnote

[1]   SWIFT is the Society for Worldwide Interbank Financial Telecommunications established in Belgium in 1973. Fedwire is the Federal Reserve's Fund Transfer System. CHIPS is the Clearing House Interbank Payments System based in New York and established in 1971. CHAPS is the Clearing House Automated Payments System based in London and established in 1984.

Section II

Financial Markets in the IT Age

Chapter V

Malliavin Calculus for the Estimation of the U.S. Dollar/Euro Exchange Rate When the Volatility is Stochastic

Ahmed Abutaleb, Cairo University, Egypt

Michael Papaioannou, International Monetary Fund, USA

Abstract

The tendency of exchange rates to fluctuate markedly and regularly is often referred as currency market volatility. The extent of currency market volatility is a major element of market risk. For financial transactions, volatility represents both costs and profit opportunities. Increased currency market volatility implies higher currency option premia and, therefore, higher hedging costs for investors and importers/ exporters. However, for banks and other investment houses dealing in options, an increase in option prices may contribute to higher profits. It has been well established that the volatility of exchange rates changes with time. In recent years, various stochastic volatility models have been proposed in the literature that try to capture the exchange-rate volatility dynamics. In turn, several methods have been developed to estimate the parameters of such stochastic volatility models, with varying results. In this chapter, we propose another method for the estimation of the parameters of an exchange rate function when the volatility follows a stochastic process. Stochastic volatility is represented by a geometric Brownian motion. Using Malliavin calculus, we are able to find an explicit expression for the likelihood function of the observations. Numerical integration methods (Monte-Carlo simulations) and numerical optimization methods (generic algorithms) enable us to find an estimate for the unknown parameters and the volatility. This estimation method is then applied to the U.S. dollar/euro exchange rate. Specifically, first we formulate a U.S. dollar/euro exchange rate equation with a stochastic volatility model. We assume that the observed U.S. dollar/ euro exchange rate follows a stochastic differential equation with random volatility, while the unobserved volatility follows a different stochastic differential equation. Then, we obtain the likelihood function of the observations by applying Malliavin calculus. The estimation of the unknown parameters is achieved through the maximization of the likelihood function. Using weekly U.S. dollar/euro exchange rates for the period April 28, 2000, to March 26, 2001, we obtain estimates of the parameters of the U.S. dollar/euro exchange rate function (i.e., the constant of the drift) and the assumed stochastic volatility model (i.e., the constants of the diffusion process). Application of the estimated model to out-of-sample data for the U.S. dollar/euro exchange rate shows a significantly high accuracy of the proposed method, as indicated by the very low root mean square error for the estimated exchange rate. This method can also be applied to other models of financial variables that follow similar processes.

Introduction

The magnitude of fluctuations among currencies is often called exchange rate volatility. It has been well established that currency market volatility could change rapidly over time. The extent of currency market volatility is a major element of market risk. For financial transactions, it represents both costs and profit opportunities. Currency market volatility raises the costs of hedging, for example, as indicated in the pricing of options. Increased volatility implies higher option premia and therefore higher hedging costs for investors and importers/exporters, but it may also contribute to generally higher profits for banks and other investment houses dealing in options (Papaioannou, 2001).

The observed instability in currency markets during the last two decades has been seen as a consequence of at least five identifiable factors: (i) The present floating exchange rate system, which allows for wide currency fluctuations; (ii) The increased global financial integration caused by the emergence of free trade blocks and new currencies such as the euro; (iii) The growth in capital flows as a result a result of the liberalization of trade in goods and services; (iv) The increased response of financial markets to emerging opportunities from interest rate differentials, misalignments and market inefficiencies; and (v) The spread of information technology.

Several methods have been developed in recent years to estimate the parameters of stochastic volatility models (in continuous time) that try to capture volatility dynamics:

1.   Method of moments (Hanson, 1982; Genon-Catalot, Jeantheau & Laredo, 1998).

2.   Estimation based on simple approximation to the marginal distribution of the observations (Genon-Catalot, Jeantheau & Laredo, 1999).

3.   Prediction-based estimation functions (Sorensen, 1999).

4.   Bayesian-based methods (Elerian, 1999; Elerian, Chib & Shiphard, 2001; Ait-Sahalia, 1996a, 1996b, 2002).

5.   Auxiliary-based models (Gourieroux, Monfort & Renault, 1993).

6.   Extended Kalman Filter (Nielsen, 2000).

7.   Approximate maximum likelihood estimation (Sorensen, 2000).

These methods have increasingly been used in exchange rate applications with varying results (Abutaleb, Kumasaka, & Papaioannou, 2003).

In this chapter, we propose a method for the estimation of the parameters of a behavioral function when the volatility follows a stochastic process. Stochastic volatility is represented by a geometric Brownian motion. Using Malliavin calculus, we are able to find an explicit expression for the likelihood function of the observations. Numerical integration methods (Monte-Carlo simulations) and numerical optimization methods (generic algorithms) enable us to find an estimate for the unknown parameters and the volatility. This estimation method is then applied to the U.S. dollar/euro exchange rate.

Specifically, first, we formulate a U.S. dollar/euro exchange rate equation with a stochastic volatility model. We assume that the observed U.S. dollar/euro exchange rate follows a stochastic differential equation with random volatility, while the unobserved volatility follows a different stochastic differential equation. Then, we obtain the likelihood function of the observations by applying Malliavin calculus. The estimation of the unknown parameters is achieved through the maximization of the likelihood function.

Using weekly U.S. dollar/euro exchange rates for the period April 28, 2000, to March 26, 2001, we obtain estimates of the parameters of the U.S. dollar/euro exchange rate function (i.e., the constant of the drift) and the assumed stochastic volatility model (i.e., the constants of the diffusion process). Application of the estimated model to out-of-sample data for the U.S. dollar/euro exchange rate shows a significantly high accuracy of the proposed method, as indicated by the very low root mean square error for the estimated exchange rate. This method can also be applied to other models of financial variables that follow similar processes.

The chapter is organized as follows: In the second section, we describe the problem of parameter estimation when the volatility is random. In the third section, we introduce the proposed method based on Malliavin calculus. In the fourth section, we apply the method to the exchange rate between the U.S. dollar and the euro. Finally, in the fifth section, we present a summary and conclusions. There are two appendices that introduce the Malliavin calculus.

Problem Formulation:
Stochastic Volatility

Consider the classical model for the exchange rate X^t at instant t:

$$dX^t = \beta X^t dt + \tau X^t dW_t^1 \tag{II.1}$$

where β is an unknown constant and τ is an unknown positive constant, and W_t^1 is a standard Brownian motion. In stochastic volatility models, the linearity of the drift and diffusion is retained, but an additional source of noise is introduced. The constant term τ is replaced by the value of a diffusion process $\sqrt{v_t}$. The process v_t is unobserved, and it is interpreted as the volatility. The modified model is then given by:

$$dX^t = \beta X^t dt + \tau X^t dW_t^1 \tag{II.2}$$

$$dv_t = b(v_t;\underline{\theta}_1)dt + \sigma(v_t;\underline{\theta}_1)dW_t^2 \tag{II.3}$$

where $\underline{\theta}_1$ is a vector of unknown parameters, W_t^2 is a Brownian motion independent of W_t^1, and the exchange rate X^t is observed at certain time periods. It is desired to find an estimate for $\underline{\theta}_1 = [\underline{\theta}'_1, \beta]$. Equations (II.2) and (II.3) have the following integral form:

$$X^t = X^0 + \beta t \int_0^t X^s ds + \int_0^t \sqrt{v_s} X^s dW_s^1 \tag{II.4}$$

The stochastic volatility could assume one of several models (Lipton, 2000):

$$\frac{dv_t}{v_t} = \alpha dt + \gamma dW_t^2 \tag{II.5a}$$

which has a solution:

$$v_t = v_t(t, W_t^2) = v_0 \exp\left[\left(\alpha - \frac{1}{2}\gamma^2\right)t + \gamma W_t^2\right] \tag{II.6}$$

$$dv_t = (\beta_0 - \beta_1 v_t)dt + \sigma_0 dW_t^2 \tag{II.5b}$$

$$dv_t = k(\alpha - v_t)dt + \varepsilon\sqrt{v_t}\,dW_t^2 \tag{II.5c}$$

where W_t^2 is a Brownian motion. Other models are also available (Elerian, 1999). Substituting the expression for of equation (II. 6) into equation (II. 2) we get:

$$X^t = X^0 + \beta\int_0^t X^s ds + \sqrt{v_o}\int_0^t \sqrt{\exp\left[\left(\alpha - \frac{1}{2}\gamma^2\right)s + \gamma W_s^2\right]}X^s dW_s^1$$

which is reduced to:

$$X^t = X^0 + \beta\int_0^t X^s ds + \sqrt{v_o}\int_0^t \left\{\exp\frac{1}{2}\left[\left(\alpha - \frac{1}{2}\gamma^2\right)s + \gamma W_s^2\right]\right\}X^s dW_s^1 \tag{II.7}$$

that is, $X^t = X^t(t, W_t^1, W_t^2)$.

Equations (II. 2) and (II. 5a) could be written in a vector form as:

$$\begin{bmatrix} dX^t \\ dv_t \end{bmatrix} = \begin{bmatrix} \beta X^t \\ \alpha v_t \end{bmatrix}dt + \begin{bmatrix} \sqrt{v_t}\,X^t \\ 0 \end{bmatrix}dW_t^1 + \begin{bmatrix} 0 \\ \gamma v_t \end{bmatrix}dW_t^2 \tag{II.8}$$

which has the form $\quad d\underline{Z}_t = \underline{B}(\underline{Z}_t)dt + \sum_{k=1}^{d=2} A_k(\underline{Z}_t)dW_t^k \tag{II.9}$

where $Z_t^1 = X^t = $ exchange rate, $Z_t^2 = v_t = $ volatility,

$$\underline{B}(\underline{Z}_t) = \begin{bmatrix} \beta X^t \\ \alpha Z_t^2 \end{bmatrix}, A_1(\underline{Z}t) = \begin{bmatrix} Z_t^1\sqrt{Z_t^2} \\ 0 \end{bmatrix}, A_2(\underline{Z}t) = \begin{bmatrix} 0 \\ \gamma Z_t^2 \end{bmatrix} \tag{II.10}$$

$$\frac{\partial A_1(\underline{Z}_t)}{\partial Z_t^1} = \begin{bmatrix} \sqrt{Z_t^2} \\ 0 \end{bmatrix}, \frac{\partial A_1(\underline{Z}_t)}{\partial Z_t^2} = \begin{bmatrix} \frac{1}{2}Z_t^1/\sqrt{Z_t^2} \\ 0 \end{bmatrix}, \frac{\partial A_2(\underline{Z}_t)}{\partial Z_t^1} = \begin{bmatrix} 0 \\ 0 \end{bmatrix}, \frac{\partial A_2(\underline{Z}_t)}{\partial Z_t^2} = \begin{bmatrix} 0 \\ \gamma \end{bmatrix} \tag{II.11}$$

$$\frac{\partial B(Zt)}{\partial Z_t^1} = \begin{bmatrix} \beta \\ 0 \end{bmatrix}, \frac{\partial B(Zt)}{\partial Z_t^1} = \begin{bmatrix} 0 \\ \alpha \end{bmatrix} \qquad\qquad (II.12)$$

Let $\underline{\theta} = [\beta, v_0, \alpha, \gamma]$ be the vector of unknown constants that we need to estimate. A number of econometric methods have recently been developed to estimate the parameters.

The Proposed Malliavin Calculus-Based Method

Using Malliavin calculus we derive an expression for the likelihood function of the observations. This will be valid only for the volatility models that have a closed-form solution (as explained below).

So far in the literature, it is not possible to find a closed-form expression for the stochastic differential equation (SDE) of X^i for the general case. Instead, using Malliavin calculus, we will derive the joint likelihood function of the observations $X^1, X^2,..., X^n$ at instants t_1, $t_2,..., t_n, f[X^1, X^2,..., X^n]$ To proceed, assume that the volatility v_t follows a geometric Brownian motion process and can be represented by the following stochastic differential equation (SDE):

$$\frac{dv_t}{v_t} = \alpha dt + \gamma dW_t^2 \qquad\qquad (II.5a)$$

where W_t^2 is a Wiener process and the unknowns are α and γ. A typical set of simulated volatility, v_t, is given in Figure 1 for the values $\alpha = 4$, $\gamma = 2$, and the sampling interval is 0.001. The solution of the SDE of has the form:

$$v_t = v_0 \exp\left[\left(\alpha - \frac{1}{2}\gamma^2\right)t + \gamma W_t^2\right] \qquad\qquad (II.6)$$

Malliavin Calculus

In this section, Malliavin calculus is applied within the framework of the stochastic processes. For definitions and properties of Malliavin calculus we draw from various articles (Bally, 2003; Kohatsu-Higa & Montero, 2003). The observation period is [0,T].

Figure 1. Typical set of simulated volatility, v(t), modeled as geometric Brownian motion.

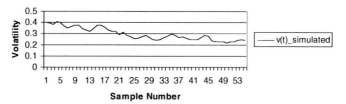

Note: The parameters are: alfa = 4, gama = 2, and the sampling interval is 0.001.

Let $W = \{W_t\}_{t \in [0,T]}$ be a standard one-dimensional Brownian motion defined on a complete probability space (Ω, F, P), where we assume that the random variable $F = \{F_t\}_{t \in [0,T]}$ is generated by W. We shall first introduce the Malliavin derivative and the Skorohod integral. We then present the derivation of the integration-by-parts formula of Malliavin calculus. During the derivation we digress to find a useable expression for the joint probability density function (PDF) of the observations. It is this expression that will be used in finding the maximum likelihood estimates of the parameters. Several examples are given using the derived joint PDF. Finally, we apply this formula to estimate the parameters of the stochastic volatility model when the volatility follows a stochastic process, such as the geometric Brownian motion.

Malliavin Derivative and Skorohod Integral (Bally, 2003)

The operator, D, the Malliavin derivative and its adjoint operator, also known as the Skorohod integral, δ or D^*, is introduced. Let us consider a random variable of the form $F = f(W_{t_1}, ... W_{t_n})$, where f is a smooth function of the arguments. The Malliavin derivative of F, $D_t F$ is given as:

$$D_t F = \sum_{i=1}^{n} \frac{\partial}{\partial x_i} f(W_{t_1}, ..., x_i, ..., W_{t_n}) |_{x_i = W_{t_i}} \, 1_{[t_i, T]}(t) \tag{III.1}$$

where $\quad 1_{[ti,T]}(t) = \begin{array}{ll} 1 & ti \le t \le T \\ 0 & elsewhere \end{array}$

Since D operates on functions in the form of partial derivatives, it shares their general properties, for example, linearity, the chain rule, and the product rule.

The adjoint operator, δ or D^*, behaves as a stochastic integral. Letting $u = u(t, w) = \{u_t\}_{t\in[0,T]}$ be a stochastic process defined on (Ω, F, P), we can then write:

$$\delta(u) = D^*(u) = \int_0^T u_t dW_t \tag{III.2}$$

Both operators D and D^* are linked by the following duality principle:

$$E\left[\int_0^T (D_t F) u_t dt\right] = E\left[F D^*(u)\right] = E\left[F \int_0^T u_t dW_t\right] \tag{III.3}$$

The above formula is the basis of the integration-by-parts formula for Malliavin calculus. It allows us to interchange the stochastic derivative acting on F, by a stochastic integral that does not affect F. This formula is also the basis for the derivation of the joint probability density function of the observations (the likelihood function). For the sake of simplicity, we shall first derive an expression for the likelihood function of the observations in the scalar case. Later, we will deal with the more general vector case.

Derivation of the Integration-by-Parts Formula and the PDF for a Single Random Variable

Consider the random variables X, Y, Z where $Z = f(X)$. Then the Malliavin derivative of Z, $D_s Z$ is given as:

$$D_s Z = \frac{\partial f(X)}{\partial X} D_s X = f'(X) D_s X \tag{III.4}$$

Multiplying both sides by $Y D_s X$, we get:

$$(D_s Z) Y (D_s X) = f'(X) Y (D_s X)^2 \tag{III.5}$$

Integrating this for $s \in [0,T]$, we have:

$$\int_0^T (D_s Z) Y (D_s X) ds = \int_0^T f'(X) Y (D_s X)^2 ds = f'(X) Y \int_0^T (D_s X)^2 ds \qquad \text{(III.6)}$$

By rearranging, we get:

$$f'(X) Y = \frac{\displaystyle\int_0^T (D_s Z) Y (D_s X) ds}{\displaystyle\int_0^T (D_s X)^2 ds} = \int_0^T \frac{(D_s Z) Y (D_s X)}{\displaystyle\int_0^T (D_s X)^2 ds} ds \qquad \text{(III.7)}$$

Let $\quad u_s = \dfrac{Y (D_s X)}{\displaystyle\int_0^T (D_v X)^2 dv}$ \qquad\qquad\qquad\qquad\qquad\qquad\qquad (III.8)

then $\quad f'(X) Y = \displaystyle\int_0^T (D_s Z) u_s \, ds = < DZ, u >$ \qquad\qquad\qquad (III.9)

Taking expectations of both sides, we get:

$$E[f'(X) Y] = E\left[\int_0^T (D_s Z) u_s \, ds\right] = E[< DZ, u >] \qquad \text{(III.10)}$$

From the duality principle of Malliavin calculus we have:

$$E\left[\int_0^T (D_s Z) u_s \, ds\right] = E[< DZ, u >] = E\left[Z D^*(u) \right]$$

Thus, we end up with the formula:

$$E[f'(X) Y] = E\left[f(X) D^* u \right] = E[f(X) H(X,Y)] \qquad \text{(III.11)}$$

$$\text{where } H(X,Y)=D^*u=\frac{\displaystyle\int_0^T Y(D_sX)dW_s}{\displaystyle\int_0^T (D_vX)^2\,dv} \tag{III.12}$$

Another expression of the left hand side of equation (III. 11) can be derived using standard calculus. If the unknown joint probability density function of (X, Y) is given by $p(x,y)$ then:

$$E[f'(X)Y]=\int f'(x)\, y\, p(x,y)\, dx\, dy \tag{III.13}$$

Using the standard-calculus-integration-by-parts-formula, we get:

$$=-\int f(x)\, y\,\frac{\partial \log p(x,y)}{\partial x}\, p(x,y)\, dx\, dy$$

$$\tag{III.14}$$

$$=-E[f(X)\, Y\,\frac{\partial \log p(X,Y)}{\partial X}]$$

Also, $E\left[f'(X)Y\right]=E\left[f(X)H(X,Y)\right]$ \hfill (III.11)

This suggests a possible formula for $H(X,Y)=D^*u=\dfrac{\displaystyle\int_0^T Y(D_sX)dW_s}{\displaystyle\int_0^T (D_vX)^2\,dv}$ as follows:

$$H(X,Y)=-Y\frac{\partial \log p(X,Y)}{\partial X} \tag{III.15}$$

Thus, if one knows $H(X,Y)$, one could be able to derive an expression for $p(x,y)$ to a scale factor; that is:

$$\log p(X,Y) = -\frac{1}{Y}\int H(x,y)dx + constant \qquad \text{(III. 16)}$$

where the constant is independent of X but could be function of Y.

$$\text{Thus,} \quad H(X,Y) = D^*u = \frac{\int_0^T Y(D_sX)dW_s}{\int_0^T (D_vX)^2 dv}$$

And, finally, we get an expression for the joint PDF $p(x,y)$; that is:

$$p(X,Y) \propto \exp\left[-\frac{1}{Y}\int H(x,y)dx\right]$$

$$\propto \exp\left[-\frac{1}{Y}\int \frac{\int_0^T Y(D_sX)dW_s}{\int_0^T (D_vX)^2 dv} dx\right] \qquad \text{(III. 17)}$$

Notice that $H(X,Y)$ is not unique. Thus, the derived joint PDF, $p(x,y)$, is not unique.

Example

Let X be a random variable that is a function of the Wiener process. Let $X = \beta + dW_t$, where dW_t is white Gaussian noise with zero mean and unity variance. This means that X is Gaussian random variable with mean β and variance 1. We need to use the integration-by-parts formula of the Malliavin calculus to find the PDF of x, $p(x)$, which we know as:

$$p(X) = \frac{1}{\sqrt{2\pi}}\exp\frac{-(X-\beta)^2}{2}$$

Following the previous steps, we get:

$$D_v X = D_v(\beta + dW_t) = D_v(dW_t) = \delta(v-t)$$

where $\delta(v-t) = \begin{array}{cc} 1 & v=t \\ 0 & elsewhere \end{array}$,

and $\displaystyle\int_0^T \delta(v-t)dv = 1$, $\displaystyle\int_0^T \delta(v-t)dW_v = dW_v$

Then, $\displaystyle H(X,Y) = D^*u = \frac{\int_0^T Y(D_s X)dW_s}{\int_0^T (D_v X)^2 dv} = \frac{\int_0^T Y\delta(s-t)dW_s}{\int_0^T [\delta(v-t)]^2 dv} = Y\, dW_t = Y(X-\beta)$

where in the last expression we have substituted $dW_t = X - \beta$.
And as proven before, we have:

$$p(X) = p(X,Y)|_{Y=1} \quad \propto \quad \exp\left[-\int H(x,1)dx\right]$$

Thus, we have:

$$p(X) = p(X,Y)|_{Y=1} \quad \propto \quad \exp\left[-\int H(x,1)dx\right] = \exp\left[-\int(x-\beta)dx\right]$$

that is, $\displaystyle p(X) \propto \exp\left[-\frac{1}{2}(x-\beta)^2\right]$

This is the expression for the PDF of X, with the constant of proportionality being the

term $\dfrac{1}{\sqrt{2\pi}}$.

One Random Variable and n Observations (Snapshots)

We may now derive an expression for the joint PDF of n observations/snapshots. For n snapshots we have $Z = f(X^1, \ldots X^n) = f(\underline{X})$, and we need to find the joint PDF of $X^1, \ldots, X^n$. Let $\underline{W} = [W^1, \ldots W^k]$ be a k-dimensional Wiener process. Each of the snapshots, X^i, is a function of the Wiener process vector $\underline{W}$. Notice that the shape of f is not important when deriving the joint PDF.

Let $\nabla f(\underline{x}) = [\dfrac{\partial f}{\partial x^1}, \ldots, \dfrac{\partial f}{\partial x^n}]$

Using Malliavin calculus chain rule, we get:

$$D_s^j Z = D_s \underline{X} \, \nabla f(\underline{X}) = \sum_{i=1}^{n} \frac{\partial f}{\partial x^i} D_s^j X^i \tag{III.18}$$

Let $u_s^{jl} = D_s^j X^l$ \hfill (III.19)

As we did in the scalar case, by multiplying the equation for DZ by a smooth nxn matrix process $\underline{u}$ we get:

$$\langle DZ, u \rangle = \langle (D\underline{X})\nabla f(\underline{X}), u \rangle$$

$$= \sum_{i=1}^{n}\sum_{j=1}^{k}\int_0^T \frac{\partial f(\underline{x})}{\partial x^i}(D_s^j x^i)u_s^{jl}\,ds = \sum_{i=1}^{n}\sum_{j=1}^{k} \frac{\partial f(\underline{x})}{\partial x^i}\int_0^T (D_s^j x^i)(D_s^j x^l)\,ds \tag{III.20}$$

$$= A\nabla f(\underline{X})$$

where $A^{il} = \sum_{j=1}^{k}\int_0^T (D_s^j x^i)(D_s^j x^l)\,ds$ \hfill (III.21) is defined as the Malliavin matrix. Suppose that there is another matrix B such that $BA = I$, then if we multiply both sides of equation (III. 20) by the matrix B from the left and by the $nx1$ vector $\underline{Y}$ from the right, we get:

$$B\langle DZ,u \rangle \underline{Y} = BA\nabla f(\underline{X})\underline{Y} = \nabla f(\underline{X})\underline{Y} \tag{III.22a}$$

Taking expectations of both sides, we obtain:

$$E\left[(B\langle DZ,u \rangle)\underline{Y} \right] = E\left[\nabla f(\underline{X})\underline{Y} \right] \tag{III.22b}$$

Using the duality principle in the vector case [Nualart; 1995], we get:

$$E\left[\nabla f(\underline{X})\underline{Y} \right] = \sum_{l=1}^{n} \sum_{m=1}^{n} \sum_{j=1}^{k} E\left[f(\underline{X})D^{*j}\left(B^{ml}Y_m D_s^j X^l \right) \right] \tag{III.23}$$

The left-hand side of equation (III. 22b) can also be expressed as:

$$E\left[\nabla f(\underline{X})\underline{Y} \right] = \int \nabla f(\underline{x})\underline{y}\, p(\underline{x},\underline{y})\, d\underline{x}\, d\underline{y}$$

$$= -\int f(\underline{x})\underline{y}[\nabla \log p(\underline{x},\underline{y})] p(\underline{x},\underline{y}) d\underline{x}\, d\underline{y} \tag{III.24}$$

$$= -E\left\{ f(\underline{X})\underline{Y}[\nabla \log p(\underline{X},\underline{Y})] \right\}$$

This suggests, as in the scalar case with setting $\underline{Y}$ to unity vector, the following relation for the joint PDF:

$$\nabla \log p(\underline{X}) = -\sum_{l=1}^{n} \sum_{m=1}^{n} \sum_{j=1}^{k} D^{*j}\left(B^{ml}D_s^j X^l \right) \tag{III.25}$$

that is, $\quad p(\underline{X}) \propto \exp{-\sum_{l=1}^{n} \sum_{m=1}^{n} \sum_{j=1}^{k} \int D^{*j}\left(B^{ml}D_s^j X^l \right) dX^l} \tag{III.26}$

Equation (III. 26) is the likelihood function, and it is the desired result. Maximizing this quantity with respect to the unknown parameters will yield the maximum likelihood estimates. The same results will be obtained if we maximize the expression of equation (III. 25). Note that in this way we do not need to perform the integration. For the estimation of the parameters of the stochastic volatility model, one has to find the different elements of equation (III. 26). This is done in the next section.

Estimation of the Parameters of the Stochastic Volatility Model Using Malliavin Calculus

In many situations in parameter estimation the stochastic processes of interest follow some known shapes such as the geometric Brownian motion, the Ornstein-Uhlenbeck process or others. The observations, in our case the exchange rate, are usually nonlinear functions of these processes. We are mainly interested in the parameters of these processes. If we follow the standard procedure of Ito calculus and use Girsanov theory, one would not be able to find the likelihood function of the observations except for some special cases (Abutaleb, 2004). This is where the Malliavin calculus becomes relevant. As in the second section of this chapter, assume that the volatility, v_t, follows the geometric Brownian motion and can be represented by the following stochastic differential equation (SDE):

$$\frac{dv_t}{v_t} = \alpha \, dt + \gamma \, dW_t^2 \qquad \text{(II. 5a)}$$

The solution of the SDE of v_t has the form:

$$v_t = v_0 \exp\left[\left(\alpha - \frac{1}{2}\gamma^2\right)t + \gamma \, W_t^2\right] \qquad \text{(II. 6)}$$

The Malliavin derivative of v_t is derived as:

$$D_s^2 v_t = \gamma \, v_t 1_{[0,t]}(s) = \gamma \, v_0 \exp\left[\left(\alpha - \frac{1}{2}\gamma^2\right)t + \gamma \, W_t^2\right] 1_{[0,t]}(s) \qquad \text{(III. 27)}$$

We will study the general case where X^i, the observed exchange rate at instant t_i, defines the nonlinear observation of the volatility v_t, at instant t_i. X^i is a random variable that is function of the Wiener processes $[W_t^1, W_t^2]$. We need to find a SDE for $D_r^i X^t$. Solving this SDE will yield an expression for $D_r^i X^t$ which is what we will be using in the derived joint PDF of the observations $p(X_1, ..., X^n)$ of equation (III. 26). To this end, one could use the general expressions, for the SDE of, derived in Appendix B. Instead we could use the special properties of the geometric Brownian motion of the volatility and directly derive the desired SDE for $D_r^i X^t$. Specifically:

$$X^t = X^0 + \beta \int_0^t X^s ds + \sqrt{v_0} \int_0^t \left\{ \exp \frac{1}{2} \left[\left(\alpha - \frac{1}{2} \gamma^2 \right) s + \gamma \ W_s^2 \right] \right\} X^s dW_s^1 \qquad (II.7)$$

that is, $X^t = X^t(t, \ W_t^1, W_t^2)$

$$D_r^i X^t = \beta \int_0^t D_r^i X^s ds + D_r^i \int_0^t \sqrt{v_0 \exp \left[\left(\alpha - \frac{1}{2} \gamma^2 \right) s + \gamma \ W_s^2 \right]} X^s dW_s^1$$

or, $D_r^i X^t = \beta \int_0^t D_r^i X^s ds + D_r^i \int_0^t \sqrt{v_s} \ X^s dW_s^1$ \qquad (III.28)

If $u(t,w)$ is an adapted square integrable process, then (Bally, 2003):

$$D_t^i \left[\int_0^T u(s,w) dW_s^j \right] = u(t,w) \delta_{ij} + \int_t^T D_t^i u(s,w) dW_s^j \qquad (III.29)$$

$$D_t^i \left[\int_0^T u(s,w) ds \right] = \int_t^T D_t^i u(s,w) ds \qquad (III.30)$$

Let $u(t,w) = \sqrt{v_t} \ X^t = \sqrt{v_t(t,W_t^2)} \ X^t(t, \ W_t^1, W_t^2)$

Then, $D_t^i u(s,w) = \sqrt{v_s} \ D_t^i X^s + X^s D_t^i \sqrt{v_s} = \sqrt{v_s} \ D_t^i X^s + \dfrac{X^s}{2\sqrt{v_s}} D_t^i v_s$ (III.31)

$$= \sqrt{v_s(s,W_s^2)} \ D_t^i[X^s(s,W_s^1,W_s^2)] + \frac{X^s(s,W_s^1,W_s^2)}{2\sqrt{v_s(s,W_s^2)}} D_t^i[v_s(s,W_s^2)]$$

Notice that $D_t^i[v_s(s,W_s^2)] = 0$, i=1

$$D_t^2 v_s = \gamma \ v_s 1_{[0,s]}(t) = \gamma \ v_0 \exp\left[\left(\alpha - \frac{1}{2}\gamma^2\right)s + \gamma \ W_s^2\right]1_{[0,s]}(t) \tag{III.18}$$

Substituting equation (III. 18) in equation (III. 31), we get:

$$D_r^i\left(\int_0^t \sqrt{v_s} \ X^s dW_s^1\right) = \sqrt{v_r(r,W_r^2)} \ X^r(r,W_r^1,W_r^2)\delta_{i1}$$

$$+ \int_r^t \sqrt{v_s(s,W_s^2)} \ D_r^i[X^s(s,W_s^1,W_s^2)]dW_s^1 + \int_r^t \frac{X^s(s,W_s^1,W_s^2)}{2\sqrt{v_s(s,W_s^2)}} D_r^i[v_s(s,W_s^2)]dW_s^1 \tag{III.32}$$

Substituting in $D_r^i X^t = \beta \int_0^t D_r^i X^s ds + D_r^i \left(\int_0^t \sqrt{v_s} \ X^s dW_s^1\right)$, we get:

$$D_r^i X^t = \sqrt{v_r(r,W_r^2)} \ X^r(r,W_r^1,W_r^2)\delta_{i1} + \beta\int_0^t D_r^i X^s ds$$

$$+ \int_r^t \sqrt{v_s(s,W_s^2)}D_r^i[X^s(s,W_s^1,W_s^2)]dW_s^1 + \int_r^t \frac{D_r^i[v_s(s,W_s^2)]}{2\sqrt{v_s(s,W_s^2)}} X^s(s,W_s^1,W_s^2)dW_s^1 \tag{III.33}$$

Thus, $D_r^2 X^t$ has the following SDE:

(III. 34)

$$d(D_r^2 X^t) = \beta(D_r^2 X^t)dt + \left[\sqrt{v_t(t,W_t^2)}(D_r^2 X^t) + \frac{D_r^2[v_t(t,W_t^2)]}{2\sqrt{v_t(t,W_t^2)}} X^t(t,W_t^1,W_t^2) \right] dW_t^1$$

with initial conditions $D_r^2 X^0 = 0$. Notice that the SDE of $D_r^2 X^t$ has two components:

$$d(D_r^2 X^t) = \left\{ \beta(D_r^2 X^t)dt + \left[\sqrt{v_t(t,W_t^2)}(D_r^2 X^t) \right] dW_t^1 \right\}$$
$$+ \left\{ 0dt + \left[\frac{D_r^2[v_t(t,W_t^2)]}{2\sqrt{v_t(t,W_t^2)}} X^t(t,W_t^1,W_t^2) \right] dW_t^1 \right\}$$

Since the initial condition is zero and $D_r^2 X^t$ is multiplied by the drift and the diffusion, then the first term will yield zero value. The second term will yield:

(III. 35)

$$D_r^2 X^t = 1_{[0,t]}(r)\int_0^t \frac{D_r^2[v_s(s,W_s^2)]}{2\sqrt{v_s(s,W_s^2)}} X^s(s,W_s^1,W_s^2)dW_s^1$$
$$= 1_{[0,t]}(r)\int_0^t \frac{\gamma v_s 1_{[0,s]}(r)}{2\sqrt{v_s}} X^s(s,W_s^1,W_s^2)dW_s^1 = 1_{[0,t]}(r)\frac{\gamma}{2}\int_0^t \sqrt{v_s} 1_{[0,s]}(r)X^s(s,W_s^1,W_s^2)dW_s^1$$

And $D_r^1 X^t$ has the following SDE:

$$d(D_r^1 X^t) = \beta(D_r^1 X^t)dt + \left[\sqrt{v_t(t,W_t^2)}(D_r^1 X^t) + \frac{D_r^1[v_t(t,W_t^2)]}{2\sqrt{v_t(t,W_t^2)}} X^t(t,W_t^1,W_t^2) \right] dW_t^1$$

(III. 36)

And since $D_r^1[v_t(t,W_t^2)] = 0$, then:

$$d(D_r^1 X^t) = \beta(D_r^1 X^t)dt + \left[\sqrt{v_t(t,W_t^2)}(D_r^1 X^t) \right] dW_t^1$$

that is, $\dfrac{d(D_r^1 X^t)}{(D_r^1 X^t)} = \beta\, dt + \left[\sqrt{v_t(t, W_t^2)} \right] dW_t^1$ (III. 37)

with initial conditions $D_r^1 X^0 = \sqrt{v_r(r, W_r^2)}\; X^r(r, W_r^1, W_r^2)$. This means that $D_r^1 X^t$ has a geometric Brownian motion process with random and time-varying diffusion coefficient:

$$\sqrt{v_t(t, W_t^2)} = \sqrt{v_0}\, \exp \frac{1}{2}\left[\left(\alpha - \frac{1}{2}\gamma^2 \right) t + \gamma\; W_t^2 \right]$$

The nxn Malliavin matrix has elements A^{ij} (Kohatsu-Higa & Montero, 2003; Bally, 2003) given by:

$$A^{il} = \sum_{j=1}^{k} \int_0^T (D_s^j X^i)(D_s^j X^l)\, ds = \int_0^T (D_s^1 X^i)(D_s^1 X^l)\, ds + \int_0^T (D_s^2 X^i)(D_s^2 X^l)\, ds$$ (III. 38)

Thus, the Malliavin matrix A is symmetric, has a complicated shape, and is a function of the data at different snapshots. It is obtained numerically from the expressions of $D_s^j X^i$ for j=1,2, and for different instants of time (see equation (III. 34) and equation (III. 37)). Its inverse, $B = A^{-1}$, has also a complicated shape and it is also obtained numerically. We need to find an expression for $D^{*j}\left(B^{ml} D_s^j X^l \right)$ in order to find the joint PDF. Remember that:

$$D^{*j}\left(B^{ml} D_s^j X^l \right) = \int_0^T B^{ml}(D_s^j X^l)\, dW_s^j$$ (III. 39)

$$p(\underline{X};\underline{\theta}) \propto \exp - \sum_{l=1}^{n} \sum_{m=1}^{n} \sum_{j=1}^{k=2} \int D^{*j}\left(B^{ml} D_s^j X^l \right) dX^l$$ (III. 26)

The evaluation of both equations (III. 39) and (III. 26) is achieved numerically and through Monte-Carlo simulation.

Summary of the Algorithm

We now present a brief summary of the proposed algorithm to find the maximum likelihood estimate of the parameters of the exchange rate under a stochastic volatility model; the latter is represented by a geometric Brownian motion. The algorithm uses the following steps:

1. Initialize, at random, an estimate θ for the unknown parameters.

2. Use Monte-Carlo simulation to find an estimate for the Malliavin derivatives of equations (III. 34) and (III. 37).

3. Use Monte-Carlo simulation to find an estimate for the Malliavin matrix of equation (III. 38) A and its inverse B.

4. Use Monte-Carlo simulation to find an estimate for $D^{*j}\left(B^{ml}D_s^j X^l\right)$ of equation (III. 39) for j=1, 2.

5. Use Monte-Carlo simulation to find the joint PDF of the observations, the likelihood function, of equation (III. 26) or its derivative of equation (III. 25).

6. Go to step 1 and change the estimates of the unknown parameters θ using the genetic algorithm (Abutaleb, 1997) where the cost function is the likelihood function of equation (III. 26).

7. Stop when there is no change in the estimates of the parameters or the set number of iterations is exceeded.

This algorithm can also be applied to other models of financial variables that follow similar processes.

Monte-Carlo Simulations

Many of the equations we deal with are analytically hard to solve. Thus, one has to resort to numerical methods such as Monte-Carlo simulation (Jackel, 2003). The stochastic volatility could be represented by one of several models:

$$\frac{dv_t}{v_t} = \alpha\, dt + \gamma\, dW_t^2 \tag{II. 5a}$$

which has a solution: $v_t = v_t(t, W_t^2) = v_0 \exp\left[\left(\alpha - \frac{1}{2}\gamma^2\right)t + \gamma\, W_t^2\right]$ (II. 6)

One could use the Euler method of discretization for the simulation of the trajectory of the volatility (Kloeden & Platter, 1992):

$$v_{l+1} = v_l + \alpha\, v_l \Delta + \gamma\, v_l \Delta W_l^2 \qquad\qquad\qquad (III.40)$$

where Δ is the sampling interval, and ΔW_l^2 is Gaussian with zero mean and variance Δ. Euler approximation is used for the different integrations according to the following formulas:

$$\int_0^t h(s, z(s))ds = \sum_{i=0}^{N-1} h(i, z(i))\Delta_i$$

$$\qquad\qquad\qquad (III.41)$$

$$t = \sum_{i=0}^{N-1} \Delta_i$$

where $z(i)$ is the value of $z(t)$ at instant i, $h(i, z(i))$ is the value of $h(s, z(s))$ at instant i, and Δ_i is the sampling interval between the ith sample and the $(i+1)^{th}$ sample. Δ_i is usually constant, and,

$$\int_0^t h(s, z(s))dz(s) = \sum_{i=0}^{N-1} h(i, z(i))\, \Delta z(i) \qquad\qquad\qquad (III.42)$$

where $\Delta z(i) = z(i+1) - z(i)$. Other more accurate but computationally intensive discretization methods are also available (Kloeden & Platen, 1992).

In the design of Monte-Carlo integration, we make use of the formulas (Jackel, 2003, ch. 3):

$$\int_{t=0}^T f(t)dW_t \sim N\left[0, \int_0^T [f(t)]^2\right] \qquad\qquad\qquad (III.43)$$

where $f(t)$ is a deterministic quantity, and

$$W_T = \int_{t=0}^T dW_t \sim N(0, T) \qquad\qquad\qquad (III.44)$$

Testing Using Real Data

To test the proposed approach, we use the weekly U.S. dollar/euro exchange rate for the period April 28, 2000, to March 26, 2001. The exchange rate, $x(t)$, and the volatility, $v(t)$ follow the equations:

$$dx(t) = \mu \, x(t)dt + x(t)\sqrt{v(t)}dB(t) \tag{II.1}$$

$$\frac{dv(t)}{v(t)} = \alpha \, dt + \gamma \, dB_2(t) \tag{II.5a}$$

where μ, α, and γ are unknowns to be estimated. The Malliavin calculus-based method, as explained in the third section of this chapter, was used to find the desired estimates. The average values of the unknown parameters are given in Table 1.

The observed exchange rate and the typically estimated exchange rate, using Malliavin calculus, are shown in Figure 2. The root mean square error (RMSE) for the estimated exchange rate using the Malliavin calculus-based method is 0.027.

Table 1. Estimated parameters of the exchange rate, μ of equation (II. 1), and the stochastic volatility model, α and γ of equation (II. 5a); estimates using Malliavin calculus-based method

Estimated μ	Estimated α	Estimated γ
1.5	-8.2	0.38

Figure 2. Observed exchange rate and typically estimated exchange rate using Malliavin Calculus

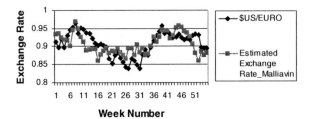

Summary and Conclusions

In this chapter we introduce a new method for the estimation of the parameters of the exchange rate equation when the volatility follows a stochastic process. Using Malliavin calculus, one is able to find an explicit expression for the likelihood function of the observations. Using numerical integration methods (Monte-Carlo simulations) and numerical optimization methods (genetic algorithms), we are able to find an estimate for the unknown parameters and the volatility. The estimation method is applied to the U.S. dollar/euro exchange rate. As indicated by the very low RMSE statistic, the obtained out-of-sample simulation results show a significantly high accuracy of the proposed method.

References

Abutaleb, A. (1997). A genetic algorithm for the maximum likelihood estimation of the parameters of sinusoids in noisy environment. *Circuits, Systems, and Signal Processing, 16*(1), 69-81.

Abutaleb, A. (2004). Stochastic calculus and bootstrapping for instantaneous frequency estimation. Submitted to *IEEE Trans. Circuits and Systems, Part I*.

Abutaleb, A., Kumasaka Y., & Papaioannou, M. (2003). Estimation and prediction of the Japanese yen/U.S. dollar rate using an adaptive time-varying model. In J. Choi & T. Hiraki (Eds.), The Japanese finance: Corporate finance and capital markets in changing Japan. *International Finance Review, 4*, 425-441.

Ait-Sahalia, Y. (1996a). Nonparametric pricing of interest rate derivative securities. *Econmetrica, 64*, 527-560.

Ait-Sahalia, Y. (1996b). Testing continuous time models of the spot interest rates. *Review of Financial Studies, 9*, 385-426.

Ait-Sahalia, Y. (2002). Maximum likelihood estimation of discretely sampled diffusions: A closed form approximation approach. *Econometrica, 70*(1), 223-262.

Bally, V. (2003). *An elementary introduction to Malliavin calculus*. Research report, Nº 4718, INRIA, Rocquencourt, France.

Elerian, O. (1999). *Simulation estimation of continuous-time models with applications to finance*. Ph.D. dissertation, University of Oxford, Nuffield College.

Elerian, O., Chib, S., & Shiphard, N. (2001). Likelihood inference for discretely observed nonlinear diffusions. *Econometrica, 69*(4), 959-993.

Friz, P. (2002). *An introduction to Malliavin Calculus*. Retrieved from http://www.math.nyu.edu/phd_students/

Genon-Catalot, V., Jeantheau, T., & Laredo, C. (1998). Limit theorems for discretely observed stochastic volatility models. *Bernoulli, 4*, 283-303.

Genon-Catalot, V., Jeantheau, T., & Laredo, C. (1999). Parameter estimation for discretely observed stochastic volatility models. *Bernoulli, 5*, 855-872.

Gourieroux, C., Monfort, A., & Renault, E. (1993). Indirect inference. *Journal of Applied Econometrics, 8*, S85-S118.

Hansen, L. (1982). Large sample properties of generalized method of moments estimators. *Econometrica, 50*, 1029-1054.

Jackel, P. (2003). *Monte Carlo simulation methods in finance.* New York: John Wiley.

Kloeden, P., & Platen, E. (1992). *Numerical solution of stochastic differential equations.* New York: Springer-Verlag.

Kohatsu-Higa, A., & Montero, M. (2003). Malliavin calculus in finance. Retrieved from econ.upf.es/docs/papers/downloads/672

Lipton, A. (2000). *Mathematical methods for foreign exchange: A financial engineer's approach.* New York: World Scientific.

Nielsen, J., Vetergaard, M., & Madsen, H. (2000). Estimation in continuous time stochastic volatility models using nonlinear filters. *International Journal of Theoretical and Applied Finance, 3,* 279-308.

Nualart, D. (1995). *The Malliavin calculus and related topics.* Berlin: Springer.

Papaioannou, M. (2001). Volatility and misalignments of EMS and other currencies during 1974-1998. *International Finance Review, 2*, 51-96.

Sorensen, H. (1999). *Prediction-based estimating functions.* Preprint 1999-5. Copenhagen, Denmark: Department of Theoretical Statistics, University of Copenhagen, Denmark.

Sorensen, H. (2000). *Inference for diffusion processes and stochastic volatility models.* PhD thesis, University of Copenhagen, Denmark.

Appendix A: Differential and Integral Operators in Malliavin Calculus (Bally, 2003)

Let (Ω, F, P) be a probability space, $\underline{B} = [B_t^1, ..., B_t^d] = (B_t)_{t \geq 0}$ a d-dimensional Brownian motion. Let $(F_t)_{t \geq 0}$ be the filtration generated by $\underline{B}$.

Simple Functionals and Simple Processes

Let $t_n^k = \dfrac{k}{2^n}$ and $I_n^k = [t_n^k, t_n^{k+1})$, where the period of interest is $[0,1]$. We denote the vector $\underline{\Delta}_n^k = \underline{B}(t_n^{k+1}) - \underline{B}(t_n^k)$. Component-wise we have: $\underline{\Delta}_n^k = [\Delta_n^{k,1}, ..., \Delta_n^{k,d}]$ with $\Delta_n^{k,i} = B^i(t_n^{k+1}) - B^i(t_n^k)$. Notice that $\Delta_n^{k,i}$ is Gaussian with zero mean and some variance and so is the vector $\underline{\Delta}_n^k$. We define the simple functionals of order n to be the random variables of the form:

$$F = f(\underline{\Delta}_n^0, ..., \underline{\Delta}_n^{m-1})$$

where $m = 2^n$, $f: R^{m \times d} \to R$ is a smooth function with polynomial growth. In particular, F has finite moments of any order. We denote by S_n the space of all the simple functionals of order n, and $S = \bigcup_n S_n$ is the space of all the simple functionals. We now define the simple processes of order n to be the processes of the form:

$$u(t, w) = \sum_{k=0}^{m} u_k(\Delta_n^0, ..., \Delta_n^{m-1}) 1_{I_n^k}(t) \tag{A.1}$$

where $u_k: R^{m \times d} \to R$, $k = 0, ..., m\text{-}1$ are smooth functions with polynomial growth.

Malliavin Derivatives and Skorohod Integral

We define the Malliavin derivative D^i, $i = 1, ..., d$ by:

$$D_t^i F = \sum_{k=1}^{m-1} \frac{\partial f(\Delta_n^0, ..., \Delta_n^{m-1})}{\partial x^{k,i}} 1_{I_n^k}(t) \tag{A.2}$$

We have $x = [x^0,...,x^{m-1}]$ with $\underline{x}^k = [x^{k,1},...x^{k,d}]$.

From an intuitive point of view, $D_t^i F$ represents the derivative of F with respect to the increment of B^i corresponding to t, that is,

$$D_t^i F = \frac{\partial F}{\partial \Delta_t^i} \tag{A.3}$$

where $\Delta_t^i = B^i(t_n^{k+1}) - B^i(t_n^k) = \Delta_n^{k,i}$, which is Gaussian with zero mean and $t_n^k \leq t < t_n^{k+1}$. The Skorohod integral δ^i or D^{*i} for $i = 1,...,d$ is defined as:

$$\delta^i(u) = \sum_{k=1}^{m-1} u_n^k(\Delta_n^0,...,\Delta_n^{m-1})\Delta_n^{k,i} - \sum_{k=1}^{m-1} \frac{\partial u_k^n(\Delta_n^0,...,\Delta_n^{m-1})}{\partial x^{k,i}} \frac{1}{2^n} \tag{A.4}$$

A central fact is that the operators D^i and δ^i or D^{*i} are adjoint, that is:

$$E\left[\int_0^\infty (D_t^i F)u(t,w)dt\right] = E\left[F\delta^i(u)\right] \tag{A.5}$$

The proof is interesting in itself. The sampling interval is $\Delta t = \frac{1}{2^n}$

$$E\left[\int_0^1 (D_t^i F)u(t,w)dt\right] = E\left[\sum_{k=1}^{m-1} \frac{\partial f(\Delta_n^0,...,\Delta_n^{m-1})}{\partial x^{k,i}} 1_{I_n^k}(t)u_n^k(\Delta_n^0,...,\Delta_n^{m-1})\frac{1}{2^n}\right]$$

$$= E\left[\sum_{k=1}^{m-1} \frac{\partial f(\Delta_n)}{\partial x^{k,i}} 1_{I_n^k}(t)u_n^k(\Delta_n)\frac{1}{2^n}\right] \tag{A.6}$$

Using the integration by parts formula:

$$E\left[\frac{\partial f(\Delta)}{\partial x^i}g(\Delta)\right] = E\left[f(\Delta)[g(\Delta)\frac{\Delta^i}{\sigma^i} - \frac{\partial g(\Delta)}{\partial x^i}]\right] \tag{A.7}$$

where $F = f(\Delta^1, \ldots \Delta^m)$, $G = g(\Delta^1, \ldots, \Delta^m)$, $\Delta = [\Delta^1, \ldots, \Delta^m]$, and $\Delta^1, \ldots, \Delta m$ are independent zero mean Gaussian random variables with variances, not standard deviation, $\sigma^1, \ldots, \sigma^m$, then with $g(\Delta) = u_n^k(\Delta_n)$

$$E\left[\sum_{k=1}^{m-1} \frac{\partial f(\Delta_n)}{\partial x^{k,i}} 1_{I_n^k}(t) u_n^k(\Delta_n) \frac{1}{2^n}\right]$$

$$= E\left[f(\Delta_n)\left[\sum_{k=1}^{m-1} u_n^k(\Delta_n)\Delta_n^{k,i} - \sum_{k=1}^{m-1} \frac{u_n^k(\Delta_n))}{\partial x^{k,i}} \frac{1}{2^n}\right]\right] = E[F\delta^i(u)] \tag{A.8}$$

which is the desired result.

For F and G scalars and function of the Brownian motion vector $\underline{B}$, we get:

$$\langle DF, DG \rangle = \int_0^\infty \sum_{i=1}^d D_t^i F D_t^i G \, dt \tag{A.9}$$

and the Ornstein-Uhlenbeck operator L is defined as:

$$L(F) = -\sum_{i=1}^d \delta^i(D^i F) \tag{A.10}$$

and since $F = f(\Delta_n) = f(\Delta_n^0, \ldots, \Delta_n^{m-1})$ we have:

$$L(F) = \sum_{i=1}^d \sum_{k=0}^{m-1} \frac{\partial^2 f(\Delta_n)}{\partial(x^{k,i})^2} \frac{1}{2^n} - \sum_{i=1}^d \sum_{k=0}^{m-1} \frac{\partial f(\Delta_n)}{\partial x^{k,i}} \Delta_n^{k,i} \tag{A.11}$$

For the random variables F and G we have:

$$E[FL(G)] = E[GL(F)] = -E\left[\langle DF, DG \rangle\right] \tag{A.12}$$

For the vectors $\underline{F}=[F^1,...,F^k]$, $G=[G^1,...,G^k]$ and the scalar function $\varphi\in C^1_p(R^k;R)$ we have:

$$D^i_t\varphi(\underline{F})=\sum_{j=1}^{k}\frac{\partial\varphi(\underline{F})}{\partial x^j}D^i F^j \qquad\qquad (A.13)$$

$$L\varphi(\underline{F})=\sum_{i,j=1}^{d}\frac{\partial^2\varphi(\underline{F})}{\partial x^i\partial x^j}\left\langle DF^i,DF^j\right\rangle+\sum_{i=1}^{d}\frac{\partial\varphi(\underline{F})}{\partial x^j}LF^i \qquad\qquad (A.14)$$

For an adapted square integrable process $u(t,w)$ we have:

$$D^i_t(\int_0^T u(s,w)dB^j_s)=u(t,w)\delta_{ij}-\int_t^T D^i_t u(s,w)dB^j_s \qquad\qquad (A.15)$$

$$\text{and}\quad D^i_t(\int_0^T u(s,w)ds)=\int_t^T D^i_t u(s,w)ds \qquad\qquad (A.16)$$

where δ_{ij} is the Kronecker delta. The above formula is actually a relation between the Skorohod integral and the Malliavin derivative of the process $u(t,w)$; that is:

$$D_t(D^*u)=-D^*(D_t u)+u(t,w) \qquad\qquad (A.17a)$$

$$\text{that is,}\quad D^*(D_t u)=-D_t(D^*u)+u(t,w) \qquad\qquad (A.17b)$$

Appendix B: Malliavin Calculus on the D-dimensional Wiener Space (Friz, 2002)

For an m dimensional random vector $X=(X^i)$ we have the mxd matrix:

$$D\underline{X}=[D^1\underline{X},...,D^d\underline{X}]=(D^j X^i)_{ij} \qquad\qquad (B.1)$$

where $D^j\underline{X}=[D^j X^1,...,D^j X^m]$, and $DX^i=[D^1 X^i,...,D^d X^i]$ \qquad (B.2)

The Malliavin covariance matrix is given as:

$$\Lambda_{ij} = \left\langle DX^i, DX^j \right\rangle = \sum_{k=1}^{d} \left\langle D^k X^i, D^k X^j \right\rangle \tag{B.3}$$

which is rewritten as:

$$\Lambda = \left\langle D\underline{X}, (D\underline{X})^T \right\rangle \tag{B.3}$$

Given vector fields $A^1,..., A_d, B$ that belong to R^m consider the SDE:

$$d\underline{X}_t = B(\underline{X}_t)dt + \sum_{j=1}^{d} A_j(\underline{X}_t)dW_t^j \tag{B.4}$$

and component-wise is given as:

$$dX_t^i = B^i(\underline{X}_t)dt + \sum_{j=1}^{d} A_j^i(\underline{X}_t)dW_t^j \tag{B.5}$$

For simplicity consider the case m=d=1. The solution of the SDE is given as:

$$X_t = x + \int_0^t a(X_s)dW_s + \int_0^t b(X_s)ds \tag{B.6}$$

where $a(X_s)$ and $b(X_s)$ are scalar quantities. We need to find the Malliavin derivative of X_t. This is derived as:

$$D_r X_t = a(X_r) + \int_r^t D_r a(X_s)dW_s + \int_r^t D_r b(X_s)ds$$

$$= a(X_r) + \int_r^t \frac{\partial a(X_s)}{\partial X_s}(D_r X_s)dW_s + \int_r^t \frac{\partial b(X_s)}{\partial X_s}(D_r X_s)ds \tag{B.7}$$

For fixed r and setting $\tilde{X}_t = D_r X_t$ we find the linear SDE for the Malliavin derivative of X_t as:

$$d\tilde{X}_t = \frac{\partial b(X_t)}{\partial X_t}\tilde{X}_t dt + \frac{\partial a(X_t)}{\partial X_t}\tilde{X}_t dW_t \quad , \; t>r \tag{B.8}$$

with initial conditions $\tilde{X}_r = a(X_r)$.

In the multidimensional setting we have $\tilde{X}_t = D_r X_t \in R^{mxd}$ with initial conditions $\underline{X}_0 = \underline{x} \in R^m$.

The Malliavin derivative of X_t^i is the solution of (Bally, 2003):

$$\tag{B.9}$$

$$D_s^q X_t^i = \left[A_q^i(\underline{X}_s) + \sum_{j=1}^d \int_s^t \sum_{l=1}^m \frac{\partial A_j^i(\underline{X}_r)}{\partial x^l} D_s^q X_r^l dW_r^j + \int_0^t \sum_{l=1}^m \frac{\partial B^i(\underline{X}_r)}{\partial x^l} D_s^q X_r^l dr \right] 1_{[0,s]}(t)$$

In vector format we have:

$$d\underline{X}_t = \underline{B}(\underline{X}_t)dt + \sum_{k=1}^d \underline{A}_k(\underline{X}_t)dW_t^k \tag{B.10}$$

which has a solution:

$$\underline{X}_t = \underline{x} + \int_0^t \underline{B}(\underline{X}_s)ds + \sum_{k=1}^d \int_0^t \underline{A}_k(\underline{X}_s)dW_s^k \tag{B.11}$$

Taking the Malliavin derivative of both sides we get for the mxd matrix $D_r\underline{X}_t$:

$$D_r\underline{X}_t = D_r\underline{x} + D_r\left[\int_0^t \underline{B}(\underline{X}_s)ds\right] + \sum_{k=1}^d D_r\left[\int_0^t \underline{A}_k(\underline{X}_s)dW_s^k\right] \tag{B.12}$$

Remember that $D_r\underline{X}_t = \begin{bmatrix} D_r^1X_t^1 & D_r^2X_t^1 & \dots & D_r^dX_t^1 \\ D_r^1X_t^2 & D_r^2X_t^2 & \dots & D_r^dX_t^2 \\ \dots & \dots & \dots & \dots \\ D_r^1X_t^m & D_r^2X_t^m & \dots & D_r^dX_t^m \end{bmatrix}$ (B.13)

which is expanded to yield:

$$D_r\underline{X}_t = \int_r^t \frac{\partial B(\underline{X}_s)}{\partial\underline{X}_s}(D_r\underline{X}_s)ds + \sum_{k=1}^d A_k(\underline{X}_r) + \sum_{k=1}^d \int_r^t \frac{\partial A_k(\underline{X}_s)}{\partial\underline{X}_s}D_r(\underline{X}_s)dW_s^k \qquad \text{(B.14)}$$

where $\dfrac{\partial A_k(\underline{X}_t)}{\partial\underline{X}_t} = \begin{bmatrix} \dfrac{\partial A_k^1(\underline{X}_t)}{\partial X_t^1} & \dfrac{\partial A_k^2(\underline{X}_t)}{\partial X_t^1} & \dots & \dfrac{\partial A_k^m(\underline{X}_t)}{\partial X_t^1} \\ \dfrac{\partial A_k^1(\underline{X}_t)}{\partial X_t^2} & \dfrac{\partial A_k^2(\underline{X}_t)}{\partial X_t^2} & \dots & \dfrac{\partial A_k^m(\underline{X}_t)}{\partial X_t^2} \\ \dots & \dots & \dots & \dots \\ \dfrac{\partial A_k^1(\underline{X}_t)}{\partial X_t^m} & \dfrac{\partial A_k^2(\underline{X}_t)}{\partial X_t^m} & \dots & \dfrac{\partial A_k^m(\underline{X}_t)}{\partial X_t^m} \end{bmatrix}$ (B.15)

Thus, we end up with the linear SDE for the mxd matrix $D_r\underline{X}_t$ as:

$$d(D_r\underline{X}_t) = \frac{\partial B(\underline{X}_t)}{\partial\underline{X}_t}(D_r\underline{X}_t)dt + \sum_{k=1}^d \frac{\partial A_k(\underline{X}_t)}{\partial\underline{X}_t}D_r(\underline{X}_t)dW_t^k \qquad \text{(B.16)}$$

with initial conditions $D_r\underline{X}_0$.

Chapter VI

Evolution of the Euro and Currency Competition in the Global ICT Age

Sadayoshi Takaya, Kansai University, Japan

Abstract

This chapter focuses on the function of international currencies as foreign exchange vehicles, which has a character of the network externality. On January 1999, the euro was introduced in Europe where the functions of the euro are limed as a currency. After January 2002, the euro had perfect functions, while the competition between the euro and the U.S. dollar was keen as the dominant international currency. We present the currency competition model with a decreasing transaction cost that reflects the character of the network externality, to investigate the competition between the euro and the dollar. We suggest the impact of introduction of the euro is the determinant for competition winner between the euro and the dollar.

Key Currency and International Monetary Regimes

International monetary regimes are arrangements that are made for agents to carry out foreign official and private settlements. These regimes include provisions pertaining to the use of international currencies as settlement currencies, exchange rates regimes and degree of capital mobility in order to decide the availability of foreign settlements. In particular, the international currency that is used primarily in international settlements is referred to as a key currency. Furthermore, there exists an inherent asymmetry in international monetary regimes between the key-currency country and the non-key currency countries. In other words, although the country providing the key currency can make foreign settlements using its home currency, the country providing a non-key currency cannot. Therefore, the key-currency country does not face exchange rate risks.

Since the key-currency country is secure in the independence of its own policy objectives, it has the option of altering the exchange rates regime and the degree of capital mobility depending on the global economic situation. The degree of flexibility of the fiscal policy is also a criterion for the choice of an international monetary system. If a government intends to expand its fiscal deficits, it would be inclined to opt for a system wherein it is easier to raise finance from foreign agents. In brief, if liberalization is faced with a difficulty in sustaining a fixed exchange rate regime, the government will be able to liberalize capital controls in order to alter the flexible exchange rate regime.

Non-key currency countries use the key currency because of its easy availability and for international settlements. Under this circumstance, non-key currency countries choose an exchange rates regime and the degree of capital mobility taking into consideration the effects that exchange rates and capital mobility have on their economies. The choice of an international monetary system depends on the preference of the country or the government. For example, if a government prefers to stabilize exchange rates, it will not hesitate to restrain capital mobility. If a government prefers to import foreign capital, it will opt to liberalize capital controls and adopt a fixed exchange rates regime. However, such countries will face a difficulty in maintaining a consistency between free capital mobility and fixed exchange rates regime.

Historically, the international gold standard persisted before World War I with free capital mobility and fixed exchange rates. The pound sterling of Great Britain was the key currency at that time. The gold exchange standard survived through the interval period with unstable exchange rates and capital controls. Although the pound sterling continued to be the key currency during this period, its significance was diminished. Post World War II saw the emergence of the Bretton Woods regime with fixed exchange rates and capital controls. The U.S. dollar has since been the key currency. Since the 1970s, most major countries have experienced the flexible exchange rates regime. Although international capital movements were formerly restrained, these have gradually been liberalized in developed countries since the 1980s. This liberalization led to the emergence of a global financial economy and intensified capital mobility by hedge funds, mutual funds, pension funds and so forth.

The evolution of the euro in the 1990s is considered to be a prominent characteristic of the globalized economy. The emergence of a single currency area accelerated the further integration of money and financial markets in the European Union (EU) to promote the possibility of the euro emerging as not only an international currency but also the key currency. As a non-national but common currency, the euro is currently not used in most countries in the EU, but only in the periphery countries of the EU. It is possible that the euro will compete with the U.S. dollar, which has been the key currency globally since World War II. This chapter investigates the possibility and conditions for the euro to emerge as the key currency by presenting the dynamic currency competition model.

The primary functions of an international currency are described in terms of its three roles. It acts as (1) a unit of exchange, (2) a means of payment, and (3) a store of value. These three functions of the international currency are not independent of each other. Any currency or medium of exchange has the function of being a store of value, which implies purchasing power. Money cannot work as a medium if currency does not play the role of a unit of account. Therefore, any currency must perform these perfect functions.

On the other hand, the functions of the international currency include six roles, which are classified by users, the private sector, the official sector, and traders in foreign exchange markets. In the private sector, the international currency is used as denomination currency, vehicle currency, payments currency and investment currency for portfolio allocation. The denomination currency is used when private agents write an invoice to denominate prices in trading goods and services with foreign countries. In addition, agents use this currency for domestic trading in high-inflation countries. This case is referred to as currency substitution. Vehicle currency is used for trading with foreign agents, and payments currency is used for trading settlements. Private agents also use the international currency when they prefer global portfolio allocation. If capital movements are liberalized, it will be possible for private agents to invest in foreign assets or currencies. The international currency for portfolio allocation is the currency that these assets or moneys are denominated in.

As mentioned above, in foreign exchange markets, traders use the international currency as a foreign exchange vehicle. In the foreign exchange markets, official agents use international currencies to intervene in the markets to restore the stability of exchange rates. Hereafter, we will refer to the international currency as "intervention currency" in the context of this function.

International currencies do not always perform all six functions. At present, only the key currency, such as the U.S. dollar, has these perfect roles. However, the U.S. dollar does not always play a dominant role as an international currency. Private agents in industrialized countries prefer to use their home currency for exchange risks or transaction costs. This results in a decline in the private use of the U.S. dollar as the denomination and the vehicle currency.

The determinants of international currencies are transaction costs, security issues, policy incentives, policy instruments and risk[1]. From among these determinants, this chapter will focus on transaction costs because they are related to the settlement system, which is dependent on Information and Communication Technology (ICT). The transaction cost of international currencies implies a bid-ask spread, which becomes low if the market for the foreign exchange vehicle is large and deep. Further, as pointed out by

Hartman (1997), high exchange volatility increases the transaction cost. Monetary authorities tend to use the same currency for intervention.

One of the determinants of international use for a currency is safety, which depends on the settlement system between cross-border banks. This is because global risk and more importantly, systemic risk that arises from currency crisis and contagion, result in a cross-border bank failing to run other banks not only in the same country but in other countries as well. Since cross-border banking is always faced with systemic risk, banks with cross-border operations pay particular attention to safety settlement networks. Further, risk-averse investors tend to select the currency without systemic risk, resulting in the use of banks participating in safety settlement networks or RTGS.

The Economic Monetary Union (EMU) in Europe now has a settlement system between banks in EMU and non-EMU member countries-Trans-European Automated Real-time Gross settlement Express Transfer (TARGET). TARGET is a pan-European system interlinking EU real-time gross settlement systems. It allows large euro payments to be made in real time across EU countries. Although private banks in EMU member countries have deposits in each central bank for settlement purposes, the central banks of member countries share information on settlements through the EMU in order to connect to a common information platform, or TARGET, which is a decentralized system, not through the European Central Bank (ECB) but through interlinking or bilateral linking. EMU member countries can connect with each other through this system with low risk. The real-time gross settlements system (RTGS) is sustained by ICT, which provides the potential to conduct massive settlement procedures between banks in EMU and non-EMU member countries.

In addition to TARGET, private foreign settlement systems such as EURO1 by the Euro Banking Association (EBA), RTGS[Plus] in Germany, and Paris Integrated Settlement (PIS) in France provide payments services.

EURO1 is not a gross settlement but a net settlement system operated by EBA, which was a former ECU clearing system. The use of TARGET incurs a high transaction fee because it employs RTGS; however, the transaction fee incurred for EURO1 is lower because it employs a netting payment system for large transactions. In addition, the STEP1 system connected to EURO1 is a netting payment system for small transactions.

The Euro Access Frankfurt (EAF), a net settlement system operated by Landesbank Hessen, has been substituted by RTGS[Plus] following its declining usage since the introduction of the euro. RTGS[Plus] has two payments systems, express payments and limit payments. The former is for emergent settlements and the latter for regular settlements. RTGS[Plus] is open to banking institutions not only in Germany but also in other European countries.

PIS is a liquidity bridge between two net settlement systems: the Paris Net Settlement (PNS) and RTGS in France and Transfers Banque de France (TBF). PNS carries out continuous daily bilateral settlements. Meanwhile, the system makes multilateral netting unsettled volume. PNS is connected to TBF, which is operated by Banque de France and is also interlinked with TARGET.

On the other hand, the Clearing House Interbank Payment System (CHIPS) sustains international settlements by using the U.S. dollar. CHIPS is installed in the New York

Clearinghouse, where net settlement amounts are calculated. Finally, the amounts are cleared through Fed Wire in the Federal Reserve Bank of New York, where 21 member banks make settlements through deposits in the Reserve Bank. Non-member banks can use deposits in member banks for domestic and international settlements. In addition, information can be obtained regarding agreements and confirmations of international settlements, such as trade payments, international investments, loans and deposits, and transmits through the Society for Worldwide Interbank Financial Telecommunication (SWIFT), which is a computerized system for information transfer.

TARGET, like RTGS, differs from CHIPS as a net settlement system in real-time risk management. Worldwide users of international settlements would make a choice between the euro and the U.S. dollar for risk management. In other words, because the development of ICT sustains the safety of the settlement system, ICT would be one of the determinants of the international currency.

If the role of the U.S. dollar as a foreign exchange vehicle declines, an alternate international currency has the potential to emerge as a dominant currency in foreign exchange markets. We attempt to investigate the conditions for the shift of the key currency from the U.S. dollar to the euro. In the next section, we develop a model with decreasing cost function.

The remainder of this chapter is organized as follows. In Section 2, the model is introduced in order to explain the characteristics of the foreign exchange vehicle function of the international currency and discuss the competition between the euro and the U.S. dollar. Section 3 is a summary that discusses the future role of the euro.

The Model of the Currency Competition

Framework of Our Model

We focus on constructing the model of exchange vehicle currency among foreign exchange traders. This is done for following reasons. First, the use of international currency as exchange vehicle currency is dominated in foreign exchange markets, while the share of trade vehicle currency is small in the markets. This situation is resulted by a series of exchange control liberalization in developed and developing countries. Second, Krugman (1980) suggests the exchange vehicle currencies are the most important factor of the character of international currency, which has a network effect including increasing return. However, Krugman doesn't indicate the dynamic model of international currency. So, his suggestion is not sufficient to explain why a currency becomes the international currency. We assume a dynamic model in this chapter, which basically has same structure in Takaya (2005).

The increasing return model is applied to explain the characteristic of the network effect of exchange vehicle role of international currency in the foreign exchange markets. The network effect means that the more of an international currency trader of foreign exchange use, the smaller the transaction fee for the international currency becomes. To explain this, the decreasing cost model that applies the increasing return model is introduced. Recent studies by Krugman (1991), Matsuyama (1992) and Murphy, Shleifer and Vishny (1989) have attempted to derive multiple equilibrium to mention economic development when the paths both to good development and to bad development. Their studies suggest roles of expectation for future return and historically initial equilibrium. In this chapter, the increasing return model is applied to our non-linear decreasing transaction model to describe the network effect of the international currency. Krugman (1991) constructs the linear model with increasing return to investigate the characteristic of local equilibrium. Krugman's model is expanded to non-linear model in our model.

We assume two relevant currencies. These are international currencies traded in the foreign exchange markets, for example, the euro and the U.S. dollar. Here, we introduce currency speculators in the third country, who maximize their returns in each period. 1 denotes the currency or assets denominated in the euro, 2 ones denominated in the U.S. dollar. The third countries' currencies are not international currency, therefore, traders in the countries trade the euro or the U.S. dollar for international transactions. They decide on which currency they investment inter-temporally without considering interest rate differentials. Here, δ_j denotes interest differentials between interest rate in j country and home country.

Since traders face the volatility of exchange rates between international currencies and home's, they make expectations on exchange rates. ε_j represents expected fluctuation of exchange rates. While ε_j generally depends on volume of trade in foreign exchange markets, we assume ε_j is constant at first. We relax this assumption later[2].

All of trade are assumed to be charged the ratio of transaction fee c_j (j=1, 2) which is decreasing function of the total assets balances, B_j (j=1, 2) denominated by each currency. In the practical markets, there are differentials between bid rate and ask rate, so called bid-ask spreads, which are though to be reflected in the search cost of each currency trade. Since the search cost assumed to be depend on convenience of meeting currency which trader intend to buy and sell it, the more the volume of transaction increase, the smaller the transaction fee decrease. That is, the transaction cost has the character of economy of scale. Form the other view, difference of ICT innovation related with settlement system results in different structure of transaction cost. We assume z as the ICT innovation parameter by the euro. z represents TARGET system, which is superior to CHIPS. The flows not only of transactions in the foreign exchange markets but also of potential transactions affect the cost, which are the asset positions. Then, we assume c_j decreasing function[3]. However, each trader deals with c_j exogenously because economy of scale is externality. The cost function is as follows;

$$C_1 = zc_1(B_1).$$

$$c_j' = \frac{\partial c_j}{\partial B_j} > 0, \quad c_j'' = \frac{\partial^2 c_j}{\partial B_j^2} < 0. \tag{1}$$

where α is assumed to be the parameter representing technology for transaction by using the euro.

We assume each trader also faces the adjustment cost ϕ, depending on investment volume N. Adjustments of asset position assume to be expense increasingly. The function ϕ is a following increasing function;

$$\phi = \phi(N).\tag{2}$$

Here, we assume $\phi' = \dfrac{\partial \phi}{\partial N} > 0$, $\phi'' = \dfrac{\partial \phi''}{\partial N^2} > 0$.

The number of traders in the third countries is assumed constant. For simplicity, trader's investment volumes are supposed to be constrained constant instantaneously. When each trader determines whether they invest in assets denominated in the euro or the U.S. dollar, she or he faces the constraint:

$$n_t = n_{1,t} + n_{2,t},\tag{3}$$

where n_t denotes constraint of each speculator's total investment in period t, n_1 investment to assets denominated in the euro, n_2 investment to assets in the U.S. dollar. Total investments in this whole economy are defined as N in each period, which is assumed to be constant for simplicity. In other words, we assume accumulation rate of total assets is given. Investment constraint in this whole economy is as follows:

$$N = N_1 + N_2,\tag{4}$$

where N_1 denotes investments in the euro assets, N_2 investments in the U.S. dollar assets. Stock constraint of each trader is as follows:

$$b = b_1 + b_2,$$

where b denotes total holding assets of each speculator, b_1 holding euro assets, b_2 holding U.S. dollar assets. Aggregated stock constraint in whole economy is as follows:

$$B = B_1 + B_2,\tag{5}$$

where B denotes aggregate assets in this economy, B_1 aggregate the euro assets, B_2 aggregate the U.S. dollar assets.

Let an individual speculator's profit function be represented by π as follows:

$$\pi = (\varepsilon_1 + \delta_1)b_1 + (\varepsilon_2 + \delta_2)b_2 - zc_1(B_1)n_1 - c_2(B_2)n_2 - \phi(N_1 + N_2).$$

We can aggregate each speculator's profit function to get a profit function in this whole economy:

$$\Pi = (\varepsilon_1 + \delta_1)B_1 + (\varepsilon_2 + \delta_2)B_2 - zc_1(B_1)N_1 - c_2(B_2)N_2 - \phi(N_1 + N_2). \tag{6}$$

Π denotes an aggregate profit function. The change of asset denominated by the 1 currency is as follows:

$$\dot{B}_1 = N_1 \tag{7}$$

Each trader maximizes inter-temporal profit subject to the change of asset denominated by the euro. Trader's maximization problem is as follows:

$$\max \int_t^\infty \Pi_t e^{-\rho(s-t)} ds \tag{8}$$

s.t. $\dot{B}_1 = N_1$.

Each speculator in each period determines the volume of investment in euro assets or U.S. dollar assets, while she or he regards transaction cost function as given.

We can define the current value Hamiltonian as follows:

$$H = (\varepsilon_1 + \delta_1)B_1 + (\varepsilon_2 + \delta_2)B_2 - zc_1(B_1)N_1 - c_2(B_2)N_2 - \phi(N_1) + \lambda N_1 \tag{9}$$

where γ denotes co-state variable. Necessary condition is as follows;

$$\frac{\partial H}{\partial N} = 0, \tag{10}$$

$$\dot{\lambda} = \rho\lambda - \frac{\partial H}{\partial B_1} . \tag{11}$$

Transversality condition is as a follows:

$$\lim_{t\to\infty} \lambda_t B_{1,t} \exp(-\rho t) = 0 . \tag{12}$$

From (10),

$$-\alpha c_1 (B_1) N_1 - c_2 (B_2) N_2 - \phi'_{N1} + \lambda = 0 ,$$

which can be written by a form of inverse function as follows:

$$N = N(\lambda, B_1), \tag{13}$$

where we note $\dfrac{dN}{d\lambda} = \phi'' > 0$, $\dfrac{dN}{dB_1} = -\dfrac{zc_1' + c_2'}{\phi''}$ for our assumptions.

From (13), Equation (11) yields:

$$\dot{\lambda} = \rho\lambda - \left(\Omega - zc_1' (B_1) N_1 + c_2' (B_2) N_2 \right), \tag{14}$$

where we note $\Omega = (\varepsilon_1 - \varepsilon_2) + (\delta_1 - \delta_2) = const.$ from our assumption. With attention to (12), equation (14) can be solved as follows:

$$\lambda = \int_t^\infty \left(\Omega + \alpha c_1' (B_1) N_1 - c_2' (B_2) N_2 \right) \exp\left((-\rho)(s-t)\right) ds , \tag{15}$$

where γ represents a current value of a series of difference of expected gains and transaction cost between both two currencies. This suggests determinants of investment are current and future gains from both assets and transaction costs. In other words, difference of future transaction costs depends on other speculator's expectation for future transaction costs for a reason of externality.

A simple way of exploring how speculations to the assets denominated in the euro determine is to take a linear approximation to the two-equation system in a neighborhood of the steady state. The result is:

$$
\begin{pmatrix} \dot{B_1} \\ \dot{\lambda} \end{pmatrix} = \begin{pmatrix} A_1 & \phi''_\lambda \\ A_2 & \rho \end{pmatrix} \begin{pmatrix} B_1 - \overline{B} \\ \lambda - \overline{\lambda} \end{pmatrix},
$$

(16)

where we define $A_1 = \dfrac{\partial N}{\partial B_1} < 0$, $A_2 = \alpha c''_1 N_1 + c''\left(\overline{N} - N_1\right) + z c'_1 N'_{B1} + c_2 N'_{B1}$. The sign of A_1 is negative, but that of A_2 is ambiguous.

The transaction cost c assumed to be a decreasing function of B. Then, the sign of A_2 is negative, which is shown above. Trace (tr.) and determinant (det) of matrix (16) are as follows:

$$
tr. = A_1 + \rho = -\phi''^{-1}\left(z c'_1 + c'_2\right) + \rho,
$$

(17)

$$
\det = A_1 \rho - A_2 \phi''^{-1}
$$
$$
= -\left(\phi''^{-1}\left(z c'_1 + c'_2\right)\right)\left(\rho - \phi''^{-1}\left(\alpha c'_1 + c'_2\right)\right) - \phi''^{-1}\left(\alpha c''_1 N + c''_2\left(\overline{N} - N_1\right)\right).
$$

(18)

Both of signs of trace and determinant are ambiguous a priori. Here, we suppose *trace* is positive. That is:

$$
\rho\phi'' - \left(\alpha c'_1 + c'_2\right) > 0,
$$

(19)

is assumed[4]. This inequality implies that the size of ρ and ϕ is sufficient large, or the technological innovation z is large. z means ICT innovation speed in the euro might be higher than that in the U.S. if the innovation causes the cost decrease through the construction of rigid sage and convenience system. Now, we can make a distinction between some cases below, according to parameters of the determinant because the sign of determinant is ambiguous a priori.

Figure 1. The phase diagram in the case of decreasing function of transaction cost (1)

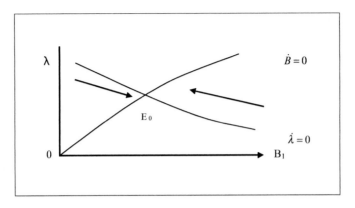

Case 1

We assume the following inequality:

$$\left|-\left(zc_1'+c_2'\right)\left(\rho-\phi''^{-1}\left(zc_1'+c_2'\right)\right)\right|>\left|\left(zc_1''N_1+c_2''\left(\bar{N}-N_1\right)\right)\right|. \tag{20}$$

This inequality (20) means that the degree of decreasing cost of transaction is smaller. In case 1, the network effect of an international currency as the foreign exchange vehicle is not strong.

In case 1, two equilibriums E_1 and E_2 are saddle because the determinant of each equilibrium is negative. Because det is negative in this case, the equilibrium is saddle point with unique stable arm, which we have explored in the previous section. The phase diagram is shown as Figure 1.

Case 2

In case 2 of the parameters of the determinant, the following inequality is assumed:

$$\left|-\left(\alpha c_1'+c_2'\right)\left(\rho-\phi''^{-1}\left(\alpha c_1'+c_2'\right)\right)\right|<\left|\left(\alpha c_1''N_1+c_2''\left(\bar{N}-N_1\right)\right)\right|. \tag{21}$$

This inequality (20) means that the degree of decreasing cost of transaction is larger. In case 1, the network effect of an international currency as the foreign exchange vehicle is strong.

Figure 2. The phase diagram in the case of decreasing function of transaction cost (2)

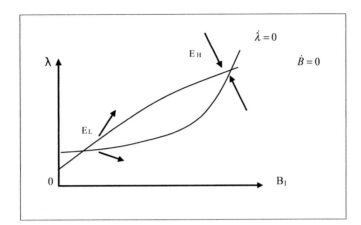

Figure 2 shows the phase diagram of $\dot{\lambda} = 0$ and $\dot{B}_1 = 0$. The lines of $\dot{\lambda} = 0$ and $\dot{B}_1 = 0$ are right upper slope with two equilibrium E_L and E_H. E_H is equilibrium where share of the euro is highest in the equilibrium. Also, E_H is saddle point. The reason is that determinant of matrix of coefficients of (16) is negative since c_1'' is smaller for the bigger B_1 from our assumptions. The share in E_L is lower than one in E_H. The determinant of matrix of coefficients in E_L is positive since is bigger for the reason of relatively smaller B_1. Thus, this point is source. The point 0 is also equilibrium, where the share is zero. The determinant of matrix of coefficients in zero point is positive as we mentioned above.

Thus, smaller uses of the euro can move to high uses in case 3 by speculator's expectations. At the beginning of introduction of the euro, frequency of use is lower than that of the U.S. dollar. However, the share of the euro could be higher if expectation of use of the euro is evolved in the near future, to higher frequency than the U.S. dollar.

Implications for the Future of the Euro

This chapter investigated the conditions for the euro to dominate the U.S. dollar as the key currency in foreign exchange markets. When the euro was first introduced, technical innovations in dealing in the euro significantly decreased the transaction costs due to network effects. We focus only on the foreign exchange vehicle function of the international currency because this is more important a factor than the other factors. Even if there were no technical innovations in dealing in the euro, the large increase in the transaction volumes in the euro could still be regarded as technical progress.

Table 1 lists recent statistics on the current use of major currencies. As evident from this table, the U.S. dollar has the largest share in terms of international use, but not a dominant share, except in the case of foreign exchange turnover. Therefore, today, the U.S. dollar

Table 1. The recent statistics on the present international use of the main currencies

Market Share	USD	Yen	Euro	Others*
Foreign exchange turnover (2001)	90.4	22.7	37.6	49.3
Gross issuance of long-term international debt securities (2003q3-2004q2)	43.1	7.0	32.0	17.9
Official reserves (2003)	63.8	4.8	19.7	11.7

Source: ECB, Review of the International Role of the Euro, 2005; BIS, Central Bank Survey of Foreign Exchange and Derivatives Market Activity.

Notes: Other currencies include pound sterling, French franc, Netherlands guilder and ecu.*

Table 2. Spot foreign exchange transaction costs ($ for a 10,000 transaction, assuming zero volatility)

$/DM	4.06
DM/Yen	4.37
$/Yen	4.16
FF/$	4.61
/$	4.27

Source: Alogoskoufis, Portes and Rey (1997)

as the key currency is sustained by its role as a foreign exchange vehicle. In this chapter, we focus on this role. We attach importance to the foreign exchange vehicle function since it is the dominant function in foreign exchange markets. In particular, the currency that function as a vehicle of trade between small volume currencies in foreign exchange markets emerges as an international currency. The logic that applies here is the same as that applicable to the evolution of money. Alogoskoufis, Portes and Rey (1997) use Hartman's estimates to compute the bid-ask spreads with zero volatility, which are shown in Table 2 as spot foreign exchange transaction costs. Although the difference in transaction costs due to difference in liquidity is very small for a ten thousand dollar transaction, the actual amount of the difference is very large because the number of daily transactions in foreign exchange markets is very high. Therefore, these differences are very important for traders dealing in currencies.

The U.S. dollar is likely to retain its current status for some period of time even after the introduction of the euro. The hysteresis effect or the history of the use of the U.S. dollar causes traders to deal in the dollar. However, if the areas using the euro expand — if Central and Eastern Europe accept the euro as their currency — it will result in the euro being used more frequently as the denomination or vehicle currency. If Asian or other countries prefer to hold assets denominated in the euro, its importance as portfolio currency will increase. This will result in a decline in transaction costs for the euro, making it more convenient to use. Once the use of the euro becomes more frequent, the transaction costs will dramatically decrease, and its share will increase correspondingly as it will be able to compete with the present key currency — the U.S. dollar. Therefore, the euro has the potential to emerge as the key currency of the world.

With regard to a bipolar key currency regime, we have historical experience of the sterling-dollar regime during the interwar period, when massive capital flow resulted in instability in the sterling/dollar exchange rates. Furthermore, the international monetary regime became unstable due to the competition in devaluation in order to take advantage of lower prices in foreign trade. Theoretically, exchange rates are indeterminate if capital mobility is deregulated to become perfect between symmetric countries. If capital mobility became perfect between the areas using the euro and the U.S. dollar, and the network effect diminished, the bipolar regime would become unstable through speculative capital flows between these areas.

As a method of preventing these instabilities, the following points may be considered: (1) implementation of capital controls, (2) introduction of a fixed exchange rates regime, and (3) promotion of discretionary economic policy coordination. The first proposal — implementation of capital controls — is expected to be resisted under current globalizing capital flows and the ICT age. Although controls by different governments may succeed in restraining globalizing capital, profit-seeking entities such as hedge funds, mutual funds, pension funds, and individual investors object to the implementation of capital controls. Second, if a fixed exchange rates regime is introduced, macroeconomic policies will be restrained in the concerned country. Therefore, the government may hesitate to introduce the fixed regime. The areas using the euro have decided upon a macroeconomic policy mix of price stability by the European Central Bank and fiscal deficit by the Stability and Growth Pact, leaving no scope to commit to exchange rates stability. Third, policy coordination is the only way to prevent instability; however, in some ways, this constrains room for discretion in macroeconomic policies. Agreement on policy coordination is a comparatively easier option because it does not require strict rules. Thus, policy coordination is the only realistic solution to prevent an unstable international monetary regime. To be more precise, the current key-currency country, the United States, should control its twin deficits, namely, its current account deficits and fiscal deficits. On the other hand, the areas using the euro should pay attention not only to price stability but also to economic growth in order to have an impact on world business cycles.

Although policy coordination among these areas may enable the realization of a stable situation, this coordination has the potential to become a moral hazard for the U.S. government. The government may have an incentive to suffer fiscal deficits as a consequence of the facility to finance these deficits. Therefore, the U.S. government should commit to policy coordination in order to decrease its current account and fiscal deficits. If traders in foreign exchange markets realize the U.S. government's reluctance to coordinate its policies with the areas using the euro, they may shift the massive funds they own from the United States to other countries, thereby resulting in unstable exchange rates and real economy. As suggested by our model in the previous section, a small change in the expectations of traders, arising from mistrust regarding policy coordination, can cause massive capital flows and a switch in the key currency.

In the global ICT age with globalizing capital, the stability of the international monetary system may depend on appropriate policy coordination between the U.S., which provides the existing key currency, and the areas using the euro, which have the potential to provide the next key currency.

References

Alogoskoufis, G., Portes, R., & Rey, H. (1997). The emergence of the euro as an international currency. *CEPR Discussion Paper*, 1741.

Bénassy-Quere, A., Mojon, B., & Schor, A.-D. (1998). The international role of the euro. *CEPII, Document de Travail*, 98-03.

Cohen, D. (1997). How will the euro behave? *CEPR Discussion Paper*, 1673.

Goodhart, C. (1988). The foreign exchange market: A random walk with a dragging anchor. *Economica*, 55, 437-60.

Guckenheimer, J., & Holmes, P. (1986). *Nonlinear oscillations, dynamical systems and bifurcations of vector fields*. New York: Springer-Verlag.

Hartman, P. (1998a). *Currency competition and foreign exchange markets: The dollar, the yen and the euro*. Cambridge, UK: Cambridge University Press.

Hartman, P. (1998b). Do Reuters' spreads reflect currencies' differences in global trading activity? *Journal of International Money and Finance*, 17, 757-784.

Howitt, P., & McAfee, P. (1988). Stability of equilibria with externalities. *Quarterly Journal of Economics*, 103, 261-277.

Kingman, P. (1991). History versus expectations. *Quarterly Journal of Economics*, 106, 651-667.

Kiyotaki, N. (1988). Trade, accumulation and uneven development. *Journal of Development Economics*, 103, 695-714.

Krugman, P. (1980). Vehicle currencies and the structure of international exchange. *Journal of Money, Credit, and Banking*, 12, 503-526.

Matsuyama, K. (1991). Increasing Returns, Industrialization and Indeterminacy of Equilibrium. *Quarterly Journal of Economics*, 106, 17-650.

Matasuyama, K. (1992). A simple model of sectoral adjustment. *Review of Economic Studies*, 59, 375-388.

Murphy, K., Shleifer, A., & Vishny, R. (1989). Industrialization and the big push. *Journal of Political Economy*, 97, 1003-1026.

Romer, P. (1986). Increasing returns and long-run growth. *Journal of Political Economy*, 94, 45-75.

Takaya, S. (2005). Competition between the euro and the U.S. dollar. *Kansai University Review of Business and Commerce*, 7, 41-62.

Tavlas, G. S. (1997). The international use of the U.S. dollar: An optimum currency area perspective. *The World Economy*, 20, 709-747.

Endnotes

[1]   See Bénassy-Quere, Mojon and Schor (1998) for details.

[2]   We extend this model with endogenously expected fluctuation of exchange rates in Takaya (2005).

[3]   We explain the increasing function case in Takaya (2005).

[4]   Negative case is ignored here, because the system is stable.

Chapter VII

Co-Integration of the International Capital Markets with the Use of Information Technology:
The Case of Europe

Argyrios Volis, Athens University of Economics and Business, Greece

Abstract

The purpose of this study is to explore the "revolution" that was caused by the rapid spread of information technology towards the development and co-integration of financial markets, especially capital markets. The main issue is that the IT progress and facilities enabled the last years the overreaction of the capital markets, and this phenomenon had as a result to offer to the investors a variety of investment choices. The study shall focus on the European capital markets and the impact of information technology to the key activities the capital markets implement: the structure of the trading platforms, the cross-border cooperation of the markets and the financial intermediaries, at a theoretical and practical framework.

Description of the Basic Applications as a Result of the IT Development

The basic means of technology that are widely used in the financial industry and lead to the co-integration of the financial markets are a) the Internet and b) the implementation and use of sophisticated trading platforms by the majority of the capital markets. Both means serve most of the participating groups in the market, namely the investors, the issuers and the intermediaries.

Internet

"Internet is a system of linked computer networks, international in scope, that facilitates data transfer and communication services, such as remote login, file transfer (FTP), electronic mail (e-mail), newsgroups and the World Wide Web. The Internet greatly extends the reach of each connected computer network" (www.netlingo.com).

Internet technology has brought a huge evolution to everyday activities. The financial services industry is also influenced by the tools and accessories that Internet offers to the activities of the industry. With the use of the Internet, the nature of securities transactions becomes "non-physical", while it offers interactivity and dissemination of information to every direction. IT allows vast quantities of financial information to be available anywhere anytime. The importance of this issue is significant, because the information business is one of the fundamental services provided by financial intermediaries. Moreover, it offers more opportunities for diversification, as the investors can trade not only domestically, but globally as well. Foreign competitors can penetrate the local markets, and as a result the process of price formation is more transparent. The market transparency results to more volatile stock prices and financial flows, because market participants can react immediately to new information.

The main characteristics of the Internet, as far as the financial industry is concerned, are the following:

1. First of all, the cost for both acquiring information about the markets and the issuers, as well as the trade of shares, is decreasing (a parameter that applies to the European Markets). The World Wide Web provides the investors with all the necessary information they need in order to proceed to securities transactions. As far as the issuers are concerned, they can attract new investors by disseminating detailed information about their company, quickly and with low cost.

2. The second issue to be addressed is the communication between the market participants. Internet provides important tools, such as the electronic mail, the Web sites and the "File Transfer Protocol", well known as FTP, which assist the market participants to communicate, to provide information about the services they offer, (for the issuers) to present their company, its activities and the future potentials,

and to receive the kind of information they need, in order to take investment decisions.

3.   Moreover, the Internet offers the opportunity to both investors and companies to gain access to markets that are not domestic. For the investors, Internet and online brokerage services offer the opportunity to diversify even more, by having the opportunity to buy shares for their international portfolio, and reduce their risk exposure. For the financial intermediaries, Internet is the communication channel for getting access to other markets and attracting foreign clients, or even financial alliances. The development of cross-border European alliances on joint financial products is the result of the impact of IT on the means of communication among intermediaries all over the world.

4.   Finally, in terms of market competition, the evolution of the information technology reduces barriers to entry, facilitating entry by non-financial entities, and resulting to the increase of the competition, especially in services provided by banks and brokerage firms. Moreover, financial intermediaries have to set new technological standards to the services they offer, standards which can be used as prerequisites by the investors, such as mobile brokerage or market monitoring.

One of the main targets for the capital markets is how the technology and especially the Internet can improve the activities taking place after the trading occurs, namely the clearing and settlement process. In most of the capital markets, the "T+3" rule of clearing and settlement exists. With the new technology, the "T+0" rule is what the markets are targeting to, in order to eliminate the risks associated with the day trading and the flow of information.

The specific advantages for the participants (the investors, the issuers and the financial intermediaries) of the market can be summarized as following:

Investors

Investors can retrieve a significant amount of information through the Internet. The most important type of information is reports about the traded companies (in domestic and global markets), research reports offered by the companies that provide freely their research reports and historical data. Where available, the investors can open accounts online and perform trading activity through the brokerage company that offers such service. Moreover, Internet provides to the users — investors educational material, which concerns general principles of portfolio theory, how to set up investment strategies, as well as the use of historical prices and their scientific interpretation. The brokerage companies that offer Internet services usually offer tools to the investors for monitoring their portfolio, retrieving historical prices and news concerning the markets they are interested, as well as gaining access to all available information. Finally, the World Wide Web offers unique opportunities to the investors to communicate each other and exchange ideas and opinions on the financial markets.

Issuers

Apart from the investors, issuers can also benefit from the wide use of the Internet. The first important advantage for the issuers is that they can expand the dissemination of information to a greater number of investors, and to big geographical areas (domestically and globally). Through Internet, the issuers can attract a wide number of potential small investors, with low cost, and they are able to transfer the kind of information that they provide to the large, institutional investors. Especially in the cases of initial public offerings (IPOs), all the marketing activities (presentation of the company, purposes for going public, investment scheme for the forthcoming years, benefits from investing in such company) that concerns the attraction of new investors, can be implemented through the Internet (Web site and e-mails). Through "direct stock purchase schemes", which are provided directly through the Internet by the issuers, the investors are not obliged to contact a brokerage company, but the issuer directly.

Financial Intermediaries

The companies that offer financial services have extensively benefited by the use of the Internet, and the evolution of the technology. In this section we shall present the benefits that arise from the use of Internet, and in the next section we shall focus on the impact of the technology evolution concerning the sophisticated trading platforms and the unique systems of clearing and settlement. As far as the Internet is concerned, the financial intermediaries can develop marketing tools that they can offer to the investors, such as:

- *Dissemination of information with the use of e-mails or Web sites.* The brokerage companies can provide the investors with various reports concerning analysis of trading companies, summary of the trading day, corporate news, information for new public offerings, news about the evolution of the financial industry and the macroeconomic environment in general.

- *Daily monitoring tools of the market.* Most of the brokerage companies provide facilities for the online monitoring of the market (with a small delay) and a summary of the orders for all the shares. This of course is a tool that provides most of the capital market's Web sites, including facilities such as online portfolio monitoring, currency converter and adjusted historical data.

- *Online order placement.* A group of brokerage companies offers the possibility of online order placement, for investors that are subscribed to the specific service. The advantages of this service is mainly that there is not loss of time, and the cost is significantly reduced for the investors.

- *Marketing of services provided.* Finally, the financial intermediaries can implement big advertisement projects, locally and globally, and present the services they offer without harming their budget.

Capital Markets

Apart from the main participants, an extensive analysis has been conducted for the impact of the new technology and the World Wide Web to the capital markets. The impact on the markets however can be analyzed through two technological innovations: the Internet and the electronic trading platforms that are used, in order to execute trades and to enable the clearing and settlement process.

The Internet in brief has offered the following advantages to the capital markets:

1.   First of all the markets can disseminate a significant amount of information concerning both the market (regulation, procedures, products), and the exchange members (brokerage companies and financial houses). The official markets, through the Internet, can provide to the investors the trading rules, all the laws applied to the market, online quotation, as well as press releases and financial results of the listed companies. Most of the Web sites of the exchanges provide to the investors detailed presentation of the listed companies, including field of activity, main shareholders and financial results for a number of recent years.

2.   Education is also one basic characteristic of the tools to be offered by the markets. Through Internet, the markets try to provide to the investors "investment culture" and tutorials about the investment strategies, as well as fundamental issues of the capital markets (expected return, associated risk, fundamental and technical analysis, purpose of index existence).

3.   Internet has offered the opportunity to the markets to become "non-physical". The financial intermediary companies are directly connected to the trading system and forward their orders. That issue was the revolution of the capital markets especially during the '80s.

In the case of cross-border trading, where the issuer and the investor is located to different geographical areas, the Internet is the only mean of implementing cross-border transactions fast and securely.

Definition: *A cross-border trade is defined as the trade between counterparties (buyer and seller) located in different countries, whereas a cross-border settlement occurs when the security settlement is realized in a distinct country of one or both counterparties.*

Compared to the local securities trade, where securities are traded and settled by participants of the same Central Securities Depository (CSD), cross-border transaction infers complexity due to the increasing number of relationships that the international investor must have to gain access to the settlement system. Bilateral links between CSDs have been established in order to facilitate the cross-border transfer of securities and to use them for the transfer of collateral for the Eurosystem's credit operations.

Global custodians typically have sub-custodians in different countries that hold access to the local CSD. They are most dealing with equities, a market where ICSDs are less active. In general, global custodians concentrate more in institutional investors (e.g. mutual and pension funds) and private banks, while ICSDs attend wholesale financial clients (e.g., investment banks). The competitive advantage of the global custodians relies on the customization of services attending the clients' needs. Global custodians may have a great number of clients enabling settlement of securities to occur in their own book-entry system.

Associated Risks

The risks however that are associated with the use of Internet and the tools provided are mainly the following: in one hand (issues concerning the participants), fraud and money laundering, privacy and identity management, and on the other hand (issues concerning the IT industry), the growth of viruses and limited security for specific communication channels and protocols.

Another issue that arises from the use of electronic services is the existence and liability of electronic signatures, for both issuers and investors. In that case, the technology can ensure secure communication channels, which prove that the sender of financial information of trading orders is valid, and the message is actually transmitted the way it is formed. The IT industry spends a substantial amount of money in order to ensure that the transmission of any kind of information between markets and brokers, markets and investors, as well as investors and issuers is secure through the World Wide Web.

Regulatory Issues

"Transparency of trading information is a very important factor in helping markets function effectively."

Apart from the participants, the securities regulators, such as the markets and the market authorities use the advances of the technology in order to serve their activities. The main issue of regulators across capital markets, when electronic trading is concerned, is transparency, especially of information about the trading process. The second issue is investment education for existing and future investors.

Electronic trading can be the prerequisite for transparency in the trading process, as the trading systems can disseminate all the available information to all the participants of the market, and can facilitate greater pre- and post-trade transparency. Transparency of the markets through electronic trading satisfies also the demand for anonymous trading, as most of the electronic markets can accept "iceberg" orders, that are automatically matched if hit, but are not visible in an order book.

On the other hand, electronic systems can avoid information leakage, as they allow to the traders not to reveal their strategy in the framework of the electronic order book. In such case, the orders should be filled in accurately, minimizing the disclosure of information that should not be revealed (for example by splitting the trade, in order to reduce the observable information content).

The first case concerns the initial public offering of a company, where most of the paperwork involved in such activity (information dissemination, filling in documents) can be implemented electronically. Moreover, the markets and the authorities promote the legal framework and all the regulatory issues of their operations in their Web sites, so as to inform the current and potential investors. Moreover, news and press releases are daily uploaded, information that has an impact on the investment strategy of the investors.

Moreover, through the Internet, the regulators and authorities can offer educational schemes to the broad group of investors, namely investment strategies, basic elements of portfolio theory and methods of risk diversification. In most of the markets an integrated support center operates, which provides the investors with information on implicit questions and market news.

Most of the securities market laws and regulations require certain information by the listed companies to be delivered to investors. The Internet provides such facilities, while regulators ensure that the quality of such information is equal with any other mean of delivery.

E-Trading

The most important service provided by the financial intermediaries to the investors, within the framework of Internet tools and applications, is electronic trading.

Within this framework, the definition of online brokerage is introduced:

Online brokerage is the purchasing and selling securities online, on the Internet. Online brokers offer security transactions to their customers, and online access to investment information, by opening an online account.

Effects of E-Trading
in Market Architecture

We can summarize the effects of electronic trading to market architecture to the following:

a.   *Market access:* as previously explained, the electronic trading can widen access to trading systems across several dimensions. More users can now participate to the markets at a relatively low cost, while the increase of the financial intermediaries that participate increases the competition, the liquidity and forces them to focus on other value added services, such as consultant services, corporate finance and risk control.

b.   *Transparency:* Electronic trading facilitates and increases the transparency of the market, as explained in the previous section. Such characteristic can lead to more efficient price formation, as investors and intermediaries can incorporate all the available information and act accordingly, leading the market to the formation of efficient prices.

c.   *Trading cost:* In a trading environment, fully modernized and technologically innovated, both the trading explicit and implicit costs are reduced. Explicit costs include overheads, fees, commissions, taxes, clearing costs, while implicit costs concern bid-ask spreads and market impact costs. Especially for the explicit costs, the electronic systems involve lower setup and operating costs (in most of the cases it can reach a level of 50%). One reason is because the orders can follow STP (straight through processing) arrangements, without further intervention.

d.   *Liquidity:* Finally, electronic systems have the ability to link to financial intermediaries' order management systems, so as to search for orders, cross matches and consequently produce liquidity. Electronic systems can also cause liquidity, especially when non-frequently traded issues are involved, as the systems can enable their trading (this is mainly observed to the fixed income markets).

Theoretical Framework

Before presenting the impact of IT evolution to the capital markets and the trading systems, a theoretical framework is presented that concerns the co-integration of the capital markets.

Co-Integration of the Markets

Two markets are considered to be co-integrated when no barriers exist that prevent the free transfer of capital among the markets. In terms of expected returns, if two markets are co-integrated, the shares that are traded in such markets and have similar risk exposure, have similar expected returns. One way to test for co-integration of the markets is to explore parameters that prevent arbitrage among markets (for example the capital markets laws or the taxation).

An alternative way to test for co-integration, is to test the hypothesis that shares with similar risk characteristics have the same expected returns in different markets, by using a benchmark efficient portfolio. In that case, the shares traded in co-integrated markets have expected returns that are determined by the beta coefficients. The parameter to be retrieved is the efficient portfolio (in order to measure the characteristics of the risk associated).

Campbell and Hamao (1992) examine a model in order to test for market co-integration, and they apply for the markets of New York and Japan. The model consisting of k parameters is the following:

$$r_{i,t+1} = Et[r_{i,t+1}] + \sum_{1}^{K} \beta_{\iota\kappa} f_{\kappa,t+1} + e_{i,t+1}$$

where

$$Et[r_{i,t+1}] = \sum_{1}^{K} \beta_{\iota\kappa} \lambda_{\kappa t} \quad (\text{ë is the market price of risk of K factor}).$$

If we suppose that at period t, the total information consists of N variables and the restricted expected prices are linear to these variables, then:

$$\lambda_{kt} = \sum_{1}^{K} \theta_{kn} X_{nt} \quad \text{and if we comprise,}$$

$$Et[r_{i,t+1}] = \sum_{1}^{K} \beta_{\iota\kappa} \sum \theta_{kn} X_{nt} = \sum_{1}^{N} a_{in} X_{nt}$$

we regress i excess returns to N variables.

There are two ways to test this model: Either we consider that there is a variable that proxies for the international factor to the asset pricing, or there is not. The model examines the case where there is a portfolio with the following characteristics: its [2] coefficient of the first factor is 1, and 0 otherwise. If the returns of the portfolio are denoted by $r_{1,t+1}$, then:

$$r_{i,t+1} = \beta_{i1} r_{1,t+1} + \sum_{2}^{K} \beta_{\iota\kappa} \sum \theta_{kn} X_{nt} + \sum_{2}^{K} \beta_{\iota\kappa} f_{k,t+1} + e_{i,t+1} =$$

$$\ldots\ldots = \beta_{i1} r_{1,t+1} + \sum_{1}^{N} a^{*}_{in} X_{nt} + u_{i,t+1}$$

The intuition of the formula is the following: Suppose that the model is going to explain the returns of the capital market of Japan. This model is applied by considering that the first factor is an international factor (an international index) and some domestic variables.

The variance of the factor $\sum_{1}^{N} a^{*}{}_{in} X_{nt}$ related to the factor $\sum_{1}^{N} a^{*}{}_{in} X_{nt}$ is a measure of variability of the domestic factors risk prices, compared to the total factors risk prices.

For the specific study, two indices were used (NYSE index for the New York and a combination of Nikkei and TOPIX for Japan). The variables that are used in both markets are the following: a dummy variable for January effect, the dividend yield (D/P ratio), the 'relative short rate' (difference between the current short-term interest rate and its moving average) and the spread between the short-term and long-term interest rates.

Two models are examined in two different alternatives:

BASIC 1 (3 variables)		ADDITIVE 1 (5 variables)	
January Dummy		January Dummy	
D/P ratio		D/P ratio	
Short-term interest rate		Short-term interest rate	
		Previous excess Returns	
		Interest Rate spread	
BASIC 2 (5 variables)		ADDITIVE 2 (9 variables)	
January Dummy		January Dummy	
D/P ratio	(domestic and foreign)	D/P ratio	(domestic and foreign)
Short-term interest rate	(domestic and foreign)	Short-term interest rate	(domestic and foreign)
		Previous excess Returns	(domestic and foreign)
		Interest Rate spread	(domestic and foreign)

The results for the markets of Japan and New York are the following:

1. The excess returns can be estimated using domestic variables.

2. The variables of United States can predict the excess returns of Japan (which means that the markets are co-integrated).

3. The international index that was used instead of the local indices (MSCI index) is quite important when explaining the markets' returns (the index explains 70% of the variability of returns in New York and 60% in Japan).

Another approach concerning the portfolio construction and the risk pricing in a global economy is presented by Harvey (1993), and it is based on conditional asset pricing restrictions. According to CAPM, the conditional expected return of a share is proportional to the covariance with the world market portfolio. In this case we must define the country risk: it is the conditional sensitivity of the country return to a world stock return.

The model is the following:

$$E(r_{jt} \mid \Omega_{t-1}) = \frac{E[r_{mt} \mid \Omega_{t-1}]}{Var[r_{mt} \mid \Omega_{t-1}]} Cov[r_{jt}, r_{mt} \mid \Omega_{t-1}]$$

where r denotes the excess returns, r_{mt} denotes the excess returns of a world portfolio and r_{jt} denotes the excess returns of country j.

The research tries to identify the purposes why differences in countries performance exist, and define the country specific risk parameters. Without any further elaboration on the proposed methodology, it is clear that investors can benefit by the differences between stock returns among different countries. The existence of Internet facilities and consolidated markets provide, on one hand, the opportunity to investors to measure the risk of the shares as part of a global portfolio and further identify investment opportunities, and on the other hand, the chance to minimize the spreads among prices of companies that are traded in different capital markets.

Impact of Information Technology Evolution in the European Markets

The analysis concerning the European capital markets shall be based on two major areas. The first area is the impact of the technology to the financial markets and the participants, namely the investors, the issuers and the financial advisors, and how the technology enabled the trading process in the European markets. The second area of interest is the evolution of the markets, the trading platforms and the clearing and settlement process. The key concepts are the Internet, the sophisticated trading platforms and Web applications for the communication of the financial intermediaries and the market, and finally the subsequent consolidation of the capital markets that took place the recent years. The examples of "EURONEXT", and "OMX Exchanges", are cases to be analyzed in the next sections.

Figure 1. Number of personal computers per EU member (Source: Eurostat Yearbook 2004, The Statistical Guide to Europe - Data 1992-2002, European Communities 2004)

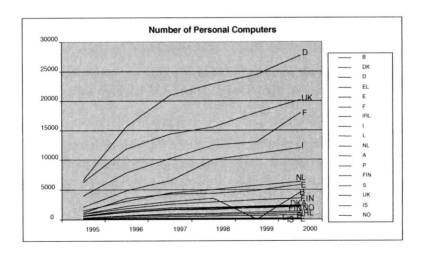

Figure 2. Evolution of Internet users the last decade in EU (Source: Eurostat Yearbook 2004, The Statistical Guide to Europe - Data 1992-2002, European Communities 2004)

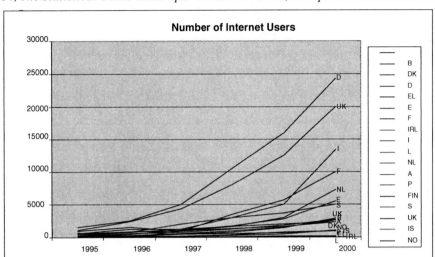

The first topic to be analyzed, however, is the use of technology and its evolution the past years in the European area, and especially the groups of people that use personal computers and Internet facilities.

Use of Personal Computers

One basic parameter that affects the daily operations of companies, persons, and in our case the markets are the number of personal computers used by the population of a country. Figure 1 presents the evolution of the number of personal computers per country.

It is obvious that the use of personal computers has increased significantly at the end of the century, for all the countries included in the European Union. This is a result of various parameters, such as the inclusion of informatics to the basic courses delivered to students, the advantages that the PCs offer, and the development of numerous applications and tools available to anyone.

Internet in the European Union

Internet is the communication channel of the future. In the previous section we examined the advantages that Internet offers to the capital markets and the international cooperations, by eliminating the distance and bringing in a common "non-physical" place the investors and the issuers.

Figure 3. Number of Internet hosts per EU member (Source: Eurostat Yearbook 2004, The Statistical Guide to Europe - Data 1992-2002, European Communities 2004)

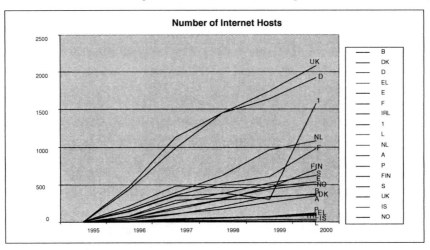

Table 1. Current situation in the European Union - Internet use (Source: www.InternetWorldStats.com)

EU	Population (2005 Est.)	Internet Users, Latest Data	User Growth (2000-2005)	Penetration (% Population)	% Users in EU
Austria	8,163,782	3,730,000	77.6 %	45.7 %	1.8 %
Belgium	10,443,012	3,769,123	88.5 %	36.1 %	1.8 %
Cyprus	950,947	250,000	108.3 %	26.3 %	0.1 %
Denmark	5,411,596	3,375,850	73.1 %	62.4 %	1.6 %
Finland	5,246,920	2,650,000	37.5 %	50.5 %	1.3 %
France	60,293,927	25,046,299	194.7 %	41.5 %	12.1 %
Germany	82.726,188	46,455,813	93.6 %	56.2 %	22.5 %
Greece	11,212,468	1,718,400	71.8 %	15.3 %	0.8 %
Hungary	10,083,477	2,400,000	235.7 %	23.8 %	1.2 %
Ireland	4,027,303	1,319,608	68.3 %	32.8 %	0.6 %
Italy	58,608,565	28,610,000	116.7 %	48.8 %	13.9 %
Luxembourg	455,581	170,000	70.0 %	37.3 %	0.1 %
Malta	384,594	120,000	200.0 %	31.2 %	0.1 %
Netherlands	16,316,019	10,806,328	177.1 %	66.2 %	5.2 %
Poland	38,133,891	8,970,000	220.4 %	23.5 %	4.4 %
Portugal	10,463,170	3,600,000	44.0 %	34.4 %	1.7 %
Spain	43,435,136	14,095,451	161.6 %	32.5 %	6.8 %
Sweden	9,043,990	6,722,553	66.1 %	74.3 %	3.3 %
United Kingdom	59,889,407	35,309,524	129.3 %	59.0 %	17.1 %
EU	459,938,780	206,196,749	121.3 %	44.8 %	100.0 %

The Internet users have increased dramatically during the period 1995-2000. It is quite indicative the fact that in 1995, Internet users in the European Union where 6.712.000, while in 2000, users exceeded the 100.000.000. One of the reasons was first of all the fact that the cost of getting an Internet connection was decreasing, while the providers of Internet services were significantly increasing. Figure 3 presents the number of hosts for the same period.

Figure 4. Current situation in the European Union - Internet use (Source: www.InternetWorldStats.com)

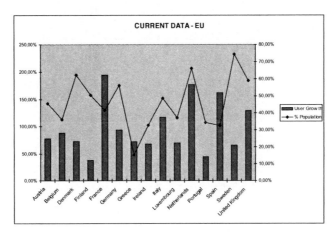

Table 1 provides the current situation of the Internet users, as well as the growth that occurred for the last five years, from 2000 to 2005. On average, the increase is more than 100% for the European area. However, it is important the fact that the percentage of population dealing with Internet and the services that are offered through the World Wide Web, is a rather increasing parameter.

It is obvious from the previous analysis that the target group of companies that provide electronic services in the European Union is still increasing. All the holders of Internet connection have access to all the companies and markets that offer electronic services, and especially electronic financial services through the Net. As a result, the number of potential investors that can open an account and make trades through the Internet is increasing, and this is a fact that is going to be examined in the next section.

European Capital Markets and IT Evolution

Brief History

The first signals of the information technology impact on the European capital markets appeared during the mid-'80s. The transformation process led to the disappearance of floor trading and the existence of electronic order book. Actually this evolution altered completely the nature of financial transactions, becoming dematerialized (electronic trading systems do not require the existence of "physical" shares). At that period, all the capital markets invested in automated trading systems, that would enable the activities

Table 2. Initiation of electronic markets in the European Union (Source: Internet - Sites of European Exchanges)

European Exchange	Electronic since
Amsterdam	1994
Austria	1999
Borsa Italiana	1994
Brussels	1996
Copenhagen	1999
Deutsche Borse	1992
Finland	1997
London Stock Exchange	1997
Madrid	1989
Oslo	1999
Paris Bourse	1994
Stockholm	1989
Greece	1999
Switzerland	1996

Table 3. Commission fees - European Union (1996-1999) (Source: Institutional Investor)

Country	1996	1997	1998	1999
		basis points		
Austria	40.3	39.9	54.1	42.7
Belgium	37.1	31.1	33.9	27.9
Denmark	35.7	45.4	43.4	41.1
Finland	41.9	42.3	44.0	40.7
France	29.9	26.7	26.6	24.9
Germany	39.3	33.3	27.6	28.7
Greece	64.4	66.9	63.6	87.3
Ireland	153.3	105.1	99.4	71.9
Italy	36.1	29.7	30.4	34.2
Luxembourg	75.5	73.0	70.0	102.3
Netherlands	69.3	25.8	30.0	28.4
Norway	46.1	34.0	36.4	34.4
Portugal	62.7	59.9	41.1	42.7
Spain	47.1	34.9	43.0	42.3
Sweden	36.1	30.6	30.9	31.5
Switzerland	37.1	44.0	46.0	36.5
UK cell	32.8	30.1	34.2	30.5

of a "non-physical" market, and reduce the cost trading for the investors. In contrast to the United States, most electronic trading facilities have developed within the existing exchanges.

At the late '90s, a growth of Internet-based retailed brokerage is observed, which has as a result the reduction of number of brokers. At that time, in the European era, the banking system plays an important role in the industry, by acquiring a major part of the activities traditionally implemented by brokerage companies.

Table 2 depicts when the traditional European stock markets became technologically advanced and electronic.

The introduction of automated financial markets had as a result the increase of the competition and the decrease of the transaction costs. One of the basic issues analyzed in the first section is that automation of the capital markets has as a result the reduction of cost that the investors bear. This fact, combined with the Internet facilities provided by the brokerage companies, led to the cost reduction. Table 3 presents estimation of the average costs in the European Union.

Two researches conducted for this issue prove the fact that the trading cost decreased in the European Capital markets, when these became automated. The first research is by Domowirz (2001) for the worldwide markets. Using dummy analysis techniques, it is proved that markets that are automated have total average trading costs on average 33 to 46 basis points lower than those of the non-automated markets, for the period 1996 to 1998. Degryse and Van Achter (2002), focusing in the European equity markets, show that in automated markets, the total trading cost is on average eight basis points lower than the non-automated markets. So it is obvious that the trading costs in Europe has been reduced, increasing simultaneously the liquidity for the high capitalization stocks.

However, although the trading process was becoming quite innovative, the back office activities and clearing and settlement process did not follow the stream of technology, especially for cross-border trading, which resulted in the increased cost for such trading.

As far as the trading activities are concerned, the main evolution is the cross-border merger of major European capital markets into a single market. In 2000, the French, Belgian and Dutch national stock exchanges merged into a single entity called Euronext. Further expansion of Euronext took place in 2001, when it took over the London Derivatives Market LIFFE and in 2002 the Portuguese Stock Exchange and Derivative Market merged with Euronext. Cross-membership was signed with HEX, the Helsinki Exchange, in 2001, while Swiss Stock Exchange acquired Tradepoint and launched Virt-x in the same year. Finally, OMX Exchanges (with its headquarters in Sweden) possess the Stockholm Stock Exchange and the Helsinki Stock Exchange. The consolidation of stock exchanges in Europe has an impact on the integration of financial markets in Europe. Specifically, it fosters the further development towards interoperability of clearing and settlement systems provided by different depositories, resulting in a cost-efficient euro area-wide mechanism.

The European Capital Markets and the Euro Introduction

One event that expected to change the way the markets were operating in the European Union, and lead to the creation of a single capital market, was the euro denomination and the use of the currency to most of the countries of the European Union. Eleven national currencies were converted into one single currency overnight. The successful launch of the euro has also boosted the integration of financial markets in the euro area. This process of integration in European financial markets coincided with the trend towards globalization. In January 1999, foreign exchange and interbank markets immediately switched over to the euro. At the same time, a single monetary policy was established, with a policy implementation framework for all euro area countries.

The most important advantage of a single currency is to erase currency differentials, which were one of the major barriers to cross-border trading and competition, as well as to reduce foreign exchange risk. For institutional investors, investment in the euro area is no longer restricted by foreign currency requirements, thereby simplifying cross-border investments. In addition, with financial institutions competing across national borders, financing and transaction costs are expected to decline. The process of trading, settlement and clearing becomes more efficient when a single denomination is used. Moreover, the existence of a single currency causes transparent pricing comparisons for the investors and the issuers.

Finally, the use of a single currency leads to the existence of national stock exchanges, considered as part of a single market. That phenomenon allows for economies of scale among markets and companies: On the supply side, the euro has stimulated a growing number of issuers and larger volumes of issues which have appealed to a larger investor base. The euro has increased the importance of the equity markets and attracted a number of new companies, mainly from IT-sector companies, which demonstrate a significant growth. On the demand side, the elimination of the exchange rate risk has helped the currency matching rule requirements imposed on many institutional investors for assets and liabilities. This has led to a shift to the national portfolio allocation in favor of assets from larger euro-zone members, and countries from outside the euro zone.

As far as the other markets are concerned, the deposit markets and the derivatives markets became fully integrated in early 1999. Moreover, the need to redistribute liquidity among euro area countries, including liquidity provided by the Eurosystem as part of its refinancing operations, fostered the development of area-wide transactions in the money

Figure 5. Number of online accounts 2001 - Europe (Source: JP Morgan 2000)

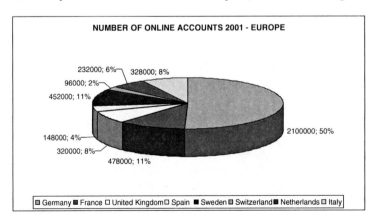

market. Another sector in which changes have taken place following the introduction of the euro is the euro-denominated bond market. Following the introduction of the euro, the euro-denominated component of international bond markets played a larger role than the predecessor currencies of the euro.

E-Brokerage in Europe

The significant growth of Internet in Europe had an important impact on securities markets. The markets demanded new forms of intermediation, which could take advantage the Internet technology, as well as innovation to the actual trading systems of the capital markets. As a result, new companies, belonging to the IT sector, or traditional financial intermediaries, that made agreements with IT vendors, started offering online trading alternatives to the investors, from the mid-'90s. The e-brokerage companies started to grow, but until 2000, their main target group was the domestic investors, without taking advantage of the cross-border trading they could offer using their online facilities. The next section briefly presents the top companies that offer online trading facilities in the European Union.

a.   *Online brokerage markets in Europe*

According to the data until 2000, Germany is the leader concerning the number of total online accounts for trading purposes, holding almost 50% of the European market. Germany is the largest market for online brokerage in Europe, while Sweden and France follow, holding approximately 11% each.

The industry has presented a substantial growth during 2001 (almost 25%), but the expectations for the next years are that the online services shall be increased.

Figure 6. Top 10 brokerage companies in Europe - 2001 (Source: JP Morgan 2000)

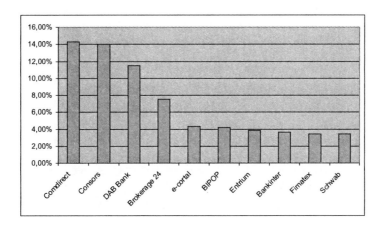

Table 4. Top 5 companies per country 2001 (Source: Internet - JP Morgan, 2000)

GERMANY	FRANCE	ITALY	SWEDEN	UK
Comdirect	e-cortal	BIPOP	SEB	Charles Schwab
Consors	Fimatex	IMI Web	Handelsbanken	Barcleys
DAB Bank	Selftrade	Medio SIM	HQ.SE	Halifax
Brokerage 24	ConSors	Directa	Nordnet	TD Waterhouse
Entrium	Ferri online	Sella it.	Netrade	DLJdirect

The reasons for such an evolution are already explained in the previous section: first of all, the wide use of Internet, that helped new providers and investors to gain access in the market, and secondly, the cost reduction, which allowed providers to start their operations without the necessity of building a branch network.

b.   *Top online brokers in Europe*

As far as the key players are concerned, most of the leading online brokerage companies operate in Germany. Figure 6 presents the top 10 online brokers in Europe, for 2000. Comdirect (a company owned by Commerzbank) and ConSors (73% owned by Schmidt) hold 30% of the total number of accounts in Europe.

Most of these companies operate a rather sophisticated Web site, where the online clients can open an account and send orders for execution.

Description of Major European Capital Markets

Until recently, each country in Europe had its own stock exchange, legal and regulatory framework. This fragmentation has led to low trading volumes and transactions conducted primarily among local investors, leading to higher settlement costs. Gradually, Europe has consolidated some of its stock exchanges and settlement institutions, such as the cross-border merging of stock exchanges. In early 2000, the first pole formed when the Paris, Amsterdam and Brussels exchanges began to allow trading of stocks listed on the other two exchanges. The same year, the exchanges merged into Euronext. A second pole is centered on Germany's Deutsche Borse Exchange. In 1999, the German securities depository, Deutsche Borse Clearing, and the other main international depository, Cedel, merged to become Clearstream. Although a central counterparty has not yet been established within this pole, the Deutsche Borse and Eurex, the large German derivatives exchange, have discussed an arrangement whereby Eurex would provide a central counterparty service for cash market transactions executed on the Deutsche Borse. A third pole exists in the United Kingdom. Although the London Stock Exchange, the London ClearingHouse, and CREST maintain separate ownership and governance structures, these organizations have aligned their operations more closely.

The most important mergers to be analyzed are the EURONEXT and OM Exchanges.

EURONEXT

Participating Markets:
Amsterdam Exchanges
Brussels Exchanges
Paris Bourse
London International Financial Futures and Options Exchange
Portuguese Stock Exchange

	NETHERLANDS	BELGIUM	FRANCE	PORTUGAL
Trading Markets	Euronext Amsterdam	Euronext Brussels Nasdaq Europe	Euronext Paris	Lisbon Trading MTS Portugal
Clearing and Settlement	Clearnet Amsterdam Euroclear Netherlands.	Clearnet SA Brus. NBB SSS Euronext CIK	Clearnet SA Euroclear France	InterBolsa SITEME
PARTICIPANTS				
No of Domestic Banks	24	64	391	2
No of Foreign Banks	23	65		0
No of Domestic Brokers	49	42	182	22
No of Foreign Brokers	52	15		1

Source: European Central Bank 2004, Frankfurt

Euronext is the first pan-European market, the result of the merger among the Amsterdam, Brussels and Paris stock exchanges. The market was announced in March 2000, and it was initiated by its financial alliances on September 22, 2000, with the incorporation of the company Euronext N.V. Shareholders of the Amsterdam Exchanges, Brussels Exchanges and ParisBourseSBF SA received shares in this new company in exchange for their existing interests. Following an agreed offer in October 2001, Euronext NV acquired LIFFE (the London International Financial Futures and Options Exchange) in January 2002, while BVLP, the Portuguese Stock Exchange joined Euronext in February 2002.

The market operators, subsidiaries of Euronext N.V., retain their identity under the new names Euronext Amsterdam N.V., Euronext Brussels S.A./N.V. and Euronext Paris S.A., so as to meet regulatory requirements, in particular as regards listing, and to ensure the integration of Euronext in the business culture of each country. Euronext's activities include:

- The drawing up common market rules, subject to approval by regulators in each of the countries concerned;

- The admission of securities and financial products to listing;

- Membership granding;

- Operation of electronic trading systems, trading information publishing and prices dissemination;

- Registration of trades between members with a clearing house, its subsidiary Clearnet, which acts as a central counterparty guaranteeing payment for securities sold and delivery of securities bought; and

- Provision to issuers with services for listing and trading of their securities.

Euronext combines a single trading platform serving all trading members and providing access to all shares, a single order book for each stock, a change which makes for greater market transparency and liquidity, a single clearing house acting as a central counterparty to guarantee payments and deliveries, and a single payment and delivery system.

The market indices are:

- AEX, BEL 20 and CAC 40 (calculated and disseminated the same way they did, before the initiation of Euronext).

- Euronext 100 Index, representing the first 100 companies on the Euronext market, ranked by market capitalization.

- Next 150 Index, representing the next 150 companies following those included in the Euronext 100.

- FTSEurofirst indices were launched on April 29, 2003, by Euronext and FTSE Group: FTSEurofirst 80 covers the current Eurozone and provides a basket of 80 stocks, and FTSEurofirst 100 provides a pan-European selection of 100 stocks, using only two currencies and offering a much easier way to trade across borders in Europe.

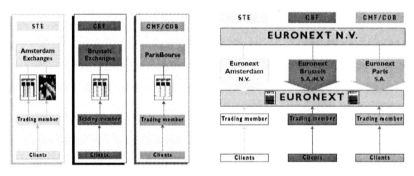

Source: www.euronext.com

Market Authority

The Market Authority is an independent authority constituted within Euronext Brussels under the Law of April 6, 1995. Its responsibilities include (a) transparency, integrity and security of Euronext Brussels securities markets and the public auctions market, and (b) compliance with the disclosure requirements in respect of share repurchases under the Belgian company code.

The Market Authority is also the competent authority as defined in Article 9(1) of the Listing Directive. To carry out its duties, the Market Authority has powers of investigation and may require any information or document that it deems necessary.

OMX Exchanges

Participating Markets:
Copenhagen Stock Exchange
Helsinki Stock Exchange
Stockholm Stock Exchange
Tallinn Stock Exchange
Riga Stock Exchange
Vilnius Stock Exchange

	DENMARK	**FINLAND**	**SWEDEN**
Trading Markets	Copenhagen Stock Exchange	Helsinki Securities and Derivatives Ex.	CLICK and SAXESS
Clearing and Settlement	VP A/S	Finnish Central Securities Depository	VPC AB
PARTICIPANTS			
No of Domestic Banks	17	6	8
No of Foreign Banks	9	3	NA
No of Domestic Brokers	4	11	26
No of Foreign Brokers	13	23	NA

Source: European Central Bank 2004, Frankfurt

OMX Group is a company that is established in Sweden and owns and operates one of the largest integrated securities market in northern Europe and is a leading provider of marketplace services and solutions for the financial and energy markets. OMX Group has two divisions: OMX Exchanges and OMX Technology:

- OMX Exchanges is the integrated Nordic and Baltic marketplace, that offers customers access to 80% of the Nordic and Baltic securities markets through its stock and derivatives exchange operations within the Stockholm Stock Exchange, the Helsinki Stock Exchange, the Riga Stock Exchange, the Tallinn Stock Exchange and the Vilnius Stock Exchange.

- OMX Technology is a provider of solutions and services — transaction technology, processing and outsourcing — based on advanced technology.

Trading Systems

Equity trading on OMX Exchanges is powered by the electronic trading system SAXESS™ developed by OMX Technology. SAXESS is an order-based system in which orders are electronically matched to a trade when price and volume match.

The trading process on OMX Exchanges' derivatives market is carried out in CLICK XT™ trading system, developed by OMX Technology. CLICK XT is a fully integrated electronic trading system that supports all trading from securities, derivatives, commodities and electricity contracts to cross-border trades, supporting multiple markets simultaneously on a single platform.

NOREX Exchanges

NOREX is the strategic alliance between the Nordic stock exchanges. NOREX has implemented a single trading platform for securities trading and by having harmonized rules and requirements with respect to trading and membership. The Alliance currently consists of the Copenhagen Stock Exchange, Iceland Stock Exchange, Oslo and Stockholm.

When Copenhagen and Stockholm originally formed the alliance, the focus was on moving equity trading to the joint trading system SAXESS (OMX Exchanges). The four NOREX markets comprise more than 800 companies. The electronic trading platform that NOREX uses is SAXESS. SAXESS offers to the members access to an electronic order book for each financial instrument with a number of facilities that supports liquidity. SAXESS offers functionality to support both order driven markets and price driven markets.

EDX London

EDX London is a derivatives exchange based in London that is jointly owned by the London Stock Exchange (76%) and OMX (24%). Combining the strength and liquidity of LSE with the advanced technology of OMX, EDX London is now considered a leading market for equity derivatives. In addition to offering trading services in derivatives products and access to trading and clearing services, EDX London is providing clearing and confirmation services for OTC deals in the derivatives market, based on OMX's SECUR technology.

Brief History of LSE and DB Cooperation

Since 2000, the London and Frankfurt Stock Exchanges were planning to cooperate in order to create the greatest European capital market, the "International Exchanges". Such agreement would mean a big step towards the creation of a unique European system of equity trading and a world market. For example, the capital markets of Milan and Madrid had signed an agreement for their future incorporation to "International Exchanges". The new market would have listed 135 of the best European companies in terms of market capitalization, and the volume would represent 53% of the total European volume. However, this agreement never led to the implementation of the International Exchanges. The next section describes the recent events:

- **May 2001:** LSE and Deutsche Boerse announce plans for pan-European bourse called iX (International Exchanges).
- **August 2001:** Sweden's OM bids for LSE, forcing it to withdraw from iX deal.
- **September 2001:** LSE bids for derivatives exchange LIFFE, which is eventually bought by Euronext.
- **December 2004:** Deutsche Boerse bid for LSE rejected.
- **December 2004:** Euronext says it is also interested in bidding for LSE.
- **January 2005:** Deutsche Boerse sets out its bid. (Source: BBC News)

References

Barber, B., & Odean, T. (2001). The Internet and the investor. *Journal of Economic Perspectives, 15*(1), 41-54.

Barclay, M., Hendershott, T., & McCormick, T. (2003). Competition among trading venues: Information and trading on electronic communications networks. *The Journal of Finance, 28*(6), 2637-2665.

Campbell, J., & Hamao, Y. (1992). Predictable stock returns in the United States and Japan: A study of long-term capital market integration. *The Journal of Finance, 17*(1), 43-67.

Degryse, H., & Van Achter, M. (2002). *Alternative trading systems and liquidity.* Working paper.

Domowitz, I. (2001). *Liquidity transaction costs, and intermediation in electronic markets.* Working paper.

European Central Bank. (2004). *Payment and securities settlement systems in the European Union.* Blue Book.

Eurostat Yearbook. (2004). *The statistical guide to Europe: Data 1992-2002,* European Communities.

FIWG. (2002). *Internet and securities market position paper.* FIWG.

Giordano, F. (2002). *Cross border trading in financial securities in Europe: The role of central counterparty.* European Capital Markets Institute, Madrid.

Harvey, C. (1993). The world price of covariance risk. *The Journal of Finance, 18*(1), 111-157.

JP Morgan. (2000). *Industry update – European online investor*. London: JP Morgan.

Levecq, H., & Weber, B. (2002). Electronic trading systems: Strategic implications of market design choices. *Journal of Organizational Computing and Electronic Commerce, 12*(1), 85-103.

Lin, L., Geng, X., & Whinston, A. (2001). *A new perspective to finance and competition and challenges for financial institutions in the Internet era*. BIS Papers 7.

Marshall, B., Crutchley, C., & Lending, D. (2004). Early Internet IPOs versus subsequent entrants. *Journal of Economics and Finance, 28*(1), 104-117.

OICV-IOSCO. (2001). *Report on securities activity on the Internet II*. The International Organization of Securities Commission, Internet Task Force Report, III.

OICV-IOSCO. (2003). *Report on Securities Activity on the Internet III*. The International Organization of Securities Commission.

Sahut, J. (2003). On-line brokerage in Europe: Actors and strategies. *Journal of Internet Banking and Commerce, 8*(1).

Schuler, M. (2002). *Integration of the European market for e-finance – Evidence from online brokerage*. Discussion paper 02-24. Centre for European Economic Research, Mannheim.

Web sites:

www.eurostat.org

www.euronext.com

www.omxgroup.com

www.londonstockexchange.co.uk

www.economist.com

Chapter VIII

International Capital Movements, Currency Crisis, and ICT Innovation

Sadayoshi Takaya, Kansai University, Japan

Abstract

This chapter investigates the effects generated by the currency crisis. The countries experienced the currency turmoil confronted financial crisis, economic deterioration, and increase of unemployment. This chapter empirically examines the effect of currency depreciation on the real GDP and the unemployment rates in those countries by employing the structural vector autoregressive model, which attempts to clarify whether identified supply or demand shocks can be caused by exchange rate depreciation. This study suggests currency crisis might generate demand shock, to result in harmful impacts to real economy in those countries. Those could be considered as negative effects of the ICT innovation.

Figure 1. Recent evolution of capital movements (Source: International Financial Statistics CD-ROM)

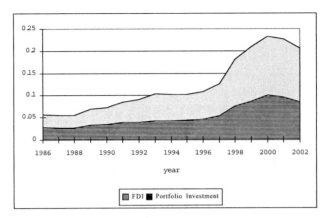

Note: Chart plots the sum of FDI and portfolio investments as a share of aggregate GDP for a sample of industrial countries including: Australia, Austria, Belgium, Canada, Finland, France, Germany, Italy, Japan, Netherlands, Spain, Sweden, Switzerland, United Kingdom and United States.

Introduction

In the 1990s, the currency turmoil exerted a great impact on emerging market countries such as Mexico, East Asian countries, Russia, Brazil, Argentina and so on. The crisis affected a broad spectrum of countries including not only those with prodigious signs but also those with sound economic conditions. Developments of theories on the currency crisis suggest self-fulfilling expectations and fundamental economic deterioration as the factors responsible for the crisis.

However, the institutional and technical changes such as liberalization of capital movements in the emerging countries or developments of information and communication technology (ICT) are noteworthy in an analysis of the currency turmoil. These changes caused instantaneous movements of capital among the countries. This chapter discusses the relationship observed between ICT innovation and the currency crisis in the 1990s.

This chapter emphasizes on the effects caused by the currency turmoil. It resulted in financial crisis, economic deterioration, and increase of unemployment in these countries. I will perform an empirical study on the effect of currency depreciation on the real GDP or the unemployment rates by employing the structural vector autoregressive model. Although, for this purpose, I essentially employ the model developed by Blanchard and Quah (1989), my empirical work attempts to clarify whether identified shocks or supply and demand shocks can be caused by exchange rate depreciation. This chapter uses this method to focus on the negative impact caused by ICT innovation.

Enormous financial globalization is observed toward the end of the 20th century (see Figure 1). Although, from a historical perspective, globalization is not a new phenomenon, Geiger (2001) reports the evolution of some new aspects as follows[1]:

Presently, globalization is not a stand-alone development but rather a manifestation of the six fundamental forces of change: (1) information and communication technology (ICT) advancements, (2) liberalization, (3) value orientation, (4) new demographic trends, (5) progress in the theory of finance and (6) Euroland.

1. ICT bridged the gap between neighboring countries and shortened the transaction time in the 1990s.

2. Recent liberalization of cross-border financial transaction facilitates gross capital flow not only between the developed countries but also between the developed and the developing countries in order to decrease the costs of financial transactions.

3. The economic value orientation has shifted from social democracy to neo-liberalization in numerous countries. This implies that the governments liberalize financial transactions to promote market-oriented policies.

4. The demographic trend of developed countries such as Japan is decreasing, while that of developing countries such as China is increasing. These opposite movements require a flow of labor from the developed to the developing countries, which results in the globalization of migration.

5. Progress in the theory of finance provides rational measures of domestic and international investments to investors in numerous countries. Meanwhile, the growing recognition of the theories of finance misleads amateur investors who easily invest their money in speculative financial assets.

6. The evolution of the euro in the EU is a new aspect of globalization in the 1990s because it might pose a currency competition in the near future between the current key currency — the U.S. dollar — and a new currency — the euro. This new aspect of globalization would cause an enormous capital shift between the euro and the U.S. dollar.

Globalization and ICT are ongoing trends. Particularly, as pointed out in (2), financial globalization is significant determinant of the some adverse impacts such as currency crisis, which is considered to be a major example. Globalization is characterized as large amounts of not only net but also gross movements of capital since the 1990s. Gross capital movements imply two types of capital flows; ones are the flows among intra-developed countries such as intra-industry trades and others are the flows between developed and developing countries. The latter pattern is represented by traditional theory of capital movements. The former pattern is recent one that would be explained by application of intra-industry trade theory. The former case cannot be explained by traditional theory because the rates of return among the developed countries do not differ greatly. Therefore, the determinants of capital movements are identified as follows:

1. rates of return,
2. taxation,
3. liquidity,
4. maturity,
5. geography, and
6. risk (sovereign, corporate, currency, etc.).

In general, capital flow depends on the difference in the rates of return between two countries, which also pertains to tax rates or other transaction costs such as liquidity and maturity. Under the uncertainty of asset prices and defaults, investors and speculators are obliged to take risks into account. Due to these risks, there exists a variety in issuers, which includes governments and corporations in numerous countries. Developed countries have large financial markets in which diversified securities in risks are seen circulating, whereas developing countries do not have them due to the lack of liquidity. Therefore, capital movements among the developed countries are more frequent than between the developed and the developing countries. These are known as gross capital movements[2].

ICT and globalization accelerate these gross capital movements through the transaction of hedge funds and mutual funds. They also reduce the currency turmoil or financial crisis in the more financially open countries. Explanations for the crisis are provided by using

Figure 2. Factors of international capital movements

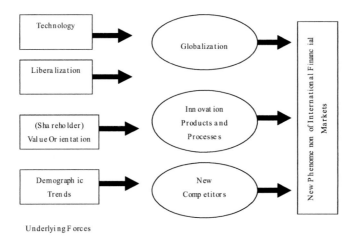

Underlying Forces

Source: Greiger (2001) and author

the following three models: first-generation model, second-generation model, and third-generation model. The first-generation model explains the crisis based on the deterioration of fundamentals such as fiscal deficits, money supplies, saving rates and so forth. The second-generation model accounts for the crisis through a change in the level of confidence in fixed exchange rate regimes; this model generally includes multiple equilibriums[3]. The third-generation model simultaneously links the crisis with a financial crisis within the same country. The model provides the logic of genesis of twin crisis such as the Asian currency crisis[4].

This chapter focuses on the effects of the crisis on the economic fundamentals, not on the explanations of the crisis, because these effects are the negative consequences arising from ICT innovation and globalization.

Before I empirically investigate the effects of the currency crisis in the next section, a theoretical background has to be provided on an economic basis. I suppose a Keynesian type open macro model or a sluggish price model such as the Dornbush-type model for this purpose.

On the supply side, because the product function is supposed to depend on imported capital goods and labor, the supply function depends on real wage and real exchange rate. A supply shock is induced by innovation and/or real exchange rate fluctuation. On the other hand, the aggregate demand side includes trade (exports and imports of goods and services), consumption, and investment. Trade depends on the real exchange rate, which is exogenous in this case. The interest rate is decided by the money market. The aggregate demand is subject to a demand shock that is induced by increased money supply, real exchange rate fluctuation, and/or fiscal deficit. Price is supposed to be sluggish so that the demand shock may effectuate a temporal positive movement of production.

Does depreciation induce a negative supply shock or a positive demand shock? Which of the two shocks induced larger effects before and after the currency turmoil in the 1990s? This is the empirical problem pertaining to the effects of the currency crisis.

The remaining chapter is organized following the following manner. In section 2, the empirical model is explained for analyzing the effects of the currency turmoil on the real economies of the developing countries. I employed the structural VAR model for this purpose, which can easily identify exogenous shocks. In section 3, I regress the identified shock on the change of exchange rates in order to analyze the direction and magnitude of currency crisis with respect to the GDP and unemployment rates. Section 4 concludes.

SVAR Model and Impulse Reaction Function

A typical restriction, compatible with the Keynesian type model, is that demand shocks have zero impact on output in the long run. Blanchard and Quah (1989) show that this long-run restriction can be used to identify the underlying structural shocks — demand shock and supply shock — in the vector autoregressive model. I employed their long-run restriction to identify the shocks in the countries before and after the currency crisis.

Consider a system where the model can be represented by an infinite moving average representation of a set of variables, z_t, and shocks ε_t. Using a lag operator L, the variables can be written as:

$$\Delta z_t = A_0 \varepsilon_t + A_1 \varepsilon_{t-1} + A_2 \varepsilon_{t-2} \cdots$$
$$= A(L)\varepsilon_t \qquad (1)$$

where $z_t = (y,p)'$, $A(L) = A_0 + A_1 L + A_2 L^2 + \ldots$, represents the matrix polynomial in the lag operator L. $\varepsilon_t = (\varepsilon_{st}, \varepsilon_{dt})$ is serially uncorrelated, and $E[\varepsilon_t, \varepsilon_t']$ is normalized to the identity matrix. I assume that the structural shocks are orthogonal and that their variances are normalized to unity. The VMA representation of the VAR can be written as follows:

$$\Delta z_t = C(L)u_t, \qquad (2)$$

where $C(L) = C_0 + C_1 L + C_2 L^2$ and the first matrix in the polynomial $C(L)$ is the identity matrix. The disturbance vector $u_t = (u_{st}, u_{dt})'$ is a vector of reduced form disturbances with $E(u_t) = 0$ and $E[u_t u_t'] = \Omega$. u_t has an estimated covariance matrix Σ.

Equations (1) and (2) imply a linear relationship between ε_t and u_t:

$$u_t = C_0 \varepsilon_t, \qquad (3)$$

where C_0 is selected to satisfy

$$C_0 C_0' = \Sigma. \qquad (4)$$

Equation (2) can be written as:

$$\Delta z_t = D(L)e_t$$
$$= D(1)e_t + D^*(L)\Delta \varepsilon_t,$$

where $D(L) = C(L)R$ and $D(L) = D(1) + D^*(L)(1-L)$. On integrating, we get:

$$z_t = z_0 + D(1)\tau_t + D^*(L)\Delta \tau_t,$$

Table1. Estimation period

Countries	Beginning	Ending
Indonesia	1994q1	2000q3
Korea	1994q2	2000q4
Malaysia	1994q1	2000q3
Philippines	1994q1	2000q3
Thailand	1994q1	2000q3
Ireland	1989q2	1995q4
Italy	1989q2	1995q4
Sweden	1989q2	1995q4
United Kingdom	1989q2	1995q4
Argentina	1998q4	2004q1
Brazil	1995q2	2001q3
Mexico	1991q4	1998q2

where $\varepsilon_t \Delta\tau$ and $\tau_t = (\tau_{1t}, \tau_{2t})'$ is a vector of uncorrelated common stochastic trends. Equation (3) does not identify C_0 uniquely. Therefore, when z_t is an $n \times 1$ vector, we need $n^2 = 4$ restrictions. Blanchard and Quah (1989) provide an economic theory that suggests this restriction. The symmetric matrix Σ imposes three of the four required restrictions, therefore, one additional identifying restriction is required, which implies that the cumulative effect of demand shocks on the change of output should be zero. Long-run restriction implies that $D(1)_{12} = 0$.

Data

This chapter aims to separate demand shocks from supply shocks in order to regress their shocks on exchange rate fluctuations. Therefore, I consider a VAR on the variables, growth rates and inflation rates. I obtained monthly data for the study, which is directed toward Asian countries under the currency turmoil, such as Indonesia, Korea, Malaysia, the Philippines and Thailand; European countries under the ERM crisis, such as Ireland, Italy, Sweden and the United Kingdom; and Latin American countries under the crisis, such as Argentina, Brazil and Mexico. Table 1 shows individual samples for estimation.

I retrieved data for two types of monthly series that is, seasonally adjusted industrial production and consumer prices from the *International Financial Statistics CD-ROM*. Data is available for samples from countries under consideration for 13 time points before and after currency crisis.

Table 2. Optimum lag

Countries	Optimum Lags of VAR
Indonesia	4
Korea	1
Malaysia	2
Philippines	1
Thailand	2
Ireland	1
Italy	4
Sweden	1
United Kingdom	4
Argentina	1
Brazil	4
Mexico	2

*Optimum lag order is determined by Akaike information criteria (AIC) in our model.

Unit Roots

It is essential to determine whether the variables are stationary around the stochastic or the deterministic trends. We examine the augmented Dickey Fuller (ADF) test and Phillips-Perron test, and their statistics are confirmed to be lesser than 10% critical value for the variables[5]. Therefore, the growth rate of output and inflation rate of all interested countries are stationary. In other words, I cannot reject the hypothesis of nonstationarity of the growth and inflation rates.

Estimation Results

This section shows the estimation results obtained by employing the stationary reduced-form VAR models, which were estimated with OLS. The VAR models have an optimum lag order that is determined by Akaike Information Criterion (AIC), and the lags are listed in Table 2.

Next, we examine the impulse response of each of the explanatory variables to a unit positive innovation in each of the fundamental shocks using a variety of specifications. Initially, I conducted an analysis of a VAR system of output growth rates and inflation rates. The impulse responses of the explanatory variables are shown from Figures 3 to 6.

First, the responses of growth rate to supply shocks are presented in Figure 3, which are classified by regional areas. Figure 3a shows the responses of growth rate to supply shocks in the Asian countries that were affected by the Asian currency turmoil in 1997. Among these Asian countries, the shocks in Korea are noted to have the greatest effects

Figure 3a. Accumulated response of growth rate to supply shock

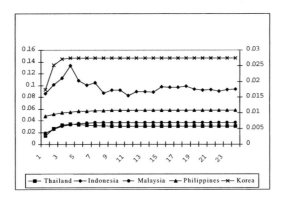

Figure 3b. Accumulated response of growth rate to supply shock

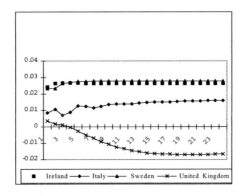

Figure 3c. Accumulated response of growth rate to supply shock

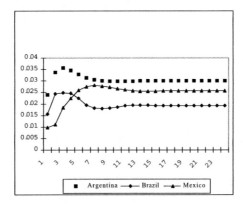

on the growth rate. The shocks in Indonesia are noted to have the next greatest impact. Third greatest impact is noted in a group including Malaysia, Philippines and Thailand.

Figure 3b presents the accumulated response of growth rate to supply shock in the European countries under the ERM currency crisis, that is, Ireland, Italy, Sweden and United Kingdom. Among the four European countries, Ireland and Sweden are noted to have the greatest impact on the growth rate followed by Italy. United Kingdom is initially noted to have a positive effect; however, it is noted to have a negative effect after a four-period lag.

Figure 3c shows the responses of growth rate to supply shocks in the Latin American countries that were affected by the currency turmoil in the 1990s. The responses of all three countries are similar in size and pattern.

The responses of growth rate to supply shocks in the Asian countries are greater than those of the other countries. This implies that the supply shocks mostly affect the growth rates of the Asian countries.

Figure 4a. Accumulated response of growth rate to demand shock

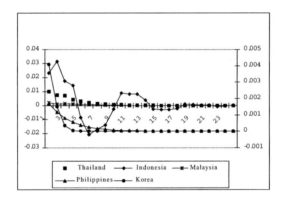

Figure 4b. Accumulated response of growth rate to demand shock

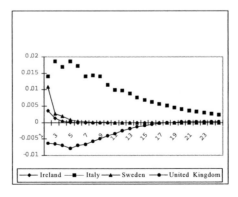

Figure 4c. Accumulated response of growth rate to demand shock

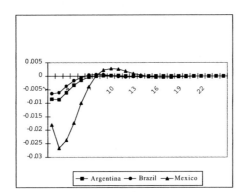

The accumulated responses of growth rate to demand shocks are presented in Figure 4. Figure 4a shows the response of growth rate to demand shocks in the Asian countries. Korea's response is initially positive; however, it is noted to be negative after a three-period lag. Indonesia's response is noted to have a cyclical effect with damping. Thailand's and Malaysia's responses are noted to have minimal effects. Philippines' response is noted to be negative.

Figure 4b presents the response of growth rate to demand shocks among the European countries. Italy is noted to have the greatest positive effect. Ireland and Sweden are noted to have minimal positive effects. United Kingdom initially is noted to have a large negative effect; however, it is gradually noted to become positive.

Figure 4c shows the responses of growth rate to demand shocks among the Latin American countries, which initially indicate all negative effects. The size and pattern of

Figure 5a. Accumulated response of inflation rate to supply shock

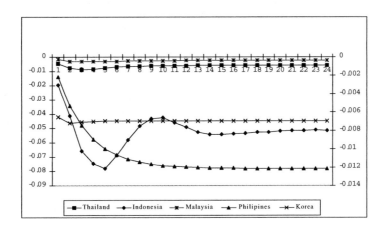

5b. Accumulated response of inflation rate to supply shock

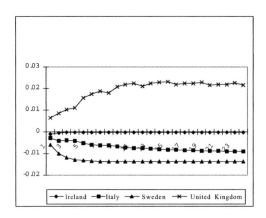

5c. Accumulated response of inflation rate to supply shock

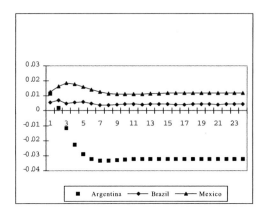

their responses are also similar. Therefore, positive demand shocks in the Latin American countries experiencing the currency crisis have negative impacts on the growth rates.

The responses of inflation rate to supply shocks are presented in Figure 5. Figure 5a shows that all responses of inflation rate to supply shocks in the Asian countries are negative. These results are consistent with the theoretical background, that is, standard Keynesian model with sticky prices. In the event of a positive supply shock such as technical innovation, a firm is able to produce more for the price to decrease. If one must equate the countries with the firms, the response of prices will be identical to that explained in the Keynesian model with sticky prices.

Figures 5b and 5c present the responses of inflation rate to supply shocks in the European countries and the Latin American countries, respectively. Excluding United Kingdom, the effects for all other countries are negative, which is consistent with the theoretical insights. The response of inflation rates to supply shocks in the United Kingdom has a positive effect.

The responses of inflation rate to supply shocks in the Latin American countries are presented in Figure 5c. Argentina's response is consistent with the theory; however, Brazil and Mexico are noted to have adverse responses. The abovementioned results indicate that the responses of inflation rate to supply shocks are ambiguous in Latin American countries.

The responses of inflation rates to demand shocks are presented in Figure 6. Figure 6a shows the response of inflation rates to demand shocks in the Asian countries. Indonesia's response is indicated to be greater than the other countries, which in turn are noted to have minimal responses. Figures 6b and 6c present the responses of European countries and Latin American countries, respectively. These figures imply that demand shocks cause inflation in all countries.

Figure 6a. Accumulated response of inflation rate to demand shock

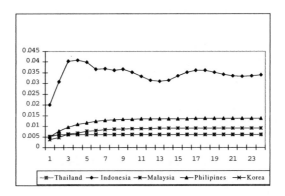

Figure 6b. Accumulated response of inflation rate to demand shock

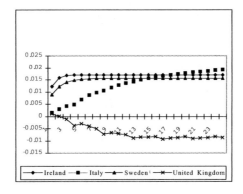

Figure 6c. Accumulated response of inflation rate to demand shock

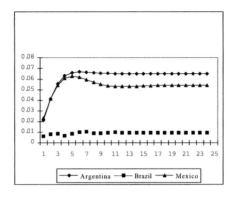

Using the restriction suggested by Blanchard and Quah (1998), I have identified the exogenous shocks as supply and demand shocks. However, I have not analyzed the relationship between the currency crisis and these exogenous shocks. If the real economy remains unaffected by the currency turmoil, then currency depreciation does not cause exogenous shocks. In other words, if depreciation causes significant shocks, then currency turmoil affects not only financial markets but also the real economy. Therefore, I present a regression analysis of exchange rate fluctuations on exogenous shocks.

Shocks and Exchange Rate Behaviors

I estimate the effects of exchange rate behaviors on the supply and demand shocks in order to examine whether the macroeconomics of a country affected by the currency turmoil is actually disturbed.

The supply and demand shocks derived in the previous section are regressed on the rates of change in exchange rates. The data pertaining to exchange rates are collected from the *International Financial Statistics CD-ROM*.

The results are presented in Tables 3 and 4. Table 3a shows the results of the regression of supply shocks on the rates of change in exchange rates. The intercepts of Korea, Thailand, Indonesia, Malaysia, Philippines or the East Asian countries under the Asian currency turmoil (symbolized as Const) are insignificant, and the rates of change in exchange rates (symbolized as Exr) are all significant because the probabilities are smaller than that at the 5% level. Further, all signs are negative. This implies that the changes in exchange rates are able to cause negative supply shocks. As examined above, the Asian currency crisis led to a reduction in output in five countries through the supply function, in which the real exchange rates are taken into account as imports of capital goods.

Table 3a. East Asia

dependent variable:Supply Shock										
Country	Thailand		Indonesia		Malaysia		Philippines		Korea	
	Coefficients	Prob.	Coefficients	Prob.	Coefficients	Prob.	Coefficients	Prob.	Coefficients	Prob.
Const.	0.028	0.803	0.069	0.599	0.049	0.472	0.086	0.513	0.094	0.224
	(0.111)		(0.531)		(0.068)		(0.130)		(0.075)	
Exr	-3.044	0.044	-1.877	0.013	-5.009	0.001	-5.180	0.046	-6.428	0.000
	(1.434)		(2.603)		(1.376)		(2.507)		(1.097)	
Adj.R-squared	0.119		0.135		0.239		0.077		0.594	
S.E. of regression	0.567		0.782		0.422		0.779		0.468	
Sum squared resid	8.029		22.012		6.769		23.053		5.477	
D.W.	2.094		2.117		2.161		2.209		2.451	
Sample	1994q1:2000q3		1994q1:2000q3		1994q1:2000q3		1994q1:2000q3		1994q2:2000q4	
Obs.	27		27		27		27		27	
Option									N.W.	
Standard errors are reported in parenthesis										
N.W. means that coefficient covariance of Newey-West was used in estimation.										

dependent variable: Supply Shock

Table 3b. Latin America

dependent variable:Supply Shock						
Country	Mexico		Brazil		Argentina	
	Coefficients	Prob.	Coefficients	Prob.	Coefficients	Prob.
Const.	0.129	0.252	-0.024	0.889	0.002	0.995
	0.110		(0.167)		(0.228)	
Exr	-3.295	0.000	1.393	0.430	-1.253	0.129
	(0.306)		(1.730)		(0.769)	
Adj.R-squared	0.186		-0.017		0.014	
S.E. of regression	0.656		0.697		0.934	
Sum squared resid	9.898		9.716		10.467	
D.W.	2.500		1.951		2.468	
Sample			1996q2:2001q4		2000q2:2003q4	
Obs.	27		27		15	
Option	N.W.				N.W.	
Standard errors are reported in parenthesis						
N.W. means that coefficient covariance of Newey-West was used in estimation.						

dependent variable: Supply Shock

Table 3c. Western Europe

dependent variable:Supply Shock								
Country	Ireland		Italy		Sweden		UK	
	Coefficients	Prob.	Coefficients	Prob.	Coefficients	Prob.	Coefficients	Prob.
Const.	0.035	0.864	0.097	0.611	-0.032	0.863	0.008	0.924
	(0.201)		(0.188)		(0.184)		(0.084)	
Exr	-4.690	0.461	-1.447	0.812	-1.314	0.799	-1.384	0.634
	(6.266)		(6.010)		(5.092)		(2.871)	
Adj.R-squared	-0.033		-0.038		-0.037		-0.030	
S.E. of regression	0.846		0.905		0.931		0.407	
Sum squared resid	17.892		20.465		21.660		4.149	
D.W.	1.628		2.161		1.913		2.072	
Sample	1989q2:1995q4		1989q2:1995q4		1989q2:1995q4		1989q2:1995q4	
Obs.	27		27		27		27	
Option	N.W.							
Standard errors are reported in parenthesis								
N.W. means that coefficient covariance of Newey-West was used in estimation.								

dependent variable: Supply Shock

Table 3b shows the results of the regression of supply shocks on the rates of change in exchange rates of Latin American countries, which suggests that all intercepts are insignificant and that the change in exchange rates is significant for Mexico but insignificant for Argentina and Brazil.

Table 3c presents the results of the regression of supply shocks on the rates of change in exchange rates of European countries. It indicates that all intercepts and the change in exchange rates are insignificant. This indicates that the ERM crisis did not affect supply shocks; in other words, the crisis did not cause long-term real shocks in these countries. In our opinion, supply functions of developed countries, such as the European countries, are not composed of real exchange rates because these countries do not usually depend on the imports of capital goods. There may be an asymmetric effect on output through the supply function between the developing and the developed countries.

Table 4a. East Asia

dependent variable:Demand Shock										
Country	Thailand		Indonesia		Malaysia		Philippines		Korea	
	Coefficients	Prob.	Coefficients	Prob.	Coefficients	Prob.	Coefficients	Prob.	Coefficients	Prob.
Const.	-0.015	0.751	-0.003	0.987	-0.032	0.573	0.051	0.676	-0.062	0.711
	(0.048)		(0.186)		(0.056)		(0.121)		(0.164)	
Exr	1.353	0.066	0.081	0.902	3.225	0.006	-3.076	0.195	5.932	0.000
	(0.715)		(0.652)		(1.118)		(2.333)		(1.101)	
Adj.R-squared	0.062		-0.028		0.130		0.019		0.217	
S.E. of regression	0.296		1.133		0.378		0.725		0.941	
Sum squared resid	3.333		46.227		5.443		19.956		22.117	
D.W.	2.186		2.045		1.712		2.018		2.305	
Sample	1994q1:2000q3		1994q1:2000q3		1994q1:2000q3		1994q1:2000q3		1994q2:2000q4	
Obs.	27		27		27		27		27	
Option					N.W.				N.W.	
Standard errors are reported in parenthesis										
N.W. means that coefficient covariance of Newey-West was used in estimation.										

dependent variable: Demand Shock

Table 4b. Latin America

dependent variable:Demand Shock						
Country	Mexico		Brazil		Argentina	
	Coefficients	Prob.	Coefficients	Prob.	Coefficients	Prob.
Const.	-0.410	0.430	-0.024	0.889	-0.081	0.658
	(0.511)		(0.167)		(0.179)	
Exr	10.503	0.000	1.393	0.430	0.580	0.440
	(1.361)		(1.730)		(0.727)	
Adj.R-squared	0.080		-0.017		-0.044	
S.E. of regression	3.027		0.697		0.704	
Sum squared resid	210.698		9.716		5.950	
D.W.	2.437		1.951		2.254	
Sample			1996q2:2001q4		2000q2:2003q4	
Obs.	27		27		15	
Option	N.W.				N.W.	
Standard errors are reported in parenthesis						
N.W. means that coefficient covariance of Newey-West was used in estimation.						

dependent variable: Demand Shock

Table 4c. Western Europe

dependent variable:Demand Shock									
Country	Ireland		Italy		Sweden		UK		
	Coefficients	Prob.	Coefficients	Prob.	Coefficients	Prob.	Coefficients	Prob.	
Const.	-0.072	0.335	0.045	0.602	-0.031	0.864	0.026	0.933	
	(0.073)		(0.086)		(0.182)		(0.305)		
Exr	-38.386	0.000	1.068	0.700	5.566	0.280	0.243	0.982	
	(3.082)		(2.739)		(5.039)		(10.476)		
Adj.R-squared	0.646		-0.034		0.008		-0.040		
S.E. of regression	0.411		0.412		0.921		1.487		
Sum squared resid	4.232		4.249		21.214		55.252		
D.W.	2.240		2.190		1.930		1.896		
Sample	1989q2:1995q4		1989q2:1995q4		1989q2:1995q4		1989q2:1995q4		
Obs.	27		27		27		27		
Option	N.W.								
Standard errors are reported in parenthesis									
N.W. means that coefficient covariance of Newey-West was used in estimation.									

dependent variable: Demand Shock

Table 4a shows the results of regression of demand shocks on the rates of change in exchange rates of East Asian countries under the Asian currency turmoil. The intercepts of all five countries are insignificant. The changes in exchange rates of Malaysia and Korea are significantly below the 1% critical value and that of Thailand is significantly below the 10% critical value. The changes in exchange rates of Indonesia and Philippines are insignificant. Since depreciation theoretically promotes exports to increase outputs with prices stickiness, the outputs of Malaysia, Korea and Thailand were stimulated post crisis; however, the outputs of Indonesia and Philippines were not stimulated by the currency crisis.

Table 4b shows the results of regression of demand shocks on the rates of change in the exchange rates of Latin American countries under the currency turmoil in the 1990s. The intercepts of all three countries are insignificant. The changes in exchange rates of Mexico are significant, whereas those of Argentina and Brazil are insignificant.

Table 4c presents the results of regression of demand shocks on the rates of change in the exchange rates of European countries under the ERM crisis. The intercepts of all three countries are insignificant. The changes in the exchange rates of Ireland are significant, while those of the other countries are insignificant.

If exchange rate fluctuations cause these shocks, then depreciation crisis has not only nominal but also real economic effects. As mentioned above, the Asian currency crisis caused real effects on the economies. Supply shocks induced by exchange rate depreciation caused negative shocks in Asian countries by decreasing the imports of capital goods, whereas demand shocks induced by depreciation caused a positive shock by promoting exports. As a result, Thailand, Malaysia and Korea recovered almost two years post crisis, while Indonesia and Philippines did not recover quickly in the absence of positive demand shocks induced by the depreciation.

The ERM crisis did not result in supply and demand shocks induced by the depreciation. It implies that European countries had economic structures that could not be influenced by external monetary shocks. These countries have developed economic structures that do not usually depend on imports of capital goods. Therefore, the effects of the crisis were limited in these countries, whereas East Asia and Mexico were noted to have serious effects caused by the currency crisis. The economic structures of the latter countries depended on their imports in order to control the supply of industrial goods.

The economic structures of countries contributed to difference of impacts of the crisis. If a country has the structure of a developed economy, it will not be seriously affected by the large depreciation, whereas another country that has the structure of a developing economy will be seriously affected by the depreciation.

Conclusions

It may not be possible for any individual or institution to discontinue the trend of ICT development as it is considered to be one of the historical aspects. In a similar manner, globalization is also another historical aspect since nothing can ever discontinue the trend, although the rate at which the trend continues can be decreased. However, these trends bear serious impacts on developing economies through the currency crisis, which is occasionally a political and social turmoil such as the cases seen in Indonesia.

Since a currency turmoil is expected in such conditions, the establishment of an international financial architecture to robustly avoid the crisis will be required. On the other hand, the developing countries, particularly those with emerging markets, have to establish a rigid economy that does not depend on the imports of capital goods, as investigated by us in the previous sections.

The East Asian countries developed a new international financial architecture post 1997, which is known as Chiang Mai Initiatives that include the swap agreement of central banks among East Asian Countries, Japan, China, Thailand and so on. The initiatives had the capability to temporally counter massive speculative attacks in these countries but not necessarily forefend the economies from the attacks. Developments of ICT and globalization may launch the attacks in small open economies that are fragile toward the crisis, despite a well-designed architecture.

Needless to say, although the current international financial architectures, which are vulnerable to the speculative attacks, should be re-formed for prevention against currency crisis, it is not sufficient for the 21st century system that has a substantial amount of speculative capital flows. Therefore, it is imperative for these countries to have a robust economy even if the speculations attack the exchange rate regimes in these countries. In other words, these economies are required to step up their initiatives for endurance against the currency turmoil.

References

Blanchard, O., & Quah, D. (1989). The dynamic effects of aggregate demand and aggregate supply shocks. *American Economic Review, 79*, 655-673.

Committee on the Global Financial System. (2001). *The implications of electronic trading in financial markets*. Basle: Bank for International Settlements.

Geiger, H. (2001). Globalisation and payment intermediation. In M. Balling, E. H. Hochreiter & E. Hennessy (Eds.), *Adapting to financial globalisation* (pp. 191-209). London: Routledge.

Gordon, R. (2000). The aftermath of the 1992 ERM breakup: Was there a macroeconomic free lunch? In P. Krugman (Ed.), *Currency crisis* (pp. 241-284). Cambridge, MA: MIT Press.

Lane, P. R., & Milesi-Ferretti, G. (2004, October). *Financial globalization and exchange rates*. Mimeo. International Monetary Fund.

Miller, V. (1996). Speculative currency attacks with endogenously induced commercial bank crises. *Journal of International Money and Finance, 15*, 383-403.

Obstfeld, M. (1994). The logic of currency crises. *Cahiers Economiques et Monétaires, 43*,189-213.

Obstfeld, M. (2004). External adjustment. NBER working paper 10843.

Radelet, S., & Sachs, J. D. (1998). The East Asian financial crises: Diagnosis, remedies, prospects. *Brookings Papers on Economic Activity, 1*, 1-74.

White, W. R. (1998). *The coming transformation of continental European banking?* Basle: Bank for International Settlements.

Endnotes

[1]   We refer to Geiger (2001) for enumeration; however, the evolution of new aspects of globalization is described in this chapter from my perspective.

[2]   Gross capital movements can be explained by logic similar to the intra-industry trade. See Obstfeld (2004) for details.

[3]   For details, see Obstfeld (1986).

[4]   For details, see (1997).

[5]   The results are omitted to restrict the total number of pages.

Chapter IX

Volatility Spillover Structure of Stock and Foreign Exchange Market between Korea, Japan, and Hong Kong

Masayuki Susai, Nagasaki University, Japan

Abstract

Highly developed IT technology can be the source of volatility spillover between markets located in other countries. In this chapter, we investigate the interrelationship between stock returns in North East Asian countries and the effect of foreign exchange rate volatility on the interrelationship between stock returns. We bring out clear simultaneous interrelationship between stock return and foreign exchange volatility. Focusing on covariance of each asset returns, if we do not take foreign exchange rate volatility into account when we evaluate our international portfolio, the portfolio risk might be underevaluated. The analysis shows that foreign exchange market turbulence might be accompanied by increase in covariance between stock returns. Just after the Asian currency crisis, the relationship between stock returns and foreign exchange turbulence might have changed. For managing international portfolio risk, we should be aware of foreign exchange risk and structural change in covariance between stock returns.

Introduction

Information technology in financial industry has been developing at amazing speed. The information inflowed into a particular financial market can be transferred to other market within a minute or even a couple of second through many kinds of Internet tools. In this circumstance, volatility in any particular market can be transmitted to other markets, which is located even in other countries, caused by informational trade if traders act following efficient market hypothesis. This volatility transmission mechanism has been investigated in many articles[1]. IT technology development has been accelerating this tendency in world financial market. The more IT technology develops, the closer the financial asset returns might co-move. Contagion in volatility co-movement during currency attack can be one of the important results arising from this mechanism.

In a globalized financial world, the importance of international capital flow has been stressed to afford the good opportunity to invest and finance. For investing and financing internationally, we have to be careful about the portfolio risk. Many methods to manage international portfolio risk are proposed from finance and economics field. To manage the portfolio risk in the first step, we should recognize the risk itself or the source of the risk. Cross-country stock return or those volatility covariances are one of the most important respects in international portfolio risk management in highly developed IT technology days from the reason just mentioned above. In this chapter, we try to explore the volatility structure between financial markets located in different countries and the effect of foreign exchange rate change on those structures. If the IT technology breeds information transfer between the markets, we might expect that there exist some kind of volatility relations.

Karolyi and Stulz (1996) emphasize the importance of stock return covariances between countries in some respects. As these covariances increase, internationally diversified portfolio risk increases. Financing cost for individual firms also rise through covariance increase. One of the important components, which may effect the international relationship between stock markets, is foreign exchange rate.

Some theoretical articles infer that the stability of foreign exchange rate may induce higher asset price variability with a given random shocks[2]. This tendency can be called volatility transfer hypothesis. A lot empirical study is showing that the stability of foreign exchange rate contributes to ease volatility of asset prices[3]. Fratianni and Hagen (1990), Artis and Taylor (1994) used EMS and related data to test this relationship.

Multivariate GARCH with constant correlation is used in Longin and Solnik (1995) to investigate whether the correlation of international equity returns is constant. They suggest that the conditional covariance structure of international equity returns may change over time. And the correlation increases in periods in high volatility.

With the EMS experience, Bodart and Reding (1999) explores the relationship between exchange rate stability and international correlation of asset returns. They use bivariate GARCH model with constant conditional correlation and bring out that credible peg system can reduce bond market volatility, and an increase in exchange rate volatility is accompanied by a decline in international correlation between stock returns.

The transmission and spillover structure of foreign exchange rate volatility is studied by multivariate GARCH model in Kearney and Patton (2000). In Kearney and Patton (2000), they use up to five variable multivariate GARCH with BKKK (Baba, Engle, Kraft, & Kroner, 1990) parameterization. Within the EMS, Deutsche Mark played a dominant role and transmitted more volatility to other currencies. ECU also transmitted volatility to other currencies through covariance terms. Another objective in Kearney & Patton (2000) is to check for specification robustness in multivariate GARCH model and they chose multivariate GARCH (1,1) model[4].

In this chapter, we focus on the covariance structure of volatility in stock returns and foreign exchange depreciation rate. The volatility in each asset returns will be estimated with non-linear time series method.

Because the covariance of asset return volatility here reflects complex mutual influences, we use multivariate GARCH model to estimate volatility of each return. Multivariate GARCH can capture the dynamic structure between returns. Verifying the effect of foreign exchange rate volatility, we incorporate foreign exchange rate volatility in multivariate GARCH and estimate this model simultaneously. We can confirm the foreign exchange effect by comparing the result of GARCH estimation with and without foreign exchange rate.

Besides the fact above, we show the effect of foreign exchange market turbulence on the covariance structure between stock returns. As we know, many articles state the possibility that foreign exchange volatility may effect the covariance between macro economic indices. If the stock market is efficient, stock price must reflect the change of macro economic conditions that may have an effect on future firms' performance in some countries. Therefore, investigating the effect of foreign exchange turbulence on stock return covariance is meaningful in risk management for international portfolio. If the foreign exchange turbulence increases covariance between stock returns, foreign exchange volatility might be a global shock to both stock markets in the sense of Karolyi and Stulz (1996)[5]. If the increase in foreign exchange volatility is accompanied by decline in covariance, foreign exchange volatility could be understood as a competitive shock to domestic stock market.

The rest of the chapter is preceded as follows. In the next section, we explain our models to be estimated and the statistical method we use. In the third section, we present our data. Estimated results are shown in the fourth section. We confirm our findings and discuss those significant in the fifth section. The last section concludes the chapter.

Methodology

When we plan to conduct internationally diversified investment, it is important to affirm that the direction of each market index return change and the covariance among them. If the covariance is negative, we can reduce our portfolio risk by weaving those indices into our portfolio. Therefore, the information on the variability of each market index return and covariance plays a concernment role in risk management for international investment. The development of IT technology may have some effect on the co-movement of financial market in different countries.

For exploring the interrelations among three markets (Korea, Hong Kong and Japan), linear and non-linear time series analysis methods will be applied. As we mentioned above, not only stock return risk but also foreign exchange rate risk should be taken into consideration when we invest internationally. This is because we need to assess our portfolio in terms of our home currency at the end of the investment period.

Before estimating an empirical model, we have to confirm the stationality of the our data. For checking this condition, the ADF (augmented Dickey-Fuller) test is employed as the unit root test. It is well known that the simple Dickey-Fuller unit root test is valid only if the series is an AR (1) process. If the series is correlated at higher order lags, the assumption of white noise disturbances is violated. The ADF test constructs a parametric correction for higher-order correlation by assuming that the series follows an AR (p) process and adding p lagged difference terms of the dependent variable to the right-hand side of the test regression. If the data used in this research is not stational, we have to translate those data into stational data by taking log differences. The test can be written as follows:

$$\Delta y_t = \alpha \, y_{t-1} + x^{'} \gamma + \sum_{i=1}^{p} \beta_i \Delta y_{t-i} + \varepsilon_t$$

$$H_0 : \alpha = 0$$
$$H_1 : \alpha < 0$$

where x_t in the equation above are optional exogenous regressors which may consist of constant, or a constant and trend.

The data, which is translated into the log difference, can be treated as return of each asset. In this chapter, we investigate daily return movements and those interrelations mainly.

To estimate the volatility of stock return and foreign exchange depreciation rate, the non-linear time series analysis method, GARCH, is employed. The simple GARCH (1,1) model is written as follows:

$$y_t = \mu_t + \sqrt{h_t} \, v_t \quad v \sim N(0,1) \tag{1}$$

$$h_t = \lambda + \alpha \left(y_{t-1} - \mu_{t-1} \right)^2 + \beta h_{t-1} \tag{2}$$

According to the articles in finance field, we treat h_t, conditional variance, as volatility. In equation (1), stock index return and foreign exchange depreciation rate depend on the deterministic (μ) and stochastic ($\sqrt{h}v$) component. We can divide the stochastic component into two parts, one is so called white noise, v_t, and the other is the element that depends on past information of its own $(h_{t-1}, (y_{t-1} - \mu_{t-1})^2)$. From the risk management view, we cannot predict the future change of v_t, but the future value of h_t can be forecasted through the equation (2). Therefore the volatility here can be recognized as the foreseeable part of error term in equation (1). This specification, especially equation (2), is often interpreted in a financial context, where an agent or trader predicts this period's variance by forming a weighted average of a long term average (λ), the forecasted variance from last period $(\alpha(y_{t-1} - \mu_{t-1})^2)$, and information about volatility observed in the previous period (βh_{t-1}). If the stock price movement was unexpectedly large in either the upward or the downward direction, then the trader will increase the estimate of the variance for the next period. This model is also consistent with the volatility clustering often seen in financial returns data, where large changes in returns are likely to be followed by further large changes. In the next section, we use log difference of stock indices and foreign exchange rate as y_t in the equation (1) because of nonstationality of our data. Estimating GARCH model in this chapter, quasi-maximum likelihood method is employed with BHHH algorithm.

Attaining our goral, we need to verify the interrelationship between stock market volatilities and the effect of foreign exchange volatility on the stock market volatility interrelationship. Multivariate GARCH model is proposed to explore the complex dynamic structure of the volatility and the model can be written as follows:

$$Y_t = N_t + \sqrt{H_t}\Psi_t \ , \ \ \Psi \sim N(0, I) \tag{3}$$

$$H_t = \Lambda'\Lambda + A'(Y_{t-1} - N_{t-1})(Y_{t-1} - N_{t-1})'A + B'H_{t-1}B \tag{4}$$

where I in equation (3) is identity matrix.

This model is extended version of simple GARCH (1,1) model. All variables and parameters in equation (3), (4) are matrices. With this multivariate non-linear time series model, we can discuss dynamic relationship between volatility processes of multiple variables and hence elucidate the interrelationship among three stock and foreign exchange markets.

After estimating the GARCH model, we calculate the variances and covariance among volatilities, h_t, for each variable in equation (4). If the covariance of any of two stock index volatilities is negative, we had better include these stock indices into our portfolio simultaneously from the viewpoint of risk reduction. To check the interrelationship between stock returns, we focus on the effect of foreign exchange rate risk on those covariances. In order to explore the effect of foreign exchange risk, three variables, a pair of stock indices returns and bilateral foreign exchange depreciation rate, are incorporated into the trivariate GARCH model (Y_t in equation (3)) simultaneously.

Foreign exchange volatility turbulence may have some effect on the stock return interrelationship[6]. Checking the role of foreign exchange rate volatility turbulence, we try to investigate the relation between volatility turbulence of foreign exchange market and interrelationship among stock returns by simple OLS model. In this OLS model, covariance from trivariate GARCH estimation results among stock returns is used as an independent variable and variance of foreign exchange rate appreciation rate from the

GARCH results are used as the dependent variable. For extracting a foreign exchange turbulence effect, a dummy variable will be introduced. The OLS model to be estimated is as follows:

$$\text{cov}_t = \alpha + \beta_1 \, \text{var}_t + \sum_{i=2}^{3} \beta_i \, dum_i \, \text{var}_{it} + \varepsilon_t \tag{5}$$

Where cov_t represents the covariance between stock return volatilities from equation (4) and var_t is the variance of bilateral foreign exchange rate appreciation rate volatility. Dum_i is the dummy variable and takes one for a given period, say turbulent period, and otherwise zero. ε_t is error term and follows normal distribution.

Data

The data that we use here is daily stock market indices in each country and foreign exchange rate. KOSPI Composite Index (KOSPI) is chosen as Korean financial market data, and HANG SENG INDEX (HIS) as Hong Kong data, and TOPICS (TOPICS) as Japanese data. Though we should use SSE Composite Index as the Chinese data, we cannot use long historical data enough. The foreign exchange rate in these three countries is usually dominated by each home currency against the U.S. dollar. When investors in Japan want to assess their portfolio composed of these three financial market indices, they need to convert the total value of the portfolio into JPY term. In doing this procedure, we need to use Korean won (KRW_D) and Hong Kong dollar (HKD_D) rate against JPY, and we call converted rate against JPY as bilateral rate (KRW, HKD respectively). To calculate these rates, we use triangular arbitrage rate. Hong Kong dollar is pegged to U.S. dollar, so it looks unchanged when we draw a figure as usual. But from the viewpoint of evaluation of the portfolio here, the calculated bilateral exchange rate is flexible. Figure 2 and Figure 3 are showing this fact. Notations of each data are in the parenthesis.

The empirical work analyzes the data collected from each stock exchange and foreign exchange market from January 4, 1994 to December 30, 2002. Each data is closing data.

Table 1. Basic statistics

	TOPICS	HIS	KOSPI	JPY	HKD_D	KRW_D
Mean	1364.54	11591.90	740.47	113.88	7.76	1059.69
Std. Dev.	223.62	2524.13	191.54	12.41	0.03	235.25
Skewness	-0.42	0.60	-0.45	-0.03	0.47	0.22
Kurtosis	2.21	2.50	2.42	2.94	1.55	2.06
Jarque-Bera	113.98	144.99	97.22	0.75	252.08	92.67
(Probability)	0%	0%	0%	69%	0%	0%
Observations	2046	2046	2046	2046	2046	2046

Figure 1. Stock indices

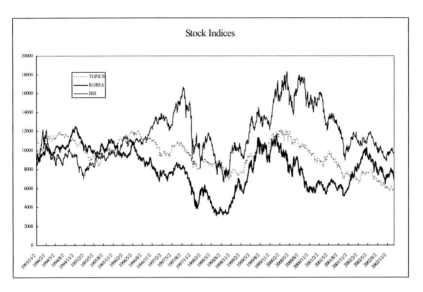

Figure 2. Foreign exchange rate

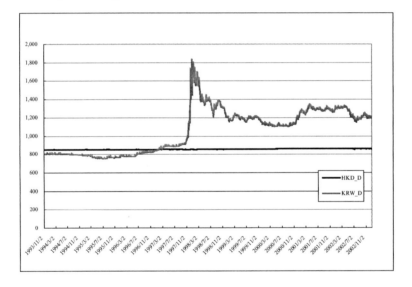

As we know, closing time in these markets is not same, there might be some bias caused by this fact[7]. We exclude the date when at least one market is closed due to holidays[8] or any other reasons.

In our sample, the Asian currency crisis period is included. This effect was especially strong in Korea. In addition to all sample analysis, we employ three subsamples: the pre-

Figure 3. Foreign exchange rate (denominated in JPY)

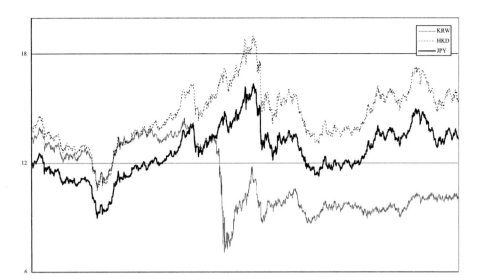

Asian currency crisis, during Asian currency crisis and post Asian currency crisis. The empirical result of the subsample period can show how the Asian currency crisis makes an impact on this three-market interrelationship and brings out how the turbulence in the foreign exchange market effects stock market volatilities relations in these three markets.

Table 1 shows descriptive statistics. Jarque-Bera is a statistical test for checking whether the series is normally distributed. The test statistics measures the difference of the skewness and kurtosis of the series with those from the normal distribution. From this result, all data except JPY are not normal.

Figure 1 shows time series of three stock indices. During the pre-Asian currency attack period, the degree of movement was rather small. During the Asian currency crisis, KOSPI and TOPICS were declining but HIS was rising. After the Asian currency crisis, the degree of movement is getting bigger and bigger. The extent of the movement of TOPICS is the smallest in the whole sample. This fact is also clear from the standard deviation in Table 1.

Figure 2 is describing HKD_D and KRW_D (dominated against USD) time series. HKD_D has been pegged to USD, whereas Korea abandoned pegged foreign exchange system in 11/1997. During 1997, reflecting the Asian currency crisis, KRW_D jumped up dramatically and declined a lot just after reaching the peak of the rate.

In Figure 3, the Korean won (KRW) and the Hong Kong dollar (HKD) are dominated against the Japanese yen. The Hong Kong dollar fluctuates in this setting and only the Korean won was devaluated during the Asian currency crisis.

Table 2. Unit root test result

Variable	Coefficient	Std. Error	t-Statistic	Prob.
HIS(-1)	-0.0040	0.0020	-2.02	27.8%
KOSPI(-1)	-0.0032	0.0018	-1.79	38.4%
TOPICS(-1)	-0.0020	0.0017	-1.18	68.5%
HKD(-1)	-0.0028	0.0016	-1.76	40.0%
KRW(-1)	-0.0025	0.0016	-1.58	49.2%
JPY(-1)	-0.0027	0.0016	-1.74	40.9%
HKD_D(-1)	-0.0025	0.0027	-0.93	78.1%
KRW_D(-1)	-0.0030	0.0015	-1.94	31.2%
DLOG(HIS(-1))	-0.9617	0.0221	-43.55	0%
DLOG(KOSPI(-1))	-0.9451	0.0221	-42.74	0%
DLOG(TOPICS(-1))	-1.0017	0.0303	-33.09	0%
DLOG(HKD(-1))	-0.9195	0.0221	-41.69	0%
DLOG(KRW(-1))	-0.8100	0.1066	-7.60	0%
DLOG((JPY(-1)))	-0.9173	0.0221	-41.60	0%
DLOG(HKD_D(-1))	-2.8418	0.1131	-25.12	0%
DLOG(KRW_D(-1))	-0.7166	0.1005	-7.13	0%

Empirical Results

Unit Root Test

Before estimating an empirical model, the stationality of the data must be checked. ADF test is employed for the unit root test. The result is shown in Table 2. The stationality of all variables is rejected. Log differential of all variable follows stational process. Consequently we adopt log differential data for estimating the model. The notation DLOG(x) in Table 2 means the log differential of x and the parenthesis after the variable, (-1), means 1 period lagged. HKD and KRW are dominated against JPY. Hereafter the log difference of each asset is called "return".

Multivariate GARCH Model Estimation and Volatility Relationship

A lot type of multivariate GARCH models is proposed[9]. Basic multivariate GARCH models are the models with constant correlation and time-varying correlation in conditional variance equation. The model we use here is time-varying correlation model. This is because we want to focus on dynamic volatility relationship among three markets, the relationship may change over time. Especially in our sample, we cover Asian currency

Table 7. Covariance of the volatility among stock market

	KOSPI/HIS	KOSPI/TOPICS	HIS/TOPICS
All Sample	5.64E-06	-2.25E-06	1.07E-05
Pre_Attack	8.43E-06	-3.65E-06	9.52E-06
Attack	8.54E-05	-8.17E-06	8.62E-06
Post_Attack	-2.75E-05	3.57E-06	2.17E-06

Table 8. Volatility covariance among foreign exchange rate

	KRW_D/HKD_D	KRW_D/JPY	HKD_D/JPY
All Sample	3.92E-07	8.67E-06	3.36E-08
Pre_Attack	9.02E-08	1.20E-06	4.83E-08
Attack	5.67E-07	1.76E-05	7.70E-08
Post_Attack	2.91E-07	8.80E-06	7.01E-09

crisis. We had better take into account the structural change in relationship among these markets.

Here we chose the BEKK model as the time-varying correlation multivariate GARCH (equation (4), (5)). Three variables are introduced in our model simultaneously, we will estimate trivariate GARCH model.

Among stock index returns, foreign exchange depreciation rates, and two stock returns and bilateral foreign exchange depreciation rate between the countries, we develop five combinations of variables.

First, we review the relationship among the three stock returns. The combination in which the sign of covariance is minus contributes to reduce portfolio risk. The sign of the combination of HIS and TOPICS is positive consistently. On the other hand, KOSPI and TOPICS returns move oppositely except after the Asian currency crisis period. The relationship between KOSPI and HIS returns may have changed since the Asian currency crisis. We should remind here that these results do not reflect any foreign exchange rate risk effect.

Foreign exchange depreciation rate has been moving in the same direction over our sample period. The sign of all combination is positive in all periods. All currencies here

Table 9. Covariance between Korea and Japan with foreign exchange risk

	KOSPI/TOPICS	KOSPI/FX	TOPICS/FX
All Sample	-1.39E-06	6.31E-06	-1.79E-05
Pre_Attack	-2.40E-06	2.60E-06	-1.63E-05
Attack	-1.03E-05	3.20E-05	-8.89E-06
Post_Attack	3.07E-06	2.44E-06	-1.11E-05

Table 10. Covariance between Korea and Hong Kong with foreign exchange risk

	KOSPI/HIS	KOSPI/FX	HIS/FX
All Sample	5.55E-06	3.24E-06	-4.37E-06
Pre_Attack	9.56E-06	2.35E-07	4.09E-07
Attack	8.40E-05	-6.94E-06	-2.57E-05
Post_Attack	-2.83E-05	9.70E-06	-2.66E-07

Table 11. Covariance between Hong Kong and Japan with foreign exchange risk

	HIS/TOPICS	HIS/FX	TOPICS/FX
All Sample	1.10E-05	1.40E-06	-1.15E-05
Pre_Attack	1.16E-05	-2.81E-06	-2.03E-05
Attack	1.12E-05	1.65E-05	1.93E-05
Post_Attack	6.38E-06	-9.84E-07	-1.19E-05

are dominated against the U.S. dollar. If one of three currencies appreciates against the U.S. dollar, the other two currencies also appreciate likewise. Incorporating these currencies into same portfolio, we suffer bigger foreign exchange rate risk against the U.S. dollar than when we take position separately.

Hereafter, we incorporate the effect of foreign exchange risk into the relationship between stock market returns. The first column shows the relationship between stock market volatility. Comparing Table 7 with Table 9, the sign of covariance in each period is same. But the value of them is not same. Except after the Asian currency crisis period, the value in Table 9 is bigger than those in Table 7. From the risk management viewpoint, the extent of the risk reduction effect in a portfolio is much bigger in the case of Table 7 as compared to Table 9. We should be aware that if we do not take account of foreign exchange risk, we might overvalue the risk reduction effect of this combination of stock market returns.

According to Table 10, the tendency of the difference of the covariance with foreign exchange risk and without it is not the same as in Table 9. Also, this result shows there might be a structural change in the relationship among these financial markets before and after the Asian currency crisis.

Same as Table 7, the covariance between HIS and TOPICS is positive in all subsample periods. After the Asian currency crisis, the covariance with foreign exchange risk is much bigger than the value without the foreign exchange risk. Here we can find the structural change among these financial markets and the importance of the foreign exchange risk to evaluate portfolio risk.

Foreign Exchange Rate Turbulence and Stock Return Volatility Relationship

Stock volatility interrelationship may change around the Asian currency attack period. The results from Table 7 to Table 11 are indicating this scenario. In this section, we try to explore the effect of foreign exchange turbulence on interrelationship between stock returns volatilities by estimating equation (5). We show equation (5) here again.

$$cov_t = \alpha + \beta_1 \, var_t + \sum_{i=2}^{3} \beta_i \, dum_i \, var_{it} + \varepsilon_t \qquad (5)$$

Where cov_t represents the covariance between stock return volatilities at time t and var_t is the variance of bilateral foreign exchange appreciation rate volatility at time t. Dum_i is the dummy variable and takes one for subsample i, and otherwise zero. Dum_2 covers

Table 12. ADF test result for covariance and variance

	t value	p_value
KOSPI/TOPICS	-9.81	0%
KRW/JPY (var)	-6.15	0%
HIS/TOPICS	-9.81	0%
HKD/JPY (var)	-6.15	0%
HIS/KOSPI	-6.30	0%
HKD/KRW (var)	-6.31	0%

Figure 4. Covariance and variance

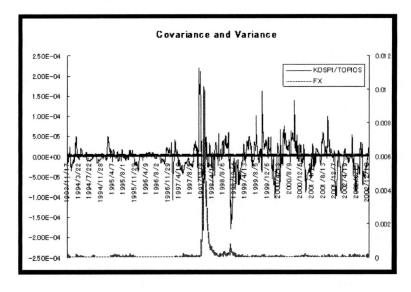

Figure 5. Covariance and variance

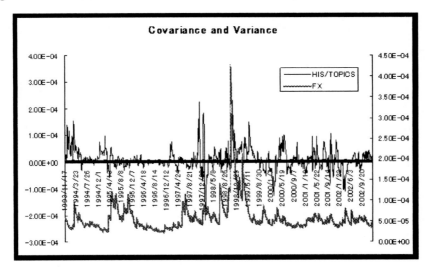

Figure 6. Covariance and variance

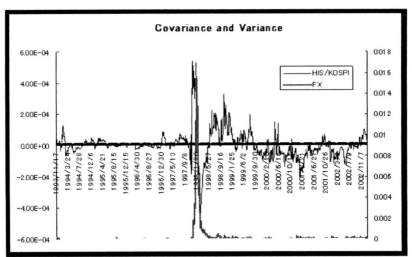

Pre_Attack period, Dum_3 covers Attack period. OLS is employed for estimating equation (5).

Before estimating (5), we have to check the stationary of the data with the ADF test.

The variables which are followed by "var" in parentheses are variance, and others are all covariance. Table 12 is showing that all covariance and variance are following a stationary process. Then we can use OLS to estimate (5). Figure 4 to 6 show covariance and variance in three pairs of stock return and its bilateral foreign exchange volatilities.

Table 13 shows the estimation result of equation (5) for KOSPI/TOPICS and bilateral foreign exchange rate volatilities. β (showed above the bold line) is the coefficient without dummy variables. Three βs below the bold line are the estimated coefficient of dummy variables and all parameters are estimated significantly. If we do not distinguish

Table 13. OLS result between KOSPI/TOPICS and bilateral foreign exchange rate

	Coefficient	Std. Error	Prob.
β	-0.0085	0.001	0.0%
β₁	-0.0642	0.024	0.8%
β₂	0.060	0.027	2.7%
β₃	0.055	0.024	2.1%

Table 14. OLS result between HIS/TOPICS and bilateral foreign exchange rate

	Coefficient	Std. Error	Prob.
β	0.257	0.022	0.0%
β₁	0.212	0.037	0.0%
β₂	0.052	0.036	15.5%
β₃	0.049	0.032	12.7%

Table 15. OLS result between HIS/KOSPI and bilateral foreign exchange rate

	Coefficient	Std. Error	Prob.
β	0.027	0.002	0.0%
β₁	-0.431	0.065	0.0%
β₂	0.427	0.255	9.5%
β₃	0.457	0.064	0.0%

the turbulence period, the rise in foreign exchange market turbulence may reduce stock return interrelation between KOPSI and TOPICS. During the turbulence period, the reducing effect of the foreign exchange rate is significant but smaller (β_3).

Between HIS and TOPICS, the turbulence of the foreign exchange market may amplify the volatility relationship between these stock returns. All dummies are estimated insignificant. Focusing on the turbulence effect, we may point out that the turbulence of volatility magnifies the positive covariance, but the extent of the risk increasing effect might be small because the dummy during this period (β_3) is not significant.

From Table 15, the turbulence of the foreign exchange rate volatility gives rise to the covariance incrementation between HIS and KOSPI. Only β_2 (Pre_Attack period) is insignificant. Especially in the turbulence period, the foreign exchange volatility magnifies the positive interrelation between stock return volatilities.

Discussion

In the internationally diversified portfolio, we have to take into account the foreign exchange rate risk. We investigate the relationship among the return and volatility in KOSPI, HIS and TOPICS with and without foreign exchange risk. This research can bring out how the foreign exchange risk affects the stock return relations among North East Asian financial markets, and structural change before and after the Asian currency crisis.

The multivariate GARCH model can trace a dynamic volatility structure. We use a trivariate GARCH model to check the volatility relations among three stock returns and between two stock returns with bilateral foreign exchange depreciation rate. Estimating volatility for each stock returns or foreign exchange depreciation rate, we calculate covariance between these volatilities to confirm if the combination of stock returns of any pair out of three can reduce the volatility of portfolio.

The results without foreign exchange rate show that the combination of KOSPI and HIS can reduce the volatility risk after the Asian currency crisis period. If we invest KOSPI or HIS with TOPICS simultaneously, the volatility of portfolio will be bigger than if we hold each index independently, especially during post-Asian currency crisis period. The structural change can be seen in the pair of KOSPI/HIS and KOSPI/TOPICS just after the Asian currency crisis. As for the volatility structural change, KOSPI may be the key market.

Those mutual volatility relations do not reflect the effect of foreign exchange volatility. Investing abroad, we usually evaluate our portfolio in terms of domestic currency. Even if the stock index we invest does not move, the change of foreign exchange rate affects the value of our portfolio in domestic currency term. To explore the foreign exchange volatility effect, we use two stock returns and bilateral foreign exchange depreciate rate in the trivariate GARCH model simultaneously.

The effect of foreign exchange depreciation rate on the volatility relation between stock returns depends on the combination of the stock market. But the sign of all covariance does not change even if we introduce foreign exchange depreciation rate into the multivariate GARCH model.

The covariance of KOSPI/HIS and KOSPI/TOPICS combination show distinct structural change just before and after the Asian currency crisis, more specifically the sign of covariance is different. As for HIS/TOPICS covariance, the sign in all subsample is same. From the viewpoint of volatility relations, we may deduce that the volatility of KOSPI has changed since the Asian currency crisis even though we take account of the foreign exchange effect.

The risk reducing effect of KOSPI/HIS has been increasing since the crisis. In KOSPI/TOPICS and HIS/TOPICS, covariance decreases also after the crisis. Because the sign of those covariance is positive, if we incorporate those indices into our portfolio, the risk will be bigger compare to investing independently. The risk just referred above might be

Table 16. Variance of KOSPI, TOPICS, KRW/JPY

	KOSPI	TOPICS	KRW/JPY
All Sample	0.57	0.18	0.18
Pre_Attack	0.16	0.12	0.04
Attack	1.08	0.2	0.77
Post_Attack	0.63	0.21	0.06

Table17. Variance of HIS, TOPICS, HKD/JPY

	HIS	TOPICS	HKD/JPY
All Sample	0.4	0.18	0.06
Pre_Attack	0.24	0.12	0.04
Attack	0.85	0.2	0.11
Post_Attack	0.32	0.21	0.05

Table 18. Variance of KOSPI, HIS, KRW/HKD

	KOSPI	HIS	KRW/JPY
All Sample	0.57	0.4	0.18
Pre_Attack	0.16	0.25	0.01
Attack	1.09	0.83	0.98
Post_Attack	0.64	0.32	0.03

overvalued if we do not care about foreign exchange effect. Therefore, if we rule out the foreign exchange effect, the portfolio risk might be overvalued in all cases after the crisis.

In order to investigate the effect of the turbulence of the foreign exchange market, we check the variance of volatility in each period.

As we imagine, the variances of all variables in all cases are highest in the Asian currency crisis period. In Bodart and Reding (1999), they found an increase in foreign exchange rate volatility is accompanied by decline in international correlation between stock markets in Europe. Variance in the attack period is highest in any bilateral foreign exchange rate, the second highest value of variance is in the Post_Attack period in any case. Here we try to conduct comparable studies among North East Asian financial markets to test whether foreign exchange turbulence increases international relationship between stock returns.

From Table 9 to Table 11, the foreign exchange turbulence is accompanied by an increase in absolute value of covariance in KOSPI/TOPICS and KOSPI/HIS. In the Asian currency

Table 19. Summary from Table 13 to Table 15

	KOSPI/TOPICS	HIS/TOPICS	HIS/KOSPI
β_1	-0.064[*]	0.21[*]	-0.43[**]
β_2	0.060[**]	0.052	0.43
β_3	0.055[**]	0.049	0.46[*]

* significant at 1%
** significant at 5%

crisis period, covariance in absolute value is the biggest in all the market. From these facts, we can infer that foreign exchange market turbulences are accompanied by increase in covariance but the direction of each market response is not same[10].

From the estimation result of equation (5), the comparison of our result to Bodart and Reding's (1999) findings can be carried out. Table 19 summarizes the effect of the foreign exchange market turbulence on stock return interrelations. β_3 is representing the effect during the Asian currency crisis, a turbulent period especially in the foreign exchange market. In KOSPI/TOPICS and HIS/KOSPI case, the parameter β_3 is significant and positive.

As we know, we need to add the value β_3 to the value β_1 to capture the parameter value for variance in the attack period. After adding both values, the parameters are positive in HIS/TOPICS and HIS/KOSPI. This fact suggests that the volatility in foreign exchange induce an increase in the covariance between these stock markets volatilities especially in foreign exchange turbulent period. This result is the same as in the previous analysis in this chapter.

Another tendency can be pointed out by parameter β_1. This value represents the parameter for variance in the Post_Attack period. In the two pairs, KOSPI/TOPICS and HIS/KOSPI, β_1 is significant and negative. We can infer that the turbulence in the foreign exchange market is associated with smaller covariance and minus in sign in these stock markets after the Asian currency crisis. This change of the foreign exchange volatility effect may be an evidence for structural change between stock returns in these countries.

In HIS/TOPICS case, the turbulence in foreign exchange market has consistent effect on interrelationship between stock return volatilities in all subsample. An increase in foreign exchange rate volatility is accompanied by an increase in covariance between stock markets in Hong Kong and Japan.

If the sign of the parameter of variance is positive, turbulences in the foreign exchange market is accompanied by an increase in the volatility of the stock return. Positive volatility jump in foreign exchange rate gives rise to positive jump in both stock return volatilities. The rise in foreign exchange rate risk affects domestic stock market in both countries likewise. The turbulence in the foreign exchange market is interpreted as global shock in Karolyi and Stulz (1996). Investors assess that the revenue of the firms in both country will be influenced by foreign exchange fluctuation. The rise in foreign exchange volatility can be considered as common component, which affects the domestic stock market.

The turbulence in foreign exchange market is accompanied by decline in portfolio risk when the sign of variance parameter is negative. A rise in volatility of foreign exchange depreciation rate has positive impact on one country's stock market and has negative impact on the other stock market simultaneously. These kinds of factors, which effect domestic stock markets, are referred to as competitive shock in Karolyi & Stulz (1996). The portfolio risks in KOSPI/TOPICS and KOSPI/HIS may be getting smaller with the rise in foreign exchange volatility.

In this analysis, the Korean market might play a special role in these three countries. As we know, Korea suffered a severe impact from the Asian currency crisis. After this crisis, the financial market structure in Korea and its relation to markets abroad might change. Foreign exchange volatility can reduce the risk of the portfolio that contains KOSPI especially after the Asian currency crisis.

Summary

In a highly IT developed world and market, information inflowed into a particular market can be transmitted into other markets very quickly. This phenomenon might cause volatility spillover between financial markets. If traders follow an efficient market hypothesis, an information transfer mechanism can be one of the contributory sources of volatility spillover.

The relationship among stock indices in Korea, Hong Kong and Japan with and without foreign exchange movement has been examined to see that the volatility spillover phenomenon can be found. Because of the non-stationality of the data, we focus on the result using log difference of each daily data.

Simultaneous volatility relationship has been explored by a trivariate GARCH model. From the estimation result, the existence of a volatility spillover phenomenon is confirmed in North East Asian financial markets. To see the spillover structure in more detail, covariance between a pair of stock returns volatilities is calculated with GARCH estimation results.

First of all, structural change before and after the Asian currency crisis can be found out especially in the portfolio containing KOSPI. After the crisis, risk-reduction affects have been increasing in KOSPI/HIS and risk-accruing effects have been decreasing in KOSPI/TOPICS and HIS/TOPICS. Therefore, the international portfolio with these indices may afford the opportunity to reduce investment and financing risk.

Furthermore, we have to be aware that foreign exchange rate volatility should be incorporated to evaluate an international portfolio risk. We show that covariance between stock returns is high when the foreign exchange market is turbulent in KOSPI/HIS and HIS/TOPICS. This suggests that international diversification does not provide as much diversification against large foreign exchange turbulence as one might have expected. But this relationship might change over time, especially after the Asian currency crisis. The portfolio risks in KOSPI/TOPICS and KOSPI/HIS are reducing with rise in foreign exchange market volatility after the Asian currency crisis.

Therefore, in the risk analysis, it is not appropriate to assume that covariances between these three stock markets are constant over time and move independently against foreign exchange market volatility. In some cases, decline in foreign exchange volatility will be accompanied by decreasing portfolio risk. In this case, a foreign exchange rate stability policy may contribute to reduce portfolio risk, and consequently reduce the cost of capital for firms in this area.

References

Artis, M. J., & Taylor, M. P. (1994). The stabilizing effect of the ERM on exchange rates and interest rates. *International Monetary Fund Staff Paper, 41*, 123-148.

Baba, Y., Engle, R. F., Kraft, K., & Kroner, K. (1990). *Multivariate simultaneous generalized ARCH*. Unpublished manuscript. University of California, San Diego.

Bessler, D. A., & Yang, J. (2003). The structure of interdependence in international stock markets. *Journal of International Money and Finance, 22*, 261-287.

Bodart, V., & Reding, P. (1999). Exchange rate regime, volatility and international correlations on bond and stock markets. *Journal of International Money and Finance, 18*, 133-151.

Bolersrev, T., Engle, R. F., & Nelson, D. B. (1994). ARCH models. In R. F. Engle & D. McFadden (Eds.), *The handbook of econometrics,* (Vol. 4, pp. 2959-3038). Amsterdam: North Holland.

Engle, R. F. (2000). *Dynamic conditional correlation: A simple class of multivariate GARCH models.* Mimeo. Retrieved from http://weber.ucsd.edu/~mbacci/engle/index_recent.html

Engle, R. F., Ito, T., & Lin, W. (1990). Meteor showers or heat waves? Heteroskedastic intra-daily volatility in the foreign exchange market. *Econometrica, 59*, 525-542.

Engle, R. F., & Kroner, K. F. (1995). Multivariate simultaneous generalized ARCH. *Econometric Theory, 11*, 122-150.

Flood, R. P., & Rose, A. K. (1995). Fixing exchange rate: A virtual quest for fundamentals. *Journal of Monetary Economics, 36*, 3-37.

Fratianni, M., & von Hagen, J. (1990). The European monetary system ten years after. *Carnegie Rochester Conference Series in Public Policy, 32*, 173-242.

Frenkel, J. A., & Mussa, M. L. (1980). The efficiency of foreign exchange markets and measures of turbulence. *American Economic Review, 70*, 374-381.

Karolyi, G. A., & Stulz, R. M. (1996). Why do markets move together? An investigation of U.S.-Japan stock return comovements. *Journal of Finance, 51*, 951-986

Kearney, C., & Patton, A. J. (2000). Multivariate GARCH modeling of exchange rate volatility transmission in the European monetary system. *The Financial Review, 41*, 29-48.

Koutmos, G., & Booth, G. (1995). Asymmetric volatility transmission in international stock markets. *Journal of International Money and Finance, 14*, 747-762.

Longin, F., & Solnik, B. (1995). Is the correlation in international equity returns constant: 1960-1990? *Journal of International Money and Finance, 14*, 3-26.

Lrdoit, O., Santa-Clara, P., & Wolf, M. (2002). Flexible multivariate GARCH modeling with an application to international stock markets. *Review of Economics and Statistics, 85,* 735-747.

Susai, M. (2005, March 3). The spillover structure of the volatility of financial market between Korea, Japan and China. *Proceedings of the 12ᵗʰ International Conference on Regional Cooperation in Northeast Asia, "Peace, Prosperity and Regional Community in Northeast Asia."* Institute of East and West Studies, Yonsei University.

Teyssiere, G.. (1998). *Multivariate long-memory ARCH modeling for high frequency foreign exchange rate.* Paper presented in the Proceedings of the Conference "High-Frequency Data in Finance." Olsen & Associates.

Tsay, R. S. (2002). Analysis of financial time series. In *Wiley Series in Probability and Statistics.* New York: Wiley & Sons.

Endnotes

[1]   For example, see Engle, Ito, and Lin (1990).

[2]   See, for example, Frenkel and Mussa (1980), Flood and Rose (1995) and Rose (1995).

[3]   See also Flood and Rose (1995) and Rose (1995).

[4]   Other empirical methods can be used to study an international asset return relationship. See, for example, Bessler and Yang (2003).

[5]   Global shocks are those that effect the stock price in both countries in the same direction. Competitive shocks increase the stock price in one country relative to another country. See Karolyi and Stulz (1996), p. 952, for details.

[6]   See Bodart and Reding (1999) and Karolyi and Stulz (1996).

[7]   There might remain some effect of nonsynchronous trading time. But this effect is relatively smaller than when we examine the relation between U.S. and Japanese markets.

[8]   There might be some from the day of the week and holiday effect. New Years holidays in the Hong Kong market is longer than in any other markets, so we may suffer a stronger holiday effect just before and after this period. See Karolyi and Stulz (1996).

[9]   See Bolersrev, Engle and Nelson (1994) for details.

[10] The sign of covariance is not same. Only the sign of covariance in KOSPI/TOPICS is minus.

Section III

Financial Innovations and IT

Chapter X

Trade Liberalization and International Performance of Australian Manufacturing Industries and ITs

Andrew Marks, University of Western Sydney, Australia

Abstract

Trade liberalization has played a pivotal role in improving the export orientation of the various Australian manufacturing industries (at the two-digit level) in the period 1974/75-2000/01. However, those industries subjected to industry-specific assistance measures — for example, the textile, clothing and footwear and the machinery and equipment industries (motor vehicle industry component) — have exhibited a superior export-oriented performance. The important lesson emanating from this result for the information technology sector is that although it is also subjected to these measures, their expansion can help alleviate the weak and stagnant export performance in information technology goods thereby helping to combat the projected large balance of trade deficit. Moreover, stronger output and employment growth will arise because of the significant contribution of these goods to the economy.

Introduction

The trade liberalisation process in Australia, which began in 1971, has exposed the manufacturing sector to stronger import competition, which, in turn, has played a pivotal role in stimulating economic efficiency and more generally an improvement in international competitiveness. The higher export profile has been reflected by an acceleration in the real rate of growth of exports from this sector as revealed by Garnaut (1991), Swan and Zeitch (1992), the Mckinsey Report (1993), the Economic Planning Advisory Council (EPAC) (1993), Bullock, Grenville and Heenan (1993), Menzies (1994) and Athokurala (1995).

However, an important limitation of these studies is that they do not indicate whether the improved manufacturing export performance is sustainable. A study by Marks and Sadeghi (1998) has utilised both co-integration and regression analyses to reveal a statistically significant inverse relationship between falling levels of import protection and the rising export orientation of the manufacturing sector's production in the period 1980:1-1996:2. The stronger international focus as reflected by rising proportion of manufacturing output exported in turn indicates sustainable manufacturing export growth.

The present study seeks to build on this latter result by assessing the impact of trade liberalisation on the degree of export-oriented production at the two-digit level of the manufacturing sector[1]. The outcome of this exercise will indicate the relative output and hence employment growth prospects of these manufacturing industries. Emphasis will also be placed on the export performance of the Australian information technology sector. This objective is important as international trade in this area has been exhibiting above average growth in the last 20 years (e.g., see UN Trade Statistics). Hence, a positive export performance by the Australian information technology sector will generate not only higher levels of output and employment growth, but also stronger growth in export receipts.

The Manufacturing Sector's Export Oriented Response

The (real) export-oriented performance of the various manufacturing industries at the two-digit level that will be gauged include the food, beverages and tobacco (FBT), textile, clothing and footwear (TCF), metal products (MP), machinery and equipment manufacturing (MEM), chemical, petroleum and related products (PCC & AS) and miscellaneous manufacturing (MM) industries[2]. Movements in the export orientation of the manufacturing sector (MS)) is also included. This task is undertaken for the period 1974/75-2000/01 with the assistance of Diagram 1[3].

Diagram 1 depicts all the manufacturing industries to have improved their export orientation in the period 1974/75-2000/01, that is, an increasing proportion of output is being exported. The same result applies to the manufacturing sector. The TCF, metal

Diagram 1. Export-oriented production (Source: A.B.S. Cat. No. 8221.0 Manufacturing Industry, A.B.S. Cat. No. 5204, National Income Expenditure and Product, I.C. (1995) Australian Manufacturing Industry and International Trade Data 1968/69-1992/93 and data provided by the A.B.S. on request.)

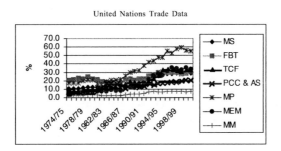

Table 1. Level of export orientation at the two-digit manufacturing level (Source: A.B.S. Cat. No. 8221.0 Manufacturing Industry, A.B.S. Cat. No. 5204, National Income Expenditure and Product, I.C. (1995) Australian Manufacturing Industry and International Trade Data 1968/69-1992/93 and data provided by the A.B.S. on request.)

Two-Digit Manufacturing Industry	Level of Export Orientation in 1974/75	Average Level of Export Orientation 1975/76-2000/01	Percentage Change 1974/75- Compared to Average of 1975/76-2000/01
1. TCF	5.1	18.7	266.7
2. Machinery & Equipment Manufacturing	7	17.2	146.0
3. Chem., Petrol. & Related Products	5.6	13.5	140.6
4. Metal Products	17.4	34.0	95.5
5. Miscellaneous Manufacturing	2.7	4.7	73.1
6. Food, Beverages & Tobacco	20.4	23.9	17.2
Total Manufacturing	**10.9**	**29**	**166.1**

products, machinery and equipment manufacturing and to a lesser extent chemical, petroleum and related products industries have exhibited the largest improvement. The food, beverages and tobacco and miscellaneous industries have displayed the weakest improvement in export-oriented production.

However, it is difficult to ascertain an accurate assessment of each industry's export-oriented response to trade liberalisation during the period 1974/75-2000/01 because of the different export orientation levels prevailing at the beginning of this period and in particular 1974/75. This problem however can be overcome by comparing the base year (1974/75) with the average movement over the subsequent years (1975/76-2000/01) for each of the manufacturing industries. The results of this exercise are displayed in the Table 1.

Table 1 depicts the TCF and machinery and equipment industries exhibiting the strongest improvement in export-oriented production of 266.7 and 146.0% respectively in the period of 1974/75 as compared to the average of the period 1975/76-2000/01. The chemical, petroleum and related products industry follows with a 140.6% improvement. The metal products industry improvement in export orientation was 95.5% with the miscellaneous manufacturing and food, beverages and tobacco industries' improvement being of the order of 73.1 and 17.2% respectively. These results at the two-digit level compare with the improvement in the export orientation of the manufacturing sector of 166.1. It is noteworthy that only the improvement in the TCF industry's export orientation of 266.7% has surpassed that of the manufacturing sector of 166.1%.

Industry-Specific Assistance Measures

An interesting feature of the TCF industry result is that, unlike the other manufacturing subdivisions, the trade liberalisation process has been reinforced with industry-specific assistance measures so as to intensify the drive to penetrate the world market. For example, subsidies have been provided for investment and research and development expenditure, whilst the state and federal governments have also provided finance to upgrade the skill level of the labor force in this industry.

The machinery and equipment industry is devised by the motor vehicle and parts, other transport equipment, photographic, professional and scientific equipment, appliances and electrical equipment, and the industrial machinery and equipment components. Of these components, only the motor vehicle and parts segment has been characterised by the same policy stance as the TCF industry, that is, trade liberalisation and industry-specific assistance measures. This situation therefore encouraged the substitution of the motor vehicle industry for the machinery and equipment manufacturing industry in order to assess the impact of industry-specific assistance measures on the motor vehicle industry's export orientation[4]. Table 2 depicts the results of this exercise[5].

The replacement of the machinery and equipment industry with one of its components, namely the motor vehicle industry, has led to export orientation rising from 146 to 147.5% in the period 1974/75 as compared to the average of the period 1975/76-2000/01. Since the motor vehicle industry is the only part of the machinery and equipment industry that was subjected to industry-specific measures, this implies the effectiveness of these measures, as in the case of the TCF industry, in reinforcing the efforts of trade liberalisation to sharpen export focus[6]. Indeed, Conlon and Perkins (1995) and Owen (1995) both emphasise the critical importance of industry-specific assistance measures, within the context of free trade, in reorienting motor vehicle production form the domestic to international market. Furthermore, it is worthwhile noting that the relatively stronger export-oriented response of the motor vehicle industry has also narrowed the difference

Table 2. Level of export orientation at the two- and three-digit manufacturing levels (Source: A.B.S. Cat. No. 8221.0 Manufacturing Industry, A.B.S. Cat. No. 5204, National Income Expenditure and Product, I.C. (1995) Australian Manufacturing Industry and International Trade Data 1968/69-1992/93 and data provided by the A.B.S. on request.)

Manufacturing Industry	Level of Export Orientation in 1974/75	Average Level of Export Orientation 1975/76-2000/01	Percentage Change 1974/75- Compared to Average of 1975/76-2000/01
1. TCF	5.1	18.7	266.7
2. Motor Vehicle Industry	5.9	14.6	147.5
3. Chem., Petrol. & Related Products.	5.6	13.5	140.6
4. Metal Products	17.4	34.0	95.5
5. Miscellaneous Manufacturing	2.7	4.7	73.1
6. Food, Beverages & Tobacco	20.4	23.9	17.2
Total Manufacturing	**10.9**	**29**	**166.1**

as compared to the overall manufacturing sector's export orientated performance, that is, by 1.4 percentage points.

It is also noteworthy that the extremely low export orientation of the TCF and motor vehicle industries in the-mid 1970s, as depicted by Table 2, mirrored the deeply ingrained economic inefficiency and more generally lack of international competitiveness that prevailed. The significant turnaround in the export orientation of these two industries therefore reinforces the complementary nature of the trade liberalisation and industry-specific assistance measures in constituting a sufficiently strong incentive to drive a higher export profile.

The Export Performance of the Australian Information Technology Sector

The information technology sector is of critical importance to the Australian economy according to the Goldsworthy Report (1997) because its effective use will enhance the economy's international competitiveness[7]. Furthermore, the output of this sector constitutes approximately 7% of GDP which in turn makes a significant contribution to overall output and employment growth in the economy. Finally, this report highlights the need to promote exports in this area so as to overcome a projected $A46 billion trade deficit in information technology goods by 2005. Promoting an improved export performance of the Australian information technology sector is of particular significance because international trade in this area has been exhibiting above average growth in the last 20

Table 3. Export performance of the information technology industry (Source: A.B.S. Cat. No. 5422, International Merchandise Trade)

Year	Exports of IT Goods $A Millions	IT Exports as a % of Total Manufacturing Exports
1989/90	1100	4.5
1994/95	2532	5.8
1999/00	2365	4.1
2002/03	2790	4.2

years (e.g., see UN Trade Statistics). Hence, a positive export performance by the Australian information technology sector will not only improve international competitiveness and generate higher levels of output and employment growth, but also lead to stronger growth in export receipts. This importance of this latter objective is highlighted by Australia's projected large trade deficit in information technology goods, thus concurrently helping to ease Australia's persistent large current account deficit.

Table 3 depicts the Australian information technology sector's export performance since 1989/908.

The first interesting feature of Table 3 is a sharp increase in the value of information technology exports from 1989/90 to 1994/95. While the small base from which these exports began is an important factor in explaining this development, numerous other factors have also been responsible. For example, the major form of assistance for the computer hardware industry has been the government offsets program where the Australian government purchases computer hardware from foreign suppliers in exchange for their direct investment in the local hardware industry. The central objective has been to use Australia as a base for higher export-oriented production. An important aspect of this arrangement has been the benefit that local hardware companies could derive from their cooperation with the international companies which also dominate the international hardware market, in order to increase export penetration. The Industry Assistance Commission (IAC) (1984) also notes the provision of export subsidies to encourage information technology exports. Nevertheless, exports from this sector have stagnated. A similar trend has materialised with the contribution of information technology exports to total manufacturing exports thereby indicating a structural weakness of the Australian economy.

Industry-Specific Assistance Measures for the Australian Information Technology Sector

The international market is dominated by large imperfectly competitive firms possessing a cost advantage due to technological superiority and large scale production (e.g., see

Spencer & Brander, 1983, & Krugman, 1986). The international information technology market is no exception to this characteristic. The Australian information technology companies, however, are small to medium in size due to the relatively small magnitude of the Australian economy. This situation therefore places the Australian information technology companies (and indeed export activity generally) at competitive disadvantage on the international market.

Australian governments have been providing industry-specific assistance measures to the information technology sector over a period. For example, the (IAC) (1984) notes the provision of export subsidies whilst the Goldsworthy Report (1997) has encouraged the provision of investment incentives in order to compete against other nations which provide similar incentives. Moreover, indirect assistance measures have also been provided such as infrastructure support in the form of government providing a labour force with the appropriate skills, economy wide incentives for research and development and corporate tax relief. However, these assistance measures do not appear to have been sufficient in helping this sector overcome the inherited barriers to greater export penetration as indicated by the stagnant export performance in the period 1994/95-2002/03. Hence, there is a need to expand the assistance measures provided to the information technology sector.

The need to intensify the industry-specific assistance measures is consistent with the positive response of the TCF and motor vehicle industries to these measures by sharply improving their export orientation. Moreover, the critical importance of industry-specific assistance measures for the Australian information technology sector's export performance is highlighted by the OECD (1998) which identifies the dominance of low tech manufacturing itself in discouraging domestic and foreign resource flows into high technology areas in Australia. This situation therefore reinforces the need for industry-specific assistance measures to promote the growth of not only the information technology sector, but more generally medium to high technology activity in Australia. The success of such a policy will help "break" the vicious circle of low tech manufacturing deterring investment in medium/high tech manufacturing which in turn maintains the status quo.

The need for an expansion of industry-specific assistance measures for the Australian information technology sector is harmonious with the effectiveness of general assistance measures in promoting overall international competitiveness, exports and hence GDP growth in Australia, as highlighted by the Mortimer Report (1997). For example, this report highlights that the use of incentives for higher investment and R and D and the successful role of Austrade (a government organisation to assist with international marketing) have all been significant in promoting overall exports. In addition, the Mortimer Report (1997) has emphasised the importance of economywide assistance measures in encouraging foreign investment in the Australian economy. Such an outcome will also benefit the Australian information technology sector by promoting its growth and export drive as a result of the access to higher levels of technology and managerial expertise.

Conclusion and Policy Implications

Trade liberalization has played a pivotal role in improving the export orientation of all the (two-digit) manufacturing industries in the period 1974/75-2000/01. However, those industries concurrently subjected to industry-specific assistance measures (e.g., the TCF and motor vehicle industries) have exhibited the quickest improvement in export-oriented production relative to the other manufacturing industries that were not subjected to these measures.

The effectiveness of industry-specific assistance measures in helping to turnaround the TCF and motor vehicle industries' production from the domestic to international market also indicates the possibility of implementing such policy measures in order to achieve an improved export performance of the Australian information technology sector. Although industry and more general assistance measures have been used, an expansion of these measures is nevertheless required as the export growth of this sector has stagnated, whilst the contribution of information technology exports to total manufacturing exports has remained at very low levels.

The expansion of industry-specific assistance measures for the information technology sector however is likely to be more effective than in the past because of the substantial falls in import protection levels for the economy generally. The resulting intensification of import competition is therefore likely to encourage firms in this sector to consider utilising these measures so as to raise their international competitiveness in order to cushion themselves from the stronger import competition. This improvement in international competitiveness in turn will simultaneously enhance export growth. An improved export performance of the Australian information technology sector will not only impact favourably on the trade balance of this sector, but simultaneously enhance the economy's output and employment growth performance given the magnitude of this sector's contribution to GDP. It is also important to note an improvement in international competitiveness also implies higher economy efficiency which will keep the price of information technology goods lower than otherwise, thereby combating the input costs of the manufacturing sector and economy more generally as a result of the significance of the goods as inputs in the generation of output.

However, Krugman (1983) argues that industry-specific assistance measures are more likely to distort the efficient allocation of resources as reflected in over or under allocation of resources. He cites the example of the Japanese steel and semi-conductor industries where the provision of industry-specific assistance measures accelerated the inflow of resources as a time when the market was already achieving this result, ultimately leading to excess productive capacity being installed and hence falling rates of return. Nevertheless, Krugman (1983) also argues that the introduction of industry-specific assistance measures can be effective if clear-cut criteria are established. He argues that these criteria constitute market failure based on:

- Positive externalities
- Dynamic economies based on R&D activities and "learning by doing"

The above two criteria are further justified when used to capture the high rents on the international market.

It would appear that the Australian information technology sector can achieve the above three objectives with the expansion of industry-specific measures for this sector. For example, higher levels of output in information technology goods and services will have positive externalities as a result of their use to help the economy produce higher levels of output. Moreover, the higher production of information technology goods and services will assist export growth in these goods. The importance of this latter objective is highlighted by the fact that international trade in the information technology area has been exhibiting above average growth in the last 20 years.

References

Athukorala, P. (1995). Internationalisation and structural adoption. *Economic Papers, 14*(1), 1-11.

Australian Bureau of Statistics. Various issues. Cat. no. 5204, Australian System of National Accounts.

Australian Bureau of Statistics. Various issues. Cat. no. 5302, Balance of Payments and International Investment Position.

Australian Bureau of Statistics. Various issues. Cat. no. 5422, *International Merchandise Trade.*

Australian Bureau of Statistics. Various issues. Cat. no. 8221, *Manufacturing Industry.*

Building a competitive Australia. (1991). Canberra: A.G.P.S.

Bullock, M., Grenville, S., & Heenan, G. (1993). The exchange rate and the current account in the exchange rate, international trade and the balance of payments. *Reserve Bank of Australia*, 85-140.

Button, J. (1984, May 29). *Motor vehicle policy statement.* News release no. 37/34. Canberra, Australia: Minister for Industry Technology and Commerce.

Button, J. N. (1987, June). Statement to Parliament on the textiles, clothing & footwear industries by Senator The Honourable John N. Button. *Minister for Industry, Technology & Commerce.*

Conlon, R. M., & Perkins, J. A. (1995). Automotive industry policy in Australia: Origins, import and prospects. *Economic Papers, 14*(3), 49-68.

Economic Planning Advisory Council. (1993). *Issues In competition policy.* Canberra, Australia: A.G.P.S.

Garnaut, R. (1991). Trade and industry policy. *Economic Papers, 10*(2), 18-33.

Goldsworthy Report. (1997). *The global information economy: The way ahead.* Canberra, Australia: A.G.P.S.

Industries Assistance Commission. (1984). *Computer software and hardware, typewriters and office machines.* Report no. 338. Canberra, Australia: A.G.P.S.

Industry Commission. (1995), *Australian manufacturing industry and international trade data 1968/69-1992/93.* Canberra, Australia: A.G.P.S.

Krugman, P. (1983). Targeted industrial policies: Theory and evidence. *Federal Reserve Bank of Kansas City,* 123-55.

Krugman, P. R. (1986). Introduction: New thinking about trade policy. In P. R. Krugman (Ed.), *Strategic trade policy and the new international economic order.* Cambridge, MA: MIT Press.

Marks, A., & Sadeghi, M. (1998). Testing the Olson hypothesis within the Australian context. *Australian Economic Review, 31*(2), 130-144.

Mckinsey and Co. (1993). *Emerging exporters: Australia's high value added manufacturing exporters.* Final report to the Australian Manufacturing Council.

Menzies, G. (1994). Explaining the timing Of Australia's manufactured export boom. *Australian Economic Review, 10*(4), 72-86.

Mortimer Report. (1997). *Going for growth: Business programs for investment, innovation and export.* Canberra, Australia: A.G.P.S.

Organisation for Economic Cooperation & Development. (1998). *Human capital investment.* Paris: Centre for Educational Research and Innovation.

Owens, D. (1995). The button plan in restrospect. *Economic Papers, 14*(3), 69-79.

Spencer, B. J., & Brander, J. A. (1983). International R and D rivalry and industrial strategy. *Review of Economic Studies, 50*(7), 20-31.

Swan, P., & Zeitch, J. (1992). The emerging Australian manufacturing export response to microeconomic reform. *Australian Journal of Management, 17*(1), 21-41.

Endnotes

[1]   It is important to emphasis that this study has been restricted to the two-digit level because of the inconsistent classification of manufacturing exports (SITC basis) and turnover in the manufacturing sector (ANZIC basis). This, in turn, has generally prevented the calculation of the value of export-oriented production at the three- and four-digit manufacturing subdivisions. In particular, whilst data is available on the value of turnover at the one-, two-, three- and four-digit levels on an ANZIC basis, data on the value of manufacturing exports is only available at the one- and two-digit levels on an ANZIC basis.

[2]   The Australian Bureau of Statistics (ABS) has initially collected data for the variables related to the two-digit manufacturing level on an Australian Standard International Classification (ASIC) basis from 1968/69-1991/92 and on the Austra-

lian and New Zealand International Classification thereafter. The data collected on an ASIC basis has therefore been converted to an ANZIC basis. In addition, the "miscellaneous manufacturing category" has amalgamated the relatively smaller industries (on the basis of the value of turnover) so as to accommodate the availability of data on such a basis and for simplicity. In relation to the former, this amalgamation has also been enforced due to data on the value of turnover and exports not been available for the printing publishing and recorded media and wood and paper product manufacturing before 1991/92 because of the restructuring of these industries thereafter. This category therefore comprises the "other manufacturing", "printing publishing and recorded media", "wood and paper and product manufacturing" and "non metallic mineral product manufacturing" industries.

[3]   Data limitation has prevented the extension of the analysis to the earlier trade liberalisation period of 1971/72-1973/74. For example, no data was available for the non-rural export price deflator which was necessary to calculate the real value of exports for the various manufacturing industries.

[4]   The motor vehicle industry has been considered as opposed to the motor vehicle and parts industry because it has been relatively easier to obtain data for the former. Moreover, the parts industry is appreciably smaller than the motor vehicle industry.

[5]   The introduction mentioned that data is unavailable to calculate the value of export-oriented production at the three- and four-digit manufacturing subdivisions. However, the SITC classification of exports does provide data on the value of motor vehicle exports. The availability of data on the value of turnover for all four manufacturing subdivisions has therefore made it possible to calculate the value of export-oriented production in the motor vehicle industry.

[6]   Apart from the motor vehicle and TCF industries, pharmaceuticals, shipbuilding and information technology industries were the other manufacturing industries subjected to industry-specific assistance measures. However, data is unavailable for key variables of these industries during the period under consideration. For example, no data was available for the level of turnover to help calculate export orientation.

[7]   Information technology is defined as computing and telecommunications equipment, which corresponds to SITC 75 and 76, respectively.

[8]   Data on the value of turnover for the information technology sector is not available. This has therefore prevented the calculation of export orientation for this sector.

Chapter XI

Recent Developments of Digital Cash Projects in Japan

Nobuyoshi Yamori, Nagoya University, Japan

Narunto Nishigaki, Okayama University, Japan

Abstract

Most discussions and analyses regarding Japanese financial institutions during the 1990s have focused on the lingering effects of the collapse of the bubble economy, including huge non-performing loans and large-scale bank failures. Thus, it is natural for foreign observers to fail to acknowledge that many Japanese banks and other non-bank enterprises have conducted forward-looking projects despite their financial difficulties. One of these projects has been to develop digital cash technology and promote its usage. Because people in Japan tend to use cash for daily payments more often than people in other nations, if the Japanese begin using digital cash instead of traditional cash (i.e., Bank of Japan's notes and coins), we anticipate that digital cash will have a larger potential effect on the society and economy in Japan than in other nations. Efforts to establish digital cash projects made discernible progress in the early 2000s, and digital cash is more commonly used now in Japan than in other IT-advanced countries. This chapter attempts to provide an overview of the recent development of digital cash projects in Japan, and to discuss the issues involved in the further growth of digital cash usage. This chapter is organized as follows. Section 1 presents the introduction. In Section 2, we explain the historical developments of digital cash projects in Japan. Section 3 discusses what factors led to remarkable progress in digital cash usage in the early 2000s. Section 4 describes the remaining issues that must be addressed for further growth of digital cash usage. Finally, Section 5 concludes the chapter.

Introduction

Foreign observers who know that Japan suffered prolonged financial difficulties and an economic slump in the 1990s may be surprised to find that the use of digital cash as a tool of payments or settlements has grown rapidly in Japan. In fact, an increasing number of people in Japan use digital cash for shopping. In addition, most Japanese people know the names used for digital cash, such as "Edy" or "Suica", even if they do not use digital cash themselves. The Japanese have become familiar with digital cash.

Only several years ago, financial economists thought that the diffusion of digital cash or electronic money would not easily occur[1]. The reason was that there were many obstacles to the spread of digital cash. As we indicate in this chapter, a significant number of those obstacles have been eliminated by the government and through the efforts of many private enterprises. The main purpose of this chapter is to examine the factors affecting digital cash diffusion in Japan. For this purpose, we would like to examine the history of various digital cash projects in Japan during the past decade.

We would like to point out that many problems remain to be solved before further growth of the digital cash business in this country can occur. One of the characteristics of the digital cash business in Japan is that digital cash schemes are mainly managed by the private sector rather than the public sector, and issuers of digital cash are not limited to banks. In other words, non-financial firms can issue "cash" now. In relation to such circumstances, it is necessary to consider what restrictions or policies are needed to maintain a stable payment system.

This chapter is organized as follows. Section 2 examines the history of digital cash projects in Japan during the past decade. Section 3 examines the factors for the spread of digital cash in Japan. Section 4 indicates the problems that must be solved for further growth and stability of the digital cash system in this country. Section 5 presents the conclusion.

History of Digital Cash Projects in Japan

Start-Up Period: 1995-1997

1. *High Potentiality of Information Technology*

The three years from 1995 to 1997 can be considered the start-up period of electronic money or digital cash projects in Japan. Remarkably, innovative technologies like multi-functional-type or remote-type IC cards, which made digital cash businesses in Japan superior to that in other countries in the early 2000s had already been developed in Japan before 1995. It is well known among digital cash researchers that Tim Jones and Graham Higgins, who are the parents of "Mondex", the first smart card-type digital cash, entrusted the development of the card system to Japanese enterprises such as Dai Nippon Printing, Hitachi, Matsushita Electric Industrial and Oki Electric Industry in 1991. These corporations had researched and been developing IC-card payment technologies since the mid-1980s. For example, Oki Electric Industry had been involved in developing the IC-card system "Apron Card" in Kyoto City since 1986, which became an actual usable card in April 1992, when Mondex was still under experimentation[2].

2. *Governmental Initiative*

However, it was governmental initiatives, beginning in 1995 that led nationwide experimental activities in electronic payment and settlements in Japan. At the initiative of the Ministry of Finance (MOF), the Bank of Japan (BOJ), Fuji Bank[3], Nippon Telegraph and Telephone (NTT) and Fujitsu Corporation organized a council for the introduction of digital cash in October 1995. The council discussed whether there would be a strong demand for digital cash in Japan, how they would be able to avoid forgeries and robberies, and how they would be able to prevent money laundering.

In 1996, many private Japanese banks launched their own digital cash projects. For example, in April 1996, Daiichi Kangyo Bank, Sakura Bank and Asahi Bank[4] introduced the use of a smart card for digital cash in the Waterfront Area of Tokyo, as an experiment. Additionally, in October of the same year, the Ministry of Transport (predecessor of the Ministry of Land, Infrastructure and Transport) together with Tokyo-Mitsubishi Bank, Sumitomo Bank and Sanwa Bank took part in this Waterfront Area experiment. The goal of the project was to develop an IC-card commuter ticket system that would allow passengers not only to pay for an override charge, but also to buy food and other consumer goods in and around train stations. This technology afterward provided a technological base for "Suica", which is one of the most diffused and popularized types of digital cash in Japan. The other digital cash-related projects that started in this period are summarized in Table 1.

As other private sector projects, in February 1996, the Hitachi group, using their experiences obtained in the United Kingdom, began to focus on developing their own

Table 1. Early digital cash projects in Japan (-1997)

Year	Month	District	Content
1992	Apr	Kyoto City, Nishi-shindo -nishikikai shopping street	An IC-card system, "Apron Card," was introduced for use along a local shopping street.
1995	Oct	Metropolis, Tokyo	Daiichi Kangyo Bank and NTT Data Communications jointly develop an ATM that could handle digital cash.
1996	Mar	Metropolis, Tokyo	Sakura Bank established a special section devoted to the development of digital cash technology.
	Apr	Waterfront Area, Tokyo	Daiichi Kangyo Bank, Sakura Bank and Asahi Bank began an experiment with the Smart-card type of digital cash.
	June	Ogaki City, Gifu Pef.	An IC-card experiment was begun at a multimedia center "Soft-pier Japan".
	Oct	Komagane City, Nagano Pref.	An IC-card system, "Tsuretette Card" was introduced for use on a local shopping street.
	Nov	Ina City, Nagano Pref.	An IC-card system, "Iina-Chan Card" was introduced for use on a local shopping street.
	Dec	Shizuoka Pref.	Shizouka Prefecture organized a society for the study of Electronic Commerce.
1997	Apr	Metropolis, Tokyo	Asahi Bank and Matusushita Electric Industrial introduced IC-card type digital cash on the campus of Waseda University in cooperation with the University Co-op.
	July	Mitaka City, Tokyo	An experiment of digital cash in the shopping street in front of JR Mitaka Station.
	Aug	Yamagata Pref.	Nippon Arcadia Network, the third sector of the Prefecture, started an experiment using digital cash and e-commerce.
		Aomori Pref.	Michinoku Bank took part in the Business of Mondex International.
	Sept	Fukuoka Pref.	An IC-card experiment in which Fujitsu took a leading part began.
	Oct	Kobe City	An IC-card experiment with multi-functions including prepaid, credit and online payments was initiated.
	Nov	Kanto-Koshinetsu District	A new settlement system was established through the cooperation of 59 universities in the Kanto-Koshinetsu District collaborating with NTT Data and several city banks.

digital cash technology in Japan. In competition with Hitachi, the Mitsubishi group decided to invest in the subsidiary of Mondex in Japan, which was established in June 1996 by the Industrial Bank of Japan, Sakura Bank, Asahi Bank, NTT and Hitachi.

3. *Collaborations with Overseas Firms*

The most remarkable development in the period after the second half of 1996 was that many Japanese firms began collaborating with foreign firms to start digital cash projects. In August 1996, Japan Information Printing, whose main business was to print prepaid cards, collaborated with Switzerland's *Kaldak* to produce IC cards. Moreover, in December, Hitachi took an order for an in-bank settlement system from *Westpac Trust*, the largest bank in New Zealand[5]. In the first half of 1997, Sumitomo Credit Service collaborated with *Microsoft*, *Veriphon* and *GTE* to develop a new electronic settlement service system on the Internet, and this consortium of companies strove to be the first to commercialize such a system in Japan[6]. *GTE* also established a new company with Nomura Research Institute, NTT Mobile Communications and B.U.G.[7], and they issued electronic certificates for Sumitomo Credit and JCB in April 1997. *Microsoft*, on the other hand, competing with *GTE*, suddenly announced its participation in the project with Sumitomo Credit, and it collaborated with JCB to develop a new settlement system. *Microsoft* intended to overcome its rival company, *Netscape Communications*, which had collaborated with *VISA International* and Toshiba Corporation on digital cash experiments.

4. *General Public Attitude During This Period*

In the early stage of electronic money projects and e-businesses in Japan, consumers seemed hesitant to use digital cash. According to a survey on the opinions of financial institutions' customers conducted in August 1996 by the Institute for Posts and Telecommunication Policy, one-third of respondents answered that they were worried about innovations in finance such as digital cash and home-banking. Only 2% of respondents used home-banking services. Forty-one percent of them did not anticipate using home-banking services in the future, while 13% showed interest in using the services. Also, an astonishing 69% believed that home-banking services were not necessary, and 54% also said that they were not interested in using digital cash.

Moreover, according to a questionnaire conducted by Nihon Keizai Shinbun in October 1996, 74% of respondents in the United States anticipated significantly greater use of digital cash during the next ten years, compared to only 36% of Japanese respondents.

These results suggest that Japanese consumers in the mid-1990s did not value the convenience offered by digital cash and were concerned about the security of information and payments transmitted through new electronic settlement systems. To promote the general acceptance of digital cash, legislative activities seemed necessary.

5. *Legislative Activities*

Policy makers had recognized that related laws and regulations should be reformed to correspond to new technologies. In May 1996, the MOF organized a committee to review the Prepaid Card Regulations, and asked another committee to review the Foreign Exchange and Foreign Trade Control Act, which allowed only authorized foreign exchange banks to deal with foreign exchange transactions. The MOF then began to prepare for the revision of these laws and regulations. Moreover, in the same month, the Center for Financial Industry Information System, which was an affiliated organization of the MOF, concluded in its research report on electronic settlement that digital cash should be made available to the general public as soon as possible.

In July 1996, the Financial Research Council and the Committee on Foreign Exchange and Other Transactions, which was an advisory body of the MOF, established the Joint Conference on Digital Cash and Electronic Settlement to examine how to diffuse digital cash. At the first meeting of the month, it began discussion on revising the Prepaid Card Regulations and the Act Concerning Acceptance of Contribution, Deposit and Interest[8]. Following the first meeting, the conference was held every month. At these meetings, the necessity of a new legal infrastructure concerning digital cash, the prevention of forgery and the improvement of users' security were discussed[9]. However, at the 11th meeting in May, while some members still asserted that a new law that regulates what firms are able to issue digital cash was needed in order to prevent illegal transactions, others claimed that such legislation would make it difficult for new firms to enter digital cash businesses.

The MOF and the BOJ in particular thought that they did not have to hasten new legislation, because they believed that digital cash would not be widely used that soon in Japanese society, since the use of cash was so widespread and established. Of course, some argued that it was the lack of the legislation that had prevented the diffusion of digital cash in Japan. Whether this was true or not, the beliefs of the MOF and the BOJ have been proven to be wrong[10].

In September 1997, the MOF debated the creation of a new banking license (the Type 2 banking license), which would permit digital cash issuers to engage primarily in the settlement business, thus leaving traditional banks to engage in other businesses like deposit taking and loan offering. The MOF intended to promote the new entry of manufacturers and distributors into the digital cash business by introducing a laxer license. In the same month, the government established a research section on e-commerce in the Advanced Information and Telecommunication Society Promotion Headquarters and held the first advisory meeting to discuss the following subjects:

1.   substantive laws and electronic confirmation,

2.   cipher technologies, and

3.   means of electronic settlement such as digital cash.

Furthermore, the Committee for Financial System Research, at its general meeting late in the same month, decided to set up a conference to consider new legislation that would become necessary due to the diffusion of digital cash and electronic settlement in the future. The conference discussed the standards required of a digital cash issuer and an attestation institute as well as user protection. However, the focus of the discussion was not on the legislation itself, but rather on preparing for future legislation.

Subsequently, the movement of legislation became stagnant. As indicated in sections 3 and 4, it was due to other efforts, rather than legislation, that led to the promotion of diffusing electronic payment means (e.g., digital cash).

Period of Large-Scale Experiments (1998-2000)

The last three years of the 20th century were characterized by several large-scale experiments on the electronic settlement system and digital cash. One of the reasons that large-scale experiments were necessary was to collect as much data on consumers as possible. Another important reason was related to the intrinsic nature of money, the very object of the experiments. Digital cash cannot be regarded as functioning like money until it circulates to a large enough extent. Thus, it is possible to state that banks and firms would never obtain meaningful data about digital cash as long as consumers use digital cash in a narrow *laboratory*.

1. *Large-Scale Experiments in the Metropolis of Tokyo*

The "Shibuya Smart Card Society" was begun on July 16, 1998 (and was completed at the end of October 1999). This project was important for the following reasons. First, it was the largest digital cash experiment in Japan in those days. Second, its experimental area was the center of the Tokyo metropolis.

In this project, customers were able to use a smart card named "Visa Cash" issued by *VISA International* at about 800 locations (such as department stores and restaurants) within a radius of one kilometer from Shibuya Station. Forty-six institutions, including domestic city and regional banks, credit associations, manufacturers, credit card corporations and *VISA International* took part in this project[11].

The records of the project achieved by its completion were reported as follows: Visa Cash was used 89,935 times, the total amounts of the transactions were 116.452 million yen, the cards were reloaded 12,808 times, the total amount of reloading was 103.959 million yen, and the number of IC cards issued was 120,626[12]. It is difficult for us to judge only by these results whether the experiment was successful or not. However, it is at least possible to say that the Shibuya Project did not immediately and directly lead to practical businesses. For example, Tokyu Department Store, one of the participants of the project, had already announced in February 1999 that it would dismantle all of the exclusive terminals at the time of the project's completion. Furthermore, except for internal credit card corporations and a small number of city and regional banks, most financial institutions and all manufacturers proclaimed their intention to withdraw from the system by the end of the project. It is possible that the introductory costs and maintenance costs proved to be significant expenses for the participants, and offset the increase in income. Nevertheless, *VISA International* and other several domestic financial institutions likely gained useful data and operational experience from this experiment.

In parallel with the Shibuya project, another large digital cash experiment in the metropolitan area named "Shinjuku Super Cash" was implemented. Twenty-four private financial institutions in cooperation with NTT established an incorporated body called the "Super Cash Council" and began an empirical experiment with 100,000 monitors at department stores, convenience stores, gas stations and other stores in the Shinjuku area. Regrettably, without reporting on its results, the experiment finished as scheduled in May 2000.

2. *The MPT's Project in Saitama Prefecture*

Before these large experiments within the Tokyo Metropolitan area began in October 1997, the Ministry of Posts and Telecommunications (MPT) began its five-year experiment on a new type of digital cash developed by the BOJ and NTT. The intention was to use digital cash at both real and virtual malls. City banks (including Asahi, Daiwa and Tokai Bank), the Zenshinren Bank, Shinchosha (a large publisher), and several telecommunication companies (NTT and KDD) cooperatively participated in this project. This experiment was first begun at virtual malls, and in February 1998 the real side experiment began in Ohmiya City (present Saitama City), Saitama Prefecture. Initially, only 55 stores around the JR Ohmiya Station participated. In this experiment, customers were able to use the IC card both as an ATM card for postal savings and as a prepaid card at department stores, convenience stores, large chain stores, ticket slot machines at the JR Ohmiya Station and at public telephone booths.

The MPT experiment in Ohmiya City has steadily expanded its scale and range of businesses since its inception. For example, four domestic credit card corporations (e.g., JCB) expressed the desire to participate in the experiment in October 1998, and in February 1999, MPT and VISA International came to an agreement that they would integrate the empirical experimentation in Shibuya and Kobe City into the project in Ohmiya City. According to an interim report in August 1999, one and a half years after the project had begun, the practice area had been expanded to neighboring cities (Urawa and Yono City). Two-hundred and eighty-six stores participated in this project, and about 900 terminals were equipped to handle the cards. Sixty-four thousand cards were issued, and the total transactions amounted to 103.0 million yen.

3. *Other Large-Scale Experiments During This Period*

The other large-scale digital cash projects were *Smart Commerce Japan* in Kobe City, mentioned in Table 1, and a new settlement system established by the cooperatives of 59 universities in the Kanto-Koshinetsu District collaborating with NTT Data Telecommunications and city banks such as Tokyo-Mitsubishi, Daiichi-Kangyo and Fuji. The students at these universities could use the IC card as digital cash for payment at shops of the university co-ops. In this system, a student could electronically transfer funds from his bank account to his IC card through a terminal (a special ATM) that was installed on the campus, and could use the card as a prepaid card when buying writing materials and books, food, and other items. A peculiarity of this card was that it could also be used as a student identification card[13].

4. *Provisional Evaluation for These Large-Scale Experiments*

Making a final evaluation for the large-scale projects mentioned above is impossible until digital cash diffuses sufficiently in cash-oriented Japanese societies. Nevertheless, we think it possible to point out the following at the present stage:

1. It was premature to conclude that it was possible for a nationwide diffusion of digital cash to occur based on the success of an experiment, as long as the available area of digital cash was limited to one or several cities (or wards, which are urban areas).

2. Cost problems could not be overcome by enlarging the size of a project.

3. However, in the sense that these projects together with other small and medium scale experiments could provide opportunities for examining various new and applied technologies, they might possibly contribute to the commercialization of the digital-cash-related technologies.

5. *Support by the Government*

During the period 1998-2000, the Japanese government did not reform legislation, but they did begin to support IC -card-related industries to develop an electronic settlement system in earnest. The Ohmiya project by the MPT was one of such efforts.

In August 2000, the IT revolution subcommittee affiliated with the Diet Members' Union of the Liberal Democratic Party (the LDP, which was the political party in power in Japan) concerning informational industries proposed that IC-card standardization among ministries should be progressed in order to manage individual information by a unified computer system, and that the obligation of document issue had to be exempted for electronic commerce transactions. In October 2000, the Political Responsible Persons' Conference of the Government proposed that public services, including education, transportation, medical care and other administrative services, be provided through a light-speed Internet circuit, and that IC cards would be a useful method in this type of society. These proposals encouraged the government to realize the "electronic government planning"[14] by the end of fiscal year 2003.

The other governmental efforts made for the diffusion of electronic settlement and digital cash are listed in Table 2, as are the efforts made during other periods (before 1998, and after 2000). To varying degrees, these efforts seemed to have led to the full-scale practical use of digital cash in the private sector with a time lag of several years.

Period of Real Commercialization (2001 - Present)

With regards to electronic settlement and digital cash, we can regard the period since 2001 as a time of commercialization. We would like to explain several representative cases below.

1. *The Appearance of the Japanese Original Digital Cash – "Edy"*

One of the most remarkable cases is that of "Edy". It does not mean an IC card, but an electronic value, which can be filled up using various kinds of IC cards and potable telephones with built-in ICs that adopt a non-touching (or remote) technology method called "FeliCa," which was developed by Sony. The empirical experiment of Edy was begun at Gate City Ohsaki in front of JR Ohsaki Station in July 1999, and the genuine commercial service of Edy began in November 2001 after several successful experiments were conducted. The management and promotion enterprise of Edy is Bitwallet, which is now financed by 61 (initially 11) corporations such as Sony and NTT Docomo Telecommunications.

Edy service providers consist of Bitwallet as a core enterprise, seven IC-card issuers, two card printing makers, 13 value issuer firms (e.g., credit card corporations and city banks), 37 technical operating firms which provide Edy terminals, 27 solution firms which supply vending machines that can accept Edy, and more than 13,000 chain stores, including online shops, as of the end of December 2004. Chain stores in all prefectures now accept

Table 2. Governmental contributions related to the diffusion of IC card and e-money

Subject	Year	Content of Activity
The Government or LDP	1997	Establishment of a research section on e-commerce in the Advanced Information and Telecommunication Society promotion headquarters. (Sep)
	2000	The subcommittee of LDP Diet Member's Union for IT industries proposed the standardization of IC cards among ministries. (Aug)
		The Political Responsible Persons' Conference of the government gave the outlines of preparations to realize the Japanese version of the IT revolution. (Oct)
	2001	Establishment of the headquarters on IT strategies. (Jan)
		"E-Japan Planning" with over-priority was suggested. (May)
	2002	Three bills related to electronic government and local government were passed by the cabinet. (Jun)
Ministry of Finance	1995	Organization of a council with private banks for the introduction of digital cash. (Oct)
	1996	Established the Joint Conference on Digital Cash and Electronic Settlement. (Jul)
		Started to revise the prepaid card regulations and the act concerning acceptance of contribution, deposit and interest. (Jul)
	1998	"The Report of the Joint Conference on Digital Cash and Electronic Settlement". (Apr)
Ministry of Justice	1996	Established two small committees for studying electronic commerce. (Dec)
Ministry of International Trade and Industry (- 2000) Ministry of Economy, Trade and Industry (2001 -)	1998	Spent 42,500 million yen on 158 topics adopted in "the Developing and Collaborating Businesses of Advanced Information System". (Dec)
	2000	Set up a joint project with the European Commission for establishing standardized methods for a next generation IC-card system. (Jun)
	2001	Began online issue of an electronic autographed public document. (Jun)
Ministry of Transport (- 2000) Ministry of Land, Infrastructure and Transport (2000 -)	1996	Started supporting the development of an IC-card commuter ticket system. (Oct)
	2001	Developed a multi-functional IC card available both for getting on public transportation and for shopping. (Nov)
	2003	An empirical experiment was begun on the e-check-in system. (Jan - Mar)
		Achieved development of a system in which a potable telephone with a built-in IC was available for getting on trains and for ETC (electronic toll collection system) of a superhighway.
	2004	Started an empirical experiment for an IC-card commuter ticket in east Asian countries. (Feb)
Ministry of Welfare (- 2000), Ministry of Health, Labor and Welfare (2001 -)	2000	Began to examine changing from paper-based health insurance certificates to IC-card versions. (Apr)
		Embarked on the diffusion of an IC card as a health insurance certificate and as a resident's card. (Oct)
	2003	Began a model business for care insurance certificate IC-cards. (Sept)
Ministry of Posts and Telecommunications (- 2000) Japan Post (2003 -)	1997	Started a five-year experiment on a new type of digital cash available for both real and virtual malls, but at the beginning only in virtual malls. (Oct)
	1998	Extended its previous digital cash experiment to real malls in Ohmiya City. (Feb)
	2000	Embarked on joint development of a system in which a portable telephone could be used as an IC-card terminal, in collaboration with several manufacturers. (Mar)
	2003	*Japan Post* started to issue postal saving cards loaded with Edy's functions. (Aug)
Ministry of Internal Affairs and Communications	2002	Revised the ministerial ordinance related to radio wave laws and abolished business licenses for the remote type IC card. (Jul)

Edy. The categories of business have also been extended to various types of industries, such as food and drink, shopping, amusement parks and arcades, medical clinics and other places. A report released by Bitwallet stated that by the end of December 2004, about 6.8 million IC cards (including cellular phones) that can use Edy had been issued, and the number of transactions using Edy had gone up to about five million per month. From the Shibuya Smartcard Society's experience, where the average per-transaction amount was about 1500 yen, the amount of use per month may be about 7.5 billion yen total.

At present, Edy still remains a closed-loop system, not an open loop one[15]. All information concerning the transactions settled by Edy has been designed to be concentrated in an operational center of Bitwallet, and it is impossible to exchange Edy values freely among customers, stores and firms. However, there is an important difference between Edy and former closed-loop digital cash systems. Edy can be purchased on credit, and Edy cards can be charged in exchange for cash; thus, a bank balance equal to the amount of payment by Edy is not necessarily needed.

2. *Suica: Digital Cash Evolved from a Carfare IC Card*

Another widespread digital cash IC card in Japan is called "Suica", which has already been mentioned above. There are two kinds of Suica: a Suica-Io-Card (ticket) and a Suica Pass. East Japan Railway issues these cards. They were introduced at 424 JR stations in and on the outskirts of the Tokyo metropolis in November 2001, after several empirical experiments were conducted in the Tokyo Waterfront Area. The number of Suica holders has increased from 2 million (two months after the introduction) to more than 10 million in October 2004. The reasons for the diffusion of Suica are as follows. First, since December 2002, the card has been available outside the metropolitan Tokyo area (for example, in the Sendai district) and at many railway and Shinkansen stations. Second, the card has also been available on the Tokyo Waterfront Railway and the Tokyo Monorail stations since March 2002. Therefore, it is very convenient for people in Tokyo to use Suica. Third, since August 2004, Suica can be used as an ICOCA, which is a similar IC card ticket and commutation ticket issued by West Japan Railways (e.g., in the Osaka District).

Of course, if Suica was merely an IC card corresponding to the transport system, it would never be able to compete with Edy. However, besides functioning as a ticket and a commuter ticket, Suica can be used for financial transactions. In July 2003, "View Suica", which is a hybrid Suica card, was introduced, making it possible to credit the deficit in a carfare IC card. And in March 2004, Suica became available for shopping at station stalls and restaurants in station yards. Moreover, since September of 2004, the card can be used to pay for goods at convenience stores on the street. The number of Suica cards issued with a digital cash function (other than carfares) was up to 4,430,000 at the end of October, 2004. As of the same time, Suica could be used as a ticket or a commuter ticket at 847 stations of East JR, West JR, the Tokyo Waterfront Railway and the Tokyo Monorail, and as digital cash at 653 stores such as NEWDAYS or Family Mart. East JR intends to extend the use of the card to the Niigata area (within the 2005 fiscal year). In rivalry with Edy, "Mobile Suica," which uses a portable phone as a loading device, is also going to be introduced (within the second half of FY 2005)[16].

The way in which East JR expanded the usage of IC cards is instructive for international readers. JR first introduced the IC-card ticket (Suica) to its customers to show them how convenient and useful the card could be, and once that had occurred, East JR added digital cash functions to the Suica.

Table 3. The sizes of digital cash projects in Japan

		Number of Issue	Amount of use (1000 yen)
Experimental Projects	Shibuya Smartcard Society	120,626 (98.07-99.05)	116,452 (98.7- 99.5)
	MPT project (Ohmiya City)	64,000 (98.02-99.08)	103,000 (98.2- 99.8)
	Smart Commerce Japan (Kobe City)	24,468 (97.10-98.04)	56,000 (97.10-98.4)
Commercialized Projects	IC card corresponding to the Edy	6,800,000 (01.11-04.12)	7,500,000 (per month)
	Suica Card with prepaid function	3,070,000 (01.11-04.06)	....

*Note: *The data concerning the amounts used in commercialized projects are as of the end of 2004.*
***The amounts used in commercialized projects were estimated by the authors.*

Finally, we have observed that the scales of the commercialized projects (the Edy and Suica) have already become much larger than any former experimental projects (see Table 3).

3. *Governmental Activities Related to IC Card Since 2001*

In January 2001, the government started up the IT strategy headquarters, and in June of that year, the headquarters settled on the E-Japan Emphasis Plan aiming for the establishment of the most advanced IT nation within five years. The following applications of IT were planned. The government provided several IT model districts with a forefront electronic infrastructure. In those districts, (1) an election would be conducted by electronic ballot, (2) people would be able to receive electronic medical services (for example, receive a diagnosis via the Internet), (3) the management of emigrants and immigrants in the airport would be easily completed with IC cards, and (4) a system in which people can operate home appliances by remote control using a cellular phone would be introduced[17]. The Cabinet Council introduced three bills concerning the completion of paperwork electronically for the government and municipality, making it possible to file registrations of one's marriage and final tax returns online, and to obtain a copy of one's resident's card from one's PC.

Table 2 shows other governmental efforts made during this period. The government efforts listed in Table 2 include governmental and administrative activities, which might not seem to have any direct relation to digital cash. However, it is notable that these efforts were important in considering factors that have encouraged broad use of digital cash. Various kinds of IC cards, including digital cash smart cards, have been diffused due to the development of hybrid (or multifunction) technologies.

The Factors for the Spread of
Digital Cash in Japan

Public Sector's Leadership

As stated in the previous section, the rapid spread of digital cash in Japan has been highly dependent on the overall support provided by the national and local governments. The national and local authorities assisted in diffusing IC cards, but not in promoting electronic settlement by digital cash, which is just one of the information technologies. However, because the government provided support for the entire IC-card field, the diffusion of digital cash occurred as a result. One of the factors in this diffusion was hybrid technology, which brings about the spread of digital cash together with other IC card usages such as for transportation, medical treatment and administrative services. In addition, another factor is the fact that the increase in the demand to use IC cards in new ways has significantly reduced the production costs of IC cards. Therefore, financial institutions and other companies have found it easier to introduce IC technologies (e.g., electronic settlement) into their businesses. We describe this in detail in the next sub-section.

However, the entire support of the public sector would have resulted in failure if the private sector had not made its own efforts. First, many private enterprises had already accumulated experiences and advanced technologies related to electronic settlements before the participation of the public sector in the field (i.e., in 1995, as mentioned at the head of section 2). Examples of Japanese original technologies concerning electronic settlements are listed in Table 4. Second, private firms in Japan have made efforts to develop electronic settlement technologies to better serve the customers and market.

Table 4. Original Japanese technologies related to electronic settlement

Year	Technology name	Companies or governmental bodies	Content of system
- 1994	A remote-type IC card	Matsushita Electric and others	It can remotely read and write on an IC card.
1997	An IC-commutation ticket	Ministry of Transport and others	It allows passengers to pay for an override charge along with various purchases.
- 1997	A common card both in real and virtual malls	VISA International, Toshiba and others	It is an IC card available both in real malls and virtual malls.
- 2000	Cellular phone with digital cash function	NTT Docomo, Sony and others	Digital cash functions are built into a cellular phone.

Decrease of IC Card Issue Costs: Innovation and Expansion of the Market

As indicated in the example of the Shibuya Smartcard Society, the introductory costs and maintenance expenses of the electronic settlement system were major obstacles to the spread of digital cash. Of all such costs, the cost of issuing IC cards was especially expensive. When Ogaki-Kyoritsu Bank introduced IC-card digital cash as an experiment at Soft-pier-Japan (Ogaki City, Gifu Pref.) about 10 years ago, the issue cost per IC card was about 1,300 yen, ten times the cost of a standard cash card[18]. Now, the issue cost per IC card has fallen below 150 yen. Therefore, it has become much easier for financial institutions to begin electronic payment services.

Needless to say, the innovations in the technology have contributed a great deal to the increasing use of IC cards during the past decade. However, as mentioned above, the expansion of the IC-card market has also contributed a great deal to the decrease of IC-card issue costs through a scale merit (i.e., the reduction of manufacturing costs by mass production). Currently in Japan, there are six fields in which IC cards are in demand: (1) finances, (2) traffic and transportation, (3) administrative tasks, (4) identification (ID) cards, (5) communications and (6) medical care. Among these, the areas related to payment-and-settlement are (1), (2) and part of (6). But we have to consider the fact that by slight technical changes, an IC card production line can be corresponded to the functions in all of these areas. Therefore, even if a demand increases not in the area of digital cash but in other field of IC card, through a scale merit concerning IC cards' common components, the issue cost of digital cash could be reduced as the result. In other words, if the demand for IC cards in any field increased, the issue cost of digital cash would decrease.

What has Changed by the Introduction of the Edy and Suica Cards?

At present, there are two types of digital cash systems in Japan. One is a regional promotion type based on a local area or a local shopping street, which can only be used on a certain street or certain shops. The Apron Card for the Nishi-shindo-nishikikai shopping street (Kyoto City) and two smartcard systems in Nagano Prefecture are typical examples of this type of digital cash system. This system is self-concluded within the consumer's living space, and has been commercialized on their terms. A main purpose of this system is to prevent outflows of customers to large-scale shops in the suburbs or to the nearest large cities. Therefore, these projects seem to have reached this initial goal, at least to some degree.

However, Edy, Suica and ICOCA are used in larger areas. The plan is for this large-area type system to be used not only in Tokyo and Osaka, but throughout the entire nation. Although these systems have not been open-looped yet, their availability over the whole country will undoubtedly improve their general acceptability, which is one of the most important characteristics of money. Therefore, the wider the regions where one can use these currencies, the more people would want to use them. For example, if a businessperson travels around the whole country, he or she would be more likely to use digital cash if it is available from Hokkaido to Okinawa.

It is relatively easy for firms or stores to introduce Edy into their business because of its correspondence to all IC cards or cellular phones that use the FeliCa method. However, the advantage of Suica (or ICOCA) is that it is linked to the JR rail system. The success of Suica is due to the East JR's strategy for covering all places that businesspersons often visit.

Conveniences That Have Arisen by Multifunction (or Hybrid) Types of Smart Cards

Customers will never accept digital cash if they are unaccustomed to using it. Only after they acknowledge that its usefulness is greater than that obtained from cash or a credit card will they want to use it. Thus, whether digital cash offers greater advantages than cash or credit cards do is crucial for the diffusion of digital cash.

For example, the three regional type digital cash systems mentioned above were commonly accompanied with a point service function in addition to an ordinal prepaid function. A typical point service for shopping is to give points to customers who buy something with digital cash. For example, a customer obtains one point when he purchases something costing 100 yen. In the Apron Card and other systems, a customer's purchasing information is automatically converted into equivalent points, and these points are added to the prepaid value of the IC card. For the Apron Card, four yen points (four times the usual number of points) are given for the purchasing price of 100 yen. Thus, the point service function gives premium value to digital cash.

Therefore, the following inequality determines whether digital cash is used or not:

Utility from using cash (or credit card) <

   Utility from using digital cash + Premium value given to digital cash usage

When this inequality is satisfied, the customer will be willing to use digital cash. The premium makes up for the costs to customers for digital cash usage, costs that include inexperience, operational trouble and uneasiness. The premium makes customers feel payments by other than digital cash causing losses. The premium value makes customers feel that if they pay for things using actual cash, a credit card, or by some other means, they'll suffer economic losses. It is possible that if the Mondex (UK), the first IC card type digital cash in the world, had had a point service function (without sticking only to a prepaid function), it would have become a more popular card worldwide. Mondex's failure was inevitable, because the inequality was not satisfied because Mondex did not offer any premiums to customers.

Similarly, E-Cash (Digi-Cash Co., U.S.), the first network type digital cash in the world, committed the same kind of failure. It competed with credit card companies by using superior encryption technology on the Internet. When the bankruptcy of Digi-Cash Company was declared in November 1998, a journalist analyzed the cause of the failure as due to the following. As Internet consumers became accustomed to using credit cards for online shopping, the micro-payment market became smaller and smaller[19]. However, this analysis only presented one side of the facts. The more important cause of the failure is that a customer could use a credit card both in real shops on the street and in virtual malls on the net, while she or he was not able to use E-cash other than for online shopping. Therefore, despite the advanced anonymity provided by E-Cash, customers knew that the utility of using E-Cash was much less than that obtained from using a credit card. In Japan, hybrid technologies have been applied on synthetic IC cards that include credit, debit and cash-card functions together with a prepaid function available both at real stores and online. Japanese firms collaborating with the public sector have selected a *symbiotic* relationship rather than a *competitive* one in this respect. An interesting fact is that credit card companies have mainly promoted hybrid smart cards in Japan.

Currently, nationwide type cards function as credit, debit and cash cards. However, regional promotion type cards have an administrative function in addition to a point service function (see Figure 1). In sum, these two types of digital cash have evolved independently in Japan.

Innovations in Techniques

Hybrid and other new modes of smart cards have become available due to various technological innovations. The technologies have advanced rapidly. Recently, for

Figure 1. A comparison of functions in each digital cash system

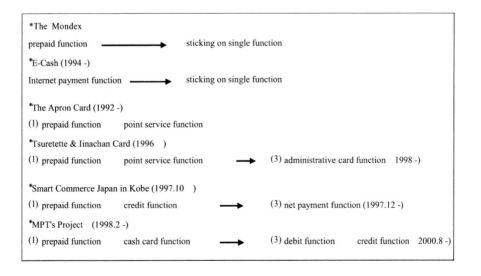

example, a new system was developed that makes it possible to transfer money directly from an ATM to a cellular phone. In addition, various ID (identification) techniques such as fingerprint attestation, face attestation, iris attestation and vein attestation have been developed in order to improve consumers' reliance on electronic settlements.

At the World Congress on Information Technology (WCIT) held in Athens in 2004, the electronic tender system applied in Yokosuka City in Kanagawa Prefecture as a public sector and East JR's Suica as a private sector were awarded the IT prizes of World Information Technology and Services Alliance (WITSA). Because the prize is reportedly the most important in the IT field worldwide, the Japanese public and private sectors were recognized as having the highest level of smart card technologies.

Summary

In this section, we consider the factors that have contributed to the rapid diffusion of digital cash in the past few years in Japan. The cooperation between the government and private companies has been the most important factor leading to the diffusion of digital cash. In addition, the following various factors also contributed to the rapid diffusion:

1. The introductory costs and operational expenses of electronic payment systems have been dramatically reduced, due to both improvements in manufacturing technologies and the increase in the demand for IC cards in various areas beyond financial fields.
2. Since the appearance of Edy and Suica, digital-cash-available regions and stores have expanded with increasing speed.
3. The development of hybrid technologies has made digital cash more convenient.
4. Remarkable innovations in attestation technology have improved reliability for consumers.

Unsolved Problems to Ensure a Stable Digital Cash System

What are the remaining issues? What problems will come to light after the spread of digital cash and other consumer electronic settlements? In this section, we consider the problems that remain to be solved to ensure stable and reliable digital cash system.

First, we should consider the problems that used to be obstacles to the diffusion of digital cash but have been forgotten because of the real spread of digital cash. In fact, these problems were not solved, but rather avoided. For example, as mentioned in the previous section, the costs of digital cash usage have been reduced and the range of regions and stores where one can use digital cash and its conveniences have significantly increased.

As a result, the commercialization of the digital cash system has greatly progressed. However, have security and privacy problems been eliminated sufficiently by the progress of ID techniques or remote-type IC-card technologies? Of course, these techniques would, to some extent, contribute to solving these problems. But remote technologies can be abused (individual information and the value of money can be stolen remotely). Additionally, ID technologies in general are also not perfect, and camouflages by various means are still possible. Furthermore, there still remain other problems, such as money laundering and tax evasion. Thus, further improvements of the technologies in this field are needed, as are solid restrictions.

Second, we should not forget confidence problems regarding digital cash issuers. Edy, Suica and other types of commercialized digital cash in Japan are all secured. The values are tentatively guaranteed by the exchange of bank deposits or the cash equivalent to the digital value. However, it is possible that an event occurs in which digital cash as a whole might lose public trust and would trigger runs upon a digital cash issuer. For example, the issuer's failure and mechanical troubles, which make digital value information destroyed or unreadable, may provoke runs on the issuers. A mechanical trouble, although not a very serious one, actually occurred. On October 26, 2002, an automatic ticket machine collected 67,380 yen in total from 290 Suica Pass users by mistake.

Finally, a money supply controllability problem accompanied with the diffusion of digital cash is of concern to the central bank. When the amount of circulation is relatively small, money supply controllability is less likely to be damaged. But it is impossible to disregard this problem once electronic money becomes widely used. It is necessary to examine the controllability problem before it is too late.

Further Government Efforts

As shown in Table 2, legal reforms by the government were made during the start-up period (1995 - 1997). However, since 1998, the government has been inactive in passing legislation. A five-year gap in administrative action in this field suggests that the primary policy of the government was to spread smart cards.

The MOF published the Report of the Informal Gathering for Discussions on Digital Cash and Electronic Settlement. Its primary goal was first to strive for the development and diffusion of electronic settlements and digital cash. The report recommended that legal and institutional frameworks be structured to encourage private firms to design and develop a digital cash system as freely as possible. The report also maintained that it would be desirable to prepare new laws to enable various firms other than depository financial institutions to issue digital cash. The Japanese government's aggressive policy contributed a great deal to the diffusion of electronic settlements all over Japan. However, we would like to note that the Japanese approach stood in contrast to the approach of the European Central Bank during the same period[20]. The ECB claimed that the issuer of digital cash should be limited to banks, whereas the MOF listed only two points as requirements for a digital cash issuer: (1) financial soundness and (2) capabilities in the technique required and in the business practices necessary. In fact, the MOF did not submit the Digital Cash Bill to the Diet. Therefore, no legislation regarding digital cash issuers has been passed.

In 2003, the Ministry of Internal Affairs and Communications and the Ministry of Economy, Trade and Industry began to study a defense plan to protect confidential information stored in an IC card. In 2004, the Financial Services Agency (FSA) also began to consider a user protection plan. For example, a digital cash issuer would be obligated to hold cash and deposits more than half of the amount of the outstanding values of the digital cash.

It is not clear how the BOJ as another financial supervisory authority evaluated the recent diffusion of digital cash. Of course, as long as the main types of digital cash in the country are the closed-loop type, it is possible to think that the monetary policy will not be influenced so soon and so severely, no matter how widely digital cash use will spread. However, the BOJ has to take the possibility into consideration that types of digital cash like Edy and Suica will open their loops after they become as popular as cash. In preparation for "that time", the BOJ must consider the following points:

1. Qualification for digital cash issuers, to ensure that the digital value is backed by cash and deposits;

2. Enhancement of the statistical data concerning digital cash;

3. Various simulations of the trends in the future.

Conclusion

In this chapter, we have examined the factors involved in the recent spread of digital cash and the problems with digital cash projects in Japan that still remain to be solved. First, we took into account the history of digital cash projects of Japan during the past decade, ranging from the initial experiments to the recent commercialization efforts.

With regards to factors accelerating the diffusion, we found that the government did not pass new laws, but instead supported the experiments and commercialization. At the same time, we found that the manufacturing costs of smart cards were significantly reduced through expansion of IC-card markets and technological improvements. Furthermore, the most fundamental causes for diffusion that we pointed out are (1) increasing convenience of digital cash usage, (2) expansion of available districts of digital cash, (3) innovations in ID technologies and (4) close cooperation between the public and private sectors.

Concerning the remaining issues, we enumerated consumer protection problems, confidence problems of digital cash issuers, the money supply controllability problem if digital cash turns into an open-loop system in the future, and other criminal issues such as money laundering. The Japan of today is not necessarily a world leader in all IT industries. However, in the digital cash field, Japan is one of the most advanced countries in the world. Thus, if Japan is to become a "good model" for other countries in this field, policy efforts must be made to remove the various factors destabilizing the digital cash system.

Acknowledgments

The authors appreciate professor Yutaka Kurihara for his valuable comments. Nobuyoshi Yamori also appreciates the Japan Society for the Promotion of Science for its financial support (grant-in-aid for scientific research).

References

European Central Bank. (1998). *Report of Electronic Money*.

Nihon Keizai Shinbun CD-ROM Versions. (1993-1998).

Senda, J. (1997). Electronic money's influences on financial system and bank management. *The Roles of Postal Savings in a Communication and Information Society*, Tokai Postal Administration Bureau, 29-41.

Yamori, N., & Nishigaki, N. (2000). Electronic money project in Japan. Working paper no. 175. Center on Japanese Economy and Business, Columbia Business School.

Web sites:

http://www.edit.ne.jp/~arita/jec/smartjapan,html

http://www.edy.jp/index.html

http://hotwired.goo.ne.jp/news/news/business/story/1594.html

http://www.jreast.co.jp/press/2004_2/20041009.pdf

http://www.jrea–#

http://www.min-iren.gr.jp/search/06press/genki/129/genki129-1.html

Endnotes

[1]   Yamori and Nishigaki (2000) reviewed these opinions.

[2]   Of course, at the same time, some digital cash projects in other developed countries were used in real economic transactions. For example, an electronic settlement service through the Internet was innovated by *First Virtual* in the United States, and IC-card type digital cash in Finland and Denmark, as well as in other countries, were in use before 1995.

[3]   It was one of the largest private banks in Japan. It was merged into the Mizuho Financial Group in 2000.

4   Like Fuji Bank, these banks were also major private banks in Japan. All of them were merged into mega financial groups later. Daiichi Kangyo and Fuji were merged into the Mizuho FG. Sakura Bank was merged into Sumitomo Mitsui Banking Corporation in 2001, and Asahi Bank joined the Resona Group in 2002.

5   These facts suggest that many Japanese industrial firms had already developed innovative techniques that were necessary for electronic finance.

6   This system consisted of two parts. The first part involved electronic attestation (i.e., inputting one's credit card number when ordering goods or services online). The second part involved credit card settlement (i.e., sending electronic information, such as the credit card number, to the credit card company). The method of settlement used was the "SET" system, upon which VISA International and Master Card had previously agreed.

7   A maker of PC-related commodities in Sapporo City (Hokkaido).

8   The regulation, abbreviated to "shusshi-hou", prohibits anyone from accepting deposits without a license. Therefore, if a non-bank issues digital cash in exchange of traditional money, the issuing of digital cash might be regarded as deposit taking, and therefore illegal for non-bank institutions.

9   The conference participants discussed in January who should be an attestation institution that proves the counter party's identity, and in March it focused on the legal rights and duties in electronic payment.

10   As another legislative action, in December 1996, the Ministry of Justice established two small committees to study electronic commerce. The committees began to discuss digital cash systems and to consider how to revise the related civil and commercial laws.

11   There were four types of smart cards: the exhaustible type, repeatable type, IC prepaid and credit card combined type, and IC prepaid and bank ATM card combined type.

12   See http://www.edit.ne.jp/~arita/jec/smartjapan.html

13   However, it did not function outside campuses.

14   It was the plan that the national and local governments would process their administrative affairs through digital or electronic systems.

15   For definitions of "closed-loop type" and "open-loop type", see the glossaries.

16   Suica, like the Edy system, still employs a closed-loop system. However, Suica and Edy cards can be charged in exchange for cash. Therefore, there is a strong possibility that Suica can replace cash as soon as it becomes open looped.

17   Most of these technologies now have been realized (i.e., at the end of fiscal year 2004).

18   See Senda (1997), p.36.

19   See http://hotwired.goo.ne.jp/news/news/business/story/1594.html

20   See European Central Bank (1998).

Chapter XII

Money is What Money Does:
Prospects for an Electronic Money Payment System in Japan

Mariusz K. Krawczyk, Fukuoka University, Japan

Abstract

Despite of amazing progress in information technology that has taken place in recent years, the electronic money failed to live to the expectations and has made little headway into payments systems. The gap between expectations and reality is especially pronounced in Japan. The reason behind the failure of electronic money in Japan is two-fold. First, typical use of electronic money is in general rather limited as long as conventional money is required as a unit of account and a store of value for the former operation. Second, Japanese financial institutions chose very limited standards for their electronic money systems that could not compete with near the monopolistic position the credit card companies enjoy in cashless payment markets. On the contrary, Germany adopted a wide standard that fully utilises the advantages of electronic money as a medium of payment.

Introduction

Technological progress has been a catalyst for great changes in human society ever since the Stone Age. From hunter-gatherer tribes, through feudal agrarian societies, to the urbanisation of the industrial age, to the information technology era the invention of the wheel, the construction of high seas going ships, the steam engine, the electricity, and computing devices each dramatically changed the route along which the human society evolves. Yet the increase in computational power has influenced the mankind in the most spectacular way. It has profoundly changed our means of communication, trade, payment and so forth.

But in spite of indeed amazing progress, the expectations associated with the information technology were, at least in some areas, actually greater than the development we have been witnessing currently. For instance, electronic money has made little headway in the payments market. Currently, most of electronic (i.e., Internet) transactions are settled using credit and debit plastic cards instead of electronic money, as it could have been expected otherwise. The cards have been designed for face-to-face real world transactions and they are by no means ideal for electronic transactions world. Let alone the fraud and moral hazard problems, they involve a lot of costly paperwork and, for that reason, they are not suitable for small transactions and person-to-person transfers. In Japan, where authorities placed a lot of political emphasis on the development of information technology as a way for achieving economic recovery (often dubbed as the "IT revolution"), the gap between the expected results and reality is especially striking.

Why, then, has electronic money failed to penetrate the payments market while electronic commerce and electronic banking seem to have been a success? In my opinion the nature of money as a network commodity helps to explain the puzzle. Looking for answers, the chapter reviews briefly the concept of money and its evolution from a commodity stage to the current form. Then the main features of conventional money are compared to those of electronic money and the prospect for adopting general electronic money payment standard are discussed. After having reviewed the current situation in Japan's payment system the concluding section provides some recommendations necessary for successful implementation of electronic money payments here.

What Money Does

The presence of money around us is so obvious that we usually do not think about what money is. The idea that a certain good may be given up for another more useful one sounds by no means strange to anyone. But the fact that a possessor of a good may be willing to exchange its utility for small seemingly useless metal discs has been always attracting attention of social thinkers who tried to define the nature of money. The answer what money is can help in providing insights what will be the future of money, too.

What is money? The simplest answer is the one given by Hicks that "money is what money does". In economic terms it means that money acts as a medium of exchange, a unit of account, and a store of value. The emergence of money can be traced down to the phenomenon that rational individuals economise on transaction costs of exchanging goods. Carl Menger (2002) quotes the experience of a European traveller in mid-19th century Africa and his encounters with barter world where no money existed.

[To proceed with the Tanganyika cruise] I discovered a good one [boat], however (...) agent wished to be paid in ivory, of which I had none; but I found that Mohammed ibn Salib had ivory, and wanted cloth. Still, as I had no cloth, this did not assist me greatly until I heard that Mohammed ibn Gharib had cloth and wanted wire. This I fortunately possessed. So I gave Mohammed ibn Gharib the requisite amount of wire, upon which he handed over cloth to Mohammed ibn Salib, who in his turn gave (...) agent the wished-for ivory. Then he allowed me to have the boat[1] (Menger, 2002).

If one bears in mind that success has been achieved with a great trouble and loss of time, and undoubtedly also with economic sacrifices then it must be clear that if there had been no money, one must have invented it. Analogously, the evolution of money from commodity money to metal money, to documents representing money, and to electronic impulses stored on plastic cards can be attributed to currency competition that manifests itself in economising on transaction costs.

The same holds for other functions of money. As soon as the money use as means of exchange broadens among a people, money becomes an asset that every economic agent requires. And, as money mediates commodity and capital transactions, there follows the necessity of measuring the value of goods to be exchanged for before any transaction takes place. Money works then as a common denominator of the value (or as a unit of account).

Finally, money allows for transfer of wealth in time and space. This requires that a good intended for such a transfer must be durable, valuable, and capable of being dispatched in space. Those properties are not necessarily found in all goods that may serve as media of exchange or units of account (animals, shells, slaves, etc.). Only a good that meets all the requirements at once can be described as money.

A Short History of Money

As shown in the preceding section, the definition of money is purely functional and disregards its form. And money, since its invention almost three thousand years ago, has appeared in numerous forms. In its most primitive forms, money materialised as salt, rice, shells, decorative beads and so forth, only later gradually assuming forms that better fitted the needs of medium of exchange. Eventually, "precious" metals assumed the role of money because of relative easiness and low cost of storage, durability, and stable rate of exchange into other goods (as our apprehension of precious metals' value less depends on individual tastes than in case of other consumer goods). Of all precious metals, gold became the most desired symbol of wealth. Once precious metals started performing as medium of exchange, unit of account, and store of value their money status became self-reinforcing. That means that the more people used money as money, the more they tended to accept it as money. It was then that the value of money began deriving not from its intrinsic value but from the confidence of those who use it as money that it will be always accepted as a form of payment.

After having assumed its metallic guise, soon money began to depart from its material form. The process began with its role as a store of value. Individuals hoarding metallic money over time needed appropriate place of storage for it. Some of the individuals were better suited to do the storage job than others and were willing to do it for a small profit. In such a way the profession of a banker (goldsmith) has been invented. The banker accepted metal and issued the depositor a note confirming the deposit. Once individuals found out that it was actually much easier to use those notes rather than metals themselves, once again the mechanism of confidence came to work and the notes replaced metal as money. At this point money has started the evolution from its material form towards a claim based on the confidence in the issuer.

As individuals used more and more of banker's notes, the deposited metal lay quietly in deposit and the banker eventually discovered that only a small part of a deposited metal was actually ever claimed back. It is only a small step from here to loaning the idle part of metal or issuing additional notes. From that moment on, the reserves of metal the banker maintained were not supposed to be equal to the total amount of notes issued but only to be sufficient to meet the expected demand for depositors' claims. That means that as the total amount of notes issued is allowed to exceed the reserves of metal some of the notes represent claims to something that does not exist at all! But again it was not the metal intrinsic value but the public confidence that decided about the value of money, and it was the confidence in the banker that decided about the value and functionality of his depository notes. In the same process as metallic money replaced other goods as means of payment, here paper money replaced metallic money. Finally, as governments took matters in their hands and severed the link between paper money and their precious metal reserves, money became fiat money; paper notes issued by central authorities that represent a claim to nothing at all. Yet even in such a form the money has been playing effectively (let aside cases of exceptionally high inflation or currency substitution) the role of medium of exchange, a unit of account, and a store of value.

Understanding the forces underlying the process of money dematerialisation helps to explain why, at the end of 20th century it was possible that money could assume yet another form; electronic zeros and ones stored on plastic cards or sometimes even without any tangible form moving somewhere in a cyberspace. The individuals and firms using money agreed to place their trust into those electronic impulses exactly as their ancestors did it for metals and paper. The dematerialised money reached another dimension going beyond physics.

Modern Money as Medium of Payment

Great expectations were associated with the emergence of electronic money. On one occasion Bill Gates said, somehow arrogantly, that banks of bricks and mortar were like dinosaurs heading for their extinction in the new era of electronic transactions. They were supposed to be replaced by electronic banks settling transactions in electronic cash. But

Table 1. Conventional payment media

	Cash	Bank cheque	Credit card	Debit card
Common acceptability	Yes	No	No	No
Legal tender	Yes	No	No	No
Payment finality	Yes	No	No	No
Anonymity	Yes	No	No	No
Intermediation costs	No	Yes	Yes	Yes
Instant settlement	Yes	No	No	Yes
Verifiability	Partial	Yes	No	Yes
Peer to peer	Yes	Yes	No	No
Offline transactions	Yes	Yes	Possible	No
Inventory	Yes	Yes	No	Yes
Risk factors	Loss, theft, forgery	Fraud, bankruptcy	Fraud, theft, data interception, forgery	Fraud, theft, data interception, forgery
Defensive solutions	Policing, anti-forgery safety features	Banking regulations	Swift detection and card cancellation	Swift detection and card cancellation

while development of electronic trading is proceeding relatively smoothly, electronic money is yet to penetrate payment systems as expected. Instead, almost all Internet transactions are settled by credit and debit card payments. They require a lot of paperwork, they are costly to operate, they are prone to fraud (i.e., data skimming as they are operated by reading devices directly at the sales point) and so forth. For that reason, credit and debit cards are rarely used for small transactions and person-to-person transfers. Yet despite this and various attempts to introduce purely electronic money into markets, there seems to be no end to their domination as payment media in the area of cashless transactions. Before turning to the realities of Japanese economy, we will review some characteristics of conventional and electronic payment media in this section.

The main characteristics of conventional payment media have been summarised in Table 1 and the properties of electronic payment media have been shown in Table 2.

Compared to cash, cheques, credit cards, and debit cards lack common acceptability and legal enforcement (a payee cannot refuse accepting payment in cash because it is a legal tender, while he can refuse accepting payment by cheque, credit or debit card). Also, while cash payment is a final step of settlement, cheques and cards require additional settlement between financial institutions. Cash payer remains anonymous while performing his transaction. On the contrary, cheques and cards reveal the payer's identity. Cash use does not result in intermediation costs while cheques and cards do. Cash payments can be verified only with the help of receipt while cheques and debit card payments are verifiable (credit card payments are not immediately verifiable). Credit and debit cards cannot be used for payments between individuals while cash and cheques can. The same applies to off-line transactions (but in some cases credit cards can be used off-line). Credit cards do not allow for positive inventories accumulation. All conventional payments media are prone to theft and forgery. Possible countermeasures include policing and frequent changes in anti-forgery features for cash, strict banking regulation for cheques, and swift card cancellation in case of both credit and debit cards.

Table 2. Electronic payment media

	Prepaid card	Smartcard	Pseudo-cash	Electronic cheque
Common acceptability	No	No	No	No
Legal tender	No	No	No	No
Payment finality	Yes	No	Yes	No
Anonymity	Yes	Partial	Optional	No
Intermediation costs	No	No	Yes	Yes
Instant settlement	Yes	Yes	Yes	Possible
Verifiability	No	No	Optional	Yes
Peer to peer	No	Yes	Yes	No
Offline transactions	Yes	Yes	No	No
Inventory	Yes	Yes	Yes	No
Risk factors	Minimal (low value)	Forgery	Fraud, double spending	Fraud
Defensive solutions		Security hardware, updates, policing	Security software, format updates	Security software, format updates

Electronic money has been intended for economising on transaction costs that the conventional payment media cannot do. Quick settlement and low operational costs are expected to be appealing to the users while electronic money issuing banks can receive an interest-free loan from customers holding their card balances (analogously to the conventional cash the issued electronic money balances pay zero interest).

Prepaid cards are designed for specific purposes (such as often used in Japan's transportation payments or public telephone system) and operate in closed systems. For that reason their risk factor is minimal. But for the same reason multipurpose use and common acceptability are impossible to achieve. Therefore their use is very limited and certainly they will not become the money of the future.

On the other hand, smartcards such as Mondex or German GeldKarte have a big advantage of multipurpose payment system and can be used for payments between individuals just like ordinary cash. At the same time smartcards do not involve costly paperwork and allow for quick settlement of payment. Although adapting the smartcards for the use on the Internet involves some security issues, they can be addressed by updating security hardware and policing.

Purely electronic cash is actually "pseudo-cash" because it involves intermediary even in transactions between individuals unlike in the real world of conventional notes and coins. For instance under Digicash's e-cash system the users buy digital "coins" (an account must be opened in a specified "mortar-and-brick" bank for this purpose) that are downloaded into their computers. Later their electronic cash can be used for purchases on the Internet with the option of anonymity[2]. Each electronic "coin" has a serial number assigned in order to avoid double spending.

Electronic cheques have all advantages and drawbacks of their paper counterpart, but as all the operations involved are paperless they are much cheaper than conventional cheques are. Electronic certificates and signatures can enhance their security, but the electronic cheques are unlikely to become a major payment medium for the same reasons the paper cheques did not replace cash; they lack finality, common acceptability, legal enforcement as payment tender and anonymity of ordinary cash.

Prospects for Electronic Money as Medium of Payment

Describing what will likely happen in (even near) future, based on information available now, always contains an element of speculation. Many predictions about the future of electronic money have proven to be of the mark (just to mention Bill Gates' comments about conventional banking).

On the one hand, the development of the Internet transactions (let it be purchase of consumer goods or file swapping operations) will certainly reveal the limits of conventional payment media as traditional credit and debit cards. Rapid development of small-scale repeat transactions is likely to call for new instruments. And it is not only the Internet that is likely to undermine the dominant position of conventional payment media. Technological progress is often forcing revisions of earlier predictions. For instance recent developments in cellular phone technology (i.e., third generation telephony) allowed for electronic payment to reach "off-road" areas where, due to the limitations of personal computer, the use of electronic pseudo-cash was not possible until now. This represents unexplored yet opportunities for the use of electronic money.

On the other hand, there are also serious obstacles to the development of electronic money. First, any forecasting about the future of electronic money must take into account the fact that money in order to become money must be generally accepted medium of exchange, unit of account, and store of value. That means the more persons use it in that way the more likely it is to become money. It is not an easy hurdle to clear. Once the critical mass of customers chooses a particular product, its presence becomes self-reinforcing (as in case of metallic money), but until then promoting a new product involves a lot of sunk costs and years perhaps before first profits turn in. Spencer (2001) cites an example of Bank of America sending millions of unsolicited credit cards, incurring costs of fraud and network building, all in order to reach a critical mass of customers for BankameriCard, the first credit card.

But once the system is established the company that blazed the trail enjoys windfall profits and near monopoly position. No surprise that after having worked for it very hard the company is going to defend its advantageous position. This means not only fighting fiercely against competitors but also quite often preventing technological progress from happening (as it would undermine the monopolist's privileged position). One of the most notorious examples of such behaviour is Microsoft that dominates market for personal computer operating systems and is often accused of unfair practices that result in slowing down improvement of existing technology (at least as long as it is introduced by the company itself). Similarly, there have been allegations that Visa and MasterCard deliberately stifled technological progress in payment systems in order to preserve their dominant position in the credit card market. This, combined with potentially high costs of switching providers creates a problem of natural monopoly that must be addressed by appropriate regulation.

Second, the emergence of electronic money is not likely to eliminate "mortar-and-brick" money as most of systems require backing up from ordinary money. The role of conventional money may be gradually limited but it will not be eliminated as long as electronic money does not reach the status of legal tender. As long as central banks take a cautious stance towards electronic money the situation is not likely to change. And central banks do have reasons to be concerned about the development of the electronic money. The issue of electronic money is likely to reduce a central bank's control of money supply, as it undermines the government monopoly on the issue of money. It has also fiscal implications as it reduces the central bank's income from seigniorage (the income from issuing domestic money that in some countries may reach up to several percent of GDP).

Third, in the era of concerns about the privacy protection, serious questions are likely to be raised about the anonymity of transactions in electronic money. In order to prevent fraud, it will take long time before, if ever, the electronic money transactions can reach the anonymity level of conventional cash transactions. As some individuals (especially in informal zones of economy) may prefer to remain anonymous, it may to some extent slow down the progress of adopting the electronic money. Another argument is that, although much cheaper than paperwork in conventional cash transactions, notational transactions in electronic money still induce some costs and, for that reason, it might be harder for the electronic money to replace conventional cash in small transactions (where the costs of notational operations weigh more than in large amount transactions).

Fourth, the spread of the Internet transactions is one of the main driving forces behind the development of electronic money. And as the Internet is intended to be a borderless network, the electronic money for the Internet transactions are also supposed to thrive in a borderless environment. And as such it is supposed to reach a high degree of compatibility around the world. The problem of compatibility has two dimensions. First concerns the interoperability of the world payment networks (i.e., protocols, hardware, software). So far no single technological standard has emerged out of numerous electronic payment systems (for instance, Digicash, Mondex, Proton, etc.). Then, if customer and merchant happen to belong to two different electronic payment systems the transaction may not be possible to materialise. The second problem is related to the foreign exchange. Naturally, borderless transactions involve numerous currencies and the exchange rates fluctuations are subject to economic policy objectives of central banks and are not related to electronic payment realities. However there are strong arguments in favour of adopting a single unit of account for electronic transactions. For transactions that tend to concentrate in regional markets it could be the unit of account of the dominating payment system, let it be the U.S. dollar, the euro or the Japanese yen. But for transactions that reach beyond the local market boundaries (and there is no reason to expect that the share of such transactions would be negligible — after all, much of the Internet appeal lies in its defiance of time and space) floating exchange rates between regional units of account may constitute a certain problem[3]. Needless to say, the stability of exchange rate between particular electronic money and the regional unit of account (and it depends very much on discretion of central banks that are not likely to participate in establishing electronic money framework) also remains a matter of concern for the participants.

To summarise, although technological progress is likely to reinforce the tendency towards the use of electronic money, there are serious systemic, technological, and economic policy related obstacles that may slow the universal adoption of electronic money as a medium of payment.

Payment Media in Japan

Cash and Cheques

Bank deposits are the most widely used means of payment in Japan, but small every day payments are settled mostly in cash. Compared to other countries cash is used extensively in Japan. The ratio of cash to nominal GDP (14.4% at the start of 2001) is the highest among the industrial nations. There are a few reasons for the high cash preference among Japanese public. First, cash has been traditionally playing a significant role in the life habits of ordinary Japanese. For instance cash gifts in clean (i.e., unused) notes that are traditionally presented at predetermined occasions increase the role cash plays in the society. Second, as Japan has a relatively low crime rate, carrying cash does not pose any serious risk. Third, due to well-developed nationwide network of ATMs[4], cash is easily and cheaply accessible. Banks, competing with nationwide postal savings network usually do not charge fees for cash withdrawals from their own ATM while the charge for withdrawals via other bank's ATM carries a small fee unrelated to the amount of cash withdrawn. Fourth, as anti-counterfeiting measures seem to have been effective and inflation rate has been very low (in fact negative for some time) the Japanese public continues to have a lot of confidence in nations cash. Finally, although not often voiced, there is also an argument that the miserable condition of the country's banking industry resulted in distrust towards financial institutions and made individuals to flee into cash away from banking deposits[5].

Needless to say, the dominant position of cash in settlement of every day transactions does not make it easy for other forms of payment to develop. Cheques, used by government agencies and firms are not common payment medium among individuals. Even though their use is in steady decline since the end of the 1980s[6]. Individual consumers often arrange their payments through direct debts or credit transfers (a tri-party agreement between the payer, the payee, and their bank) but their every day transactions are dominated by cash payments.

Credit Cards

The first credit cards were introduced in Japan in 1960 but they really took off as a major payment medium only during the 1990s. The number of cards became twice as much during that period as did the value of transactions settled by using credit card payment. There were 232 million credit cards at the end of March 2001 (almost two per one person) and the value of payments made by credit cards amounted to 23 trillion yen (almost 200 billion U.S. dollars)[7]. The transactions are cleared on line by connecting the card magnetic data reading terminal to the central Credit and Finance Information System and to the credit card company computer. After checking for lost and stolen cards and credit limit the payment is being processed. Although still limited compared to other countries, the use of credit cards increased together with recent growth in business to consumer electronic commerce.

Debit Cards

Debit cards were first introduced in Japan in 1984, when banks began providing the service known as "Bank POS". However slow and complicated use of the cards prevented the service from becoming widely used. Technological progress enabled financial institutions to reintroduce the debit card payments known as "J-Debit" in January 1999. Amid the government-sponsored "IT revolution" campaign, the "J-Debit" was quickly hailed as the payment system of the future and was expected to replace soon credit cards as small transaction personal payment medium. The expectations were high as from the beginning the system was joined by major banks (Fuji, Dai-ichi Kangyo, Sanwa and others), major department store (Seibu), oil companies (Cosmo), discount stores (Big Camera), convenience stores (Lawson) that operate round the clock, and most of all by the post office with its vast financial network. The customers were promised the convenience of cashless payment, businesses the reduction of the payment lag and lower costs of handling payments as compared with credit cards, and financial institutions were expecting the increase in number of customers and commissions charged.

The "J-Debit" uses the same terminals as credit card payments and the Credit and Finance Information System for data transmission. Payer's bank account is charged immediately after receiving the transaction data. Inter-bank settlements are cleared through inter-bank payment system two days after transaction took place. The merchant's account is credited from the third day on[8].

Despite of high expectations the "J-Debit" transactions still amount no more than a fraction of credit card payments in Japan. Although the preference for cash transactions was expected to work in favour of debit card development, the Japanese public seems to have found a new taste for credit payments. There are also other reasons but loyalty campaigns by credit card companies and high initial entry costs for merchants who have to equip themselves with new terminals and so forth are preventing wider use of debit cards.

Electronic Payment Media

Similarly to the "J-Debit", various card-based and network-based electronic money pilot projects have been conducted as a part of the "IT revolution". All of them were confined to specific geographical areas (Kyoto, Yokohama, Kobe) and all ended without even catching-up with the population of those areas.

Prepaid cards have been the only electronic money payment form that really has been widely used in Japan. Since the 1980s, they have been widely accepted for paying for public telephone (however recently in decline due to widespread use of cellular phones), railways, buses and until 2004 for public toll roads. As number of users increased, also the networks of companies using one card have been developed (originally each company had its own prepaid card system). Most of cards are simple magnetic cards but some more sophisticated instruments (including contact-less smartcards) have been introduced too. Some of cards offer new services such as possibility to reload or possibility of deferring payment as credit cards do. Prepaid cards are not subject to banking supervision, but since 1989, the card issuers have to deposit with the legal affairs bureau of the Ministry of Justice funds equivalent to half of the unused value of issued cards. This regulation is meant to protect the interests of cardholders.

Why Has Electronic Money Failed in Japan?

As explained previously, the evolution of money originates from economising on transaction costs. Therefore, in order to succeed, a new form of money must offer customers and businesses either significantly lower transaction costs, or substantial increase in convenience, or both. Meanwhile, the Japanese electronic money experiments have been confined to narrow areas or firms. This automatically precludes achieving a critical mass of users necessary for creating a self-feeding system. Another weakness of the Japanese experiments with electronic money to date is the fact that they have been based on stored value accounts. Under such system a customer cannot utilise his cash balances as long as they are not stored on a specified account. This system, currently continued in electronic toll collection system for public expressways as well as in recently announced by the Nippon Telegraph and Telephone (major telephone service providing company) system that utilises data transmission abilities of mobile phones, is rather inconvenient, as it requires "reloading" customer's account with fresh cash each time the balances approach zero. And, since in most cases there exist upper limits for balances stored on the customers account, frequent use requires also frequent "reloading" and big purchases were usually ruled out. No need of saying, none of the Japanese systems could have been used with various bank accounts. In this sense the stored value format adopted in Kyoto, Yokohama and Kobe resembles multipurpose prepaid cards with limited geographical proximity (prepaid cards do not require however time consuming applications, costly terminals etc). On the contrary, the Germany's GeldKarte allows its holder to use any account of any bank participating in the system as long as it has sufficient balances (access type of electronic money).

There is also one more often neglected more general problem that certainly has great influence of technological innovation in the Japanese financial industry. Most of the country's financial institutions have been still suffering from the outbreak of the banking crisis. The Japanese banks, unable to raise their profit margins from their main lending activities (i.e., lending to corporate customers) and suffering from the fall-out from the non-performing loan crisis are not able to invest seriously in the technological progress. For that reason they have no choice but to charge their customers with the costs of introducing new technologies. Therefore, as it often happens in Japanese consumer-business relations, it is customers and small retailers that are charged with not only banks' commissions but also with costs of purchasing terminals, connecting lines and so forth. It stands in sharp contrast to the Bank of America that was sending millions of unsolicited credit cards in order to reach a critical mass of customers. Under such circumstances, there is no surprise that customers prefer being lured by various "loyalty" perks (closely resembling the airline "mileage" programmes) offered by credit card companies (and enjoying in principle the benefits of deferred payment) instead of being confined to the limited area of "sophisticated prepaid card".

It might be interesting to compare the Japan's experience with the electronic money to the country where the new form of payment really succeeded. Sixty-two million GeldKartes circulated in Germany in 2003[9]. That means that approximately nine in 10 adults in Germany have been using their version of electronic money smartcard. The system (mostly microchip equipped Euro Cheque cards) developed by the German commercial banks' association (the Zentraler Kreditausschuss) is today the largest installed electronic money base in the world. Apparently the association utilised some elements of the already existing at that time Euro Cheque framework. The Euro Cheque used to be very popular deferred payment mechanism in Germany and some other countries (mostly Northern European) until the second half of 1980s. Its payment procedure involved a plastic card necessary for payment authorisation (i.e., cheque holder identification). As the electronic systems were gradually developing, the plastic card was used for speeding up the payment process with the paper cheque gradually becoming only a confirmation tool. In a very clever move, the banks utilised the already existing Euro Cheque cards for the purpose of creating the smartcard network. The new payment system proved to be very popular for at least two reasons. First, it involved an already familiar payment tool (the card that was formerly necessary for cheque payments) and its connection to all major banks in Germany[10]. Second, as most of European banks charge a uniform account maintenance fee regardless of the amount transactions going through the account (unlike Japanese banks that charge each transaction separately), the increasing amount of payments going via the account means decreasing marginal costs for each transaction and creates incentives for doing even small payments via the card. Currently the GeldKarte has been gradually expanding to small retail businesses, railway tickets selling machines, vending machines and so forth. Successfully competing with credit cards it is becoming a very popular payment method, at least in major German cities, and it has probably already achieved a critical mass of customers sufficient for becoming self-reinforcing payment system.

Concluding Remarks

To conclude this chapter on the prospects of electronic money in Japan as the medium of payment, let us summarise the major findings. First, the electronic money is unlikely to replace conventional money as unit of account and store of value medium. As long as its construction requires backing from conventional money (let it be creating "shadow accounts" or purchasing electronic money from provider and paying in units of conventional money) its role will be limited rather to the payment medium only.

Second, the evolution of money originates from economising on transaction costs. Therefore, in order to be able to compete against other forms of money, the electronic money must offer its users substantial efficiency gains in form of significant reduction of transaction costs and (or) significant increase of convenience. Otherwise it would be impossible to reach critical mass of users necessary for the money to reach a self-propelling stage of development.

Third, Japanese experiments with electronic money were based on stored value technology that is similar to prepaid cards. Being confined to specific geographical areas, they had very limited possibilities to compete with well established credit card systems that easily operate within world wide networks (Visa and MasterCard). In this sense, they offered customers no new quality of service while imposing at the same time a significant burden on participating retailers (costs of hardware, staff training etc). Not surprisingly, all the experiments ended quietly with no follow up.

Fourth, instead of insisting on stored value standard, it might be useful to employ an access type standard involving many banks (like in Germany's GeldKarte). Also utilising an already existing familiar payment tool (e.g., technologically enhanced "J-Debit" card) may prove helpful in overcoming customers' initial reservations.

Fifth, as establishing the electronic money standard involves a danger of creating a monopoly, the authorities may have to intervene in regulation of the newly created market. Also, as the prolonged recession in Japanese economy has weakened the country's financial system, Japanese banks have just started recovering from the non-performing loans legacy of the 1980s bubble and are not willing (not able) to engage in another costly undertaking such as investing in the electronic money business. Creating a set of proper incentives for developing costly networks etc is also a job for central authorities. Otherwise, the costs would be passed to consumers and retail businesses and the chances would be very small for the introduction of the electronic money to succeed.

References

Bank for International Settlements. (2003). *Payment and settlement systems in selected countries*. Bank for International Settlements.

Krawczyk, M. K. (2004). *Change and crisis in the Japanese banking industry*. HWWA discussion paper 277, Hamburg, Germany.

Menger, C. (2002). Money. In M. Latzer & S. W. Schmitz (Eds.), *Carl Menger and the evolution of payments systems* (pp. 25-108). Edward Elgar.

Shintani, F. (1999). *Debitto kaado* (in Japanese). Toyo Keizai Shinhosha.

Spencer, P. (2001). Regulation of the payments market and the prospect for digital money. In Bank for International Settlement's *Electronic finance: A new perspective and challenges* (pp. 69-79). BIS Papers 7.

Endnotes

[1]   V. L. Cameron. (1877). *Across Africa*, I, pp. 246 (quoted after Menger, 2002)

[2]   Spencer (2001)

[3]   It seems to be worth mentioning that similar reservations were raised 30 years ago when floating exchange rate system first emerged. The concerns proved to be quite of mark as corporations learned how to hedge against exchange rate volatility. Foreign exchange risk hedging remains however costly for individuals and, needless to say, individual transactions account for a great deal of Internet transactions.

[4]   The country has almost twice as many ATM per 1 million inhabitants as the U.S. or Germany. And since 1999 most of financial institutions have linked their ATMs with the post office ATM system that covers the entire country with its almost 26,000 ATM network.

[5]   The relation of cash to banking deposits increased by nearly one-third during the 1990s (Krawczyk, 2004).

[6]   The use of those instruments decreased by 80% between 1991 and 2001 (Bank for International Settlements, 2003).

[7]   Bank for International Settlements (2003)

[8]   Shintani (1999)

[9]   *Die Bank*, November 20, 2003

[10]   By creating a "shadow account" for loading the card, banks allow payments and transfers to be finalised no matter which bank the customer has his account with (other systems like, for instance, Mondex, can work with one bank only).

Chapter XIII

Investment in IT Stocks by Japanese Life Insurers

Takeshi Kobayashi, Chukyo University, Japan

Abstract

This chapter examined the relationship between Japanese life insurers' investment in IT stocks and conventional financial statistics, such as ROE and dividend yield, in the period from 1996 to 2003. It demonstrates that Japanese life insurers do not necessarily formulate their portfolios based on these statistics. In particular, insurers who invested in low-ROE stocks tended to be financially unstable. These findings may confirm that even after the Japanese financial crisis of the late 1990s, the primary objective of stock investment by Japanese life insurers continued to be the maintenance of business relationships with client firms, and not the maximization of investment performance.

Introduction

Since the mid-1990s, several large Japanese life insurers have been struggling under the burden of a negative spread, and six small- and mid-sized insurers — Nissan, Toho, Daihyaku, Taisho, Chiyoda and Kyoei — have since collapsed. The negative yield resulted from a sluggish stock market and a low-interest-rate policy, which was further intensified to a zero-interest-rate policy, designed to maintain short-term interest rates at virtually zero. Chen and Wong (2004) investigated the determinants of the financial

Figure 1. Shareholdings of large Japanese life insurers; Data is normalized to 1997 (= 100) (Source: Annual report of each insurer)

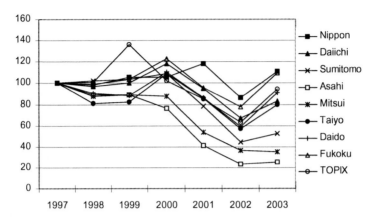

health of Asian insurers in this period, and concluded that the investment performance was significantly correlated with the financial stability of Japanese life insurers, which was not the case in several Asian countries. The failures of the life insurers resulted in a growing distrust of their stability, and a decelerating income growth due to an economic downturn also caused an increase in policy surrenders and lapses. Faced with these circumstances, the insurers sold investment securities in order to restructure their portfolios and acquire liquidity. At the end of fiscal year 1998, Japanese life insurers held 32.8 trillion yen worth of domestic stock, while this figure stood at a mere 20.9 trillion yen at the end of fiscal year 2003. The TOPIX (Tokyo Stock Price Index) declined by approximately 7% during this period, which implies that insurers sold large amounts of stocks in this period. Figure 1 shows the stock investments of major Japanese life insurers in this period. Six out of eight insurers reduced their stock holdings by an amount that exceeded the extent of decrease in the TOPIX. Figure 2 shows the proportion of stocks in insurers' securities investments. This implies that life insurers also reduced the proportion of stocks in their portfolios.

Several studies have analyzed the investment behavior of life insurers. Mei and Saunders (1997) conducted an empirical study on the real estate investments of U.S. financial institutions, including life insurers. Collins, Geisler and Shackelford (1998) examined the effects of taxes and regulations on life insurers' portfolio realizations. Okamoto (2000) indicated that Japanese life insurers preferred old and established stocks, such as utilities and steel, to growth stocks, such as communications and services.

This chapter is organized as follows. Section 2 outlines the structure of the Japanese insurance market and the typical behavior of insurers. Section 3 describes the data and the empirical methodology. Section 4 discusses the empirical results and the major findings of this study. Section 5 presents a summary and conclusion.

Figure 2. Proportion of stock in the total securities investment of each insurer (Source: Annual report of each insurer)

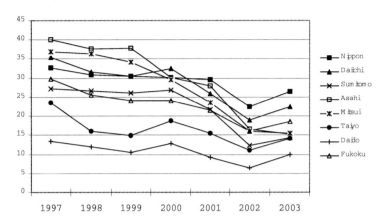

Structure of the Japanese Life Insurance Market

The Japanese life insurance market is the second largest in the world. The premium volume in 2003 was 381 billion USD, which amounts to a global market share of 22.80%. The Japanese market is characterized by the second highest per capita premium in the world, which exceeds 3000 USD[1]. The total premium amount, which is 8.61% of the country's GDP, is the third highest in the world.

Although these figures suggest that this market is very attractive for new entrants, the Ministry of Finance rarely permitted potential entrants to access it. Very few life insurers were permitted to enter the market since World War II (WWII). The life insurers currently operating in Japan can be classified into four groups, namely, domestic incumbents, domestic entrants, foreign insurers, and affiliates of Japanese non-life insurers. The domestic incumbent insurers established their businesses prior to or immediately after WWII, and they have retained a large share of the domestic market for many years. They were established as mutual companies, and some of them were recently converted into stock companies. The domestic entrants are affiliates of domestic non-insurance companies such as Sony. Foreign insurers include the domestic branches of foreign life insurers or their affiliates. Affiliates of Japanese non-life insurers were permitted to enter the life insurance market following the enactment of the New Insurance Business Law in April 1996. With the exception of the domestic incumbents, all insurers are stock companies.

The incumbent insurers hold a large share of both the individual life insurance and group insurance markets. In the individual life insurance market, they are characterized by their sales practices; they employ large sales staff, mostly comprising women. Due to a higher propensity of the people to save, these insurers sold a large number of savings insurance policies, and their assets expanded rapidly. In the group insurance market, the incumbent insurers bought and held stocks of several companies as loyal stockholders in order to sell their group insurance products to them. In contrast, the other insurers, namely, the domestic entrants, foreign insurers, and affiliates of non-life insurers, frequently sold their products to individuals by mail or via the Internet.

Stock Investment by Japanese Life Insurers

As mentioned above, Japanese incumbent life insurers hold stocks of client firms that purchase their group insurance products in order to maintain their business relationships. This practice is similar to the well-known cross-shareholding system of Japanese companies. Consequently, life insurance companies are one of the largest stock investors in the Japanese financial market. One of their primary purpose of holding stock is to sustain their business relationships, life insurers trade stocks very rarely, and therefore, their turnover is very low. At the end of fiscal year 2003, life and non-life insurers held domestic stocks worth 29.5 trillion yen, while the value of trading carried out by them in the same fiscal year was only 2.8 trillion yen. However, since the late 1990s, they began reducing their stock holdings, as shown in Figures 1 and 2. The following are the possible reasons for this. First, the economic downturn resulted in an increase in policy surrenders and lapses, which caused a decline in the total assets of insurers. Second, the negative yield reduces their risk tolerance. Therefore, insurers might have reduced their stock holdings in order to avoid financial risks.

Empirical Analysis

Public companies in Japan are required to disclose their 10 largest shareholders, and lists of the large shareholders in a company can be easily obtained from its financial statements and investor guides. Although some research companies independently refer and publish lists of their shareholders, listing even smaller shareholders, these lists do not offer sufficient data for the analysis; therefore, their data are not utilized in this study. With the exception of incumbent insurers, life insurance companies operating in Japan are so small in terms of their asset sizes that they rarely appear in the list of the 10 largest shareholders of a company. Table 1 lists the scales of operations of the major life insurers operating in Japan. Nippon, Daiichi, Sumitomo, Mitsui, Asahi, Taiyo, Daido and Fukoku are incumbent life insurers. Although Sony and AFLAC JAPAN are the largest entrant and foreign insurer, respectively, their asset sizes are smaller than that of Fukoku, the eighth-largest incumbent. Therefore, this chapter focuses on the eight large incumbent life insurers — namely, Nippon, Daiichi, Sumitomo, Mitsui, Asahi, Taiyo, Daido and Fukoku. Although Yasuda and Meiji are also large insurance companies, they have been

Table 1. Scales of operations of the major Japanese life insurers (Source: Annual report of each insurer and Standard & Poor's homepage)

Insurer	Asset[a]	Premium income[a]	S&P rating[b]
Nippon	45,492,355	5,169,262	A+
Daiichi	28,306,501	3,420,906	A-
Sumitomo	20,212,537	2,729,924	BBB-
Mitsui	7,500,103	922,091	BB-
Asahi	6,447,385	679,473	CCC+
Taiyo	6,393,428	794,168	A
Daido	5,862,325	928,260	A
Fukoku	5,004,746	740,935	A-
Sony	2,375,828	512,700	A+
AFLAC JAPAN	4,250,920	892,447	AA

Note: [a]Million yen [b]as of March 15, 2005

excluded from this analysis because of data discontinuity following their merger in January 2004.

The Tokyo Stock Exchange classifies listed companies into 33 categories by industry. Most IT firms including electronics, semiconductor, software and information services, are classified as electric appliance, precision instruments, information and communication or services. Therefore, this chapter analyzes investments by life insurers in these four categories. It should be noted that non-IT firms are also included in these categories. However, since it is difficult to separate non-IT firms from IT firms, this chapter studies all the firms in these categories.

Period of Investigation

This chapter studied the investment activities of life insurers for the period from the late 1990s to 2003. The following are the reasons for this. First, as mentioned above, since the late 1990s, life insurers have been faced with the problem of a negative yield, and some have even failed. This might have compelled them to change their investment policies. Second, IT stocks surged rapidly in 1999 and 2000, and this has been referred to as the "IT bubble". In this period, both the Tokyo Stock Exchange and the Osaka Stock Exchange established new sections for emerging stocks, a large number of young IT firms went public, and investors actively traded IT stocks. Although life insurers have primarily focused on investment in traditional industries or firms, they might have changed this policy due to the surge in IT stocks. Third, the new insurance business law enacted in 1996 relaxed the stringent regulations imposed on the Japanese insurance industry after WWII, and this stimulated market competition. It is of particular interest to examine whether insurers altered their portfolio strategies in response to the new competitive environment.

Method of Analysis

Several common investment statistics, such as return on equity (ROE), dividend yield, price-earnings ratio (P/E ratio) and percentage increase in profit over the previous year, were selected, and their effects on the investment decision regarding IT stocks by Japanese life insurers were investigated.

First, we considered those companies that were listed on either the first or second section of the Tokyo Stock Exchange (TSE) or the JASDAQ OTC market and had one or more life insurers in their lists of 10 largest stockholders at the end of fiscal year 1996. It should be noted that that most of the Japanese public companies are traded in these markets. The number of listed companies that report an insurer in their list of 10 largest shareholders is presented in Tables 2.1 and 2.2. Second, the rank of each insurer in the list of stockholders at the end of Fiscal year 1996 was compared to that at the end of fiscal year 2003. Third, the relationship between the selected investment statistics and the change in an insurer's rank in the shareholders list of each company is investigated for this period.

Table 2.1. Number of listed firms that reported an insurer as one of their 10 largest shareholders, sorted by market

Insurer	TSE 1st section	TSE 2nd section	JASDAQ
Nippon	85	24	21
Daiichi	51	10	26
Sumitomo	25	4	7
Mitsui	15	2	4
Asahi	22	11	6
Taiyo	3	0	1
Fukoku	5	3	0
Daido	4	2	0

Table 2.2. Number of listed firms that reported an insurer as one of their 10 largest shareholders, sorted by industry

Insurer	Electronic Appliances	Precision Instruments	Information and Communications	Services
Nippon	78	18	10	24
Daiichi	42	11	12	22
Sumitomo	29	2	2	3
Mitsui	13	3	0	5
Asahi	26	8	2	3
Taiyo	4	0	0	0
Fukoku	4	0	1	3
Daido	3	1	1	1

Result of the Empirical Analysis

The characteristics of the investment decisions of each insurer, in other words, the statistics that different insurers focused on when making investment decisions, were investigated. Firms that listed an insurer in their list of 10 largest shareholders at the end of fiscal year 1996 were selected. By comparing the rank of an insurer in the shareholder list of 1996 with that of 2003 for each firm, firms were classified into the UP group, wherein the rank of the insurer did not decrease in the shareholder list, and the DOWN group, wherein the rank of the insurer decreased. For example, if Nippon Life ranked seventh in the shareholder list of firm X at the end of fiscal year 1996 and ninth at the end of fiscal year 2003, firm X would then be classified into the DOWN group with regard to the investment by Nippon Life. Subsequently, the average of each statistic was calculated for firms belonging to each group, then t-test was used to compare the actual difference between the mean values for the two groups. The results are presented in Table 3. Table 3 suggests that insurers tend to prefer high-yield and low-growth stocks. As indicated by Okamoto (2000), Japanese life insurers have invested large amounts of money in "old economy" stocks, which usually yield higher dividends and have a slow growth. Table 3 reveals that even when investing in technology stocks, Japanese insurers prefer high dividend stocks to growth ones. In addition, they appear to increasingly purchase low-ROE stocks, which is contradictory to conventional financial wisdom.

It is of particular interest to discuss the effect of such a portfolio strategy on the financial stability of insurers. Table 3 shows that four out of five insurers invested in low-ROE stocks, and the credit ratings of these insurers were low. Table 1 lists the S&P credit rating of each insurer. Three insurers received a rating of BBB- or lower. In particular, Asahi, which invested in low-ROE, low-growth and high-P/E stocks experienced financial instability. It has received a rating of CCC+ from Standard and Poor's.

Table 3. Financial statistics and stock trading activity, sorted by insurer

Rank	ROE			Dividend yield			Profit growth[a]			P/E Ratio		
	Up	Down	t value	Up	Down	t value	Up	Down	t value	Up	Down	t value
Nippon	2.47	5.31	-2.13**	1.16	0.98	1.33	0.75	71.53	-1.31	67.52	51.07	0.96
Daiichi	4.00	3.33	0.39	1.37	1.07	1.47	16.5	58.08	-0.56	43.27	48.90	-0.45
Asahi	0.70	4.32	-1.12	1.34	1.24	0.23	-32.70	-2.96	-1.12	87.16	34.08	3.68***
Sumitomo	-2.22	6.59	-1.17	0.87	1.05	-0.44	-35.47	20.54	-1.17	67.01	49.03	0.72
Mitsui	0.50	4.83	-1.61	1.15	1.02	0.20	74.30	4.12	1.70	81.11	69.82	0.14

Notes: Taiyo, Daido and Fukoku are omitted because of insufficient number of samples.

[a] Rate of increase in net profit over the previous year

*** Significant at 5% level *** Significant at 1% level*

Industries and Investment Decisions

As mentioned earlier, the subject of this investigation is Japanese life insurers' investment in four IT-related industries, namely, electric appliance, precision instruments, information and communication and services. Insurers' trading activities were examined from the viewpoint of investment. In this subsection, we investigate the difference of investment decisions of life insurers among the four industries. The investigation methodology is similar to that used in the previous subsection. However, in this case, firms are sorted by industry and not by insurer. First, firms that were classified into one of the four types of industries and included at least one of the eight incumbent insurers in their list of 10 largest shareholders at the end of fiscal year 1996 were selected. Second, a company's list for fiscal year 1996 was compared with its list at the end of fiscal year 2003. If the 2003 list showed the rank of an insurer to have decreased compared to that in the 1997 list, the insurer was classified as DOWN, and UP otherwise. This was followed by the t test, which was used in a manner similar to that described earlier.

The result is presented in Table 4. Remarkably, insurers preferred low-ROE firms in both Electric Appliance and Precision Equipment industries. It should be noted that these industries include many established electronics giants, for example, NEC, Hitachi and so forth. In contrast, most firms belonging to the other two industries are relatively young and small. Okamoto (2000) argued that Japanese life insurers cannot adjust their portfolios rapidly because of their very large asset base. That is, even if they wanted to sell stocks of large companies, they could not do so rapidly due to their huge share holdings. Another reason is that they often purchase their clients' stocks in order to

Table 4. Financial statistics and stock trading activity, sorted by industry

Rank	ROE			Dividend yield			Profit growth[a]			P/E Ratio		
	Up	Down	t value	Up	Down	t value	Up	Down	t value	Up	Down	t value
Electronics	1.77	4.72	-1.82*	1.08	1.10	-0.18	-3.31	49.58	-1.06	54.49	48.35	0.65
Precision	2.60	5.41	-1.62	1.34	0.70	4.00**	16.15	-7.30	1.17	67.86	73.62	-0.21
Information and telecommunication	3.29	2.12	0.40	0.85	0.82	0.12	54.03	169.07	-0.66	35.58	32.42	0.32
Service	3.28	4.05	-0.46	1.59	1.39	0.68	-19.91	11.90	-1.93*	117.41	38.44	2.02**

Notes: [a] Rate of increase in net profit over the previous year

* Significant at 10% level ** Significant at 5% level *** Significant at 1% level

maintain business relationships with them with little focus on maximizing investment performance. Okamoto (2000) suggested that Japanese life insurers do not give significance to ROE during portfolio selection, a practice that contrasts with that of foreign investors and pension funds. The result presented in Table 4 confirms Okamoto's (2000) findings.

Market and Investment Decisions

Most of Japanese public firms are listed on the TSE first section, second section or JASDAQ market. Each of these markets has the following characteristics. Generally, large and old firms are listed on the TSE first section, and smaller firms are listed on the TSE second section. The listing requirement of JASDAQ is not tight; so emerging firms often prefer JASDAQ to the TSE. By investigating investment decisions of the insurers in each market, we can reveal the relationship between the portfolio management of insurers and their stock holdings for business relationship mentioned earlier. If the insurers attach great importance to the business relationship to old large firms, they understate financial statistics concerning these firms, which are often listed on the TSE first section. The method of analysis is similar to the preceding subsection, and now firms are sorted by market they listed. The result is shown in Table 5. As for stocks listed on the TSE first section or second section, the insurers seem to prefer low-ROE and low-growth stocks, but this is not necessarily the case with stocks listed on the JASDAQ market. They could concern the return form investment rather than business relationships with regard to JASDAQ-listed firms, since they have not had long business relationships with them, most of which are young.

Table 5. Financial statistics and stock trading activity, sorted by market

Market	ROE			Dividend yield			Profit growth[a]			P/E Ratio		
	Up	Down	t value	Up	Down	t value	Up	Down	t value	Up	Down	t value
TSE 1st section	2.23	3.58	-1.08	1.11	0.89	2.54**	5.97	47.45	-0.94	59.18	59.91	-0.07
TSE 2nd section	-0.03	7.53	-2.20**	1.24	1.11	0.47	-25.6	48.02	-0.85	164.04	38.46	2.99***
JASDAQ	4.73	4.49	0.13	1.49	1.54	-0.17	4.67	17.60	-0.75	31.45	27.26	0.30

[a] Rate of increase in net profit over the previous year

Conclusions

This chapter examined several aspects of IT-stock trading activities of Japanese life insurers from the late 1990s to 2003. It demonstrates that Japanese life insurers do not necessarily formulate their portfolios on the basis of conventional financial statistics. In particular, insurers investing in low-ROE stocks tend to be financially unstable. These findings may confirm that the primary objective of stock investment by Japanese life insurers is to maintain business relationships with firms, and not to maximize investment performance.

References

Chan, R., & Wong, K. A. (2004). The determinant of financial health of Asian insurance companies. *Journal of Risk and Insurance, 71*(3), 469-499.

Collins, J. H., Geisler, G., & Shackelford, D. (1998). The effects of taxes, regulatory capital, earnings, and organizational form on life insurers: Investment portfolio realizations. *Journal of Accounting and Economics, 24*(3), 337-361.

Okamoto, S. (2000). Sangyo kozo no henka to seiho kabushikitoshi no kadai. (In Japanese). *Semei Hoken Keiei, 68*, 26-44.

Saunders, A., & Mei, J. P. (1997). Have U.S. financial institutions' real estate investments exhibited "trend-chasing" behavior? *Review of Economics and Statistics, 79*, 248-258.

Endnote

[1]   Swiss Re "Sigma" No. 3, 2004.

Chapter XIV

The Roles of IT in the Conduct of Modern Monetary Policy

Waranya Atchariyachanvanich, Assumption University, Thailand

Kanokwan Atchariyachanvanich, The Graduate University for Advanced Studies, Japan

Abstract

This chapter reviews the roles of information technology (IT) from two perspectives. First, from the macroeconomic perspective, the IT revolution induced output growth and new financial innovations such as asset-backed securities and electronic money. However, these phenomena complicate the conduct of monetary policy, but they will not totally demise its effectiveness. Second, from the operational level, IT applications currently take roles in enhancing operational efficiency, decision-making process and innovative practice of monetary authorities in central banks throughout the world. The degree of implementing IT applications in the conduct of monetary policy, in turn, may become another determinant of monetary policy framework in the future.

Introduction

In an economy where money is required in the process of capital formation, any changes in its quantity and/or cost of borrowing (interest rate) can have an implication on macroeconomic variables, such as inflation, growth, and unemployment rates. Based on this fundamental understanding, the ultimate goal of monetary policy is to promote economic stability through manipulating monetary policy instruments that influence one or more macroeconomic variables. Effectiveness of monetary policy can be determined in terms of how precise the monetary impacts on the real economic variables compared with the target. However, each stage in the conduct of monetary policy generally deals with the problems of variable selection or priority ranking, time inconsistency between the monetary policy implementation and its feedbacks on real economy, the ability of the monetary authority, and uncertainties. The effectiveness of monetary policy, therefore, does not depend only on the type of monetary policy framework but also the environment affecting the institutional factors, the nature of the financial structure as well as degree of other uncertainties.

The revolution in information technology (IT) represents one of main engines behind rapid economic development of modern economies in this era of globalization. The near future implications of IT have already been extensively introduced to both real and financial sectors where most of transactions are now quoted in monetary units, and inevitably IT affects the conduct of monetary policy through several channels. On the one hand, IT-induced financial innovations such as electronic money (e-money) complicate the conduct of monetary policy. On the other hand, monetary authorities also have received benefits from IT, such as, in reducing time as well as resources and increasing the accuracy in compiling economic data for monetary policy design.

The objective of this chapter is to review the roles of IT on the conduct of monetary policy from the macroeconomic and operational perspectives for readers from different fields. The next section provides concise backgrounds of framework and uncertainties in the conduct of monetary policy. The third section analyzes the roles of IT on the conduct of monetary policy in macroeconomic and operational perspectives. The fourth section contains conclusions and remarks of this chapter.

Framework and Uncertainty in the Conduct of Monetary Policy

This section first provides a general overview of the conduct of monetary policy followed by a theoretical explanation of the uncertainty in monetary economics. Examples of real occurrences representing uncertainties are presented in the last subsection.

Monetary Policy Framework

The conduct of monetary policy requires deliberate understanding on the complex relationship among monetary instruments and economomic variables such as output growth and inflation rate. For each economy, the transmission process of monetary policy into changes on these variables (or monetary policy transmission mechanisms) varies in terms of time lagged and magnitude of effects. Along the long-term path toward achieving the selected monetary goal, the monetary authority has to manipulate its monetary policy instruments continually to achieve short-term policy targets that enable it to achieve an intermeditate target of the financial variable corresponding to the particular monetary goal. The comprehensive process of selecting variables for the ultimate goal, intermediate and short-term targets and the appropriate path to achieve the goal is referred to as the "monetary policy framework".

In looking at the evolution of monetary policy in most countries, it becomes clear that monetary policy goals and the type of monetary policy frameworks have changed along with the change in the structure of economy[1]. Before 1973, under the Bretton Woods system all member countries were required to peg the value of their currency to the dollar. During that period, monetary policy framework could be perceived as multiple goal-oriented and exchange rate anchored. Differences in domestic inflation rates among the member countries were the main obstacle in maintaining the Bretton Woods system.

The collapse of the Bretton Woods system of fixed exchange rate regime in 1973 has led to a search for a new nominal anchor in the conduct of monetary policy. Monetary aggregate targeting was widely adopted among industrialized countries with variations in types of intermediate variables. Until the late 1980s the monetary aggregate targeting proved to be a good nominal anchor in helping countries to achieve ultimate objective. The trend changed in the 1990s as velocity became less predictable and the price stability gained priority over growth and employment objectives. Beyond expanding the definition of the money aggregate, the Reserve Bank of New Zealand, for example, introduced inflation targeting as an alternative monetary policy framework that sets an explicit objective of price stability as the single monetary objective. Canada, the United Kingdom and Australia adopted this framework with some adjustments on target variables in terms of definitions, value specifications and length of time for target realization. Another variation in the monetary policy framework that combines main features of both inflation targeting and monetary aggregate targeting is the Single Monetary Policy of the European System of Central Banks (ESCB). France and Germany are the examples of member countries in the ESCB. Japan and the United States, on the other hand, have utilized several monetary indictors in formulating their monetary policy without setting explicit quantitative target on price stability.

Despite the diversity of monetary policy frameworks in the current era, there are two common trends in the conduct of monetary policy that have been continuing during the past decade. The first trend is the increase in the degree of central bank independence (CBI), or the extent to which a central bank has freedom in pursuing its monetary objective[2]. The main justification behind this trend is the perception that the monetary authority should be free from political influences to be effective in pursuing the long-term objective. Empirically, Cukierman (1992) asserts that industrial countries with a higher degree of CBI tend to have lower average annual inflation rates. As for developing countries, Atchariyachanvanich (2002) found a similar direction in the relationship between the degree of CBI and average annual inflation rates, however, in terms of changes in value of the two variables across time (rathar than in terms of their absolute values).

A second trend is perceptible from a survey of 91 central banks summarized by Sterne (1999) who showed that there was a significant shift towards using explicit target for money policy throughout the world from events in the 1990s (55% in 1990 to 96% in 1998)[3]. His study conveys three main messages. First, defining monetary objective narrowly and consistently with monetary objectives of price and monetary stability is perceived as a means to build credibility of monetary authority through transparency. Second, the conduct of monetary policy in this era is more rule-based rather than discretion-based, as evidenced by the current worldwide use of the explicit targets. Third, since credibility is primarily built through long-term actions and achievements of the monetary authority, along with the explicit target setting, efforts to communicate with the public about the details of the targets, the outcomes, policy changes and reasons for any target misses are also highly important.

Uncertainty in the Conduct of Monetary Policy

As pointed out previously, modern monetary authorities tend to have higher freedom in their operation and rely more on the scientific method in pursuing the objective of price stability with explicit target announced to the public. In order to achieve and maintain credibility, high precision in setting the target in addition to transparency is required. However, there have been several sources of deviation of the real outcome from the targets as seen in the evolution of monetary policy framework. Generally they can be regarded as uncertainties in the conduct of monetary policy.

As econometricians, Jenkins and Longworth (2002) explain the implications of the uncertainty of monetary policy formulation by classifying the uncertainties into five types:

1. *"additive-shock uncertainty"* representing the random errors in economic relationships,

2. *"uncertainty about the duration of a shock"* dealing with a change in the nature of the persistence and autocorrelation aspects of the shock,

3. *"data uncertainty"* arising from the chance that data are mismeasured or revised,

4. *"parameter uncertainty"* regarding the numerical value of parameter or coefficient in a given mathematical model of the economy, and

5. *"model uncertainty"* resulted from a change in the structure of the economy. Beyond this classification, it can be added that expectation is another type of uncertainty that is recognized in many monetary studies.

According to the above classification, Jenkins and Longworth (2002) assert that only the "additive-shock uncertainty" is out of control due to its randomness and has no implication for policymakers, while the other types of uncertainties depend on the efficiency of information gathering, interpreting, modeling, and analyzing. As for expectation, the degree of information symmetry along with past experience in the economy as well as lessons from other countries all have influences on the development of public's expectations. The nature of the expectation, whether it is forward- or backward-looking, is neither random nor quantifiable precisely.

Real Occurrence and Degree of Uncertainty

An example of occurrence that increases uncertainty is a sudden and unanticipated change in domestic fiscal variables. This fiscal shock can be perceived as a source of "additive-shock uncertainty" to the conduct of monetary policy because it is a random disturbance, which is uncontrollable by monetary authority. Blinder (1982) asserts that lacking of coordination between fiscal and monetary authorities can arise from differences in their objectives, economic theories and forecasts. The "additive-shock uncertainty" stemming from fiscal policy is expected to be low when there is good coordination between fiscal and monetary policies[4].

Financial liberalization is another example of an occurrence that creates uncertainty. Through processes such as deregulations on interest rate ceiling, capital movement across borders and financial innovations, the financial institutions become more motivated to compete for a higher profit. New types of financial institutions and financial products that arise from the competition promote the efficiency of fund mobilization within and across a country. Monetary authorities, therefore, have to face with higher degrees of "parameter uncertainty" and "model uncertainty" due to the change in the structure of financial sector.

A major occurrence can bring about more than one type of uncertainty to the conduct of monetary policy. A clear example is the case of the Asian Financial Crisis in 1997. The abandonment of pegged exchange rate regime to managed floating exchange regime due to speculative attacks in foreign exchange market led to capital flights and non-performing loans. It is conceivable that Thai policymakers had to face all types of uncertainty classified above. Since other neighboring countries such as Indonesia, Malaysia, the Philippines and South Korea also fell into the crisis, no analysis could precisely predict when and at which level Baht would stabilize. This represents the "additive-shock uncertainty" with "uncertainty about duration of shock" faced by Thai monetary authority. Besides, the shift in exchange rate regime and the consequences of financial reforms in the five countries after the crisis implied "parameter uncertainty" and "model uncertainty". For instance, Atchariyachanvanich (2004) asserts the need to reexamine the relative importance of channels of the monetary policy transmission mechanisms in these countries. Moreover, there were many closures, mergers, acquisitions and establishment of banks and financial institutions in both real and banking sectors during the crisis. The possibility of missing or double calculations in some accounts such as bank assets, bank credits and real value of risk assets represents "data uncertainty" in that period. Uncertainty about how the public formed their expectation was another obstacle faced by the policymakers in stabilizing the economy where rumors and subsequent panics in the public were on going.

IT and Monetary Policy

IT, in general, is a term that encompasses all forms of technology including hardware and software used in information handling, information processing, and communication[5]. Jorgenson (2001) explains that IT begins when *memory chips*, semiconductor storage devices, were invented in late 1940s and further developed in terms of speed and capacity into *logic chips* in the late 1960s. Subsequent developments and introduction of microprocessor chips, personal computers, software and communications equipment and applications along with the reduction of their prices have promoted the rapid diffusion of IT into various sectors countrywide and worldwide. This phenomenon refers to the IT revolution.

The implications of the IT revolution on the conduct of monetary policy are more complicated than the case of an onset of a crisis. Where both occurrences have affected the conduct of monetary policy through various types of uncertainty, the effects of the IT revolution both increase and decrease the degree of uncertainty to the conduct of monetary policy. This section divides the discussions into the macroeconomic and operational points of view.

Macroeconomic Perspective: Effects of IT Revolution

Cecchetti (2002) and Cette and Pfister (2003) share a common stance in believing that the IT revolution has brought about the "New Economy" in which output growth accelerated while there was a downward trend of inflation[6]. It is perceptible from their discussions that there are two main challenges to the conduct of monetary policy: First, whether the increase in output growth should be recognized as permanent or transitional one, and Second, whether the monetary policy will survive new IT-induced financial innovations.

Nature of Impact of IT Revolution on Output Growth

The first challenge matters to monetary authorities because the output growth affects prices through market adjustment mechanisms in both goods and loanable funds markets. If the output growth due to the IT revolution is transitional, then pressure on prices tends to temporary. The occurrence can be regarded as an "additive-shock uncertainty". This requires a policy response to stabilize the output to its original path and accept some inevitable deviations of inflation rate from the target without reconsideration on the entire monetary policy framework. On the other hand, if the output growth represents a permanent shift in economic structure, this will add a risk of "parameter uncertainty" to the conduct of monetary policy.

Difficulties in dealing with this first challenge concern approach and measurement. Regarding approach, a widely used framework is to decompose the source of the growth, which is the productivity into explainable and residual parts, called total factor productivity (TFP). If the IT revolution is found responsible in the explainable (TFP) part, the output growth is expected to be a permanent (transitional) one. Boucekkine and de la Croix (2003) constructed a multi-sectoral growth model with endogenous embodied technological progress to capture the viability of an IT-base economy. They concluded that a permanent effect tends to be a result of IT-boosted R&D productivity together with a permanent increase in the number of software, rather than the reliance on IT-based acceleration in production of physical capital. This implies that not only the quantity but also components in IT investment are important determinants that monetary authorities need to take into account in dealing with uncertainties regarding the magnitude and duration of the impact.

Regarding measurement, different countries employ different accounting approaches in recording spending on IT and calculating price indexes of IT equipment. Cette and Pfister (2003) give an example of the account recording for computer software that shows a "factors-costs" approach is applied to all software in France, while a "services-produced" approach is exceptionally applied to some software in the United States. The Sveriges Riksbank (2000) also addresses the hedonic type of price index for hardware investment in the United States that could be the reason for the relatively sharp fall in prices of its IT goods in the late 1990s compared to some European countries, including Sweden. These discrepancies imply the possibility for revision of accounting approaches in certain countries in the future, in turn, representing a risk of "data uncertainty" to the conduct of monetary policy.

Implications of IT-Induced Financial Innovations

The second challenge concerns fears from IT-induced financial innovations on the ability to adjust the money supply. Such ability, theoretically, relies on the monetary base comprising currency (notes and coins) held by individuals for daily transactions and deposits of commercial banks held at central banks as reserves to meet legal requirement[7]. If the demand for currency is relatively predictable and commercial banks normally lend all their excess reserves to the business sector in exchange for interest incomes, then adjusting the monetary base will lead to a predictable change on the money supply. However, the surges of IT-induced financial innovations, particularly, asset-backed securities (ABSs) and electronic money (e-money) can erode the role of the monetary base in terms of quantity and powerfulness.

According to Tran and Roldos (2003), there is an ongoing boom of ABSs in many countries such as the United States, Germany, Korea, Chile, Colombia, Mexico and Peru.[8] Conceptually, ABSs are the products of securitization process that pools assets which produce steady cash flows such as mortgage loans, credit card receivables and car loans to back an issuance of securities. As the primary source of payments is cash flows from underlying assets, ABSs can have lower credit risk than general securities from the same issuer. Continual improvements in timely and accurate data processing induced by the

IT revolution have enabled potential investors to use ABSs as a means to access cheaper funds from domestic as well as international capital markets instead of borrowing from commercial banks. Also, commercial banks gain flexibility from securitizations in raising funds and taking off assets, such as mortgage loans, from their balance. According to an empirical study conducted by Estrella (2002) on American mortgage securitizations during the late 1960s to the early 2000s, securitizations had significantly caused changes in degrees of liquidity in credit markets and demand for bank credit, in turn, affecting the effectiveness of monetary policy in influencing real output. This finding indicates risk of "parameter uncertainty" to the conduct of monetary policy.

E-money is defined as "a stored value or prepaid product in which a record of the funds or value available to the consumer for multipurpose use is stored on an electronic device in the consumer's possession" (Bank for International Settlements, 2004, p. 2). This definition covers both card-based (such as multipurpose prepaid cards and electronic purses) and software or network-based (such digital cash) devices. The spread of e-money represents a possible reduction in demand for currency. This creates two main concerns on the conduct of monetary policy. The first concern is a reduction of *seigniorage* revenue from printing bank notes and coins (Stuber, 1996; Goodhart, 2000). The second concern, raised by Friedman (2000), represents an extreme case under which e-money fully substitutes the currency and clearing systems become out of control, subsequently causing monetary authorities totally lose the ability to adjust money supply via the use of the monetary base. Although the first concern sounds theoretically plausible and unavoidable once there is an adoption of e-money at any extent, a survey on 95 central banks by the Bank for International Settlements (2004) reveals that the average value of e-money transactions is still low in most countries and, therefore, the decline in *seigniorage* revenues remain negligible.

As for the second concern, Goodhart (2000) asserts that e-money cannot become a perfect substitute for currency as long as there remain some customers who do not want their transactions to be traceable, who are not confident about the security system against data hacking, and who are not convinced in the legal value of the e-money. In short, the implications of e-money on the conduct of monetary policy are similar to those of prior financial innovations such as checks, drafts, negotiable certificate of deposits, and credit cards. These financial innovations have caused monetary authorities to set different definitions monetary aggregates and busied with monitoring their relationships with output and prices.

Woodford (2000, 2001) assert that even the "cashless" economy arrives, the monetary policy will not become totally ineffective unless it is conducted under pure monetary aggregate targeting framework. This is because monetary authorities can also influence the economy via interest rate channel (Freedmand, 2000). Adjusting discount rates charged on commercial banks at the discount window is one way to give signals to the market. A more direct way to influence market interest rate is to perform open market operations, which concern buying and selling risk-free government securities such as treasury bills. Despite the possibility of losing the ability to adjust money supply due to emergences of ABSs and e-money, the IT revolution can enhance the effectiveness in influencing the short-term interest rates. Katafono (2004) argues on this point that the emergence of electronic payment and settlement means helps activating arbitrage trading among financial assets with various term structures, resulting in possible increase in the speed at which policy interest rates affect other interest rates. It can be inferred from the study of Woodford (2000) that using overnight interest rate as the variable for operational target can help reducing "model uncertainty" because its effectiveness is not affected by the size of the monetary base as under the case of using the monetary aggregate.

Operational Perspective: IT Applications

Not only to achieve the targets corresponding to the selected monetary policy framework, the conduct of monetary policy in a central bank deals with several challenges at the operational level. Most monetary authorities have the responsibility in ensuring a good financial environment for their economies. However, like other organizations, such authorities are performing their tasks with limited resources. The key supporting elements in surviving a changing environment are high efficiency of resource utilization within the organization, high capacity of decision making and high creditability perceived by the public.

This subsection takes an operational view that presents examples of IT applications in the conduct of monetary policy in different central banks. In order to ease discussions forward, the IT applications in this chapter refer to any form of integrated use of IT components, namely hardware, software, and communications equipment[9]. Based on their potential benefits to the monetary authorities, the IT applications are divided into three groups — namely efficiency-enhancing, decision-making-enhancing and innovative IT applications.

Efficiency-Enhancing IT Applications

By looking at organization charts of most central banks, it is not difficult to imagine that there are several routine tasks within individual departments as well as interrelations among departments. The use of certain IT applications can help to improve the efficiency of some routine works and inter-department communication in terms of time or resource saving. The IT applications in this group include local area network (LAN), Intranet, electronic learning (e-learning), enterprise resource planning (ERP), electronic payment system and Web services.

In a central bank, the most fundamental computer network is LAN. It enables central banks to share the resources of several hardware and devices such as a server and printers. The server assists with file sharing storage that allows multiple computer users to access applications and data, and it is obviously practical in implementing LAN in most central banks. For example, in the Sveriges Riksbank (Sweden) there exists an IT department to operate LAN in order to provide a direct Intranet connection and allow Internet connection to staff (Sveriges Riksbank, 1999). The Intranet, in turn, can serve as a portal of applications used in the central bank in form of internal Web pages. Examples of the applications range from fundamental applications such as electronic mail to complicated applications such as e-learning, portfolio management system, and operational risk management. Among these applications, e-learning represents a potential application that helps improving the efficiency in a central bank in terms of human resource development. Since e-learning can conduct online lessons via Intranet and Internet, it represents one choice of a central bank in conducting training programs online. It would benefit both the central bank and employees because of the savings in costs and time, timely information access, and less intimidating course. Moreover, e-learning may be one channel that assists the public in understanding central bank policy with interactive education. At present, the National Bank of Poland has already launched free-access e-learning courses via the Economic Education Portal.

The ERP is another example of efficiency-enhancing IT application. For instance, the Bank of Thailand integrates ERP software package to its Intranet in order to improve processes ranging from organizational management, employee records, salary and compensation. In particular, with the ERP, the Bank of Thailand could also enhance its learning environment by providing an integrated and continuous learning approach under its Human Resource Information System and could promote the efficiency in financial and administrative operations, capital budgeting, purchasing, inventory, procurement, and cost control under its Budgeting Finance Information System (Bank of Thailand, 2002). The National Bank of Belgium (2002) also has realized the benefits of the ERP in terms of improved efficiency in operating processes such as purchasing, sales, budget management, and analytical accounting in human resources processes.

Another routine but highly important task of a central bank is to provide a payment system to facilitate clearing and settlement of transactions among participants such as financial institutions and eligible individuals. Most commercial banks prefer fast clearing process so that they can economize the required reserve (Woodford, 2001). The increase in domestic and cross-border economic activities is the main factor forcing most central banks to utilize electronic payment system in order to provide fast, reliable and efficient payment system. For example, the interbank payment system in Hong Kong was upgraded to reduce settlement risks with a more powerful and faster mainframe computer (Hong Kong Monetary Authority, 1997). Monetary unification just as in the European Union is another drive that calls for the utilization of electronic payment system.

In order to the support the flotation of the euro and the conduct of the Single Monetary Policy, the Trans-European Automated Real-time Gross settlement Express Transfer system (TARGET) was introduced in January 1999 (European Central Bank (ECB), 2004). As for new members of the European Union, another reason for improving their payment systems is to ensure the harmonization with the TARGET (Tothova, 2000). For this purpose, together with the increasing share of non-cash payments, all new member countries have improved and adjusted their domestic payment systems on various aspects such as transparency of access criteria, operating time, level of reserve requirements for each participants, transaction fees and legal and security aspects (ECB, 2002).

The electronic payment system can be further upgraded to provide other services beyond fund transfers by attaching Web services. Conceptually, Web services integrate services that can be used on Internet in order to create a complete business process though application programming interface that conforms to a particular specification format (Chung, Lin, & Mathieu, 2003; Manes, 2003). An obvious example is the BAHTNET

Web services residing in the BAHTNET System, which is an electronic high-value fund transfer network of the real gross settlements of high-value payments, foreign exchange transactions, securities trading, and funds transfers to nonresident Baht accounts between financial institutions and other organizations in Thailand. According to Tripojanee, Yamolyong, and Insuk (2002), while the enforcement of the BAHTNET System has resulted in the reduction in check usage and its clearing costs, the Web services enable BAHTNET members to access information concerning their cash and securities account from the BAHTNET System at the Bank of Thailand anytime during the service hours.

Decision-Making-Enhancing IT Applications

The second group of IT applications contains examples of the IT applications that potentially enhance the decision-making capacity of monetary authorities in the conduct of monetary policy. The applications include data warehouse, operational risk management, and portfolio management system.

Monetary authorities need accurate, consistent, detailed and timely data in performing statistical analyses for the design of monetary policy. A data warehouse represents a type of IT application that serves these needs through efficient process of collecting, extracting, transforming, distributing, storing, and retrieving data for multipurpose use (Jones, 1998). Ideally, data warehousing that allows real time access to financial institutions' records of transactions, such as value of non-performing loans, will enhance monitoring capacity of monetary authorities. There are other important benefits of data warehousing such as increasing the precision of early warning system and improving the sample selection for further on-site inspections. As for financial institutions, they receive benefits in terms of time and cost saving in preparing and submitting periodical reports. At present, several central banks such as the Banco de España (Spain), Bangko Sentral ng Pilipinas (the Philippines), the Czech National Bank, the European Central Bank, the Reserve Bank of India and the State Bank of Pakistan are developing and deploying data warehouses.

In order to maintain the credibility, the monetary authorities have to ensure sound corporate governance in their operation. Managing financial and non-financial risks is one of crucial tasks for the authorities. Sangmanee and Raengkhum (2000) posit that financial risks basically arise from international reserve management and financial market operations while non-financial risks include strategic and operational risks in the conduct of monetary policy. Managing each kind of risk requires appropriate frameworks of analysis, timely information processing, and sophisticated statistical techniques. The IT applications provide solution to assist this decision-making process. The Danmarks Nationalbank (Denmark), for example, has introduced IT applications to support its framework for operational risk management, which, "comprises a risk assessment model, a standard for procedures, physical security, IT security management and business continuity plans" (Danmarks Nationalbank, 2004, p.110).

Managing and investing foreign reserves, gold, securities in portfolio of a central bank is another important and complicated task. Basically, central banks have to hold foreign reserves to meet potential needs in intervening in the foreign exchange market and servicing foreign loans. Gold holdings, for example, are for securing the value of domestic currency. Securities that central banks usually hold are low-risk debt securities of differing maturities such as treasury bills and treasury bonds issued by government. Sales and purchases of securities enable monetary authorities to influence interest rates. As each component in the portfolio serves different purposes and has different degrees of volatility in value, portfolio management in central banks is not less difficult than in the business sector. The Danmarks Nationalbank employs a portfolio management system that helps managing all portfolios including derived products such as forward foreign-exchange contracts and structures data for all portfolios as a small number of uniform tables in the same system (Danmarks Nationalbank, 2004). The Swiss National Bank also continually upgrades the network and utilizes a central asset management application (Swiss National Bank, 2003).

Innovative IT Applications

There remain some IT applications that enable monetary authorities to perform innovative practices in the conduct of monetary policy. Examples of these applications include the World Wide Web-oriented IT applications, data mining, and the eXtensible Business Reporting Language (XBRL).

Woodford (2001) argues that the effectiveness of monetary policy in a modern economy does not only depend on the controllability of monetary instruments but also on how well the monetary authorities can influence "current expectations of future inflation" of market participants via openly informing them about current and future monetary policy actions. The emergence of the Web page (an electronic document that can be viewed via a Web browser on the World Wide Web on the Internet) helps in translating this new monetary philosophy into action. Most central banks now pay special attention on the design and details of their Web pages and allow public access. For example, the Bank of Canada and the Bank of Finland provide the public with accessibility to their Web sites which contain a huge amount of information, including speeches, press releases, explanatory notes on monetary policy and bank notes, as well as availability of statistical resources (Bank of Canada, 2000; Bank of Finland, 1997). It has also become a common practice among central banks to post and update the forecasted value of target variable (such as the Consumer Price Index), schedule for next monetary board meeting, and monetary policy board's decision. Although developing and updating user-friendly Web pages with full range of information is not a conventional task of a central bank, it represents the least costly way with timeless and borderless access to ensure the public with transparency and accountability. The ultimate objective in such practices is to serve as a means in managing the public's expectations pertaining to a higher possibility in achieving the monetary objective. The success of the Reserve Bank of New Zealand in pioneering an inflation-targeting framework was supported largely by unquestionably good preparation and effective public communication. Without IT applications like the Web page, the central bank might not be able to achieve the same level of support and understanding from the public, or it could have been more costly. Similar questions can apply to the case of the Single Monetary Policy in European Union.

So far, the conduct of the monetary policy relies on the use of macroeconomic models in capturing complex relationship among monetary and economic variables. The models normally comprise equations based on economic theories and assumptions. Considering the limited development of economic theories in relation to the dynamics of the economy that are far from the assumptions, there remain several tasks to revealing the complex relationships. In order to meet this purpose, a technique called neural networks which imitate data processing in the human brain in computer systems is gaining an interest from monetary researchers as a new method in deriving flexible and adaptive models. For example, McNelis (1998) applied artificial neural networks to estimate the *seigniorage*-maximizing inflation rates in Chile, while McNelis and McAdam (2004) applied it to forecast inflation based on the Phillips-curve formulations in the United States, Japan and the European area. The neural networks and other techniques of data mining are potential IT applications that assist the recovery of hidden behavior of the relationships among the variables. However, as the validity of the results depends on the quality and amount of data supplied, the full utilization of data mining application can occur after the successful phase of implementing data warehousing becomes linked to national statistical office.

Lastly, some central banks such as those in Germany, Japan, New Zealand and Spain are catching up with the trend in utilizing the XBRL as a standard in assigning tags on financial data in order to increase speedy automatic data handling and sharing, with less chance of errors. According to the information currently available on the XBRL International's homepage (http://www.xbrl.org), examples of other government organizations that have introduced the XBRL include national statistics authorities (Ireland), fiscal and taxation authorities (Australia, Canada, and The Netherlands), stock exchanges (Australia, Japan, and the United Kingdom), and financial institutions monitoring authorities (the United States). In Japan, the XBRL is regarded as a tool supporting financial measures in restructuring its financial system towards attending better loans pricing scheme, healthier financial institutions, better dissemination and analysis of corporate financial data, and more efficient securities markets (Fuchita, 2005).

Conclusions and Remarks

In the current era, the conduct of monetary policy in the world is shifting towards more rule-based decision making with explicit targets. The long-term credibility of a monetary authority depends on how well the authority can continually achieve the targets announced to the public; however, in a dynamic economic environment it is impossible to eliminate uncertainty in the conduct of monetary policy.

The IT revolution resulted from a rapid diffusion of IT applications into various sectors has created two dimensions of macroeconomic implications on the conduct of monetary policy. The first dimension occurs through the impacts of output growth. Whether the change in output growth tends to be permanent or transitional is crucial to monetary authorities in adjusting their policy response. A permanent effect will call for revisions on model and target values of money policy. Fewer adjustments will be needed in the case of a transitional effect. Emergence of new types of financial innovation, namely asset-backed securities and electronic money represents the second dimension of macroeconomic implications. Both products potentially undermine the role of the monetary base in influencing economic variables. However, so far, the effects are still limited because of the lagged development in legal and security aspects. From the literature, monetary policy will not completely lose its effectiveness even in cashless economy as it can be transmitted via interest rate channel.

At the operational level, the conduct of monetary policy in central banks benefits from IT applications in three main areas. First, IT applications such as local area network, Intranet, electronic learning, Enterprise Resource Planning, electronic payment system, and Web services help to improve efficiency in the organization as well as in providing services. In the decision-making process, IT applications are deployed in the areas of data utilization, risk management, and portfolio management. Lastly, IT applications provide innovative ways for monetary authorities in increasing their creditability. For instance, the emergence of the World Wide Web, Web sites and Web pages has supported the new philosophy of monetary policy that focuses on managing public expectation. Next, the advancement of data mining technique such as neural networks will enhance the capacity of the monetary authorities in formulating flexible and adaptive economic models to survive the changing economic environment. Lastly, the XBRL is becoming a potential tool for monetary authorities in restructuring financial systems.

It should be recalled here that there remain other sources of uncertainty in the conduct of monetary policy such as unanticipated fiscal actions, spillover effects from other countries through trade and investment, and non-IT-induced changes in economic structure. The IT revolution is just one of the uncertainties. On the other hand, advancements in IT applications can strengthen the capacity of and serve as pioneering tools for monetary authorities in conducting their monetary policy.

Speaking from the opposite perspective, it is becoming a *de facto* standard for modern monetary authorities to capture the trend of introducing IT applications into their operations. Failing to do so implies a risk in losing their creditability due to being unable to survive the dynamics of economic change. The degree of implementing IT applications in the conduct of monetary policy, in turn, may become another important factor in determining the appropriate type of monetary policy framework of a particular country in the future. However, the implementation requires substantial investment in terms of both infrastructure and human resources. These may not be affordable in some developing countries, and this aspect will become another source of caution for IT-deficient countries not to adopt a certain monetary policy framework from IT-advanced countries without proper adaptations. Clarification on this view calls for further research.

Lastly, but the most importantly, despite the trend towards ruled-based and more transparent monetary policy and the advancement of IT applications, the conduct of monetary policy can never be fully automated. The success of a monetary policy still highly depends on the competence and vision of the monetary authorities together with continual harmonization with other economic policies such as fiscal policy.

Acknowledgments

The authors would like to acknowledge the financial support from the Japanese Society for the Promotion of Science and valuable comments from professor Hiroshi Osada, Nagoya University, Japan. The authors are both grateful for the advice from associate professor Hitoshi Okada, National Institute of Informatics, Japan.

References

Atchariyachanvanich, W. (2002). The legal central bank independence and macroeconomic performance: An empirical study on eighteen developing countries in the 1990s. *Forum of International Development Studies, 23*, 201-221.

Atchariyachanvanich, W. (2004). VAR analysis of monetary policy transmission mechanisms: Empirical study on five Asian countries after the Asian crisis. *Forum of International Development Studies, 25*, 39-59.

Bank for International Settlements. (2004). *Survey of developments in electronic money and Internet and mobile payments*. Basel, Switzerland: Bank for International Settlements.

Bank of Canada. (2000). *Annual report 2000*. Ontario: Bank of Canada.

Bank of Finland. (1997). *Bank of Finland annual report 1997*. Helsinki: Bank of Finland.

Bank of Thailand. (2002). *Annual economic report 2002*. Bangkok: Bank of Thailand.

Blinder, A. S. (1982). Issues in the coordination of monetary and fiscal policy. *NBER Working Paper Series, 982*.

Boucekkine, R., & de la Croix, D. (2003). Information technologies, embodiment and growth. *Journal of Economic Dynamics & Control, 27*, 2007-2034.

Cecchetti, S. G. (2002). The new economy and the challenges for macroeconomic policy. *NBER Working Paper, 8935*.

Cette, G., & Pfister, C. (2003). The challenges of the "new economy" for monetary policy. *Banque de France NER Working Paper, 100*.

Chung, J.-Y., Lin, K.-J., & Mathieu, R. G. (2003). Guest editor's introduction: Web services computing: Advancing software interoperability. *Computer, 36*(10), 35-37.

Cukierman, A. (1992). *Central bank strategy, credibility, and independence: Strategy, credibility, and evidence*. Cambridge, MA: The MIT Press.

Danmarks Nationalbank. (2004). *Financial management at Danmarks Nationalbank*. Copenhagen, Denmark: Danmarks Nationalbank.

Estrella, A. (2002). Securitization and the efficacy of monetary policy. *Economic Policy Review, 8*(1), 243-255.

European Central Bank. (2002). *BLUE BOOK - Payment and securities settlement systems in accession countries*. Frankfurt, Germany: European Central Bank.

European Central Bank. (2004). *The current target system*. Frankfurt, Germany: European Central Bank.

Freedman, C. (2000). Monetary policy implementation: Past, present, and future: Will the advent of electronic money lead to the eventual demise of central banking? *International Finance, 3*(2), 211-227.

Friedman, B. M. (2000). Decoupling at the margin: The threat to monetary policy from the electronic revolution in banking. *NBER Working Paper, 7955*.

Fuchita, Y. (2005, March 18). *Japanese financial system: New initiatives and new IT infrastructures*. Paper presented at the International Conference on IT and Financial Systems in 21st Century, Hitotsubashi University, Japan.

Goodhart, C. A. E. (2000). Can central banking survive the IT revolution? *International Finance, 3*(2), 189-209.

Hong Kong Monetary Authority. (1997). *Annual report 1997*. Hong Kong: Hong Kong Monetary Authority.

Jenkins, P., & Longworth, D. (2002, Summer). Monetary policy and uncertainty. *Bank of Canada Review,* 3-10.

Jones, K. (1998). An introduction to data warehousing: What are the implications for the network? *International Journal of Network Management, 8*, 42-56.

Jorgenson, D. W. (2001). Information technology and the U.S. economy. *American Economic Review, 91*(1), 1-32.

Katafono, R. (2004). The implications of evolving technology on monetary policy: Literature survey. *Reserve Bank of Fiji: Economics Department Working Paper, 2004/02*.

Longworth, D. (2004, Autumn). Monetary policy and uncertainty. *Bank of Canada Review,* 57-62.

Mahadeva, L., & Sterne, G. (Eds.). (2000). *Monetary policy framework in global context*. London: Routledge.

Manes, A. T. (2003). *Web services: A manager's guide* (1st ed.). UK: Addison-Wesley.

McNelis, P. (1998). Money demand and seigniorage-maximizing inflation in Chile: Approximation and estimation with neural networks. *Revista de Análisis Económico 13*(2), 3-24.

McNelis, P., & McAdam, P. (2004). Forecasting inflation with thick models and neural networks. *European Central Bank Working Paper, 352*.

National Bank of Belgium. (2002). *Report 2002: Part 2 activities and annual account*. Brussels, Belgium: National Bank of Belgium.

Sangmanee, A., & Raengkhum, J. (2000, September). A general concept of central bank wide risk management. *Bank of Thailand Bulletin,* 1-10.

Sterne, G. (1999, August). The use of explicit targets for monetary policy: Practical experience of 91 economies in the 1990s. *Bank of England Quarterly Bulletin,* 272-280.

Stuber, G. (1996). The electronic purse: An overview of recent developments and policy issues. *Bank of Canada: Technical Report, 74.*

Sveriges Riksbank. (1999). *Bank annual report.* Stockholm, Sweden: Sveriges Riksbank.

Sveriges Riksbank. (2000). *Inflation report 2000:4.* Stockholm, Sweden: Sveriges Riksbank.

Swiss National Bank. (2003). *96th annual report 2003.* Wetzikon, Switzerland: Swiss National Bank.

Tothova, I. E. (2000). 5th international conference of clearing institutions of central and east Europe. *Biatec, 8*(11), 34-35.

Tran, H. Q., & Roldos, J. (2003, June 8-9). *ASIAN bond markets: The role of securitization and credit guarantees.* Paper presented at The 2nd Annual Conference of PECC Finance Forum: Issues and Challenges for Regional Financial Cooperation in the Asia-Pacific, Hilton Hua Hin Resort & Spa, Hua Hin, Thailand.

Tripojanee, S., Yamolyong, N., & Insuk, S. (2002, June). The promotion of BAHTNET on financial market development in Thailand. *Bank of Thailand Quarterly Bulletin,* 1-7.

Woodford, M. (2000). Monetary policy in a world without money. *NBER Working Paper, 7853.*

Woodford, M. (2001). Monetary policy in the information economy. *NBER Working Paper, 8674.*

Worrell, D. (2000). Monetary and fiscal coordination in small open economies. *IMF Working Paper, 00/56.*

Endnotes

[1]   The type of monetary policy framework is usually classified by the type of financial variable that proxies the monetary goal. In the *International Financial Statistics* of the IMF, it is classified into an exchange rate anchor, monetary aggregate targeting, inflation targeting, the IMF-supported or other monetary program, and other.

[2]   However, the freedom of the central bank is only on the operational method, not on the objective selection.

[3]   See Mahadeva and Sterne (2000) for detailed analyses on other aspects of global monetary policy frameworks.

[4]   Worrell (2000) describes a good coordination as the situation in which fiscal authority cooperates well with the monetary authority in designing, implementing, monitoring, and, when necessary, revising the macroeconomic policy.

[5]   This definition indicates the same meaning between the terms IT and ICTs (information and communication technologies) used in this chapter.

[6]   Cette and Pfister (2003) discussed the impacts of the IT revolution on potential output growth in terms of capital deepening effect and gains in total factor production, and claimed that the lagged wage adjustment was the source of disinflation. Cecchetti (2002) stands on the microeconomic view and argues that the IT revolution enhanced competition and resource allocation resulting in the rapid output growth. However, he believes that the decline in the inflation rate in the United States during the 1980s and the 1990s was more related to other factors rather than the IT revolution.

[7]   However, Woodford (2000) asserts that many countries today such as the United Kingdom, Sweden, Canada, Australia and New Zealand no longer set reserve requirements.

[8]   Tran and Roldos (2003) claim some factors such as unclear legal aspects of the Securitization Law and the lack of credit guarantees are the main constraints to the development of markets for asset-backed securities in some countries such as Thailand, Malaysia and Singapore.

[9]   Some IT-oriented articles may define IT applications as just software.

Chapter XV

The Role and Future of Local Currency and IT

Yutaka Kurihara, Aichi University, Japan

Akio Fukushima, Seijo University, Japan

Abstract

The use of local currency has been spreading gradually since the 1990s. It has been introduced by nonprofit organizations (NPOs) and similar groups in some countries around the world. Welfare, nursing and nonpaying work, such as childrearing, are among the most popular reasons for introducing local currency. Recently, one local currency has appeared related to preventing environmental problems and protective and nursing industries. In some countries, local currencies have supported expectations for economic recovery. Promoting the spread of local currency is thought to be important. Information technology (IT) has contributed to the spread of local currency and may create new areas of usage and value. Various problems accompany the spreading use of local currencies. Local currency will not create major obstacles to economic activity as long as the sizes of transactions do not increase greatly, so governments and financial authorities have little reason to prohibit its use unless the currency issue authority in the country is seriously threatened. The exchange of digital value through IT (e.g., IC cards and the diffusion of the local currency) has significant value but also increases risks. To promote efficiency and convenience in local currency by introducing IT, governments, public administrations and municipalities should cooperate with a strategy for the information and communication technology (ICT) development. Alliances among many institutions should be considered.

Introduction

The use of local currency has been spreading gradually. The NPOs of some countries have introduced local currency, for example, to support welfare programs, nursing and nonpaying work, such as childrearing. In some countries, expectations for economic recovery have been supported by the introduction of a local currency. Moreover, the president of Bank of Japan, Toshihiko Fukui, praised local currency for providing "economic dynamism" (*The Chunichi Newspaper*, 2003).

It is important to understand the function and the role of local currency in theoretical terms as well as its practical applications in the business world. This chapter considers the origin and examples of local currency, analyzes the economic and legal implications of local currency, and then addresses the pros and cons of local currency and its relationship with IT. The connection between IT and local currency is inevitable and provides considerable potential benefits.

Origins and Examples of Local Currency

The original local currency was the "labor note" introduced as a form of payment by Robert Owen in the 1830s. A hundred years later, stamp scripts came into use in the United States, Austria, Germany and other countries. Since that time, use of local currencies has spread all over the world. Some estimates indicate that in the early 21st century, local currencies are being introduced in 2,500 to 3,000 regions in the world. In Japan, there are some expectations for overcoming deflation (*The Nihon Keizai Newspaper*, 2002). Typical cases from around the world are described below.

The Ithaca HOURS used in the United States is a paper coupon that equates one hour with $10 U.S. and can be used to purchase goods and services in a limited region within a 20-mile radius of downtown Ithaca, New York. The purpose of this local currency is to help circulation of wealth within the community, strengthen the commitment of local enterprises to the people who live there, add to local spending power, reduce the need to transport goods and for excess packaging, and create jobs (Glover, 2002).

Similarly, time dollars are also famous in the United States. This organization equates one hour of service with one time dollar, so that time dollars is a type of currency that empowers people to convert their personal time into purchasing power by helping others and by contributing to the rebuilding of family, neighborhood and community. Every act of helping leads to another act of helping, creating a web of support and caring that rebuilds trust and enhances community. Time dollar exchanges are used in two main ways. Generalized exchanges of time dollars are most often found in neighbor-to-neighbor time dollar exchanges in which people contribute their efforts to assist their neighbors. Time dollars is also used to reward specific contributions that are deemed to be of special value to the community. In Washington, D.C., the Time Dollar Youth Court uses time dollars to recognize and reward teens that serve as jurors. In the Chicago Cross-

Age Peer Tutoring program, youth earn time dollars for tutoring younger students and the tutees also earn time dollars (Time Dollar Institute, 2004).

Toronto Dollars are used in Canada, and the method of this organization has been introduced all over the world. The scheme involves a paper ticket, or a Toronto dollar, which is equivalent to one Canadian dollar, and can be used for commercial transactions in the region. Participating community organizations are also eligible to receive 10% grants from the community fund. Any participating community and charitable organization can receive 110 Toronto Dollars for every 100 Canadian dollars by contacting their treasurer. In addition, community organizations that send volunteers to work at the booth in the St. Lawrence Market on Saturdays earn 5% of the funds exchanged for their organization, for example. Other examples of activities supported by Toronto Dollars are free dance classes for youth, nutritious breakfasts for school children, food and clothing for street people, furniture transportation for low-income people, camping trips for children, "thank-you gifts" for caring services and so on (Toronto Dollar Community Projects).

LETS (Local Exchange Trading Systems) are revitalizing communities throughout Britain. As grassroots initiatives, they are open to people of all ages, skills and abilities; local clubs and associations; voluntary groups, charities and community initiatives; housing cooperatives, small businesses and local services. LETS facilitates the give and take of currency and services, assists in the connection of its users to new resources, and in establishing a genuine community identity (UK LETS). People earn LETS credits by providing a service and then can spend the credits on whatever is offered by others using the scheme for services and products such as childcare, transport, food, home repairs or rental of tools and equipment.

Local currency can be classified into economical motives, designed to activate the regional economy and out-economical motives, designed to promote community reciprocal help and unity by facilitating personal exchanges in the region. The out-economical motive is more common than the economical motive. In some cases, the function of local currency is payment for all or part of services provided by regional shops and producers. In many cases, the use of local currency is limited to service transactions that are not easily accommodated in volunteer work and markets such as welfare, education, environment and cultural activities. This type of system helps to renew forgotten skills among community members and to champion community resources. This interweaving of service and economics helps promote prosperity and unity in the community.

Local Currency and the Economical Side

The development of local currency is progressing gradually as indicated above. The economical impact of the use of local currencies is difficult to quantify and cannot be fully analyzed. This section addresses several economic issues associated with the use of local currencies.

Economical Features of Local Currencies

Local currency is used in a defined, limited region. However, it is difficult to define the feature by this single meaning.

Regional Limitations and Non-Exchangeability with National Currency

The use of local currency is limited to a specific region and cannot be used as legal tender, as with the U.S. dollar, the euro and yen. Local currencies are not guaranteed by national governments and cannot be exchanged for the national currency. Traditional economic theory assumes that money is a value standard, a medium of exchange, a means of storing value and a means of speculation. The name *currency* is not necessarily suitable for local currency, even though it is used all over the world, because local currency does not serve the latter two functions mentioned above.

Independent Issue and Management

Local currency is independently managed and issued by the community in a specific region. It is not issued by the government or the central bank.

No Interest

Interest does not attach to local currency[1]. Some local currencies collect a "staying fee". It can be said that local currency accrues zero or negative interest.

Issue Form

Local currencies are issued in various forms, not necessarily as paper notes. There are many advantages to the use and spread of notes. Moreover, paper notes, such as the Ithaca HOURS and Toronto dollars discussed above, mimic the anonymity, for example, of paper currencies presently in use worldwide.

When the local currency can be deposited to a specific organization by the bank's book form like a present currency, convenience and safety are improved. Accurate recording and registration of currencies as well as protection against abuse are important in this form. The LETS currency discussed above is the best example.

Finally, local currency may be issued as a bond (bill and check). This method is difficult to manage though it offers many advantages.

Eco-Money and Local Development Coupons

Eco-money is one form of the regional currency that is used for limited, informal dealings such as volunteers. For instance, when welfare, nursing, cleaning and use of personal computer are performed as volunteer work, payment can be tendered with local currency.

The recipient of the local currency can then use the local currency to obtain other services or exchange it for products, as pioneered by the time dollars organization. Such local currency can be used in market and non-market dealings and for services.

The Local Development Coupon issued in 1999 in Japan were an alternative that differed from local currency in that the benefactor is public institutions, such as cities, towns and villages, rather than individuals. These coupons had limited application for specific purposes as defined by the issuing country.

Local Currency and Monetary Policy

The influence of local currency on monetary policy depends on how the local currency substitutes for the standard currency issued by the government or the central bank and its influence on demand for the standard currency.

If local currency plays the role of a second currency, the publisher of the local currency must amass reserve deposits with the central bank, which is unlikely to occur at least in the near future.

The use of local currency does not generally significantly influence monetary policy as long the role of the local currency is supplementation of the legal tender and circulation and the powers of the issuing body are limited. In this respect, local currency is substantially similar to digital cash (BIS, 1996).

Openness of the economy and the mobility of labor and capital are standards of the optimum currency area theory proffered by Mundell and MacKinnon.

For instance, consider the implications of an exchange between a national currency and local currency into the region. When the openness of the economy is low, the effect of shock on the region is large[2]. According to Reynolds (2004), the region is likely to encounter certain negative effects in this circumstance.

If the use and region of a local currency are very limited and conversion to the legal currency is not permitted, the negative effects are diminished by a common legal currency because of the small scale. Given the present economic situation in most countries, there is little advantage in local currencies exceeding the status of supplementation of the legal currency.

The Legal Implications of Local Currency

It is important to consider the legal implications of the use of local currency. There is no legal prohibition of local scrip, community currencies, or private exchange systems in the

United States. In the U.S., HOURS are legal. Federal officials have repeatedly stated that there is no prohibition of local currency, provided that it does not physically resemble dollars, the denominations are at least $1, and it is regarded as taxable income. Standard legal tender must be used to pay taxes on income in local currencies. There is, however, a possibility of colliding with the law on matters surrounding the issue form of local currencies as discussed below.

Restriction Laws

The position of financial authorities all over the world concerning local currency is that the function of currency is to serve as a means of payment for everything or settlement of transactions by everyone and anywhere. The definition of legal tender includes general availability to many people throughout the country and use to settle transactions. Because local currency circulates only in the region of issue and is limited to use by small groups, it can be argued the local currencies are not currency at all.

Private vs. Public Issue

Even with the limitation that the locally issued currency may be used only in the region of issue, it is tricky to determine whether the local public entity is legally permitted to issue local currency. One view is that the local public entity is the same as a private individual in terms of the legal right to issue currency. The chief difference between a private individual and a local public entity in terms of currency issue is public confidence, influence and power.

Whereas some believe that issuing currency is a national matter because of its impact on the nationwide monetary system, there is also some sentiment that the issue of local currency by a local public entity is a peculiar activity. No clear conclusion can be drawn regarding the legal right to issue currency.

Other Laws Affecting Local Currency

Laws concerning the restriction of prepayment-type certificates may impact the issue of local currencies. In Japan, this law is not usually applied to certificates that are limited to a six-month use period.

Laws governing acceptance of contributions, money deposits and interest, particularly those regarding transfer of value by the legal tender through local currency may limit or prohibit the use of local currency for certain types of transactions.

Labor standards law dictates that payment for labor must be for the full amount by legal tender. Trust and banking laws may likewise limit the use of local currencies in some cases for the collection, management and speculation of funds. When local currency is accepted by enterprises other than volunteer activities, it is taxable, but the laws are sometimes difficult to interpret. When individuals receive local currency as remuneration for labor, the payment becomes income and is therefore taxable as income.

If local currency is used to settle property transfers, and if a person receives local currency repeatedly or continuously, consumption tax rules may apply.

In the United States in 1996, the Federal Reserve Bank (FRB) held the opinion that the issue of Ithaca HOURS does not legally have the problem. The state of Missouri conferred tax-free status for time dollars.

Prime Minister Tony Blair himself has promoted LETS in Britain[3]. Application of global standards will help to clarify the legal status of local currencies.

Expectations and Problems Regarding Local Currency

Based on economic views such as monetary theory, local currency is inferior in terms of benefit and convenience when compared to a legal currency. The function of local currency as money is also insufficient and limited, and the trading volume is small. Introducing additional functions to parallel those of legal tender are likely to be costly and inefficient.

It is therefore natural to surmise that the use of local currency will continue in a limited way and that expectations of far-reaching use are unfounded. Yet new ventures in local currency continue to arise with increasing frequency.

The most persuasive reason for this growth seems to be that local currency has not only an economical function but also appears to encourage individual participation in the regional society. Consider the example of the public transportation. In rural or remote areas, the fiscal burden associated with public transportation systems is often prohibitive. Local currency systems can be designed to support projects for which profits are difficult to obtain, such as transportation network maintenance, the arts, regional sports and so on. Another method that bears investigation is the use of local currency to activate the economy of the region by creating a system that is not dependent on a specific purpose, such as increasing volunteerism.

These approaches benefit the region by involving larger numbers of people in community service projects, including those population segments that are sometimes disenfranchised, such as senior citizens.

Planning and operation of an efficient local currency system requires administrative resources, including hardware and software, financial support, community awareness and accurate dissemination of information about the program. In addition, to promote the spread of local currency, it is necessary to consider the design of the issue subject, organizational management and the system.

The use of local currency may encounter legal difficulties if the currency assumes roles like the deposit interest rate, such as percentage pulls. With increasing use of IT type digital cash, as the amount of circulation of a legal currency decreases, there is a possibility of decreased revenues. Serious issues also arise because of counterfeiting and problems with free riders. Countries and local administrative bodies would be wise to anticipate a spread in the use of local currencies and to clarify relevant legal points so as to prevent problems[4].

Relation to IT: Increase and Expansion

With the IT revolution gathering speed all over the world, the connection between IT and local currency bears exploration. The spread of digital cash has strengthened recently after a slower period of development for a certain period of time (Kurihara, 2003).

Because regional currency has value as money and performs many kinds of functions in addition to those provided by traditional money, issues of safety and convenience in the IC card type is inevitable. Inversely, it is thought that introducing IT may help to prevent counterfeiting and greatly contributes to the spread of local currency. The previously described Canadian LETS system offers an IC-type card.

Komagane City in Japan provides a "Take Together Card" that includes IC. A stamp card introduced early in the shopping venues in this region was changed to an IC card in 1996. Users can store one point for every purchase of 100 yen, and one point can be used as digital cash with a value of one yen. Further, some functions of traditional legal currencies are included in the card.

Government must monitor relations between local currency and its administration. City administrations have added new functions in addition to the point systems to IC cards. Various welfare services, such as kindergarten and childcare are included as the main administrative function in the IC card.

It is not a stretch to envision the local currency reaching convenience stores, supermarkets, department stores, transportation and so on as a digital cash as the range of usage expands. In addition, the linkage with other local currencies is facilitated by introducing IT. Such system connections can provide advantages to consumers, banks and enterprises through expanded business opportunities, but some problems would first have to be solved.

First of all, there is the issue of the governing body of the local currency. If "consortium government" or linkage to other areas were structured, complex problems can occur. There are no problems when a local currency is used only in a limited area. However, the usage area can be expanded easily by introducing IT. Alliances are important.

With increased use of IT-type local currency as digital cash, laws concerning electromagnetic payment records might apply. The law is not applicable when the card cannot be used to pay. In addition, there is a problem of determining the exchange rate when the money is applied to different functions such as welfare service.

The definition of the local currency is a currency used in a limited region. If the definition is modified, local currencies can be handled like a "privilege" card, for example, as with airline mileage cards. The mileage card has the value and the exchange of the value in a limited region and limited usage can be achieved. Local currency with IC can easily accommodate such transactions. The development of IC should support the growth and expansion of digital value that enables exchange of values among different kinds of money, the region and services.

Conclusions

Local currency is a means by which to activate the economy of a region, to ease the effects of recession and encourage community activism and volunteerism. Because modern society has suffered from the lack of such volunteerism, expectations for the spread of local currency are great. Local currency stands to benefit the environment, welfare, the arts, education and so on, particularly in regions that do not have dealings in the market. Local currencies are also expected to protect and to help develop local culture (*The Asahi Newspaper*, 2000).

Various problems are involved with the expansion of the use of local currencies. However, it is not necessary to think it seriously. Even if abolished or distinguished, there are no great problems with local currencies. Given a good relationship among users, the advantages are considerable. Local currency will not create major obstacles to traditional economic activity as long as the current size of the transactions does not increase greatly. Government and financial authorities have not discovered reasons to stop the use of local currencies, though that is likely to change if a country's central currency issue authority is seriously threatened by local currency.

It is important that the private sector play a leading role in developing local currencies, but for maximum benefit and a real spread of local currency, the public sector must also be involved. The value of cooperation on this front is obvious.

Use of IT is inevitable to enhance the efficiency and convenience of local currency and is beneficial for the promotion of local currency in spite of the fact that there are some concerns and problems. People who use local currency will endeavor to spread the use of the local currency, however, the public sector has significant importance for introducing IT into local currency. The infrastructure and the system of ICT will be key to the successful spread.

References

(2003, July 17). *The Chunichi Newspaper*, 12.

BIS. (1996). *Implications for central banks of the development of electronic money*, 1-20.

Breiter, W. H., & Panigirtzoglou, N. (2003). Overcoming the zero bound on nominal interest rates with negative interest on currency: Gesell's solution. *Economic Journal, 113*, 723-746.

(2000, January 18). *The Asahi Newspaper*, 15.

Glover, P. (2002). Ithaca money. *Creating community economics with local currency.* Retrieved February 14, 2005, from http://www.ithacahours.com

Goodfriend, M. (2000). Overcoming the zero bound on interest rate policy. *Journal of Money, Credit, and Banking, 32*(4), 1007-1035.

Kurihara, Y. (2003). The spreading use of digital cash and its problems. In H. Kehal & V. Singh (Eds.), *Digital economy: Impacts, influences and challenges.* Hershey, PA: Idea Publishing Group.

Lewis, S. (1996). *Rethinking our centralized monetary system: The case for a system of local currencies.* New York: Praeger.

(2002, April 7). *The Nihon Keizai Newspaper*, 20.

Reynolds, J. (2004, January 21). U.S. Indian tribes consider printing local currencies. *Knight Ridder Tribune Business News*, 5.

Time Dollar Institute. (2004). *Time dollars: A new kind of money that builds trust and community.* Retrieved February 14, 2004, from http://www.timedollar.org

Toronto Dollar Community Projects, Inc. (2005). *About the Toronto dollar.* Retrieved February 14, 2005, from http://www.torontodollar.com/about/about.php

UK LETS and Complementary Currencies Development Agency. (2005). *Pioneering complimentary currencies.* Retrieved February 14, 2005, from http://www.letslinkuk.net/

Endnotes

[1]   Some economists insist that it is necessary to use stamps to overcome a negative interest rate at a constant date. This problem was broadly analyzed by Goodfriend (2000), Buiter and Panigirtzoglou (2003) and others.

[2]   Some local currencies, such as Toronto Dollars, facilitate exchange.

[3]   In France (SEL), the government may bear part of the cost for establishing a local currency group.

[4]   HOURS are protected against counterfeiting by multicolored printing and serial numbers. The 1995 Quarter HOUR and 1997 Eighth HOUR use thermal ink, invented in Ithaca, which disappears briefly when touched or photocopied. The 1993 2-HOUR note is printed on locally made watermarked 100% cattail paper.

Section IV

Security, Law, and IT

Chapter XVI

Integrity and Security in the E-Century

Carolyn Currie, University of Technology, Australia

Abstract

E-commerce offers an enormous range of solutions to payment and settlements problems. However it also poses a myriad of regulatory issues. Understanding the technical, taxation and institutional issues posed by e-commerce that impact the ability to provide such services aids in comprehending the vast integrity and security issues surrounding this innovation. In this chapter the effect of this technological innovation is examined in the light of theories of regulation that postulate a struggle process between attempts to control innovation and further innovation and regulation. To understand how regulation of e-commerce may be counterproductive, a case study of the evolution of regulation of derivatives is used to test a hypothesis concerning social and avoidance costs. A comparative case study of regulation of e-commerce is then examined to suggest a policy approach of a private sector solution within a public policy matrix similar to private deposit insurance.

Introduction

E-commerce offers an enormous range of solutions to payment and settlements problems. However it also poses a myriad of regulatory issues. Understanding the technical, taxation and institutional issues posed by e-commerce that impact on the ability to provide such services aids in comprehending the vast integrity and security issues surrounding this innovation.

Technical features[1] involve not just whether to use specialised and portable computer hardware but also issues of consumer protection (contractual and legal relationships between consumers, retailers, issuers and operators)[2], and issues of demand by consumers and supply (in terms of issuers and merchants accepting e-money as substitutes for cash)[3]. Value can be stored in different ways, recording methods must be specified and currency choices resolved.

Taxation issues involve not only jurisdictional, administrative, identity and encryption problems, but understanding how electronic commerce could be a means for tax base erosion, tax avoidance and tax evasion, while also providing a better means of tax collection.

Institutional issues involve understanding the application of banking regulations, in terms of protective and prudential measures, concentrating on cross-border or international concerns and the necessary supervisory financial architecture. There are many unresolved policy issues[4], such as who can issue e-money differs across countries, whether seigniorage effects of e-money and effects on monetary policy could lead to central banks only issuing e-money themselves or expend reserve requirements or take other action to encourage covering of risk. As well prudential supervisory issues[5] of the risk of financial loss through fraud (manipulation or interception of electronic messages over computer networks) or accidental loss or issuer becomes insolvent, and operational risk preventing settlement, for example, expired cards, malfunctions, interoperability between products have not been solved through self regulatory measures, adequate information to consumers for risk assessment or deposit insurance.

Three types of criminal offences are made possible by the increasing use of e-processes or products: money laundering and illegal gambling[6], tax evasion[7] and counterfeiting, fraud or disruption[8], as stored value cards provide a less bulky and conspicuous means of transporting or transferring risks, although some measures such as tamper-resistant smart cards, cryptographic protocols on transactions record-keeping systems, expiration dates and value limits may alleviate problems of criminal vulnerability.

Using a systems approach[9] helps define the problem in terms of operational, liquidity, credit, market and cross-border risks. For instance consumers using prepaid cards issued in one country while travelling in another, involves problems of different legal rights in place of issue and payment and regulatory arbitrage. Policy responses by supra-regulators — the CPSS, the Basel convenors and the G-10[10] — are minimal to date. At the moment central banks are relying on existing laws but there is a concerted effort to develop supervisory cooperation to cope with the cross-border issues precipitated by electronic commerce such as settlement risk and security issues. For instance the Eurosystem, as part of its oversight role with regard to e-money schemes, is working towards establishing a harmonised approach in the areas of standard setting and assessment methodology relating to the technical security of the e-money schemes[11] and most EU member countries are in the process of transposing two new Directives into their national banking laws[12]. This involves the role of home country supervisors and the host country to assess readiness, looking as cases of local management.

Apart from issues of consumer protection, criminal and prudential supervision issues, tax issues of jurisdiction, administration, identity and encryption arising from electronic commerce (in particular internet banking and retail payments)[13], of more immediate concern to governments, in terms of loss of revenue, is tax avoidance, although the use of electronic commerce by taxation authorities has had enormous benefits in certain OECD countries such as Australia.

Before proceeding to a comparative case study of derivatives and e-commerce to illustrate the difficulties of regulating innovations, this chapter explores whether such innovations are a response to regulation, and hence will create further regulation which could be a self defeating process. This theoretical examination is made in order to formulate hypotheses so that the examination of case studies can be made within a clearly defined framework.

The Application of Theories of Regulation and Innovation to the Growth of E-Commerce

Various theories exist as to the evolution of innovative products or processes, such as the earliest financial instrument developed in the 13th century — bank deposits and bills of exchange, which were developed to circumvent usury laws which meant that interest was charged in commissions or exchange rates. Bonds were developed in France in the sixteenth century as disguised borrowings by offering a stream of income[14]. Equity evolved from the ventures of merchants — the Muscovy Company was chartered in 1553, the East India Company in 1600. The first permanent joint-stock company was the Dutch East India Company of 1602. In 1845, preference shares came to prominence in the railway mania in the United Kingdom, while in the United States the first issues of commercial paper occurred. Other major changes took place over a century later, with the first certificate of deposit in 1966, the first floating rate note in 1970, the first financial futures contract in 1972 and so on. However it was only in the 1980s that the curve of financial innovation took a steep jump (Walmsley, 1988).

Several theories of innovation allow us to put into perspective the nature, causes, risks and consequences of a very rapid growth in the diversity and the volume traded of financial instruments and the subsequent development of e-commerce. Table 1 summarises three theories that differ more in explanatory style than substance (based on Greenbaum & Higgins, 1985).

Greenbaum and Higgins (1985) note that besides government and public regulation, investor learning and the development of costly and expensive delivery systems are

Table 1. Theories of regulation and innovation

"The Linear Programming Approach" (Silber, 1975). The theory basically says little more than that financial innovation is an adaptive response by the financial system to some external shock that expresses itself in terms of the system's cost of satisfying some constraint. The system is thus maximising some (linear) objective function subject to a set of constraints which can be regulatory in origin, technological or tax based. Each constraint has a shadow price – as it rises financial innovation occurs as resources are devoted to circumventing or overcoming it. The culmination of this effort is a change in the financial system in the form of a new claim, delivery system or organisation form.
"The Hegelian Dialectic" (Kane, 1981). The financial system can be described as private participants versus the regulators with the latter attempting to restrain the financial system through some imposition of a constraint such as a price ceiling, a reserve requirement or an asset prescription. The system adapts in order to circumvent the regulatory initiative. The regulators respond by imposing yet another restriction, thereby prompting yet another adaptive initiative. The process continues ad infinitum resulting in an ever-expanding regulatory system together with an increasingly complex financial system – "the implication is that both represent a squandering of societal resources with a welter of perverse effects," (Greenbaum & Higgins, 1985).
"The Regulatory Explanation" (Greenbaum & Haywood, 1971). This view suggests regulation produces a financial system of ever-increasing complexity and fragility, with the system capable of collapse owing to the sheer weight of the system's elephantine structure. The growth of real income and cyclical increases in interest rates creates a demand for a wider variety of financial claims. After claims are brought into existence owing to high interest rates the firms producing the claims become candidates for regulatory protection. By pushing innovation to the system's periphery and then protecting financial firms, the public regulator may foster secular proliferation of claims growing out of interest rate cyclicality.

sources of irreversible innovation. Similarly Walmsley (1988) sees intensifying competition as a key stimulus since, "a reputation for innovativeness is seen as a key competitive advantage in acquiring market share." The three theories of innovation overlook such factors. The mere existence of technology such as the personal computer and electronic providers of price information and satellites facilitated the globalisation and internationalisation of markets and have also stimulated innovation, although all the above additional factors may merely comprise Silber's constraints.

Another interesting fact of the theories is that they identify regulation as a stimulus to innovations designed to circumvent it. For instance, higher capital requirements for banks drove them out of traditional business areas. Possibly due to the time at which these theories were devised, the originators were unaware of the enormous effect that

Table 2. Types of innovation

(1) **Aggressive** - Introduction of a new process or product in response to a perceived demand, used to gain a market share by displaying an ability to innovate.
(2) **Defensive** - Innovation in response to a changed environment or transaction costs, for example, the reform of the London system 1983-1985 caused by the change in the brokerage rules.
(3) **Risk transfer** - Allow the transfer of the price or credit risks in financial positions such as interest rate and foreign exchange futures and options, currency and interest rate swaps as well as tradeable loans, securitisation and credit enhancement tools. These are among the most important of innovations. Their development was stimulated by the emergence of floating exchange rates in the mid 1970s and the adoption by the Federal Reserve of its new economic policy.
(4) **Liquidity-enhancing** - Improves the negotiability of financial instruments and includes note issuance facilities, securities sold with put options and the creation of secondary markets for trading securities.
(5) **Credit-generating** - Broaden the supply of credit, either by mobilising dormant assets to back borrowings or by tapping previously untouched pockets of credit. An example of the former is securities backed by specific buildings. An example of the latter is the use of swaps to issue securities in markets, which the issuer would not normally wish to tap directly, because it would have no use for the currency or kind of funding provided.
(6) **Equity-generating** - Have been more limited than other types but include, for example, variable-rate preferred stock, which tapped an entire new market of investors and equity contract notes.

deregulation in the USA would have (e.g., abolition of fixed commissions in 1975 followed deregulation of the banking system which in turn was followed by the introduction of Rule 415 in 1982) and also in the UK, where major international banks have been allowed to buy stockbroking firms. Deregulation in New York further triggered a wave of deregulation elsewhere, notably Tokyo, Paris, Frankfurt and Zurich.

Classifying innovation by type can also assist in the analyses of the effects and risks of such growth in trading volumes as witnessed during the 80s and still occurring now. Table 2 (based on Walmsley, 1988) summarises types.

Within each category innovations can be process types (such as a new payments mechanism) or product types. In e-commerce, process innovations refer to access products that allow consumers to use electronic means of communication to access otherwise conventional payment services (for example, use of the internet to make a credit card payment or for general "online banking"). Product innovations in e-commerce are stored value or prepaid products in which a record of the funds or value available to the consumer is stored on a device in the consumer's possession, such as prepaid cards (sometimes called electronic purses) and prepaid software products that use computer networks such as the internet (sometimes called digital cash). Each type of innovation

— whether derivatives or e-commerce — which fits into the above typology will have a different impact on systemic risk levels and on the individual financial institutions.

To understand the impact of innovations Sinkey (1992) proposed a new model which combines elements of the above three theories — "the regulatory dialectic model" which postulates that exclusionary rules imposed on financial institutions, particularly rules producing non contestable markets, promote innovation to circumvent such restrictions. e-commerce fits into this theory. It is both an aggressive response (tapping new markets such as business to business) and a defensive response to requirements to control the payments systems and monitor transactions (such as the reporting of transactions over a certain limit to a regulatory body)[15], which can create both new processes (such as home banking) and new products (such as credit cards) which can be used to achieve the other four functions of innovations — transferring risk, enhancing liquidity, generating credit and equity (via digital prospectuses), and in particular by allowing e-trading in securities as well as in the provision of information on companies, securities, economies as well as on general consumer products and services.

The regulatory dialectic model on which this hypothesis is based is based on the philosopher Hegel's concept of the dialectic change (1770-1831) consists of three stages: (1) thesis, (2) antithesis and (3) synthesis (Sinkey, 1992). In this process, the thesis and antithesis clash and through an ongoing struggle evolve into a synthesis. The synthesis then becomes a new thesis, and the process of change or struggle goes on and on. Cast in a regulatory framework, the regulatory dialectic pits the regulators against the regulatees in an ongoing struggle. The regulators attempt to impose constraints on the financial system (e.g., interest rate, product, or geographic controls). The regulatees, who tend to be driven by profit or wealth-maximisation motives, attempt to circumvent the restrictions because these are implicit taxes on their profits. If the circumvention is successful — which it usually is, because profit-motivated individuals tend to move faster and more efficiently than bureaucrats — then the regulators attempt to close the window or loophole and the struggle becomes an ongoing one.

One positive aspect of the struggle process is that it tends to spur financial innovation by regulated firms and to encourage less-regulated firms to infringe on the more regulated ones. Thus, the regulatory dialectic also can be viewed as a theory of financial innovation, explaining how derivatives developed in response to regulatory rules or how in Australia in the seventies banks bought shares in non-bank financial institutions to circumvent regulations relating to the volume and type of lending. Similarly, in the '80s it is claimed that capital adequacy rules brought in to control the growth of high-risk lending resulted in a distortion in resource allocation, with banks lending more to the residential and less to the business sector.

The process of change in the financial system can be viewed as occurring autonomously or as being induced either by market forces (e.g., technology) or regulatory ones or both. To ignore any of these components presents a less than complete picture of the process of change. To focus on the interaction of technological and regulatory forces in the developing fusion of competition, the concepts of structural arbitrage and economies of scope are useful. These help explain why regulatory change may be ineffective as firms may circumvent regulation, or regulators may not understand how economies in banking are best promoted.

An important component of the reregulation process is again the contestability theory of multimarket competition[16], whereby markets are assessed in terms of barriers to entry. The financial system is characterised by an industry or marketplace that has both legislative and natural barriers to entry and exit. The natural sunk costs of entry and exit are those of technology, "learning by doing", or "know how" referred to above (Baumol, 1982). The legislative barriers are created by governments who perceive the role of the financial sector to be uniquely intertwined with the goals of governments regarding the economy, which is, "to safeguard the integrity and value of the currency — to maintain the stability of the banking and wider financial system and the integrity of payments systems, and to promote the efficiency and competitiveness of our financial markets" (Brady, 1988, p. 49).

Two key legislative barriers to entry and exit are created by governments in order to promote structural efficiency and comprise:

- regulatory bodies to supervise with charters which list specified goals, such as maintaining the stability of the currency and/or controlling inflations to a set range; and

- licences, which are required to carry on a business in the financial system for a range of financial institutions. The licence carries requirements to ensure the application of prudential and prudential measures in order to ensure uniformly prudent conduct of business for banks.

Exit conditions are governed by those licenses and regulatory bodies. Legislative barriers create sunk costs of not only entry but exit, which can also arise from both natural barriers such as the establishment cost of a financial institution in terms of technology, manpower and capital. Consider the position of any banking entrant seeking an orderly withdrawal from the markets. With restrictions on new entrants, ownership, mergers and takeovers, these financial institutions are very unlikely to be able to recover sunk costs by selling out at a profit.

Regulatory interference slows the rate of adaptation by imposing entry restrictions and corresponding avoidance costs on particular firms. In a free society in which multiple legislatures and regulatory agencies compete for regulatees, tax receipts and/or budgeted funds, authorities cannot induce either great or long-lasting divergences between the actual and the cost-minimising market structure. However this divergence may be justified if it produces greater stability. If regulatory goals in controlling the banking sector restrict entry and exit, then it is a non-contestable market where the economic principles of perfect competition cannot be applied, and economies of scale and scope may best be achieved by a smaller number of larger banks, than by the opposite (Baumol, 1982). Within such a market regulation can beget innovation both as a means of competition and as a means of reducing costs.

Hypotheses and Research Methodology

Regulations are, of course, not costless. They involve avoidance costs, which are the incremental costs of creating an unregulated substitute product or institutional arrangement, such as derivatives provided by over the counter markets, or establishing a proprietary system to allow Internet banking. In this schema, innovations are regarded as deriving from a desire to circumvent regulations — that is, they constitute avoidance activities. The other costs of regulation are also joint costs of production involved in providing innovative products in a traditional framework. However, if the benefits of joint production or the economies of scope created by providing innovations together with traditional products[17], exceeds the avoidance costs — that is, the cost of the innovation, then avoidance activities or innovations are encouraged. If regulation encourages innovation to circumvent it, then regulation produces avoidance costs.

Another cost of regulation in respect to innovation, is the social cost of a regulatory exclusion which is the sum of (1) the administrative costs of promulgating and enforcing the restriction and (2) the smaller of the forfeited economies of scope and avoidance costs. The reason for the term "smaller" is that economies of scope will only be forfeited if avoidance costs exceed economies.

Regulatory changes which may be aimed at improving the confidence and convenience functions of financial institutions, may be defeated by innovations, or by structural arbitrage (Kane, 1984), that is moving an organisation across laws and regulatory bodies to lighten its tax and regulatory burdens, or by the degree of contestability of the marketplace, that is by the degree of barriers to entry and exit.

It is thus the purpose of this chapter to test the following hypothesis:

> *H1: That regulation of innovations in financial products and services can result in both avoidance and social costs.*

The research methodology will be two case studies, one involving attempts to control the growth of derivatives and the other e-commerce, using new regulations evolved to control the payments systems in Australia as an example. Historic attempts to regulate derivatives are used as a type of control case study to illustrate what the likely future effects of similar attempts in relation to e-commerce. An additional reason is that use of derivative products in conjunction with e-commerce will provide an immense challenge to the international regulatory system.

Rather than attempting to quantify costs, the case studies will discuss them in a framework or how these innovations can raise systemic risk levels, disturbing or distorting systemic efficiency and in the worst event provoking a systemic crisis. The OECD (1991, 1992) has defined these terms in relation to systems theory, where a system is any set of interrelated parts which recognisably constitute a connected whole. Therefore any financial system is a system with components comprising trading and regulatory arrangements and market participants, and four layers starting with natural securities markets, then international securities markets, international financial markets and finally the world economy of which the latter or third systems layer is a part.

A *systemic crisis* is thus any disturbance that severely impairs the workings of the system and at the extreme causes a complete breakdown in it. *Systemic risks* are those risks that have the potential to cause such a crisis. O'Connor (1989) has narrowed the definition to those financial risks which arise from institutional and structural arrangements in markets which all participants must bear as a group.

The OECD's (1991) real concern with the characteristics, modus operandum and volume of derivatives trading or any financial innovation, is its potential to generate systemic risks sufficient to endanger the stability of the bottom system's layer, the national markets. Such a disturbance or crisis can then be spread to other systems layers by the way innovative products and processes permit rapid transmission of shocks. The effects of such shocks on the real economy can have "real damage potential" if they:

- disrupt the savings and investment processes;

- undermine the confidence of long term investors; and

- disrupt the normal cause of economic transactions due to a breakdown in the banking and payments systems as a consequence of the collapse of the securities markets (OECD, 1991).

The extent of such damage would depend on the size and duration of the breakdown as well as on the readiness and ability of monetary and other appropriate authorities to take corrective action. Overall, the OECD (1991) sees settlement mechanisms as being risky to the system in their ability to transmit members' failure to other members and thence to the financial sector more widely. Risks arise from:

- the potential insolvency of members of these systems;

- incompatibility between different settlement systems, for instance, different time-tables for collecting and paying out cash; and

- cross-border difficulties arising from mixed legal and fiscal environments, the necessity to use a home country's currency and security, time and communication differences, foreign exchange risk, exchange controls and restrictions on information flaws.

Within this scheme of market and payments mechanism lies a vital system characteristic — *systemic efficiency*. This can be defined from a microeconomic production viewpoint, as the ability to provide at high speed a product or process at a price where marginal revenue equal marginal cost, as conditions of perfect completion are assumed to exist. Oligopolistic pricing could distort the process but so could the operation of the market for derivatives on a macro level, so that capital markets do not perform their role of allocation of scarce resources amongst completing ends in an efficient manner, because security prices do not fully reflect all available information (definition of efficiency taken from Fama, 1970).

Whether a *weak form* of efficiency is used as a criteria — the information set impounded in security prices is only historical prices – or a *semi-strong* form — the information set is all publicly available information — or a *strong form* — monopolistic access to information may exist but monopolists perform a function of rapid dissemination of information — it is of concern to all supervisory authorities as to whether derivatives or e-commerce can distort any of these forms of market efficiency.

BIS (1992) using measures of volatility as the standard deviation of monthly stock market returns, and of bond yields to maturity concluded that in the United States, Japan, Germany, France, the United Kingdom and Canada that asset price and exchange rate volatility over the period 1982-1992 has increased — the exact period when deregulation and financial innovation has been at its peak.

The role of derivatives and e-commerce can best be analysed by considering how they may contribute to a systemic crisis which is defined as having four stages. Stage I begins with a sharp, sudden fall in the prices of securities and derivatives, that is, enhanced *market risk*. Stage II is the spreading of price falls from one market to another while Stage III is the effect of the preceding stages on international financial intermediaries, leading to the failure of one or more, which could endanger the system through the effects on the liquidity and solvency of interdependent participants, and hence can be analysed by consideration of effects on *liquidity risk*. Stage IV is the effect Stage III has in generating a crisis in the core banking and payments system, causing a currency run and/or collapse of financial institutions. Effects can be analysed at both an individual and systems level.

Case Studies

Table 3 using the above analysis summarises possible threats posed by e-commerce and derivatives.

The OECD and BIS recommended the adoption of regulatory solutions to the problems of derivatives that they believe will result in minimum avoidance and social costs. These are examined as they can shed light on the evolution of regulations in relation to e-commerce and whether this evolution will fulfil predictions of innovations theorists, in particular Sinkey (1992). In the next section, BIS or OECD solutions are listed next to each problem. However, as will be discussed in the concluding section the problems and solutions may be far more fundamental and of macro coverage, than what are more micro, partial, temporary, solutions discussed below and may lead to an ever-increasing cycle of further innovation and regulation.

Table 3. Threats posed by derivatives and e-commerce

1) *Liquidity risk* is the risk that it is either impossible or expensive to convert derivatives or e-money to cash. This may prevent instruments being traded or quoted, for example, perpetuals during 1987-88, or cause liquidity problems to individuals or institutions relying on an access service dependent on e-commerce, due to technological failure or fraud involving an access innovation in e-commerce. *Payment problems* occur when systems have been put under severe pressure by the dramatic increase in settlement volumes. For instance, in 1985 the CHIPS and Fedwire systems in the U.S.A. processed regularly U.S.$1 trillion in a day. The BIS (2001) survey of e-commerce concludes that its use has little or no effect on monetary policy although many countries are still not including e-money in monetary aggregates. This can contribute to a crisis, as can,

2) *market risk* which arises from instruments such as futures or options that are widely and frequently traded. Market risk is the risk that changes in market interest rates or exchange rates will lead to a capital loss. This may be less of a risk with e-commerce, but can have effects if dramatic changes in exchange rates are not factored into settlement procedures relying on e-commerce.

3) *Credit risk* has to be widespread to constitute a systemic risk contributing to a crisis, but can play a large role if a major financial institution or exchange encounters problems. Securitised products can transmit shocks, as can faulty practices such as the absence of margining or low margining in relation to derivatives. Similarly, issuers of e-money and the providers of access services can fail constituting a similar risk, in terms of counterparty default.

4) *Exchange rate fluctuations* can be precipitated by the widespread use of derivatives, due to volume trading in derivatives to enhance profitability and the taking of large positions by major financial institutions (BIS, 1992). It has yet to be shown whether e-commerce plays any role in stabilising such fluctuations by virtue of ease of convertibility and providing rapid payment mechanism. Risk transfer products and processes which use both derivatives and e-commerce can set up interconnected exposure links which can then transmit risks right throughout the system.

A Problem (Innovation) and Solution (Regulation) Matrix for Derivatives Innovative Market Mechanisms

Problem: Dealer versus auction. Dealer markets, an innovation accompanying derivatives, needed more capital for greater risk concentrations. They also had problems of generating reliable information, processing transactions, providing liquidity and a degree of automation in price quotation and order routing.

Solution: Apart from recommendations for all markets to automate settlement procedures, (claimed advantages are on line information re risk exposures, improved price
quotation and order routing), other suggestions to improve systems capacity have
focussed on measures to limit volumes of trade and volatility and enhance liquidity.

Problem: OTC (over the counter) versus ETC (exchange traded). This is where another
innovative market structure accompanying derivatives where the lack of disclosure in the
former makes insider trading and other forms of market manipulation difficult to detect.

Solution: New trading rules were needed to ensure uniformity between markets and that
price volatility does not slow order placement, routing, matching, execution and information dissemination. Confining *OTC transactions* was not a political option and would
face. opposition on grounds of reduced competition and the fact that foreign exchange
and money market transactions would still occur outside exchanges. OTC transactions
could be better risk monitored by the imposition of trade and price reporting requirements
on off exchange deals.

Problem: Programme trading. Tthe simultaneous purchase (or sale) of 15 or more stocks
with a total value of A$1 million or more. Trading strategies facilitated by programme
trading include index arbitrage, portfolio insurance, asset allocation and index substitution. The effect of *index arbitrage* is to push derivative and cash prices together in the
same direction, except where no firm prices exist for component stocks. Then the two
markets diverge, with derivatives transmitting pressure to cash markets under extreme
stress. Instead of being a means to ensure market stability and liquidity, the OECD (1991)
perceived it as a means for transmitting volatility. Similarly *portfolio insurance* (buying
or selling the derivative to protect against physical price movements) is seen by the
OECD as a trading strategy which can prolong a bull run and precipitate a bear run in both
cash and derivatives.

Solution: In the United States, restraints of index arbitrage and programme trading were
requested by the NYSE and SEC where the Dow Jones Industrial Average advances more
than 50 points. The SEC has been given a legislative mandate to regulate programme
trading. Portfolio insurance has fallen into disuse — banning is not recommended by the
OECD as they feel it will take an alternative form.

Solution: Circuit breakers are the use by regulators of the power to interrupt or restrict
trading to allow emotions to cool, information to be disseminated, and the balance of
supply and demand to be assessed more accurately. They can be related to the volume
of trading price movements and those left to market authorities. One perceived flaw is
that freezing trading in one market causes demand to be met by sales in other markets,
spreading a crisis.

Solution: Margin requirements have two purposes: prudential and reduction of highly
leveraged positions by speculators which might contribute to price volatility. The
problem is that the question of what is the right level cannot be entirely settled by formula,
as predictions bear risk themselves, other risk management safeguards may not exist, and
it is costly to cover every eventuality — there is room for an element of judgement.

Settlement and Payments Issues

Problem: Individual system risks. These comprise *capital risk*, a counterparty failing during the process of exchanging securities for money and *market risk*, or the deal having to be replaced at a different price because one or other counterparty fails before the exchange of securities for money takes place. These risks can remain with the original counterparties to a deal, or be transferred in whole or in part to third parties, who provide the payment and settlement services.

Solution: Most systems attempt to achieve transfer of delivery and payment simultaneously, irrevocably and unconditionally by three methods: *intra day finality, end-of-day finality and deferred finality*. Methods used often achieve only good enough delivery for value and payment (DVP). If DVP cannot be achieved, other methods are used to reduce, redistribute or protect against capital risk, such as monitoring of system membership, shortening settlement periods, netting arrangements, use of a central counterparty, a collateralised system, margin pledging, loss sharing arrangements and external support.

General Supervisory Problems

Problem: Capacity of central banks to regulate. Channon (1988) saw derivatives growth placing central banks in the position where lack of knowledge and lack of risk measurement techniques meant they were unable to control exposure position of banks, and had no ability to control the rest of the market place as it lay outside their arena. According to Channon, "Few central banks had supervisory departments able to understand, much less monitor these products and their effects on banks risk profiles" (p. 367).

Solution: Part of this quandary has been solved by new capital adequacy rules based on counterparty risk and will be assisted further by the extension of such rules to cover market and interest rate risk (BIS, 1992). In order to reduce the scope for regulatory arbitrage between banks and non-banks the Basle Committee on Banking, Supervision and the Technical Committee of the International Organisation of Securities Commission are working towards consistent rules to be applied to institutions on a consolidated basis and consistently between nations.

Problem: The effect of derivatives on monetary policy. Channon (1988) saw the interaction between derivatives and governmental attempts to apply monetary policy steadily towards price stability as adverse in the following respects:

1. the effect new instruments have on increasing the demand for money through their effect on monetary velocity; and

2. the effect new instruments have on blurring the distinction between traditional monetary instruments and non-monetary ones, between broad and narrow aggregates so that definitions of M_2 and M_3 have become less meaningful (Walmsley, 1988).

Solution: Due to this phenomenon, a growing number of increasingly complex systems of economic aggregates have replaced traditional measures as a basis for national financial polity, but only as guidelines, as traditional relationships no longer hold (Channon, 1988).

Problem: The growth of derivatives. This has resulted in a higher proportion of money that earns interest, which reduces the sensitivity of demand for money to changes in rates. Changes in rate levels are not reflected in interest rate differentials and an impact on monetary aggregates (Walmsley, 1988). Securitised credit and the increased alternatives open to borrowers means that policy options become fewer and fewer. Direct controls over lenders have been jettisoned in favour of internationally accepted supervisory practices, in order to avoid dramatic effects on exchange and interest rates and capital flows.

Solution: Since derivatives affect monetary policy, which if used incorrectly is one of the causes of crisis, a solution is needed which does not involve heavy handed vetting of new products, but relies on a coordinated use of indirect checks such as capital adequacy applying across all market players.

Problem: Opaqueness of derivatives markets or disclosure problems. BIS (1992) sees derivatives as leading to greater opaqueness of instruments, and relationships between instruments and markets, with regard to risks, exposure of counterparties and of market concentration.

Solution: Internationally harmonised accounting disclosure in this area.

From the above analysis two observations can be made:

- the threats posed by derivatives and e-commerce are similar in nature, except that the former's role has been evident in several systemic crises, (October, 1987, 1989, 1998) while the latter has yet to emerge; and

- the growth of derivatives has produced attempts to control derivatives which can be counterproductive — for instance capital adequacy rules produced further innovations — such as hedge funds resulting in a situation such as the Long Term Credit Bank disaster, and did not take account of other risks such as market and operational risk.

That is, regulation produced not only social costs in terms of the regulatory costs, but due to the fact that avoidance costs of hedge funds were less than the benefits conferred in the short tem, severe systemic problems resulted.

The next case study will seek to whether the hypothesis holds in relation to the regulation of e-commerce, concentrating first on tracing the development of product and process innovations in Australia and its policy responses, comparing its regulatory initiatives to those in other OECD countries.

E-Commerce and Regulations

In Australia developments have focussed around developments of card-based products, network/software-based products and electronic bill presentment, payment instruments and clearing and settlement systems[18]. Developments in these three areas and a policy response directed at these innovations are summarised below. The overview concentrates on the time period when the initial innovation was developed and the subsequent immediate policy response.

Card-Based Products

As of November 2001, usage of card-based e-money had yet to go beyond limited trials in Australia. Nevertheless, Australia is developing a smartcard industry, especially in electronic ticketing, which is internationally focused[19].

By 2001, projects were in process to supply communities using state governments as issuers with smart cards that provide a range of electronic services such as transport ticketing[20], library, parking, identification and electronic purse, with multiple-application smart cards due to be issued by early 2002, including e-cards issued to tertiary students for identification, access to restricted areas and electronic purse facilities for canteens, payphones, bookshops and library photocopying[21] or for use at retail outlets[22].

Two major banks, Westpac and ANZ Bank, have announced that they intend to upgrade their EFTPOS/retail terminals to support smartcard technology, while Telstra, Australia's largest telecommunications company started issuing disposable smart phone cards in August 1997 on the Chipper card system. The company has also conducted several trials of multifunction reloadable cards. Trials of Transcard, a multi-application contactless smart card, are still limited to certain city areas only. The technology is owned by a non-bank financial institution, with cards available from certain newsagents or the St. George Bank. The cards are reloadable up to A\$500 and also have a loyalty programme.

The Australian Mondex franchise, owed by the four major Australian banks, has not initiated any new developments in the last 12 months. Three of the banks are conducting in-house trials, of which two have been expanded to incorporate about 30 external merchants. However, the cards are still only issued to staff of the banks.

Policy Responses

Prudential supervision. In June 2000, changes were made under the Banking Act 1959 to bring all holders of stored value (i.e., entities backing stored value) in relation to purchased payment facilities, such as smartcards and electronic cash, under the regulation of either the Reserve Bank of Australia (RBA) or the Australian Prudential Regulation Authority (APRA). The change brings holders of stored value under APRA's supervision where the holder of stored value is deemed to be carrying out banking business. This is considered to be the case where the facility is available for purchase and use on a wide basis, and where all or part of the facility's unused value is repayable on demand in Australian currency. Stored value schemes outside this scope remain the regulatory responsibility of the RBA under the Payment Systems (Regulation) Act 1998. Most other policy issues arising from the development of e-money are being dealt with by existing regulation.

Issues of competition are monitored by the Australian Competition and Consumer Commission (ACCC). Consumer protection is handled under the consumer protection legislation overseen by the Australian Securities and Investments Commission (ASIC). ASIC released a revised Electronic Funds Transfer (EFT) Code of Conduct (a voluntary code) in April 2001. The code now includes rules for consumer stored value facilities and stored value transactions. The provisions of the revised EFT Code will generally bind institutions that subscribe to it from April 1, 2002.

Issues relating to law enforcement, and money laundering in particular, are being addressed by the existing agencies, including the Australian Transaction Reports and Analysis Centre (AUSTRAC). Other policy responses include changes to the criminal code ("Measures to Combat Serious and Organised Crime Act 2001") by including e-commerce in the ambit of coverage and the formation of AGEC (Action Group into the Law Enforcement Implications of Electronic Commerce)[23].

Network/Software-Based Products

Technocash, a stored value payment mechanism that allows a consumer to make purchases over the Internet or over an Australia Post outlet began operations on September 1, 2000. Customers purchase an amount (varying between A$20 and A$1,000) of Technocash along with a unique, 16-digit alphanumeric code. The code, along with the expiry details, are then required to access the Technocash for an online purchase. A password can also be applied to the Technocash as an additional security feature. Technocash is non-refundable, but is transferable to other persons and can be combined and split; it has a valid lifespan of three years. Currently, there are 28 merchants that accept Technocash.

E-cash, St. George Bank's digital cash product, continues to be used on a small scale. It is now possible for customers of other banks to purchase e-cash via the BPAY scheme. BPAY is a bank-owned, third-party bill payment service. It allows customers of participating financial institutions to arrange for the transfer of funds from their bank account using phone or Internet banking services.

Policy response: Oversight issues. Most central banks[24], including Australia, performing an oversight function of the payment system also monitor and analyse developments with regard to e-money. This includes collection of data and periodic meetings with the issuers. In other instances a wider range of activities are undertaken to study the organisational, legal, administrative, technical and security features of the product and the operator. Australia appears to rely on encryption, tamper-resistant chips and limits to stored value and does not adopt a practice of assessing whether a robust security system is in place to prevent counterfeiting and fraud.

Electronic bill presentment and payment instruments, electronic clearing and settlement systems

EBPP (electronic bill presentment and payment) is the latest innovation in Australia and might become the most influential development in the retail payment market[25]. EBPP integrates electronically the presentment and payment of bills. Therefore, EBPP is not a new payment instrument, rather a new concept that integrates different payment instruments and facilitates billing and paying. By far the most important feature of EBPP is that, depending on the model chosen, it has the ability to connect authorisation, clearing and settlement processes electronically[26]. However, the potential of EBPP does not only lie in the payment process itself but in the integration of billing and payment and connection to other information systems such as business-related software packages (eg delivery and accounting packages).

In principle, EBPP systems allow any electronic payment application to be included in the EBPP application. They are especially convenient as a replacement for paper-based giro payments or cheque payments by electronic credit transfers. Instead of using an existing data media exchange facility, recurring credit transfers can also be initiated via EBPP. On the debit payment instrument side, EBPP can also be used for direct debit transactions. Furthermore, other instruments, such as electronic money as well as credit card applications, may be included in the EBPP application. A further potential instrument of an EBPP system might be a real-time online credit transfer instrument, so to speak a substitute for a debit card on the Internet.

The consolidator is the operator of the EBPP network. Its main function consists of the processing of transaction data during the transaction process. However, an EBPP system may take over more functions than just information processing, for example an extended account management tool for private and business applications or extended interoperability between the different systems. Additionally, the EBPP system may offer clearing and settlement services. Some or all participants are connected to the EBPP network via the consolidator.

Users fall into two categories, billers (or payees) and payers (or customers), with substantial overlap. Billers include all kinds of commercial companies and public entities, while payers include consumers as well as commercial companies and public entities. Banks participate primarily as account providers, but also as users.

Based on the existing EBPP systems, two generic models can be defined: the direct or non-consolidation model and the consolidation model. The latter can be categorised in two ways, firstly according to how the customer accesses the bill, and secondly according to the clearing and settlement functions of the consolidator.

In the direct model, a biller provides its customers with its own electronic billing and payment application, offering them a single access site for viewing billing information and effecting bill payments electronically. Depending on the payment instrument used, the bill payment information is forwarded via the biller or directly to the biller's or payer's financial institution. The consolidation models are further differentiated by whether or not a direct link between biller and customer exists. In a customer consolidation model the electronic bill is delivered directly to the customer. The biller maintains control of bill details until delivery to the customer. Then customers are able to control and store the bills and to integrate this work into their off-line programs and processes. Customers initiate the payment through their consolidator.

In contrast, the service provider consolidation models establish no direct link between biller and customer. The consolidator collects bills from several billers and provides them to the payers[27]. The customer has a single access site for viewing billing information and effecting bill payments electronically, whereas the biller forwards its billing information to one or more service providers that accumulate electronic bills from a variety of billers. Two variations of the service provider consolidation model exist: the thick consolidation model and the thin consolidation model. In the authorisation by a special agency on the basis of security measures such as limits. Therefore, authorisation is reduced to checking whether or not the customer has enough funds available. The EBPP system takes care of the other steps described above (authenticity, etc). However, if insufficient funds are available, the bank rejects the payment and the customer will receive a notification.

A real-time, online credit transfer instrument might also be created for EBPP systems. Authorisation for these online transactions should be given immediately. Therefore, financial institutions must be able to confirm or reject the initiation of the payment in real time. This is equivalent to the authorisation or refusal of the payment, and procedures similar to the existing ones could be used for these transfers. Authorisation by the consolidator on the basis of daily and monthly limits and regular fund checks could be a way to circumvent time-consuming, online authorisation processes. However, the rapid development of communications technology may make this approach unnecessary.

Clearing and settlement may be executed by conventional means as well as by new arrangements known as the Bank Internet Payment System ("BIPS")[28]. This utilises either of the two consolidation models. In the service provider consolidation model, all payment processes can be connected electronically. Through customer initiation the consolidator may be permitted to hand in payment instructions directly to the ACH (Australian Clearing House), which in turn forwards payment instructions to the payment system and related information to the financial institutions. The customer consolidation model also allows for electronic straight-through processing. The consolidator executes payments in cooperation with the customers' financial institutions or an ACH. However, the details of the clearing and settlement arrangements may widely vary depending on the model. The mentioned traditional payment instruments are used as well.

Furthermore, EBPP may also allow for new ways of clearing. In a centralised open consolidation model around the world work is being undertaken on EBPP systems[29]. Cost reduction endeavours have spurred the innovation of EBPP. By 2004, a company specifically dedicated only to providing EBPP services to companies had been floated on the Australian Stock Exchange - Bill Express. The design of an EBPP system is by its very nature open to innovations. Therefore, new models may evolve over time. Although EBPP does not offer a new payment instrument its success may heavily influence the retail payment market. All in all, EBPP systems have the potential to crucially increase the efficiency of the retail payment system and its related business processes.

Policy Responses

Australian policy initiatives have concentrated on e-commerce products not the processes. For instance in the area of *monetary policy and seigniorage,* Australia together with a number of central banks including those of Austria, Belgium, Finland, Germany,

Hong Kong, Italy, Lithuania, the Netherlands, Singapore, Spain, Sweden and the United Kingdom are collecting data on the e-money issued by banks. So far no central bank has indicated an adverse impact on the size of its balance sheet due to a possible decline in the value of the banknotes in circulation as a consequence of widespread adoption of e-money. The European Central Bank (ECB) is of the view that the central banks can maintain the size of their balance sheet if necessary by imposing minimum reserves on e-money issuers or by issuing e-money themselves. Given the low average value of e-money transactions and the relatively small cap on the amounts that can be stored on stored value cards, the value of e-money float is still very low. Losses on account of decline in seigniorage revenues are also perceived to be negligible by the central banks and have so far evoked no specific policy responses from them.

General legal issues. Within the Eurosystem, a comprehensive and harmonised regulatory framework for the issuance of e-money by traditional credit institutions and a new class of credit institutions called electronic money institutions (ELMIs) is provided by two EU directives: the European Parliament and Council Directive 2000/46/EC on the taking up, pursuit of and prudential supervision of the business of electronic money institutions and the European Parliament and Council Directive 2000/28/EC amending Directive 2000/12/EC relating to the taking-up and pursuit of the business of credit institutions. Most EU national central banks accordingly envisage making suitable changes to existing legislation or new statutes in line with the two EU Directives. Elsewhere, for example in France, Hong Kong, Korea and Malaysia, it is felt that the existing legal framework is adequate to deal with issues related to e-money. In some countries specific legislation is being contemplated for regulating the issuance of e-money[30].

By comparison Australia is following an approach of using existing legislation and self-regulation, despite the fact that electronic payments and clearing has the most potential for tax evasion, money laundering and counterfeiting.

Law enforcement issues. Many of the security features of e-money schemes, including the limits on value that can be stored on the cards, make them less attractive for the purposes of money laundering and other criminal abuses. Laws combating money laundering are applicable to e-money schemes, as they are to credit institutions, which in many countries are the sole issuers of e-money. As part of the oversight function emphasis is laid on studying the features of the e-money schemes to ensure that they do not broaden the scope for possible criminal abuse. For instance, the Bundesbank cooperates with the Federal Office for Security in Information Technology to draw on the latter's expertise to assess the potential risk of counterfeiting in e-money. Some measures insisted upon by central banks which have been empowered under new banking legislation[31] are the maintenance of an audit trail, ascertaining the identity of the customer and restricting the issue of cards to account holders at the relevant credit institutions. In some countries, the supervisory role is executed by other bodies[32]. In still other countries such as Korea, Mexico and Switzerland, specific regulations on the issuance of e-money have not been issued.

However, as mentioned, abuse of electronic processes of bill presentation, payment and clearing is still wide open to abuse, as most supervision relates to e-money only, and no account has been taken of cross-border issues in Australia despite current initiatives in Europe[33].

Other issues. Some central banks are urging the market participants in their respective countries to adopt common standards on a nation wide basis to achieve the goal of standardisation and building up a common technical infrastructure such as card readers and terminals, in order to increase availability and reduce operational costs. Consumer protection issues are being addressed by some central banks (e.g., in Spain). In other countries the issue is addressed by an appropriate institutional authority different from the central bank. The emphasis in both cases remains the protection of consumer interest.

From this overview it is obvious that e-commerce in Australia is an extremely new innovation that appears as yet not to have produced enough burdensome regulation with onerous social costs sufficient to beget further innovations to overcome controls. However as a new product and process, another conclusion could be that avoidance costs are still too high to overwhelm the social costs or that both costs are preventing development and use of the product, which in Australia has been minimal. To date, e-commerce, except in the floating of companies purporting to offer huge profits through e-commerce products, does not appear to have engendered systemic crises, raised risk levels or led to deterioration in systemic efficiency.

Conclusions

Greenbaum and Higgins (1985) saw regulation as a contributor to the innovation process and hence further regulation. According to their theory, this eventually produces a financial and regulatory system of ever increasing complexity and fragility, which could culminate in collapse due to the sheer weight of the system's elephantine structure. Unfortunately, this collapse and crisis prompts basic reform, sewing further seeds for the innovation versus regulation cycle. Innovations made in response to volatility leads to a contraction of players unless volatility continues. Other theorists perceive innovations such as e-commerce and derivatives as means of promoting greater systemic efficiency and stability.

To resolve such conflicting viewpoints as to what causes crises — regulation or innovation — we examined a case study of the impact of derivatives and the growth of regulation to control such financial products, and then explored the evolution of regulation of e-commerce in Australia. An attempt has been made to assess the overall costs in view of theories of innovation and regulation that view regulation as self-defeating.

The OECD sees one aspect being of overriding importance in any solution to the debate as to the desirability of controlling innovation, which although it applied to derivatives is just as relevant in relation to e-commerce:

> *The co-ordination of regulation among the markets that trade these tightly linked instruments is important, to assess properly and contain the risks associated with various trading strategies. The absence of co-ordination among markets that are separately regulated, but effectively unified through*

market activity, can increase confusion in abnormal conditions. Co-
ordinated regulation may reduce the probability of major market
disruption.(OECD, 1991, p. 23)

Furthermore, diversity of national regulatory coverage can contribute substantially to systemic risk and crises, given one of four conditions, where:

- "inadequate standards in some countries led to a competition in laxity to attract business;

- significant risk taking activities by major intermediaries were left unsupervised; or

- diffusion of responsibility for the supervision of conglomerates either among functional supervisors and/or among different national supervisors failed to deliver sufficiently comprehensive oversight of the risk exposure of such conglomerates;

- differences in the status, coverage and objectives of the national supervisory authorities impeded international co-operation among them." (OECD, 1991, p. 38)

In view of the undeniable adverse role derivatives can play in systemic instability and crises, and the potential for e-commerce to destabilise the system, the best, most immediate solution may be internal risk management At the moment a solution of system checks on internal management is being put on trial by both public and private bodies. For instance, in Germany the central bank has developed a questionnaire that is used as a checklist to analyse the security of e-money products. A similar approach is followed in Singapore, where the monetary authority assesses whether the issuing bank has put in place a robust security system to prevent counterfeiting and fraud. In France, the central bank uses a tool called a "protection profile" to assess the security profile of the scheme. In other countries, such as Austria, the assessment of security features is entrusted to a relevant technical organisation, while in Mexico a special task force has been constituted. In Hong Kong, the central bank intends to engage outside experts to assess the security features as necessary.

Good internal risk management may best be encouraged by requiring that all issuers of e-money and providers of access services insure with an institution that is specifically established to underwrite the security and adequacy of controls. An insurance premium would be paid to this institution(s), which would come under the prudential supervision of a central regulator. Any issuer or provider not insuring would be required to carry a far higher level of capital adequacy. Disclosure of the lack of insurance would be made public to consumers. Such a private public sector partnership approach to regulation could encourage rather than inhibit the growth of innovations so that they are aggressive rather than defensive responses.

References

Bank of International Settlements (BIS). (1992, June 15). *62nd annual report, 1st April 1991-31st March 1992.* Basel: BIS.

BIS. (2001, November). *CPSS survey of electronic money developments.* Committee for Payments and Settlements Systems. Basel: BIS.

Baumol, W. J. (1982, March). Contestable markets: An uprising in the theory of industry structure. *American Economic Review,*

Baumol, W. J., Panzar, J. C., & Willig, R. D. (1982). *Contestable markets and the theory of industry structure.* San Diego: Harcourt Brace Jovanovich.

Baumol, W. J., Panzar, J. C., & Willig, R. D. (1983, June). On the theory of perfectly contestable markets. Bell Laboratories, economic discussion paper, 268.

Brady Report. (1988, January). *Report of the presidential task force on market mechanisms.* Washington, D.C.

Channon, D. F. (1988). *Global banking strategy.* New York: Wiley.

Davis, E. P. (1989, October). *Instability in the Euromarkets and the economic theory of financial crisis.* Bank of England discussion paper, 43.

Fama, E. F. (1970). Efficient capital markets: A review of theory and empirical work. *Journal of Finance, 25,* 1383-1417.

Greenbaum, S. I., & Haywood, C. F. (1971, May). Secular change in the financial services industry. *Journal of Money, Credit and Banking,* 571-89.

Greenbaum, S. I., & Higgins, B. (1985). Financial innovation. In T. M. Havrilesky, R. L. Schweitzer & J. T. Boorman (Eds.), *Dynamics of banking.* IL: Harlan Davidson.

Hogan, W. P., & Pearce, I. F. (1984). *The incredible eurodollar - Or why the world's money system is collapsing.* London: George Allen & Unwin.

Kane, E. J. (1981). Accelerating inflation, technological innovation and the decreasing effectiveness of banking regulation. *Journal of Finance, 36,* 355-67.

Kane, E. J. (1984). *Technological and regulatory forces in the developing fusion of financial services competition.* Ohio State University, Columbus, WPS, 84-85.

OECD. (1992). *Banks under stress.* Paris: OECD.

O'Connor, S. (1989, October). *Systemic risk in securities markets: A concept in search of a definition.* Bank of Canada, unpublished paper written for Ad Hoc Group.

Organisation for Economic Cooperation and Development (OECD). (1991). *Systemic risks in securities markets.* Paris: OECD.

Rose, M. (1988). *The crash: The fundamental flaws which caused the 1987-8 world stock market slump - and what they mean for future financial stability.* London: Bloomsbury.

Silber, W. L. (1975). *Towards a theory of financial innovation.* In W. L. Silber (Ed.), *Financial innovation.* Lemington, MA: D. C. Heath.

Walmsley, J. (1988). *The new financial instruments*: *An investor's guide.* New York: Wiley.

Endnotes

[1]   The Bank for International Settlements (BIS). (1996). Implications for Central Banks of the Development of Electronic Money, Basle, October, Web site: http://www.bis.org/publ.

[2]   The Bank for International Settlements and International Monetary Fund (1997), Electronic Money: consumer protection, law enforcement, supervisory and cross-border issues, Part II and III, Group of Ten, Report of the Working Party on Electronic Money, Basle, April: Web site: http://www.bis.org/publ.

[3]   Gibbons, P. (2002), Smartcards may be too clever by half, *Business Review Weekly*, January 17-23.

[4]   The Bank for International Settlements (1996), Settlement Risk in Foreign Exchange Transactions, Report prepared by the Committee on Payment and Settlement Systems of the central banks of the Group of Ten countries, Basle, March, Web site: http://www.bis.org/publ.

[5]   The Bank for International Settlements (1996), Security of Electronic Money, Report prepared by the Committee on Payment and Settlement Systems and the Group of Computer Experts of the central banks of the Group of Ten countries, Basle, March, Web site: http://www.bis.org/publ.

[6]   Bank for International Settlements(1988), Prevention of Criminal Use of the Banking System for the Purpose of Money-Laundering, Basle Committee on Banking Supervision, Basle, December, Web site: http://www.bis.org/publ. and see the Financial Action Task Force Web site on money laundering: www1.oecd.org/fatf/.

[7]   Two comprehensive documents which summarise the issues from both a national and international perspective are Australian Tax Office (ATO) (1997),"Tax and the Internet, Discussion Report of the ATO Electronic Commerce Project," (August),and ATO (1999),"Second Report," (December) — both available at www.ato.gov.au — ATO Assist.

[8]   Refer to endnote 5.

[9]   The Bank for International Settlements (2001), Survey of electronic money developments, Prepared by the Committee on Payment and Settlement Systems of the central banks of the Group of Ten countries, Basel, November.

[10]   The Bank for International Settlements (2000), Clearing And Settlement Arrangements For Retail Payments In Selected Countries, Committee On Payment And Settlement Systems Basel, September.

[11]   In order to ensure that e-money schemes are safe and efficient and that issuers are sound, the Eurosystem has defined seven minimum requirements for e-money

scheme. These are outlined in the document, "Report on electronic money," ECB, August 1998, pp. 23-27.

[12]   Both directives were implemented by member states on April 27, 2002.

[13]   Refer to endnote 7.

[14]   The first true government bond may have been the Grand Parti of France I in 1555 and was open to all lenders, not just bankers.

[15]   In Australia, this body is called Austrac, the purpose of which is linked to monitoring all types of cash transactions with the purpose of reporting criminal or tax evasion activities to the relevant authorities.

[16]   See Baumol, Panzar and Willig (1983) and Kane (1984).

[17]   Such as Internet banking, provided together with face-to-face teller withdrawals and transfers.

[18]   The Bank for International Settlements (2001), CPSS Survey of electronic money developments, Committee for Payments and Settlements Systems, Basel, November.

[19]   A study by the National Office for the Information Economy and Asia-Pacific Smartcard Forum found that, in 1999, Australia's smart card industry generated AUD $450 million, of which AUD $390 million was in exports (BIS).

[20]   For instance, ACTSMART in the Australian Capital Territory, a joint venture between two public companies, and OneLink Transit systems in Melbourne.

[21]   This is a result of an alliance between a smart card developer, a bank and a telecommunications company. Another project involves a sports group, a bank and Visa International.

[22]   An alliance between a smart card developer and a hospital insurance group.

[23]   AGEC, 2001, Mutual Assistance and Electronic Crime, Issues paper, July, 2001.

[24]   Central banks in Belgium, Finland, France, Germany, Italy, Lithuania, the Netherlands, Singapore, Spain, Sweden and Thailand include e-money schemes in the exercise of their oversight functions.

[25]   The Bank for International Settlements, 2000, Clearing And Settlement Arrangements For Retail Payments In Selected Countries, Committee On Payment And Settlement Systems Basel, September.

[26]   It is also possible to have a separated application for payment and electronic bill presentment, the simplest for the latter being standard electronic mail. If no linkages exist between these applications, the customer has to transfer the information needed to the payment application.

[27]   One provider in the United States takes paper bills (sent to the provider rather than the customer by agreement) and turns them into an electronic format. Customers pay over the Internet and the provider writes a cheque to the biller.

[28]   O'Mahony, D., Peirce, M. and Tewari, H. 2001, Electronic Payment Systems for E-commerce, Artech House, p. 148.

29   In Australia, there is currently one major EBPP scheme operating. E-Bill, partly owned by Hermes Prisidia (a large paper bill issuer in Australia) launched a service provider consolidator project in April 2000. Australia Post (a large agent for bill payment) and BPAY (a bank-owned bill payment system) are currently working on extending their services to EBPP.

30   For example, in Korea, Thailand and Venezuela.

31   In EU countries, the U.S.A., Hong Kong, Thailand, India, Lithuania, Nigeria and Singapore guidelines have been framed or vested in the central bank through legislation for the issue of e-money by banks.

32   Australia (Australian Prudential Regulation Authority), Austria (the Federal Minister of Finance), Finland (Financial Supervision Authority), Sweden (Swedish Financial Supervisory Authority, Finansinspektionen) and the United Kingdom (Financial Services Authority).

33   These are called "PACE" and "Ducato".

Chapter XVII

Legal Concerns Against Auctions and Securities Conventions:
A Japanese Perspective

Takashi Kubota, Waseda University, Japan

Abstract

This chapter introduces the two newly emerging issues in the C2C and B2B area in the Japanese IT laws: (a) anti-fraud measures in Internet auctions and (b) treatment of the Hague Securities Convention. An auction provider's liability for a tenant's fraud beyond the freedom of contracts is not clear. If consumers bear risk, adequate disclosure should be promoted. In addition, as this issue is complex, several measures including advertisement regulations against the small business consumers and development of escrow payment techniques, should be promoted. Regarding the Hague Securities Convention, the United States pushes other countries to ratify it but the EU questions to ratify it. This chapter considers that the ratification of the Hague Convention for unifying the conflict of laws and the UNIDROIT Convention for unifying the substantive laws should be done at the same time, in order to avoid some side effects.

Introduction to the Issues

Some laws do not change so often[1], but information technology (IT) laws change very often with the IT development. In the Japanese IT business markets, the business-to-business (B2B) market developed first, the business-to-consumer (B2C) market boomed second, and the consumer-to-consumer (C2C) market has started growing third within several years. Corresponding to this move, Japan has taken necessary legal measures (guidelines, laws, etc.) both in global[2] and domestic[3] contexts. Let me introduce two of new issues in the Japanese law debates.

Newly Emerged Issue in the C2C Market

In the B2C market, such as cyber-shopping malls, some laws for consumer protection have been already implemented and global policy harmonization has been discussed for several years.

However, legal discussion about the C2C markets, such as online auction, has just started in some countries including Japan because the market has just started growing rapidly. In this market, there are many varieties of consumers. Some consumers are small businesses that sell products and earn much profit regularly, but others are still normal consumers who buy products without caring much about risks. Therefore existing B2C legal framework, dichotomy of consumer and business, does not fit properly to the various consumers in the C2C market[4]. As a result, more fraud cases can be observed in the C2C auctions where the auction providers do not control of the exhibitors (fraudulent consumers and consumers like small businesses) than in the B2C cybermalls where the mall providers control their tenant shops (fraudulent businesses), although the control is not enough compared with the B2C supermarkets or department stores in the real space.

In addition, the responsibility of intermediary, not only the cybermalls in the B2C market but also the auction providers in the C2C market, is not clear against the victim consumers in the fraud cases. Suppose that you buy a camera at a new shop "A" in a famous supermarket "B" in the real space. When you find some defects, you can ask B and B will compensate you instead of A, or B will help you to contact A[5]. It is because B's famous brand is identified with B's credibility and service quality. However, in cyber space, things go differently. Suppose that you buy a camera at a new shop "C" in a famous auction site "D". When you find some defects, according to the contracts, you cannot ask D and D will *not* compensate you or D will *not* help you to contact C[6]. Should we ask cyber D to take the same responsibility as real B, or should we ask you, the consumers, to recognize that the real B and the cyber D are different? If we choose the latter, consumers need to be protected by receiving adequate risk information for starting business with the shop C.

Newly Emerged Issue in the B2B Market

On the other hand in the B2B market, global law harmonization has been sought in cross-border securities transactions[7]. As in other advanced countries, many securities transactions are shifted from paper-based to electronic-based with the IT development. When they become global, the differences of applicable domestic laws, that is, Japanese law or the U.S. law, may harm the effective and smooth transactions.

Thus two conventions are currently under discussion. First, the Hague Convention on Law Applicable to Certain Rights in Respect of Securities held with an Intermediary[8] (hereinafter "the Hague Convention") for unifying the conflict of laws rules (rules deciding governing laws) is in the final stage of ratification. Second, the Preliminary Draft Convention on Harmonized Substantive Rules Regarding Securities Held with an Intermediary[9] (hereinafter "the UNIDROIT Convention") for making domestic substantive rules (rules deciding concrete rights and duties) similar[10] is in the first stage of global formal discussion.

Most discussants will agree with the purpose of these treaties, to promote global law harmonization in cross-border securities transactions, but the European Union (EU) currently hesitates to ratify the Hague Convention[11] though the United States pushes other countries to ratify it soon. It is because the Hague Convention takes the United States law approach (agreement by the parties decides the governing law) that it may contradict the existing continental law approach (originally the place of securities decides the governing law, and currently the devised version of this principle: PRIMA) taken by the EU domestic laws. However, many discussants are confused with the interpretation and understanding of this convention articles and only some have discussed the concrete side effects in detail in the EU[12]. By contrast, though Japanese law falls in the same continental law tradition as the EU, many Japanese discussants do not concern the ratification[13, 14] and almost no one in Japan considers the side effects against Japanese securities transactions. I do insist that the effective date of the Hague Convention and that of the UNIDROIT Convention should be the same. If different, the rules of conflict of laws and substantive laws of each country change at different times for a very short period of time, legal stability collapses and the cost for corresponding systems developments and judicial-affairs will increase a lot.

This chapter introduces the Japanese discussions of the above issues in the C2C and B2B markets. To this end, this chapter considers two issues in the Japanese law context: (1) the C2C anti-fraud issues in Internet auction and (2) the B2B side effects concerned by smooth ratification of the Hague Convention.

C2C: Anti-Fraud in
C2C Internet Auctions

With the rapid growth of the e-commerce, fraudulent schemes appearing on Internet auction[15] sites, a frequently reported form of Internet fraud, are increasing not only in the United States[16] but also in Japan. As in the United States, these schemes typically purport to offer high-value items that are likely to attract many consumers. They induce their victims to send money for the promised items, but then deliver nothing or counterfeit or altered goods.

This section introduces the current initiative taken by the Japanese Ministry of Economy, Trade and Industry (METI)[17] to tackle with this fraud occurred in consumer to consumer (C2C) auctions, wherein the business hosting the auction provides a venue for transactions but is not a participant in such transactions.

To this end, this section consists of three parts. First, the statistics will show what is going on in Japan. Second, the legal relationships between auction business and users in Japan will be shown. Third, some current initiatives will be introduced.

1.   **Facts about Internet auctions in Japan**

Internet auction users are increasing. According to the METI survey on November 2004[18], 30% of Internet users have put something up at Internet auction cite, and they exhibit items averagely 19.9 times per month. Also 55% of Internet users have made a successful bid, and they do so averagely 23.5 times a month.

The biggest Internet auction site in Japan, "Yahoo! Auction", deals with more than 500 billion yen per year, which is deemed to be more than half of the total market, and traded items average per month is 6.65 million. The amounts are still increasing month by month.

With the wider the use of Internet auctions, the number of consumer disputes is also increasing. The online aternative dispute resolution (ADR) project conducted by the Next Generation Electronic Commerce Promotion Council of Japan (ECOM)[19] have committed with about 3000 disputes from November 2001 to January 2005. About 28% of the total disputes are concerned with Internet auction, and 42% are with e-mail order business, 30% are with online services, and 13% are with cross-border transactions[20]. Among the troubles of Internet auctions, as many as 77% are concerned with fraudulent sellers, while only 15% of e-mail order business troubles are caused by fraudulent sellers[21].

This is because the requirements for starting e-mail order business shops in Internet shopping mall providers are more rigid than those required for Internet auction exhibitors. In addition, law enforcement in e-mail order business is relatively easier than that in Internet auction participants. The former is a registered merchant, but the latter is ordinary person who may not even know what information should be disclosed by the law.

The typical case is as follows. Consumer A purchased a bracelet for 300 thousand yen through an Internet auction cite and paid the money before she received it. However, there was no reaction. Then she called the designated telephone number but found that the number was wrong and could not contact the seller. In such cases, consumers want to consult with the auction site providers. According to the METI survey[22] in November 2004, more than 45% of them like to consult with the site providers, about 20% with consumer affairs centers, and less than 20% with the ECOM online ADR. But providers do not adequately function for resolving disputes and the ECOM ADR is still relatively unknown to the consumers. Further, the ADR is not very effective against fraud cases or other vicious situations.

Thus litigation has occurred. The first case is against the biggest — Yahoo! Auction. In it, 572 victims from all over Japan who suffered fraud damages when goods were not delivered after paying for them appealed to the Nagoya District Court in search of reparations of a total of 115,570,000 yen on March 31, 2005, to "Yahoo!" manager of an Internet auction site. The victims are also preparing a second class-action suit against Yahoo![23].

2.   Legal relationships in Japan

The METI issued "Interpretative Guidelines of Electronic Commerce" for providing legal guidance in Japanese law context in July 2002 and updated when necessary[24]. It also focuses on the responsibility of auction business to users.

Should the auction business bear liabilities with respect to a person who incurs losses when problems such as the non-delivery of goods or non-payment arise between exhibitors and successful bidders? The auction rules usually provide that the auction business does not participate at all in sales contracts between auction users, and the actual sale is conducted under personal responsibility of the exhibitor and the successful bidder. Thus auction business is normally regarded as having no liability in regard to transaction-related problems between users. However, users tend to regard auction business as having a duty to prevent problems involving the sale of stolen goods, the non-delivery of goods, or non-payment between users of Internet auctions. In such cases, should the auction business bear some degree of liability?

The answer by the above-mentioned METI guideline is basically no, because auction businesses usually bear no contract liability in regard to transactional problems between them. Nevertheless, since an auction business provides the infrastructure for the brokering of sales information, it may be deemed to have an obligation to act with due care in accordance with the principles of good faith. However, the "due care" standards are not clear enough. What is the range of a cautions duty required for auction businesses?

The above-mentioned 572 victims insist that there is responsibility as an intermediary in Yahoo!, who operates the auction site by taking a commission. According to them, the defect lies in hosting a risky system by which victims occur frequently, and hence deserve a compensatory damage.

As this is the first case in auction, no one can predict where the judgment goes. However, some consumer protection concern may be added. As a reference, the Japanese Supreme Court ruled out in November 30, 1995, (Minshu 49-9-2972) favorably to the consumers in a shopping mall case as follows: when ordinary shoppers tend to mistake that a tenant pet shop as directly managed by a supermarket, a supermarket also takes the same responsibility as a tenant shop by analogy application of Article 23 of the commercial law. The extent of this analogy application is not clear, but the auction users in the Yahoo! Auction case use the uniform Yahoo! form under the Yahoo! Rules and they tend to mistake that they trade with Yahoo!, expecting some credibility of the famous Yahoo! brand, the literal interpretation of contracts (an auction site bears no liability) by courts is unlikely to happen.

There are several types of markets: (a) heavily regulated markets like funds and securities markets; (b) adequately controlled markets like real shopping malls with famous brand; (c) less controlled markets like cyber shopping malls with famous brand. At this moment, consumers tend to misunderstand type (c) as the same as type (b) because they do not know about their risks that cannot be easily understood by visiting cyber shopping mall sites.

To mitigate the risk of loss in the lawsuits, and also to facilitate the sound development of this rising business, the industry of auction providers needs to prepare "industry guidance" for enhancing consumer protection schemes and consumers educations for managing their risks, by consulting with consumer groups and related government agencies.

3.   **Some current initiatives**

Currently the METI hosts a study group of this issue, which consists of major IT auction businesses, mall providers, consumer groups, lawyers and scholars including me. Though the group is still in the process of discussion, I think that three dimensions are needed to consider: a) to provide enough and adequate information for consumers (successful bidders) to help them evaluate the credibility of exhibitors, b) to promote auction business to prepare consumer-friendly self-defense measures such as online escrows and auction insurances, c) to monitor exhibitors by the third parties.

(a)   *Advertisement regulations against exhibitors*

The first step is intended to help buyers' (consumers') monitoring against sellers (exhibitors) by advertisement regulation. The existing advertisement regulation under the Specified Commercial Transaction Law applies Internet auction "users." Under this law, "businesses" (exhibitors) that sell certain products are subject to obligations to display required items in advertisements (article 11), and the prohibition of misleading advertisements (article 12). The "businesses" include not only legal entities but also individuals that engaged in sales on a repeated and continuing basis with the intent of making a profit. However, many regulated "individuals" do not understand themselves as regulated under this law and may innocently fail to meet the advertisement requirements. Thus we need to educate the users by showing clear and detailed distinction between business and non-business.

(b)   *Online escrows and auction insurances*

The second step is to help consumers to defend themselves. Unlike in the U.S., online-escrows are not frequently used in Japan[25]. Though as cheap as only about three dollars per transaction[26], consumers do not like paying escrow fee. However, a kind of "offline-escrows" called "dai-biki payment" works in Japan. In dai-biki payment, you will pay when you receive the goods at the door of your house. The payment is simultaneously done with the delivery of goods, and both the seller and buyer have no default risk. If we develop the simultaneous payment method from offline to online, it can substitute online escrows.

Some auction providers offer some insurance and disclose fraud information timely. These services may be effective against frauds, but consumer education is still needed because many consumers do not fully understand how much compensated and how to use it. With the level up of fraudulent exhibitors' vicious technique, the countermeasures also should be enhanced.

(c) *Monitoring by the third party*

The third step is to introduce stronger monitoring of exhibitors by the auction providers: confirmation of exhibitors' self-information by the third party certificate authorities, checking the reliabilities of exhibitors by auction businesses and industry-wide commitments. Single measure seems not very effective against auction frauds because the issue is complicated. It needs mixture of several measures taken by the auction businesses, consumer associations, governments and so forth.

B2B: Concerns Against Smooth Ratification of the Hague Convention

Global harmonization of international transaction laws has been needed for long. Under the current legal situation, the B2B cross-border securities transactions are partly governed by the law where the securities are located (i.e., the EU, Japan), and partly by the law that participants agreed (i.e., the U.S.) and others. The national rules, from conflicts of laws to substantive laws, differ from each other and the predictability of applicable rules is not satisfactory. Recently many countries promoted electronic (paperless) securities transactions. It makes the legal relationship more complicated because the location of the electronic securities is difficult to fix.

To correspond with this change quickly, two draft treaties are currently discussed worldwide: "The Hague Convention on the Law Applicable to Certain Rights in Respect of Securities Held with an Intermediary (the Hague Convention)" and "UNIDROIT Preliminary Draft Convention on Harmonized Substantive Rules Regarding Securities Held with an Intermediary (the UNIDROIT Convention)." The Hague Convention covers the applicable law rules and the UNIDROIT Convention treats substantive ones. Unlike B2C or C2C areas, B2B financial matters, such as the Basel, tend to be promptly decided by global experts funded and enforced by the industries and the governments, because the related parties are limited.

1. **Issues**

Then let's go straight to the current issue. Should Japan ratify the Hague Convention immediately as the U.S. pushes, or oppose to it as the EU did? My answer is that Japan should wait to give its ratification until the ratification of the UNIDROIT Convention estimated to be completed in a few years. The effective date of the Hague Convention and that of the UNIDROIT Convention should be the same, in order to avoid the unnecessary trouble and cost occurred from the time difference of major law reforms in many countries for a very short period of time.

In addition, the Hague Convention itself has several technical problems. First, there remains large room for discretion by domestic laws in the name of "public policy and internationally mandatory rules" in Article 11. Extra territorial application of the U.S. Patriot Act or the Securities Exchange Act of each country may prevail over the Hague Convention. Thus the global policy coordination mechanism of "public policy and internationally mandatory rules" is needed. Second, more detailed rules about an applicable law are needed. If applicable law agreement is oral, it may cause great inconvenience for the third party and for evidence. If participants are allowed to specify the applicable laws dividedly and freely, the intermediary and related party may be in trouble. However, many issues are to be interpreted.

2. Examples

Let me show two examples to consider the possible inconveniences. If the effective date of the Hague Convention and that of the UNIDROIT Convention is the same, inconveniences may be eased.

(a) *Example 1*

Suppose that a Japanese seller A held the security to the intermediary (account management organization) X in the U.S. and triple transfers of the same security are carried out with buyer B in Japan designated as governed by Japanese law under the Hague Convention, buyer C in the U.S. governed by U.S. law and buyer D in the UK governed by UK law. Under UK law, the perfection requirement is an agreement to transfer between A and D. Under U.S. law, the perfection requirement is the occurrence of A's duty to transfer. Under Japanese law, the perfection requirement is to credit or debit to a securities account.

If A agreed with B and C and D to transfer, but did not credit to any account and went bankrupt, B cannot win under Japanese law because it is required to credit to B's account. B could win if B designated the governing law as U.S. or UK law. If market participants are careful and rational, they will avoid applying Japanese law.

However, this difference of the perfection requirements will be solved automatically when the UNIDROIT Convention is ratified at the same time as the Hague convention, because the UNIDROIT uniforms the perfection requirement as the credit or designation to an account (the UNIDROIT Convention, Article 6).

Also if A credited to B and went bankrupt, and the bankruptcy procedure began in the UK, where the securities may be considered as a claim and not a property, B may not receive the property protection that could be received in Japan. This difference of bankruptcy laws will also be solved when the UNIDROIT Convention is ratified because it covers the insolvency procedures (the UNIDROIT Convention, Article 11 and 12).

(b) *Example 2*

According to Esq. Ignacio[27], "The rule of article 7.5 will have undesired effects for existing interests in securities in case of interests over the same securities acquired after a change of applicable law, provided that the rules set out in the new law to solve conflicts between creditors do not coincide with those provided by the old law." For example, "Client A of Intermediary X grants a pledge in favour of Creditor 1 under the law applicable to the agreement — law of State A. This law states that in case of conflict between pledge Creditors, they will rank according to the time of perfection ("prior in tempore, potior in iure"), and therefore Creditor 1 is fully secured. Afterwards, Intermediary X and Client A change the law applicable to adopt law of State B, which foresees that in case of insolvency pledge Creditors rank *pari passu,* without considering the moment of perfection, and subsequently in case of enforcement they will collect on a pro-rata basis. Client A then grants another pledge over the same securities in favour of Creditor 2 under the new applicable law, that is, law of State 2, in order to secure a loan. Client 1 defaults the loan (without being insolvent) granted by Creditor 2, and the latter enforces the pledge through appropriation of half of the securities. Creditor 1 keeps his pledge, although only over the remaining half."

This difference of the laws of State A and State B will be decreased when the UNIDROIT Convention is ratified at the same time as the Hague Convention.

Final Remarks

Not only the B2C, but also the C2C and B2B markets are currently facing a tremendous structural change. Businesses, consumers and regulators (or legislators) on the global and domestic level have to take effective market-oriented measures to attain adequate consumer protection and sound development of the markets.

This research was partially supported by the Japanese Ministry of Education, Science, Sports and Culture, Grant-in-Aid for Scientific Research on Priority Areas, 16090101, 2004-2009.

References

Bang-Pedersen, U. (2004, October). *The impact on the European community states.* Retrieved April 1, 2005, from http://law.rikkyo.ac.jp/ribls/symposium/2004hague/hague.htm

Bang-Pedersen, U. (2004, October). *Investor protection in intermediary insolvency.* Retrieved April 1, 2005, from http://law.rikkyo.ac.jp/ribls/symposium/2004hague/hague.htm

Bernasconi, C. (2004, October). *Discussions in the Hague Conference and the basic structure of the convention.* Retrieved April 1, 2005, from http://law.rikkyo.ac.jp/ribls/symposium/2004hague/hague.htm

Dogauchi, M. (2004, October). *The Internet transactions and choice of law*. Retrieved April 1, 2005, from http://law.rikkyo.ac.jp/ribls/symposium/2004hague/hague.htm

European Central Bank. (2005, March). Opinion of the European central bank of March 17, 2005, at the request of the Council of the European Union on a proposal for a council decision concerning the signing of the Hague Convention on the law applicable to certain rights in respect of securities held with an intermediary (COM (2003) 783 final). Retrieved April 1, 2005, from http://www.ecb.int/ecb/legal/pdf/c_08120050402en00100017.pdf

Gómez-Sancha, I. (2005, February). Discussion paper on the effects of the Hague Convention on the law applicable to certain rights in respect of securities held with an intermediary. Retrieved April 1, 2005, from http://www.hba.gr/1234/2005/FEB-RUARY%202005/Enclosure%20to%20letter%20C0207.pdf#search='Ignacio%20Sancha%20Hague%20Convention

Hayakawa, Y. (2004, October). *Specific features of the conflict of laws rules*. Retrieved April 1, 2005, from http://law.rikkyo.ac.jp/ribls/symposium/2004hague/hague.htm

Japanese Ministry of Economy, Trade and Industry. (2003, June). *Interpretative guidelines of electronic commerce* (provisional translation). Retrieved April 1, 2005, from http://www.meti.go.jp/english/information/downloadfiles/c0306EleCome.pdf

Japanese Securities Dealers Association. (2004, November). Minutes of the 5th meeting of the promotion meeting for reform of securities clearing and settlement system. Retrieved April 1, 2005, from http://www.kessaicenter.com/now/5-a_e.pdf#search='Hague%20Convention%20Japan%20Securities%20Dealers%20Association

Kanda, H. (2004, October). *Scope of the convention*. Retrieved April 1, 2005, from http://law.rikkyo.ac.jp/ribls/symposium/2004hague/hague.htm

Kreuzer, K. (2004, October). *Innovative features of the Hague Securities Convention*. Retrieved April 1, 2005, from http://law.rikkyo.ac.jp/ribls/symposium/2004hague/hague.htm

Loon, H. V. (2004, October). *A challenge for the Hague Conference*. Retrieved April 1, 2005, from http://law.rikkyo.ac.jp/ribls/symposium/2004hague/hague.htm

Morton, G., Dupont, P., & Maffei, A. (2005, February). EU Clearing and Settlement Legal Certainty Group: UNIDROIT preliminary draft convention on harmonized substantive rules regarding securities held with an intermediary. Retrieved April 1, 2005, from http://europa.eu.int/comm/internal_market/financial-markets/docs/certainty/unidroit_en.pdf#search='Guy%20Morton%20EU%20Clearing

Morton, G. (2004, October). *A new project of the UNIDROIT*. Retrieved April 1, 2005, from http://law.rikkyo.ac.jp/ribls/symposium/2004hague/hague.htm

Morton, G. (2004, October). *Change of the applicable law and transition provisions*. Retrieved April 1, 2005, from http://law.rikkyo.ac.jp/ribls/symposium/2004hague/hague.htm

Potok, R. (2004, October). *The Hague Securities Convention: Closer and closer to a reality*. Retrieved April 1, 2005, from http://law.rikkyo.ac.jp/ribls/symposium/2004hague/hague.htm

Rogers, J. (2004, October). *Property and contract: Toward a clearer understanding.* Retrieved April 1, 2005, from http://law.rikkyo.ac.jp/ribls/symposium/2004hague/ hague.htm

Sigman, H. (2004, October). *The convention from the viewpoint of the collateral-taker.* Retrieved April 1, 2005, from http://law.rikkyo.ac.jp/ribls/symposium/2004hague/ hague.htm

Wani, A. (2004, October). *The convention from the viewpoint of the practice.* Retrieved April 1, 2005, from http://law.rikkyo.ac.jp/ribls/symposium/2004hague/hague.htm

Endnotes

[1]   Such as the Constitution, civil code and other general codes; Japanese laws did not change frequently until 10 years ago, but even the general codes including civil code, company law and conflict laws changed recently or will change soon and the constitutional reform is also currently under discussion.

[2]   Such as "guideline" setting of OECD Guidelines for Consumer Protection in the Context of Electronic Commerce, 1999, "soft law" making of UNCITRAL Model Law on Electronic Commerce, 1996, and "hard law" ratification of the Hague and the UNIDOIT Conventions as discussed below.

[3]   For details, see the homepage of the Japanese Government IT Strategic Headquarters at http://www.kantei.go.jp/foreign/policy/it/index_e.html.

[4]   Even in the B2C market, characteristics of consumers are changing and we need to update the existing legal framework that supposes consumers as week against businesses. For example, consumers sometimes have price-control powers against businesses by using "gathering" technique (if the buyers increase, the price will go down in Internet shopping).

[5]   The Japanese Supreme Court ruled out favorably to the consumers in Nov. 30, 1995, in a famous supermarket, INAGEYA case as shown below.

[6]   In practice, D sometimes voluntarily helps consumers to contact with C and pay some compensation.

[7]   In other B2B transactions, such as electronization of trade documents like the bill of lading (B/L) and letter of credit (L/C), convention is not needed and contract and standardization is promoted.

[8]   For details, see Richard Potok's "The Hague Securities Convention – Closer and Closer to a Reality," 15 JBFLP 204, 2004, available at http://law.rikkyo.ac.jp/ribls/ symposium/Potok.pdf#search='Richard%20Potok%20Hague.

[9]   For details, see morton, Dupont and Mafféi's "EU Clearing and Settlement Legal Certainty Group: UNIDROIT Preliminary Draft Convention on Harmonized Substantive Rules Regarding Securities Held With an Intermediary," 7 February 2005, available at http://europa.eu.int/comm/internal_market/financial-markets/docs/ certainty/unidroit_en.pdf#search='Guy%20Morton%20EU%20Clearing.

10   Similar, but not completely the same; Complete law harmonization is unrealistic in this field because: (1) the basic legal concepts differ much from Anglo-American law tradition such as the U.S. and the UK laws and Continental law tradition, such as the EU and Japanese laws; (2) domestic public orders and compulsory rules should be esteemed and so forth.

11   See European Central Bank's "Opinion of the European Central Bank of 17 March 2005 at the Request of the Council of the European Union on a Proposal for a Council Decision Concerning the Signing of the Hague Convention on the Law Applicable to Certain Rights in Respect of Securities Held with an Intermediary" (COM (2003) 783 final), available at http://www.ecb.int/ecb/legal/pdf/c_08120050402 en00100017.pdf.

12   Among the few, there is a paper interviewing practitioners about the side effects in detail. It is Ignacio Gómez-Sancha's "Discussion Paper on the Effects of the Hague Convention on the Law Applicable to Certain Rights in Respect of Securities Held With an Intermediary," available at http://www.hba.gr/1234/2005/FEBRU-ARY%202005/Enclosure%20to%20letter%20C0207.pdf#search ='Ignacio%20Sancha%20Hague%20Convention. His paper reflecting the inter-view results will be published in June 2005 in English.

13   The Japanese academic discussion is available at http://law.rikkyo.ac.jp/ribls/symposium/hague.htm.

14   The Japanese Securities Dealers Association declared that, "The Hague Convention earned a positive reputation that it will make a progress in conflict of laws in Japan," in November 25, 2004. See http://www.kessaicenter.com/now/5-a_e.pdf#search='Hague%20Convention%20Japan%20Securities% 20Dealers%20Association.

15   Internet auction represents a form of electronic commerce whereby people submit bids at desired prices for products introduced on Web pages, with the person submitting the highest bid by the deadline winning the auction. See p. 26, *Japanese Ministry of Economy, Trade and Industry*, "Interpretative Guidelines of Electronic Commerce (provisional translation)," June 2003, available at http://www.meti.go.jp/english/information/downloadfiles/c0306EleCome.pdf.

16   See the U.S. Department of Justice Web page at http://www.internetfraud.usdoj.gov/#What%20Are%20the%20Major%20Types %20of%20Internet.

17   The METI hosts a study group for discussing this matter. Detailed discussions and documents are disclosed in Japanese at http://www.meti.go.jp/policy/consumer/tsuuhankenkyuukai/main.html.

18   See the material in Japanese at http://www.meti.go.jp/policy/consumer/tsuuhankenkyuukai/041206/shiryou5.pdf.

19   Regarding ECOM, see http://www.ecom.or.jp/ecom_e/index.html.

      As for ECOM Online ADR, see http://www.ecom.jp/ecom_e/latest/ecomjournal_no3/topics3_e03.htm and http://www.ecom.jp/ecom_e/latest/ecomjournal_no4/wg2_e04.htm.

[20]   See the material in Japanese at http://www.meti.go.jp/policy/consumer/tsuuhankenkyuukai/050207/shiryou4.pdf.

[21]   See the material in Japanese at http://www.meti.go.jp/policy/consumer/tsuuhankenkyuukai/050404/shiryou2.pdf.

[22]   See the material in Japanese at http://www.meti.go.jp/policy/consumer/tsuuhankenkyuukai/041206/shiryou5.pdf.

[23]   See the site of plaintiffs (in Japanese) at http://web-sos.info/.

[24]   See the METI homepage at http://www.meti.go.jp.0Original version is in Japanese, but English translation is available on the Web.

[25]   Korea is reported to consider introducing a new law enforcing consumers to use online escrows or insurances or others.

[26]   Contrary to the expectations, escrow business is not currently very profitable in Japan.

[27]   Cited on p. 14 of the above-mentioned Ignacio paper.

Glossary of Terms

C

CHAPS: Clearing House Automated Payments System based in London and established in 1984.

Closed-loop type digital cash system: A system in which a digital cash issuer (an originator) should transfer the same amount of money as the sum paid by a digital cash user at a shop to the deposit account of the shop. In this system, the digital cash value exchanged for cash or deposits must be flown back to the issuer through a member bank after each transaction.

D

Data warehouse: A collection of subject-oriented and integrated data that is not volatile but relevant to some moment in time. It is designed to perform data analysis and support management's decision-making process.

DNS: The designated-time net settlement system. Systemic risks are an issue with DNS. Central banks in developed countries have been introducing RGTS as an alternative to DNS.

DVP: Delivery versus payment. This procedure is intended to reduce credit and liquidity risks in securities settlements. Its use has been spreading all over the world.

E

Electronic learning: A system supported by information and communication technology in order to conduct the online lessons on the Internet.

Electronic purse: A kind of smart card application used for small amounts of electronic payment on specified transactions of goods and services.

Enterprise resource planning: An information system that allows enterprises or organizations to automate, manage, and integrate the majority of business-related processes such as human resources, manufacturing and finance.

Export orientation: The proportion of output that is sold overseas or exported.

Export penetration: Ability to sell overseas.

F

Fedwire: The Federal Reserve's Fund Transfer System.

Financial crisis in Japan: In the late 1990s, Japan moved into deeper recession, and many banks, thrift institutions and life insurers failed. Japanese financial authorities had strictly regulated financial industries to avoid collapse of financial institutions for a long time, so this was the first serious financial crisis Japan experienced after WWII.

H

Hedonic price index: A price index that also accounts for changes in the quality of priced goods and service.

Hybrid smartcard: An IC-card which multiple functions as a credit card, debit card, cash card, prepaid card and point service function, all of which are built in. This card has multiple functions besides financial ones as well. For example, it can be used as a health care card, administrative card, ID card and so forth.

I

Imperfectly competitive firms: Firms that operate in markets that are characterized by less than full or perfect competition.

Industry specific assistance measures: Tax incentives such as tax deductibility on expenditure for research and development, investment (to purchase machines) and the training of labor. Subsidies or outright payments by the government for these types of expenses are also included.

L

Legal risk: This risk factor is uncertain in part because of insufficient or unclear legislation. Legal risks sometimes cause credit and liquidity risks.

Local currency: Introduced by non-governmental organization (NGO) or other organizations in particular regions of some countries. These currencies are used to reward volunteer and community activities, such as nursing and child-rearing.

M

Market failure: The failure of the market (forces of demand and supply) to capture the positive and negative side effects of economic activities.

Mutual company: An insurance company owned by its policyholders. Many life insurers are mutual companies, but recently some of them have been converted into stock companies to obtain access to capital market and prepare for possible M&A.

N

Negative yield: Negative yield is a negative gap between real and promised rate of returns on policies. Japanese life insurers have promised high yield to policyholders in the early 1990s, but they have suffered from low rate of return from asset due to the low-interest policy and sluggish stock market thereafter.

The New Insurance Business Law: Enacted in 1996, the law relaxed restrictions in many areas of the Japanese insurance market. For example, life and non-life insurers were permitted to enter into each other's business sphere by establish subsidiaries and insurance premiums, and products were deregulated.

Non-performing loan: A classification of bank loan in which the full payment of principal and interest is no longer anticipated because of a past due maturity date for a certain, specified number of days.

O

Open-loop type digital cash: A system in which digital cash value once paid by a customer can circulate from hand to hand without flowing back to the issuer. In this case, the digital cash provides almost the same function as real cash or deposits.

P

Payment risk: Occurs when the payer does not remit the necessary amount of money on the due date. Payment risk can be avoided by shortening of settlement times and simultaneous settlement.

P/E ratio: The price/earnings (P/E) ratio is calculated by dividing the current stock price by the net profit per share.

R

Return on equity (ROE): ROE is determined by dividing after-tax profit by net asset. High-ROE firms utilize their asset efficiently to make profit, and are attractive to investors.

RTGS: The real-time gross settlement system has been introduced in almost all developed countries and has become the mainstream in developed countries.

S

Seigniorage: The profit earned from issuing currency in terms of the difference between the face value and the cost of printing or minting the currency.

Stock market for emerging firms: In Japan, emerging firms often faced difficulties in going public since Japanese stock markets have been strictly regulated and impose tight listing requirements. To stimulate business promotion and increase the opportunity for rising money, the Tokyo Stock Exchange and the Osaka Stock Exchange founded new markets for emerging firms in 1999 and 2000, respectively.

SWIFT: The Society for Worldwide Interbank Financial Telecommunications, established in Belgium in 1973.

Systemic risk: Generated when time-designated net settlement coexists with RTGS. It can spread and introduce system downtime.

T

TARGET: The Trans-European Automated Real-time Gross settlement Express Transfer system began operating in Europe when the Euro was first introduced in 1999. It targets interbank, large-value payment systems for money market, foreign exchange and securities transactions.

TOPIX (Tokyo Stock Price Index): TOPIX was established by the TSE in 1969 and is one of the most famous stock price indices of Japanese market. TOPIX is a weighted index, and includes all stock listed on the TSE first section. Nikkei 225, another common index, is the arithmetic average of the prices of a select 225 stocks listed on the TSE first section.

Trade liberalization: The move toward free trade where there are no or minimal barriers to trade.

V

Velocity of money: The average number of times per year that a unit of money, such as a dollar, is used to purchase final goods and services.

W

Web service: An application or business logic that uses standardized XML (extensible markup language)-related technologies such as SOAP (simple object access protocol) as the communication protocol, WSDL (Web services description language) as the interface description language and UDDI (universal description, discovery and integration specification) for registering and searching services to provide connectivity and interoperability between clients and service.

X

XBRL (extensible business reporting language): An XML (extensible markup language)-based language being developed purposely as a standard means of automating business information requirements, creating financial statements and communicating information between businesses on the Internet.

About the Authors

Yutaka Kurihara is a professor of international economics at Aichi University, Japan. He has taught economics courses at both the graduate and undergraduate levels. He focuses in international economics, finance, currency integration, market integration, managerial economics, higher education and digital economy. He has published about 110 papers and some of them are in refereed international journals. His recent published books are *Business & Policy Design in the Globalization* (2003, 2004), *Intellectual Skills for Freshman* (2003) and *EU Currency Integration* (2000) (in Japanese). He is a member of the American Economic Association, Business & Economics Society International, European Economic Association, Hong Kong Economic Association and some academic associations of economics, business and higher education in Japan. He was a visiting fellow to the National Institute of Multimedia Education and was a visiting fellow to the Institute for Advanced Research at Nagoya University, Japan.

Sadayoshi Takaya was educated at Kobe University, Japan, where he graduated in 1986 with a BA in economics, and in 1991 with a master's degree in economics. He also obtained his PhD in 1998 from there. Between 1991 and 2003, he taught international macroeconomics and finance at Kinki University, Osaka, and since 2004, he has been a professor of international monetary systems and macroeconomics at Kansai University, Osaka, Japan. His recent studies are in macroeconomic policies in the Euro area; monetary policies of European Central Bank and budgetary policies of member countries representing the Stability and Growth Pact. He also researches international financial architectures and currency turmoil.

Nobuyoshi Yamori was born in 1963. He graduated from Shiga University and obtained an MA from Kobe University and a PhD from Nagoya University, Japan. He is currently a professor at Nagoya University, Japan. He has been appointed a visiting scholar at several institutions, including Columbia University, Long Island University and the Federal Reserve Bank of San Francisco. He has published many papers in international banking and financial journals, such as the *Journal of Banking and Finance*, the *Journal of Financial Research* and the *Journal of Risk and Insurance*. He also serves as an editor of several professional journals, including the *International Journal of Business*.

* * * * *

Ahmed Abutaleb is a professor at Cairo University, School of Engineering, Departments of Systems and Bioengineering, Giza, Egypt. From 1988-1991, he was a staff member at MIT/Lincoln Lab, Lexington, MA, in the radar data analysis division. From 1986-1988, he was an assistant professor at Temple University, School of Engineering, Philadelphia. From 1984-1986, he was an assistant professor at the Medical University of South Carolina, School of Graduate Studies, Charleston. He holds a PhD from The University of Pennsylvania, School of Engineering, 1984; a Masters of Science from The University of Pennsylvania, School of Engineering, 1980; a diploma in electrical engineering from MIT, School of Engineering, 1979; and a Bachelor of Science from Cairo University, School of Engineering, Dept. of Electrical Engineering, 1976. His major areas of interest are statistical signal processing, financial engineering, stochastic control, stochastic calculus and its applications, communications, applied econometrics, image processing, radar data analysis and number theory and its applications. He is a consultant with several national and international organizations.

Yoshihiro Asai was born in 1977. He graduated from Nagoya University, Japan, and obtained an MA from the State University of New York at Buffalo and Nagoya University. He is currently a PhD student at Nagoya University. He has published papers on the Japanese financial system, corporate governance and institutional investors, including the paper "Do Institutional Investors Discipline Corporate Managers in the U.S.?" (*Japanese Security Analyst Journal*, in Japanese), and "The Demise of Bank-centered Economy and Increasing Roles of Credit Ratings in Japan" with Professor Yamori (in Robert S. Uh. (Ed.). (forthcoming), *Financial Institutions and Services*. New York: Nova Science Publishers).

Kanokwan Atchariyachanvanich is a doctoral student at The Graduate University for Advanced Studies, Japan. She completed her BS in information technology at the School of Science & Technology, Assumption University, Thailand. Before pursuing her MS in information management at the Asian Institute of Technology, Thailand, she passed a six-month internship program in Denmark organized by the International Association for the Exchange of Students for Technical Experience. Her master's thesis topic was "A Comparison of Java and Microsoft Technologies in Developing an Internet Banking System." Currently, her dissertation topic is "A Cross-Country Comparative Study of B2C E-Commerce Business Model."

Waranya Atchariyachanvanich is a lecturer at the School of Business Administration, Assumption University, Thailand. She received a BBA with a double major in finance and banking and general management from Assumption University, Thailand. After completing her MA in business and managerial economics at Chulalongkorn University, Thailand, she pursued a PhD in international development, specializing in monetary economics at Nagoya University, Japan. She wrote her chapter with her co-author as a supplementary part of her postdoctoral research sponsored by the Japanese Society for the Promotion of Science on International Differences in the Determinants of Monetary Policy Framework at Graduate School of International Development, Nagoya University, Japan.

Carolyn Currie holds a PhD (USyd), MCom (Hons) (NSW), BEc (Hons), (USyd), BCom (Pass with Merit) (NSW), and is a member of the ASA, ACSA and FAIBF. She is qualified in the areas of economics, finance, banking and government. Positions held by Currie include managing director of Public Private Sector Partnerships Pty. Ltd. (current), director of D.C. Gardner PLC (1987-1990), consultant to the NSW Corporate Affairs Commission (1987-1990) and manager of Chase-NBA Group Ltd. (1976-1979). She is currently a senior lecturer in financial services at the University of Technology, Australia. She has specialized in the area of regulation of financial systems involving corporate financial analysis, public finance (monetary and fiscal policy), accounting and auditing issues and economic growth issues, and uses these skills to advise banks on topical issues such as Basel II, as well as governments on the design of financial systems in order to prevent regulatory failure and promote economic growth.

Akio Fukushima holds a Masters in Economics and is a researcher of economics at The Institute for Economic Studies, Seijo University, Japan. Economic integration and its development are some of his current research interests.

Anita Ghatak holds a BA, MA and PhD (UK) and is a professor of economics in the Department of Economics and International Business at the University of Greenwich, UK. She teaches research methods and financial economics at the postgraduate level. Money, development and time-series modeling of econometrics are some of her current research interests. She has wide teaching experience at other universities in the UK and India and a large number of publications in econometrics in the area of cointegration and structural breaks, and in macro and monetary economics in the area of budgetary deficits and finance.

Kozo Harimaya was born in 1968. He graduated from Kansai University and obtained an MA from Kwansei Gakuin University and a PhD from Kobe University. He is currently an associate professor and lecturer at Sapporo Gakuin University, Japan. His major research interest is the efficiency measurement for financial service institutions. He has published several papers in Japanese academic journals, such as *Review of Monetary and Financial Studies*.

Irene Henriques is an associate professor at the Schulich School of Business, York University, Canada. Her research interests span both economics and management and include the economics of R&D, industrial organization, environmental economics and environmental management and sustainability. She has published numerous articles in leading journals including the *American Economic Review*, the *Journal of Environmental Economics and Management*, the *Strategic Management Journal* and the *Academy of Management Journal*.

Takeshi Kobayashi is an associate professor of economics at Chukyo University, Japan. He attended Kyoto University and studied economics. After graduating, he entered the Graduate School of Economics at Nagoya University where he received his MA and PhD in economics. He joined the staff of Chukyo University in 1998. He has published papers in scholarly journals, such as *Journal of Insurance Regulation* and *Journal of Japanese and International Economies*.

Mariusz K. Krawczyk has a doctoral degree in economics from Kobe University, Japan, and is a professor at Fukuoka University, Japan, where he teaches international finance and comparative economics. He writes mainly on financial reforms in emerging market economies. His recent publications include, "On the Perils of Adopting the Euro in the New Accession Countries," *Homo Oeconomicus, 21*, 597-619 (2004) and the forthcoming, "Change and Crisis in the Japanese Banking Industry" in *Institutional and Technological Change in Japan's Economy: Past and Present,* edited by J. Hunter.

Takashi Kubota was educated at the University of Tokyo, obtaining a bachelor's degree (1990) and a master's degree (1993), at Harvard University, obtaining a master's degree (1996), and at Osaka University, obtaining a PhD (2002). He worked for the Bank of Japan from 1990 to 1998 as an economist, taught international business law at Nagoya National University from 1998 to 2004 as an associate professor, and is currently a professor of law at Waseda Law School, Waseda University, Japan, where he teaches international financial law, IT law and so forth. His recent studies include payment, electronic commerce and international financial systems; funds and securities payment laws, cyber malls and online auctions, and the Basel.

Andrew Marks holds a bachelor's degree in commerce (economics) at the honors level and master's degree in commerce (economics) from the University of New South Wales. He also holds a PhD from the University of Western Sydney, Australia. He has worked as an economist at the Commonwealth Bank of Australia, Economic Planning Advisory Council and the Department of the Prime Minister and Cabinet. He has taught economics at the University of New South Wales and the University of Western Sydney, specializing in international economics.

Narunto Nishigaki was born in 1964. He obtained an MA from Shiga University and obtained a PhD from Nagoya University. He is an associate professor at Okayama

University, Japan. He has published a book (in Japanese) and papers on the Japanese public financial system, such as "Public Financial System in Japan – Reverification of the Ballooning Theory and the Privileged Government Enterprise Theory" with Nobuyoshi Yamori (in *Public Policy Review*, 2005).

Shigeaki Ohtsuka holds an MA in economics and is currently a doctoral student in the Department of Economics at Kwansei Gakuin University, Japan. His recent studies are deposit insurance systems, especially how to avoid and/or reduce moral hazard problems. He has also taught Japanese management classes at Eichi University in Japan.

Michael Papaioannou is a senior economist in the Western Hemisphere Department since November 2000. Previously, he was a senior economist in the Treasurer's Department, Financial Relations Division (November 1990 to October 2000). While at the Fund, he served as a special advisor to the Governing Board of the Bank of Greece (September 1993 to August 1995). Prior to his employment with the International Monetary Fund (IMF), USA, he was a senior vice president and director of the Foreign Exchange Service of The WEFA Group (Wharton Econometrics Forecasting Associates) (1986 to 1990). He has served as chief economist of the Council of Economic Advisors, Ministry of Finance of Greece (1987 to 1988). He has taught at Temple University as an adjunct associate professor of finance (1989 to 1990). He was a principal research fellow at the University of Pennsylvania, Department of Economics, LINK Central (1983 to 1986), and a summer intern in the World Bank, Development Economics Department (1978 and 1979). He holds a PhD in economics from the University of Pennsylvania and an MA from Georgetown University.

Perry Sadorsky is currently an associate professor of economics in the Schulich School of Business (SSB) at York University in Toronto, Canada. He has previously taught at the University of California, Riverside, and has been a visiting international scholar at the University of California, Davis. He has published more than 35 refereed papers studying the economic, financial and managerial aspects of energy, financial markets and the economy, and corporate commitment to the natural environment. Some of these papers have appeared in leading journals like *The American Economic Review, Academy of Management Journal* and *Journal of Environmental Economics and Management*. He has also published in *Energy Economics,* which is the leading forum for economic and financial research on energy-related topics.

Masayuki Susai received an MA from Waseda University in 1987. From 1988 to 1990, Susai worked at Waseda University as assistant professor. From 1993 to 1994, Susai taught international finance and international economics at Nagasaki University, Japan, as an assistant professor. From 1994 to 2001, Susai taught international finance at the Graduate School of Economics, Nagasaki University, as an associate professor. From 1997 to 1998, Susai was a visiting scholar at the Haas School of Business, University of California at Berkeley. Since 2001, Susai has taught international finance at the Graduate School of Economics, Nagasaki University, as a professor and since 2005, has acted as executive vice president at Nagasaki University.

Argyrios Volis holds a PhD from Athens University of Economics and Business, Greece. He also received a graduate degree in economics from Athens University of Economics and Business. His second graduate degree was received at the ISMA Center, University of Reading in Finance. He is currently an adjunct lecturer of financial management at Athens University of Economics and Business. His main research activities include capital asset pricing models, seasonality effects on capital markets and efficient portfolio diversification.

Index

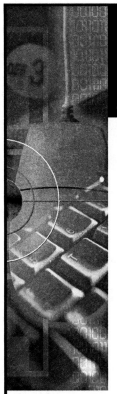